THE POLITICAL CULTURE OF MODERN BRITAIN:

Studies in memory of
STEPHEN KOSS

THE POLITICAL CULTURE OF MODERN BRITAIN:

Studies in memory of
STEPHEN KOSS

Edited by J. M. W. Bean

Foreword by John Gross

HAMISH HAMILTON · LONDON

First published in Great Britain 1987
by Hamish Hamilton Ltd
27 Wrights Lane London W8 5TZ

British Library Cataloguing in Publication Data

Political Culture in modern Britain: studies
in memory of Stephen Koss.
1. Great Britain —— Politics and government
—— 1979 –
I. Bean, J.M.W.   II. Koss, Stephen
320.941   JN231

ISBN: 0-241-12026-8

Printed and bound in Great Britain
by Butler and Tanner Ltd, Frome and London

CONTENTS

PREFACE

This volume is offered as a testimony to the admiration and gratitude for the achievements of Stephen Koss felt by friends and professional colleagues on both sides of the Atlantic. Shortly after Stephen's death, Ainslie Embree, then Chairman of the Columbia Department of History, asked me to undertake the work of editing. At the same time a Memorial Fund appeal was set up by the Department, its proceeds to be devoted to assisting Columbia students engaged on historical research on the United Kingdom. The contributors have donated any share of royalties to this fund.

The Columbia Department of History wishes to extend its gratitude to the contributors and the publishers for helping to produce this volume. As editor I am especially grateful to Christopher Sinclair-Stevenson of Hamish Hamilton for the time and trouble he has personally given to our project. Above all, all those involved thank Elaine Koss for allowing us to offer this tribute to the memory of a cherished colleague.

J.M.W.B.
September 1986

FOREWORD

Stephen Koss

John Gross

To say that Stephen Koss was deeply versed in English life and English culture may not in itself seem any great compliment: the study of modern English history was, after all, his chosen professional field. But anyone who knows his work and still more anyone who knew the man, will also know that his understanding of England went far beyond the common run of scholarly expertise. He had an exceptional feeling for the contours and inner connections of English society; his robust, unromantic sense of how things actually worked in Britain — or didn't work — was matched by a keen eye for cultural lights and shades. (I find myself zigzagging, incidentally, between references to British history, which is strictly speaking the accurate term in the context, and English history, which generally speaking seems more natural — a verbal dilemma with implications of which Stephen Koss himself, as a student of the Nonconformists, and of Lloyd George, was acutely aware.)

Was there something about England that struck a unique chord with Stephen? Not necessarily; thanks to his powers of analysis, his sound judgment and lightness of touch, he would probably have achieved the same degree of inwardness with whatever country or culture he chose to study. Still, in the event it was English history to which he was drawn; and if he came to feel at home in England, the English in turn came to feel at home with him. He and Elaine had a host of English friends, who were heartened by their visits to London or Oxford, and who sought them out in New York. I have seen personalities as different as Michael Foot and Michael Howard equally relaxed in the Kosses' company (though I should add that it could be very bracing company, too); and the memorial meeting in

London after Stephen's death vividly confirmed the affection and esteem in which he was held.

At the same time 'anglophile,' with all that it customarily implies, has never seemed to me the right term for him. He had too strong a vein of natural scepticism, for one thing, and snobbish social pretensions, where they didn't exasperate him, simply made him laugh. He also remained — in English eyes, at least — firmly and invincibly American, never more so than when he was giving rein to his ambition and drive. England being England, this didn't endear him universally, and every so often he ran into resistance — from a sluggish academic, a defiantly superficial journalist, the over-zealous guardian of a family archive. But to his English friends what they saw as his American qualities, including his dynamism, were very much part of the attraction.

American friends, I know, have occasionally been heard to express regret that he didn't devote some of his energy to American themes. But I don't think that America was in fact altogether absent from his thoughts when he addressed himself to the problems of Liberal Imperialism, or Edwardian foreign policy, or the interplay between the British political press and public opinion. A central fact — perhaps *the* central fact — about Britain in the period in which Stephen specialized is that it was a super-power doubling as a great liberal democracy. The analogy with contemporary America certainly wasn't lost on him, though whether he would eventually have developed it or built on it in his writing we will, alas, never know.

Stephen's literary skills won him a reputation in Britain that extended well beyond university circles. My first indirect contact with him was of a semi-scholarly kind: I was flattered to come across a reference to something I had written in his book on Haldane, and — since he plainly knew a good deal more about the subject than I did — grateful to him for letting me down lightly. It is characteristic, however, that the friend who subsequently brought us together should have been a political journalist, Anthony Howard. At the time we met, I was literary editor of the *New Statesman*; the reviews which Stephen wrote for that paper marked the beginning of a singularly happy working relationship which continued, and deepened, when I became editor of the *Times Literary Supplement*.

The high quality of Stephen's journalism was so readily apparent that an editor is tempted to dwell on what you might call his backstage virtues instead. He was reliable, efficient, wonderfully well organised; when occasion demanded — and crises will occur even on the best conducted papers — he could work at extraordinary speed.

Still, it is the substance of what he wrote that counts, and looking up some of his reviews and articles in the files I have found myself as impressed as I was at the time by his lucidity, his verve, his ability to enlist the curiosity of the general reader without diluting his standards. It is rather startling to learn from Isser Woloch's memoir that in his early days his writing could be clumsy and garrulous. By the time I got to know him he had thoroughly mastered his craft, and his pieces more than once reminded me of the celebrated comment of the East India Company examiners on Thomas Love Peacock's entrance papers: 'Nothing wanting, nothing superfluous.' They were also enlivened by an easy wit, which, whether or not it can be said to have had anything especially 'English' about it, was certainly appreciated by English readers.

And, I don't doubt, by American readers as well. One can make altogether too much of national categories — especially in the case of someone like Stephen Koss, whose most notable achievement was to transcend them, to set a lasting example of what can be done by scholarship and intelligence to bring one culture closer to another.

A PERSONAL MEMOIR

Isser Woloch

The accident of birth is a question, among other things, of time and place. To have been born on May 25, 1940, anywhere in Europe would scarcely have been an auspicious beginning. But Stephen Koss was born and raised across the Atlantic, and belonged to a fortunate cohort of Americans, who were destined to slide by the disasters of the twentieth century with barely a scratch — too late for the aftershocks of the Great Depression, safely removed from the Holocaust, advantaged enough under the selective service system to avoid the battlefields of Vietnam. In regard to the accidents of birth Stephen seemed lucky. But, as Napoleon liked to remark, it is one thing to be lucky, another to turn that luck to maximum advantage.

His parents, who had not had the luxury of a college education, provided him with a comfortable suburban environment. In the familiar pattern of American social mobility, this modest middle-class upbringing was to be a launching pad to an incrementally better social situation, with medicine, law, or corporate America the likely destination. For Stephen, however, time and place offered different, more exotic opportunities. The doors of American higher education had been flung open after World War II, even in the traditionally restrictive Ivy League universities. Many used this élite education as a passport to lucrative careers. But for some it proved to be more than a mere stopping place. Stephen was drawn to the life of scholarship — no doubt to the puzzlement of his family — through its most accessible port of entry, the academic career. In this momentous choice his very lack of social privilege, the seeming disadvantage of a relatively untutored background, actually proved to be an asset. For it allowed him the opportunity to become a self-made man. In the process,

1

Stephen hopped the track from a life of mere middle-class fulfilment to one of stellar achievement.

When Stephen graduated from his suburban Long Island high school in 1958 and arrived on Morningside Heights to attend Columbia College, he could not know that this physically cramped but culturally capacious community would become his permanent domain. Nor were the faculty or staff of the College particularly aware that this pleasant fellow was someone truly special. For Stephen's years in the College seem to have been entirely satisfactory without being outstanding. Perhaps the first person to have sensed his real potential before the fact was an undergraduate at Barnard College across Broadway, then as now an independent women's college nominally under the umbrella of Columbia University. Elaine and Stephen married as undergraduates, a highly unusual step in that environment. They then shared the adventure of his steady but far from painless climb upward.

Stephen received the A.B. from Columbia College in 1962 and immediately enrolled in Columbia's Graduate School of Arts and Sciences as a Ph.D candidate in history. It must be understood that the atmosphere in American universities was entirely different at that time from its rather depressed condition over the past ten or fifteen years. At least from a material perspective, the 1960s were a golden age in American academic life. Colleges and universities were expanding at a dizzying and indeed reckless pace. Numerous positions were opening up. Even in staid fields such as literature and history, departments were competing with each other to recruit promising young scholars, raising salaries from their abysmal levels, easing teaching loads, and expanding funds for research. Undergraduate teachers in the liberal arts were encouraging their brightest students to pursue academic careers — something that younger readers will no doubt find amazing. In short, it was easier to embark on an academic career at that time than it had been before or is likely to be again.

Still, one had to prove oneself. Stephen did this in a characteristic way that was to become one of his trademarks. He worked with astonishing rapidity yet with no sacrifice whatsoever of quality. In the first year of graduate work he had completed his M.A. thesis by February — probably some sort of record at Columbia. He then took his doctoral orals at the end of his second year of study, for Columbia an uncommon course. This oral examination was manifestly a turning point. His teachers had always liked and respected him, but after his awesome performance he rose above his peers. To a man, the four professors — in those days of relatively candid and uninflated evaluations — deemed it a 'brilliant', 'outstanding', and 'extraordinary' examination. This young man, known to work incessantly and with great efficiency yet always affable and low-keyed, had evidently amassed a vast fund of knowledge in British and European history and had also achieved a facility of oral expression that dazzled his

2

examiners. For once the professors, perhaps even the candidate himself, found this nerve-wracking two-hour ordeal an enjoyable experience.

It must have been with a real sense of achievement and optimism that Stephen and Elaine then sailed for England in that great rite of passage for American students of Europe, the Fulbright year. Combining his interests in British liberalism and imperial history, Stephen chose as his dissertation topic 'John Morley: A Gladstonian at the India Office, 1905 – 1910.' As usual he worked furiously. By November he was already querying his adviser about footnote form, and by the time he returned to America in the summer of 1965 he had produced a 500-page first draft.

In October his adviser, Robert Webb, read the draft and mailed off his comments. Stephen knew that something was amiss when Webb's letter began with a 'Dear Mr. Koss' rather than the accustomed 'Dear Stephen'. There followed a fourteen-page, single-spaced critique that, until its final reassuring paragraph, was absolutely unsparing. Yet in a long and increasingly close relationship, from Stephen's undergraduate days until his death, Bob Webb has probably never rendered him a greater service.

Stephen had natural talents, intense ambition, and huge potential as a researcher and writer. As a researcher he had more than proven himself already. Evidently he had much to learn as a writer. The first three pages of Webb's critique were fairly general and could serve as a text in any doctoral seminar. He taxed Stephen with striving too self-consciously to be 'readable', which, he observed, 'almost invariably results in being unreadable and artificial'. Besides exhorting his student to write more clearly and simply, he pinpoints Stephen's stylistic weakness: a faulty sense of paragraph; an excessive use of adjectives and adverbs; and above all an undue fondness for tangled metaphors. Under the rubric *substance*, Webb bluntly told him that 'I floundered through the dissertation, rarely knowing exactly where I was or where I was being taken'. He criticized Stephen for stuffing the manuscript with unnecessary quotations and references, for chronological sloppiness, and for incessant repetition. Mr. Koss had not yet acquired the discipline of discarding material amassed in the course of research — one key to the historian's craft. Worse yet, 'I don't believe that you ever really properly formulated your thesis in detail'. Webb's advice could well have applied to dissertation drafts by many of the very best students. He told Stephen to draw up a detailed outline of what he had written, to think the whole project through again, and to cut the draft by half as he rewrote it.

In Stephen's response there is only one sentence that needs to be cited: 'I intend to snap back, and your comments will not be wasted.' He was accurate on both counts. About two months later a 300-page draft reached Webb and elicited a mere page of criticisms. While he still complained that the thesis was not developed clearly enough, Webb was more or less satisfied.

3

This experience must have been harrowing but salutary for someone who cared as much as Stephen did for the joy and power of commanding the written word. Neither Webb nor anyone else would ever convert Stephen to the Strunk & White school of simple, direct prose. He continued to fashion metaphors and to manipulate adjectives and adverbs, but with increasing care and precision. The self-discipline that he always brought to his research he now imposed on his writing. The organization and argument of his books grew increasingly clear and sure-footed. His style shed all awkwardness as it became supple and elegant.

Stephen's first major foray into scholarship proved to be an even longer purgatory than usual. Having surmounted one crisis he immediately faced another problem when Stanley Wolpert published his own study of Morley and India in 1967. The prospect of publication for Stephen's dissertation clouded over ominously. His reaction to such adversity, however, was exemplary, as it would always be in matters large and small. In effect he started over again, placed the Morley manuscript in a bottom drawer, and carried out a study of Lord Haldane, another liberal politician. Through his special brand of hard work and his uncanny capacity for uncovering archival sources, Stephen ended up with two fine monographs. Both were eventually published by university presses in 1969 to favorable notice. In this unusual fashion, with two books to his name before the age of thirty, Stephen's career was launched.

For this budding British historian, commencement from Columbia as a Ph.D. in 1966 was not the end but the beginning of a long and complicated relationship with that Byzantine institution. After one year of seasoning at the University of Delaware, Stephen was called back to teach at Barnard College, where two professors who knew him (Chilton Williamson and René Albrecht-Carrié) had their principal base. He remained on Morningside Heights for the rest of his life, while acquiring a second identity as a man of letters in English scholarly and literary circles.

To the outside world Stephen's progress must have seemed steady and almost effortless. Each summer he flew off to London or Oxford for intensive research and for contact with an ever-widening circle of friends. While the British Museum never lost its charms, he was forever rooting out private manuscript collections and indeed considered this a historian's duty. His interests in the decline of British liberalism and in the British press led to a succession of four more books in six years: a biography of the Liberal Sir John Brunner; a biography of 'Fleet Street Radical' A. G. Gardiner; a study of religious Noncomformity in modern British politics; and in 1976 a concise biography of Asquith, which demonstrated the consummate skills in narrative and interpretation that Stephen had developed. In these years he also began his steady work as a book reviewer for such British periodicals as the *Times Literary Supplement* and the *New Statesman*. While making biography and political history interesting to a general audience, his reviews upheld scholarly standards, if necessary by wielding 'a mailed fist in a velvet glove', as he put it. He earned and savored his membership of the Reform Club in Pall Mall.

For most of the time, of course, he was ensconced at Barnard. After several uneventful and no doubt agreeable years at the college, however, his situation there became intolerable. For he had fallen out with a small clique of senior colleagues who ran the history department to their taste and evidently could not abide the talent, wit, and style of their most distinguished colleague. The pettiness of personal quarrels within the academy is notorious. On one level this situation was a source of amusement to Stephen, Elaine, his colleague and friend Bob McCaughey, and myself. But on another level it was scandalous and deeply wounding to Stephen. Most importantly it took a toll of his time and energy that now can only appear as incredibly wasteful.

In the early '70s Stephen was asked to offer a course 'across the street' at Columbia. Soon he began to supervise the doctoral research of certain students in British history. The competing claims of Barnard and Columbia placed Stephen in a difficult position. In effect each institution wanted two-thirds of his time. His unique situation led to charges of institutional disloyalty at Barnard, as well as a distressing inequity in salary because of the two institutions' differing pay scales. 'I despair of Columbia, and dread the prospect of returning to the Barnard situation,' he wrote from London in July 1972. His problem continued for far too long but it was finally resolved. Thanks to the determined efforts of Malcolm Bean, the chairman of Columbia's history department, prolonged and delicate negotiations for Stephen's full-time appointment at Columbia were completed in 1978. The ugly episode of harassment at Barnard was over, and Stephen could breathe freely. I was especially delighted that he now moved into the office adjoining mine in Fayerweather Hall.

II

Stephen and I had much in common. We came from the same generation and similar types of backgrounds, and had both been undergraduates at Columbia College. Our family situations were by now similar as well: we had children around the same ages and were married to feisty and literate women. Yet in other ways we assuredly formed an odd couple. We were not especially interested in each other's fields of research. Stephen, with all due qualification, seemed a complete Anglophile, while as a student of France and its Revolution I probably carried a trace of gallic Anglophobia in my baggage. Perhaps for this reason certain traits of his bothered me at first. Strangers or children would think Stephen English, and I wondered whether that did not reflect some sort of affectation. More seriously, he seemed less interested and acute about American politics and society than he ought to have been. He was more comfortable with his London *Times* than with *The New York Times*.

In fact all of this mattered very little. He was a splendid companion, informed and enthusiastic on a wide range of subjects. He loved the theater and the opera. Once we sat together through five hours of *Götterdämmerung* at the Met. For me it was an endurance contest to be experienced for the sake of *Bildung*; for him simply an enjoyable and somewhat exalting night out on the town. In 1977 he happily accepted an invitation from John Gross to write reviews of New York theater productions for the *TLS*. Above all Stephen loved to read. Naturally he had a penchant for biography, but he also devoured English fiction past and contemporary. Over the years I received from him the priceless gift of frequent recommendations, often accompanied by loans of the books themselves. One day he casually remarked that I might enjoy a book called *The Singapore Grip*, and he left it on my desk. After three nights of non-stop reading I could not imagine how Farrell's remarkable novel of British imperialism was not known everywhere. While I never came to share his fondness for books by or about Edwardians, I generally found his taste unerring. Years before the belated rediscovery of Olivia Manning, he had my wife and me reading her *Balkan Trilogy*.

Between 1973 and 1976 Stephen had been driven to desperation by his situation at Barnard. Because 'there seems to be nothing going on this side of the Atlantic', he applied for several positions in British or European history at English colleges and universities. No appropriate post materialized. Ironically, once he no longer needed this escape hatch, he had more than one opportunity to take up a major post in England. While he was gratified and perhaps tempted, it seemed to me that he never came close to accepting. No doubt family constraints had most to do with his resistance to such a move, and perhaps too a subconscious balking at expatriation. But I also believe that Stephen was actually more at home on Morningside Heights than he let on. Despite his legitimate grumbling about one thing or another, he was by now exceptionally well integrated into that community and was fast becoming one of its outstanding figures. Thus Stephen was tapped to be one of the effective organizers, the 'linchpin', of the Lionel Trilling seminars — a complex living memorial to one of Columbia's most revered scholars.

He seemed able to get along with almost everyone: timid undergraduates and precocious ones; insecure but talented graduate students; colleagues old and young; denizens of Park Avenue and Belgravia; Members of Parliament and Fellows of All Souls. With admirable social finesse he moved from being the prize student of Robert Webb and Ainslie Embree to becoming their intimate friend. He slid easily into relationships with such figures as I. I. Rabi, Lionel Robbins, and

A. J. P. Taylor — legends in their own time who found Stephen worthy of their confidence. All of this reflected something yet more fundamental and admirable about him.

Stephen's truly distinguishing trait was his interest in people. He was the antithesis of the ivory tower recluse who needs to be left alone in order to produce. Stephen always had time for his family and his friends on both sides of the Atlantic, and the Kosses' hospitality to visiting English guests was legendary. Along with the tact and grace of a born diplomat, Stephen had the ear and curiosity of a novelist. He was a connoisseur of gossip (as all who knew him will recognize) because he found people interesting. He managed to be extremely critical of pretension and foolishness without malice. It is not surprising that he was fast becoming friendly with Ved Mehta. That writer's antennae doubtless told him that in Stephen he had found a man very much on his own wave-length of sensibility.

Stephen knew that in his way he was as accomplished a historian as anyone in our large department. But he considered it his obligation to behave simply as a peer. He understood that what can make academe a special and attractive place is a measure of good citizenship and collegial egalitarianism in getting the work of the institution done. At every level Stephen was unfailing in shouldering such obligations. Never self-serving, he could always be relied on to take up university or departmental chores and to do them well. His comments on shirking colleagues were accordingly acid, while the vanity and pomposity of some never failed to amuse and infuriate him.

Stephen made no apologies for being a 'traditional' historian, for his interest in individuals, politics, and events in history. His annual lecture course was entitled 'The Political Culture of Modern Britain', and in his graduate colloquium on Victorian England the main theme was Gladstone vs. Disraeli. To the undergraduates he offered seminars on British Socialism, British society in two world wars, and the life and times of Winston Churchill. When our department created an introductory course for all graduate students in European history, each member was asked to choose the readings and run the discussion for one weekly session. The course was heavy with books by Fernand Braudel, Emmanuel LeRoy Ladurie, E. P. Thompson, and Hannah Arendt. Stephen, however, took a refreshingly playful approach, assigning cantankerous articles by Namier and Taylor concerned with the problematic role of individuals and events in history. He added chapters from Ved Mehta's *The Fly and the Fly Bottle* and let the fur fly.

In its detail his own work could be playful as well, but it was utterly serious in its import. Stephen's erudition, resourcefulness, and tenacity were all evident in his imposing *Rise and Fall of the Political Press in Britain*, whose two volumes appeared in 1981 and 1984. In Britain they were greeted not merely with interest but with excitement. Lavish praise from

7

many quarters spread across the dailies and weeklies that Stephen knew so well. He was intensely gratified. Similar recognition was bound to come in the scholarly journals with the usual delay of a year or two, and no doubt there will eventually be some respectful critiques. Whatever the case, the book was a double success: a literary event upon its appearance, and an enduring standard work to be pored over, mined, and savored for decades to come. Not a moment too soon he had completed a masterwork.

In the normal course of events this would have been a hard act to follow, and for once Stephen seemed to let up. He looked forward to accepting an invitation to spend a year in England, and had begun research on a new topic, the Anglo-American intellectual connection. As yet his commitment to this subject was relatively casual and unshaped. He was circling around it, and having a good deal of fun. One of his last ideas was to delve into turn-of-the-century American college catalogues, where he discovered the overwhelming domination of British history in their curricula. This was definitely food for thought.

His leisurely pace was interrupted by an unexpected and troubling proposition. Stephen was approached by the corporate grandees of Reuters to write their centennial history. He was of course flattered to be told insistently that he was *the* man they wanted. He was tantalized by the prospect of access to their private archives. He was challenged by the magnitude of the task. He was dazzled by the money that they proposed to throw at him, whose amount increased with each evasive response that he gave. At the same time he was apprehensive about the complete interruption of all routine that this commission would entail, and the physical demands of such global research. He was even more troubled by the prospect of being a 'house historian' and the possibility that his integrity could be compromised. And, in the final analysis, Stephen was distressed by the high-pressure style of the Reuters men who courted him. As he wrestled with the decision in the spring of 1984 it began to take on the aspect of a no-win situation. The job was too tempting to turn down with peace of mind, but too onerous and morally perilous to accept without grave misgivings. When he left for Europe in May he was still undecided, and intended to seek advice from British friends. Their counsel evidently tipped the balance and he finally said no, but only after being worn down by the stress of the whole business.

III

In 1967 Stephen had confidently noted in his Columbia placement dossier that his physical condition was excellent. He later had a minor problem with an irregular heartbeat, which cleared up and did not trouble him again until 1976. When he began to feel unduly tired at that time, he consulted doctors in London and The Hague, where he was spending the year, and was told that his heart rhythm had become irregular again. 'It's not a serious situation,' he reassured Bob Webb. 'If it does not respond to medication there is a simple treatment . . . . I quite admit that I drive myself too hard, but there really isn't any choice. I get terribly bored when I am not consumed by something.' A month later he reported that 'the medical gloom has lifted and I feel absolutely perfect . . . . The diagnosis was that I can live with the "condition" for the next 80 years, suffering no inconvenience unless I aspire to become an Olympic athlete.'

Either the diagnosis was faulty or his condition changed drastically in 1984. He had indeed enjoyed eight years of decent health and normalcy. But he returned from Europe that summer with alarming symptoms such as shortness of breath, loss of muscular power, and slurred speech. Extensive testing and consultation revealed that he was suffering from an ailment in which the heart muscle had deteriorated irreversibly. There was no prognosis whatsoever for recovery, and the greater likelihood was that it would deteriorate further. His life was being slowly snuffed out. No sooner was the gravity and hopelessness of his condition revealed, however, than modern medical technology erupted into his life. His doctors told him that there was a possible solution after all, involving nothing less than a heart transplant. They assured Stephen that he was an ideal prospect for this highly dangerous and experimental procedure: he was otherwise in fine health, emotionally mature, and intelligent. They effectively left him no choice.

Stephen's behaviour under this horrendous sequence of events was remarkable. An inner calm and serenity seemed to seize him. He had accomplished everything he hoped to do, he said, and was at peace with himself and the world. The rage and despair that would have been perfectly appropriate were suppressed. The ironic sense of life that Stephen had cultivated over the years proved to be deep-rooted and internalized. It no doubt helped that his two children had reached a point of reassuring maturity where he could visualize what they would be like in the future. Elaine's stoicism and nobility reinforced his own.

Yet there was another side to the situation. I think that Stephen inwardly rejected the idea of surrendering his being, his self to the hands of medical technology. While it may some day become a standard life-saving procedure, heart transplants at this time are almost surrealistic, dehumanizing, and remote from the range of human experience. Like the violinist in Chagall's painting, Stephen floated above this scene, detached from it while consenting to be its subject.

One way or another his equanimity and the impressive record of the physicians at Columbia-Presbyterian Hospital lulled his friends (if not his immediate family) into a false confidence. Several weeks passed as he waited for the appropriate donor. Our concern centered on the ordeal of

9

his prolonged recovery from this ultimate surgery. Then the day suddenly came. He left for the hospital, went into surgery, and died without regaining consciousness. In every respect he had been magnificent — which simply makes it harder to accept that he has left us.

1

Flying Missionaries:
Unitarian Journalists in Victorian England

R. K. Webb

In February of 1936, a young Irishman hacked his mother to death with an axe. Assuming that he might have had an accomplice, three Irish detectives paid a visit to Shrewsbury School to interview the murderer's friend and schoolfellow, Richard Cobb, by then an undergraduate at Oxford. In the course of a prudential meeting with Cobb in London, the worried headmaster, H. H. Hardy, reported on a satisfactory day's work: he had persuaded the editors of all the principal papers not to mention Shrewsbury by name in the coverage. He had, he said, still to travel north, where he expected similar success with the *Manchester Guardian*, and at the same time he would also square the *Liverpool Daily Post*, 'using his Unitarian contacts'. That an impeccably Anglican headmaster in the mid-1930s should have come naturally by, or have cultivated, Unitarian contacts is a matter of some curiosity; that he should still have found them valuable in the world of provincial journalism is a matter of historical interest.[1]

A little over forty years earlier, George Gilbert Armstrong, the son of a distinguished Unitarian minister in Liverpool, gave up hope of becoming a minister and, after a try at engineering, turned to journalism. When his first job with the *Liverpool Mercury* came to an unhappy end, finding that neither Edward Russell of the *Liverpool Daily Post* nor C. P. Scott of the *Manchester Guardian* could place him, he determined to go to London. Scott had written letters to E. T. Cook, editor of the *Daily News*, and to T. P. O'Connor, who had just left the *Star* and was about to found the *Sun*, but Armstrong's first call was on Anthony Mundella, an admirer of the elder Armstrong when he was a minister at Nottingham and the nephew of A. J. Mundella, the Liberal politician. Meanwhile, Uncle Philip

11

— Philip Henry Wicksteed, a scholarly, socially committed Unitarian minister now best remembered as a radical economist — invited Graham Wallas to dinner; Wallas did not give the hoped-for entrée to the *Daily Chronicle* but thought that both the *Observer* and the *Pall Mall Gazette* were possibilities. Mundella agreed that, if one stuck to non-political work, joining a moderate Tory paper would be no disgrace, but nothing came of either. Uncle Philip also sent George to see G. H. Perris (the son and brother of Unitarian ministers) at the *Speaker*, again without result. P. W. Clayden — R. A. Armstrong's predecessor at High Pavement, Nottingham, and now political editor of the *Daily News* and president of the Institute of Journalists — helped George to draft an advertisement for a situation wanted, but it brought no replies. During a weekend with another uncle, Armstrong attended the Unitarian chapel at Croydon, then presided over by the Rev. John Page Hopps, an inveterate publisher of Unitarian magazines and an equally inveterate writer for newspapers; Hopps sent letters of introduction to H. W. Massingham, whose refusal to see him Armstrong never forgave, and to Passmore Edwards at the *Echo*, who nearly offered a subeditor's job but then decided that the wiser course lay in the provinces. With the help of his shilling press directory, Armstrong at last landed a berth at the *Nottingham Express*, where his old Nottingham connections can scarcely have hurt. From there he went to provincial papers in Middlesbrough, Bradford, Bolton, and Darlington, before he joined the *Daily News*, first in the northern office in Manchester and then in London; he ended his career with a brief stint as editor of the Unitarian paper, the *Inquirer*.[2]

The Unitarian network so readily available to a well-connected beginner was impressively tied into the great and still burgeoning world of English newspapers on the eve of the Harmsworth revolution. Half a century or so earlier, as that freemasonry was emerging, one could also find circles that counted for something in the newspaper world and in which Unitarianism was a significant presence — in the colorful and freewheeling society that gathered around W. J. Fox, editor of the *Monthly Repository* and a Unitarian minister on his way to a wider career in politics and journalism; or the household of John Chapman at 142, Strand, a hub of radical publishing which had been George Eliot's opening to a new world. Of course, the ties of nineteenth-century Unitarians to journalism of one kind or another were not unique. Every religious group of any consequence had its denominational journals and newspapers, and adherents of every religion (and of none) played a part in the history of general newspapers, national or provincial. But if one cannot claim that Unitarians were singular in this respect, they were distinctive and so, in a pluralistic century, have some claim on the attention of historians.

As a denomination rather than a mere theological position, Unitarianism emerged in England in the last third of the eighteenth century, drawing supporters from several sectors of Dissent (and some from the Church), but most importantly from English Presbyterianism, the largest and most prestigious segment of 'Old Dissent'. The theological radicalism that swept through young Dissenters in the 1780s and the political radicalism of the 1790s drove many worshippers away, and by the 1820s the Unitarians could count only a little over two hundred congregations in England. By the early twentieth century, growth had more than balanced extinctions, and the total of congregations (a firm one now) was 293. Most of them were small in membership and even smaller in attendance. An educated guess would place total attendance in the early 1830s at around 33,000, and cautious extrapolation from a careful census of London church-going in 1902 – 03 suggests an attendance of fewer than twenty thousand in the country as a whole.[3]

There was evidence, however, in nearly every corner of Victorian England to support the Unitarian contention that, as H. S. Perris put it in 1903, they weighed more than they measured.[4] Though there were many more congregations with a working-class presence or predominance than most historians have allowed, the Unitarian claim to wealth and social position is incontestable. The ten Unitarian M.P.s returned in each of the two general elections in 1910 were but a tiny fraction of the more than 130 Nonconformists who sat in the House of Commons, but in the 1830s the fourteen or fifteen Unitarians at Westminster held a virtual monopoly of Dissenting representation. Economic historians charting the course of major firms across the spectrum and local historians counting mayors and councillors or the leaders of provincial cultural institutions regularly underline the centrality of Unitarians in town after town. By the second quarter of the century, moreover, provincial Unitarians were flocking to London to make careers and to attempt to exercise that influence on the country at large to which they believed their qualities entitled them.

Their confidence that they were in the vanguard of inevitable progress was founded not only on political ambition but, more, on the general excellence of Unitarian education and on a broad, compellingly coherent outlook. Most Unitarian ministers kept schools until well past the middle of the century, and the excellence of some of them was paralleled by other schools run by lay Unitarians, largely to cater to the children of their co-religionists. The importance of the eighteenth-century Dissenting academies in offering an education notable for openness and modernity of thought has long been recognized; for the Unitarians, Manchester College was (and is) the distinguished heir to that tradition, training both lay and divinity students as late as the 1850s. From early in the eighteenth century, some sons of Rational Dissenters found their way north to Glasgow or Edinburgh, and when the University of London was opened in 1826, the

Unitarian presence was startling. Education was the area of philanthropic activity most closely associated with Unitarians, who took the lead in founding mechanics' institutions, libraries, literary and philosophical societies, and provincial universities. And while not all Unitarians were intellectuals — far from it — the old Presbyterian ideal of a learned ministry continued to be valued well into Victorian times, and notable numbers of laymen were deeply concerned with philosophical and theological issues, debating them publicly and in the privacy of circles of like-minded people based on chapels or in the homes of congregational leaders.

Unlike their counterparts in Ireland or the United States, the English Unitarians in the first third of the century bore the impress of a single philosophical school, projected forward by men and women of that stamp who survived in active public and intellectual life at least into the 1870s. In the 1770s Joseph Priestley had published a succession of brilliantly controversial works advancing ideas that swept through the academies in the following decade and were preached and written about extensively in the generation after Priestley's death in exile in 1804, when security and confidence were restored to his beleaguered followers. To the Unitarian insistence on the full humanity of Jesus — whose learned perfection stood as an example of what anyone rightly taught and motivated could accomplish — was added the associationist psychology that Priestley (like Bentham and other radicals) drew from David Hartley. Hartleian metaphysics in turn provided a mechanism for the working of God's providence and foreknowledge, and thus a thoroughly deterministic view of the world and man's place in it. Even in the heyday of this all-encompassing philosophy, Unitarians could dissent from part or all of the Priestleyan synthesis, which was, moreover, stringently challenged within Unitarianism by James Martineau and his allies from the 1830s: they sought a different grounding for religion, in inner conviction rather than external evidences, and gradually came to question the biblical certainties — miracles and the Resurrection — that had survived the Priestleyans' criticism of the Bible and 'the corruptions of Christianity'. But these disagreements, which could become bitter indeed by mid-century, sometimes overshadowed the greater identity of views that united 'old' and 'new' schools. The long persistence of natural religion and the astonishing confirmatory advances made in science convinced thoughtful Unitarians of all stripes that more and more of God's laws would in time be discovered and that more and more of His creatures would learn to obey them; hence an early enthusiasm for political economy, for example. They were dedicated to the pursuit of truth, open to disproof and so to tolerance, and convinced of the certainty of progress and of the capacity of enlightened men and women to control it. This injunction might take the form of large-scale social engineering, as in the many educational projects Unitarians supported or in the public-health work of the minister-physician Southwood Smith; or of prescriptive

14

liberal or radical politics; or of broad public persuasion or even hectoring. It was from her early surrender to Priestleyan necessarianism that Harriet Martineau derived her mission to be a 'national instructor', a mission and a method that survived her mid-century abandonment of Unitarian Christianity for a modified Positivism.[5]

Martineau's dogmatism, with its singlemindedness and sometimes surprising results, was an extreme case, even among Unitarians, but many letters and diaries attest to the reality of lay confidence in providence and progress and to the obligation that the private beliefs and public works of two or three generations of Unitarians owed to this persuasive philosophy. In some ways even more impressive were those Dissenters with minds attuned to the imperatives of modern thought or susceptible to the corrosive effects of biblical criticism but still needing some religious anchor, who abandoned their inherited religious connections for Unitarianism, which many of them served with the especial zeal of the convert.

In the wider battle against ignorance and prejudice to establish the right way that was also the way of a rational, beneficent God, the press was a mighty engine. It was altogether characteristic that, when Joseph Barker abandoned Primitive Methodism in 1844 to espouse idiosyncratically Unitarian views, those Unitarians who welcomed him showed their gratitude by giving him a steam press, costing £390, along with an additional £144 12s. 10d. for engine, boiler, chimney, and fitting, and another hundred pounds for furniture and extra type. At the presentation of the press on July 6, 1846, John Bowring, always at the forefront of Unitarian philanthropic causes, welcomed this recruit from the people to the cause of truth. In an age, he said, that was witnessing the decay of prejudice and national hatred, a new understanding of true interests, and the beginnings of the free exchange of the bounties of Providence, the temptation of government to tyranny was giving way to moral means, and 'of all these moral influences, the greatest was the free, the irresistible, the omnipotent press,' a sentiment that Bowring later encapsulated in verse.[6]

From time to time, Unitarian papers broke out in similar praise for the promise and accomplishment of the press, praise not the less sincere because it was sometimes accompanied by an appeal for increased subscriptions. In 1847, a new editor of the *Inquirer*, scarcely a month into his tenure, welcomed the proposal for a monument to England's 'great pacific hero,' William Caxton, without whose divine art great works would have been the monopoly of the few and the newspaper 'would not have awaited the happy leisure alike of the scholar and the unlettered — the rich and the working-man.' More usual were leaders on the specific function of the religious press, seen generally as an adjunct of the pulpit, but one able to command readers in the thousands, day in and day out, as against the few hundreds that the pulpit could command for a few hours of a Sunday: 'Yes,' wrote one editor towards the end of the century, 'it is only by pen

15

and press that our over-grown modern world can effectually be reached and moved. All the magic of the eye and voice are impotent in comparison with the wide sown written sheet.' And the denomination might benefit as well. Early in 1886, borrowing the phrase from a London minister, the Unitarian paper *Christian Life* briefly billed itself as a 'flying missionary' and pushed a scheme for distributing free copies to ministers in other denominations. The notion stuck with 'A Sexagenarian Layman,' who, three years later, saw the flying missionary as a means of 'unifying and strengthening our body, [of] doing propagandist work of a truly practical and efficient kind.' [7]

The Unitarian exploitation of the press took many forms, sermons and tracts above all, and some ministers were virtually publishing industries in themselves, founding and editing periodicals, contributing to others, and turning out a steady stream of books and pamphlets. Most attention has been given to Unitarian periodicals, which had a distinguished history from Priestley's *Theological Repository*, through the *Monthly Repository* and the *Christian Reformer*, to the brilliant criticism of the *Prospective Review* in mid-century.[8] Lacking the literary importance of some of the magazines, Unitarian newspaper journalism has not received the same degree of attention, and what has been written about it is scattered and unsystematic and often little informed by an awareness of the broader dynamics of Unitarian history. This effort to pull together available information (often tantalizingly incomplete) and to place it in that wider context will not only indicate the extent of Unitarian involvement but reflect the retreat of religion from the intimate links that had bound it to the wider society in the first half or two-thirds of the century.

Even the most casual reader of studies of the provincial press will be impressed by the number of Unitarians associated with the emergence of liberal and radical newspapers. Joseph Gales, who founded the *Sheffield Register* in 1787, pioneered the leading article as a vehicle for reforming views, a coupling of technique and mission also found in the *Cambridge Intelligencer*, begun in that unpromising soil in 1792 by a handful of liberals, one of whom, the Unitarian brewer Richard Flower, persuaded his brother Benjamin to become editor. In 1794 Gales fled the country to escape what was almost certain prosecution for his radical activity and eventually became a newspaperman in North Carolina. Flower, whose paper gained a national reputation and circulation among reformers in the nineties, was imprisoned in 1799 for libelling the once-liberal Bishop of Llandaff, Richard Watson, as 'the Right Reverend time server and apostate', but he returned from Newgate to resume his editorial task, giving up in discouragement only after the resumption of war in 1803.[9]

16

In 1801, the *Leeds Mercury* was taken over by Edward Baines, with capital subscribed by eleven men, probably all Unitarians. Baines himself, from an Anglican background, was slow to associate himself formally with his wife's Congregationalism; indeed, in his early years he alternated attendance between her chapel and Mill Hill, where the Leeds Unitarians worshipped. Substantial agreement on a reforming program, perhaps even a shared sense of isolation in a town dominated by Methodists and (at a distance) Anglicans, made it possible for Unitarians and at least some Congregationalists to work together: Baines was not in favour of the disestablishment so passionately advocated by his fellow-Congregationalist Edward Miall, and he supported the Dissenters' Chapels Bill in 1844, which Parliament carried to protect Unitarian endowments from the assault of orthodox Dissenters. A similar collaboration was to be found in Sheffield, where the *Sheffield Independent*, founded in 1819 and faltering for lack of capital, was rescued at the end of 1820 by seven cutlers, probably all of whom, in Donald Read's judgment, were members of Upper Chapel. One of them, Ebenezer Rhodes, became editor for something over two years, and when he resigned, finding the work not much to his taste, he was succeeded by another of the group, the important Sheffield intellectual Thomas Asline Ward, who occupied the editorial chair until 1829, when ownership passed to Robert Leader, a Congregationalist, whose son, Robert Leader, junior, made the paper the most important in the town in the service of a radical cause he pursued with no less enthusiasm than his Unitarian fellow-citizens.[10]

The most famous of the Unitarian papers was the *Manchester Guardian*, founded by John Edward Taylor in 1821. Taylor's father had been the Unitarian minister at Ilminster in Somerset, until he turned Quaker and became a schoolmaster in Manchester; the elder Taylor's wife was the sister of Russell Scott, for many years minister to the important Unitarian congregation meeting in High Street, Portsmouth. The son, retaining his mother's Unitarianism, was apprenticed to a cotton manufacturer and then worked for a time as a cotton merchant; he married his cousin, Russell Scott's only daughter. The paper was founded with a loan of a little over a thousand pounds from eleven Manchester worthies, nine of whom are readily identified as Unitarian. Taylor was joined as co-editor by Jeremiah Garnett, another Unitarian who, having been apprenticed to a printer and having worked for newspapers, was competent to handle both production and reporting. Then in 1830, finding himself overburdened by his dual responsibility, Garnett was rescued by John Relly Beard, minister of the Unitarian chapel in Salford, who had been much impressed by the accuracy of a long account of a sermon he had delivered in Hull. Garnett at once journeyed to Hull and hired the young reporter John Harland for his paper. Like Garnett of Anglican background, Harland had sharpened his formidable skill at shorthand by taking down sermons of Hull ministers,

17

starting with the Baptist minister who spoke more slowly than the others. Impressed by what he heard in Bowl Alley Lane, he shifted his allegiance to Unitarianism.

John Edward Taylor's two sons, Russell and a second John Edward, were educated in Beard's school and at Manchester New College, then in its second Manchester residency after a crucially important period of nearly four decades in York. Garnett was left in editorial control when the elder Taylor died in 1844, but Russell survived his father by only four years. The younger John Edward, who lived until 1905, ceased to be involved in the day-to-day running of the paper after about 1870, and his cousin, Charles Prestwich Scott, entered into the inheritance, serving as editor from 1872 to 1925. Scott had intended to become a Unitarian minister, like his grandfather, but his faith grew unsettled at Oxford, and he turned to journalism. That Scott was more likely to recruit young associates from Oxford or Cambridge was a change of both symptomatic and symbolic importance, and a turning point was surely reached when, in 1884, H. M. Acton, the senior leader-writer and the son of a former Unitarian minister at Exeter, was eased out after more than thirty-five years on the staff to make way for W. T. Arnold, Matthew Arnold's nephew and one of the Oxford recruits. Unitarians were still to be found: John Frederick Smith, for example, who ministered successively at Edinburgh, Chesterfield, Mansfield, and Clifton, regularly contributed articles on theological and biblical criticism and on German political and social movements. On the other hand, while James Agate's father had been chairman of the congregation at Sale in Cheshire and James himself was secretary of the congregation when still in his teens, his colourful and productive career as a drama critic in Manchester and London owed little, if anything, to Unitarian tradition, utterly foreign to what an obituarist referred to as his 'Regency manners and a Regency deficiency of social conscience'.[11]

Unitarians were to be found in every part of the industry and in every part of the country, from T. B. W. Briggs, proprietor and editor of the *Dover Chronicle*, to George Lee, editor and later proprietor of the *Kendal Mercury*; from Thomas C. Gould, part proprietor of the *Plymouth Herald*, to an elder George Lee at the *Rockingham* in Hull, to James Clephan, publisher, editor, reporter, printer, and everything else at the *Gateshead Observer*. Clephan, from a staunch Unitarian family in Stockton, learned the newspaper trade on the *Leicester Chronicle* and took over the *Observer* in 1838, making it one of the liveliest and most distinctive papers in the country. When he retired in 1860, he joined the staff of the *Newcastle Chronicle*, edited by Joseph Cowen, a radical who had no formal religious affiliation, but who felt close sympathy with the Unitarians.

In London, the *Daily News* seemed almost as much of a Unitarian cell as the *Manchester Guardian*. Unitarians like to claim Charles Dickens, its founding (and quickly disappearing) editor, on the strength of his

18

occasional attendance at Little Portland Street Chapel, but one can be more confident, even though his Unitarian connections had grown tenuous, in pointing to W. J. Fox, a regular early leader-writer. The key figure, however, was Sir John Robinson. The son of a Congregationalist minister at Witham in Essex, Robinson was apprenticed to a printer in Shepton Mallet and worked for a time for newspapers in Bedford and Devizes. In Shepton Mallet, he had attended the Unitarian chapel presided over by the celebrated Rev. Henry Solly, through whose connections he became subeditor of the *Inquirer*, the Unitarian paper then edited by John Lalor, formerly an editor of the *Morning Chronicle*. Eventually, Robinson went to work for the *Express*, an evening paper published by Bradbury and Evans, who owned the *Daily News*, which Robinson joined as manager in 1868, remaining in that post (and serving for a time as editor) until 1901; he had become a good friend of Harriet Martineau, who had begun writing leading articles for the *Daily News* in 1852. When she retired in 1866, she recommended as her successor on American matters the Nottingham minister P. W. Clayden, who had edited the *Boston Guardian* while he was minister there and who, on moving to Rochdale, became a leader writer for the *Rochdale Observer*. Clayden joined the *Daily News* staff permanently in 1868, though he found time as well to found and edit the *Reading Observer* from 1873 to 1879 and to preach regularly up to 1884 in the Free Christian Church in Kentish Town.[12]

Briggs, the Lees, and Clayden are Unitarian instances of a phenomenon recognized in the nineteenth century but largely overlooked since — the minister as journalist, an outstanding Baptist example being Henry Dunckley, 'Verax' of the *Manchester Examiner* and *Manchester Guardian*. The motives for turning to journalism were many. It was necessary for most Unitarian ministers to find ways to add to their income. School-teaching was the usual solution, but in the more systematic educational circumstances of the last third of the century it was more likely to be an alternative to the ministry than an addition to it, whereas reviewing and leader-writing were supplementary employment much in demand when genuine talent could be offered. But journalism also offered an alternative to the ministry, one that increasingly promised large rewards in income and power. The elder George Lee was prepared for the ministry at Hoxton and Daventry academies in the 1780s, following Thomas Belsham, the divinity tutor at Daventry, into Unitarianism. He served for ten years at Belper, where the great cotton-spinning family, the Strutts, had built Field Row Chapel in 1788. He was then asked to supply at Hull, while the newly designated minister completed his college course. There he became a schoolmaster, and, though he often took services, he never again held a ministerial appointment. In 1809, with a group of fellow-citizens, he founded the *Rockingham*, which he edited until shortly before his death in 1842. George Lee, the son, attended Manchester College at York and served as minister for three years at Boston and six at Lancaster before taking up the appointment as editor of the *Kendal Mercury* in 1835.

In the case of Philip Harwood, a change of views contributed to the shift in profession. The son of a wholesale grocer and sugar refiner in Bristol, Harwood became a Unitarian while a student at Edinburgh. His sole Unitarian pulpit was in Bridport, from 1835 to 1840. Having become sceptical about miracles, he became assistant to W. J. Fox, at South Place, and later he lectured at the Beaumont Institution in Mile End until his theology offended the wealthy founder of that establishment. Through Fox's connections, he secured a subeditor's post on the *Examiner*, from which he moved to the *Spectator*. He then joined John Douglas Cook on the *Morning Chronicle*, and from 1855 was on the staff of the *Saturday Review*, first as subeditor under Cook and from 1868 to 1883 as editor. In Edward Parry's case, journalism offered an escape from a different kind of problem. Parry, who had worked for a printer in Birmingham from the age of eleven, was drawn out of his Methodism by the heterodox Baptist George Dawson. Asked to supply the Unitarian pulpit at Battle in Sussex, Parry stayed for six years as minister and schoolmaster and then took up an appointment in Kidderminster, where he was also master of Pearsall's Grammar School. The congregation at the New Meeting was split between an older generation loyal to the doctrines of Priestley and Belsham and a group of working men who had been inspired by Joseph Barker's brief passage through Unitarianism. Parry's efforts at conciliation failed and his initiatives like a Christmas Day service, standing while singing, or introducing James Martineau's hymnal, provoked more resistance, so in 1869 he resigned, to be re-elected by a majority of the congregation. His election was contested in the Court of Chancery, which decided that the trustees' concurrence was required. Parry withdrew again, and on February 12, 1870, published the first issue of the *Kidderminster Shuttle*, putting his old training to work with an unreliable second-hand steam press. The paper was soon established as a force in the community, and Parry turned to local politics, becoming mayor from 1898 to 1900. He remained editor of the paper until 1920. Similarly, in 1890 the Rev. Henry McKean, minister at Oldbury, founded with a group of schoolmasters the *Weekly News*, which grew into the Midland Printing Company, the publisher of a number of newspapers in the neighbourhood.[13]

Another minister who, like Clayden, combined politics with journalism and the pulpit was the Rev. Harold Rylett. Born in Horncastle in Lincolnshire in 1851, he studied at the Unitarian Home Missionary Board in Manchester from 1871 to 1875 and at Owens College in the two years following. He served as secretary of the Liberal Club in Regent Ward, Salford, while still a student and became a supporter and friend of Joseph Arch, the agricultural trade unionist. After a brief ministry at Reading — where he introduced Arch at a public meeting — he moved to Moneyrea,

20

near Belfast, where he plunged into the campaign for Irish Home Rule and the activities of the Land League. After five years there, during which all the major Irish leaders became his friends, he moved to Maidstone, where he became a member of the school board. When he moved to Dudley in 1887, the chairman of the meeting of welcome noted that the Old Meeting House had always been identified with progress and that John Palmer, the minister from 1833 to 1852, had been as much a politician as a preacher. In his address, the Rev. H. W. Crosskey, minister of the Church of the Messiah in Birmingham, described the local ministers as a body of fighting men, friends of liberty who were non-sectarian and willing both to disagree and to respect each other. Believing that the religious man was the highest ideal of humanity, Crosskey said, they sought to bring the blessings of life to 'the poor child in the gutter, the debased drunkard, and the inmates of the wretched household', who were as much the children of God as any other. Rylett vowed to carry on the traditions of the congregation, preaching 'a Gospel with God for its centre, Jesus Christ for its illustration, and love and self-sacrifice in every department of life for its manifestations'. His particular concern, he said, was avoiding foreign entanglements and war, but he quickly became involved with the plight of the chain- and nail-makers, giving evidence to the House of Lords Select Committee on Sweating. At this time he also became a friend of Henry George.

Rylett had been employed in his younger days on the *Birmingham Post* and re-entered journalism while minister at Flowery Field in Hyde, the magnificent church that the Ashtons had built two decades before for their workpeople. A local printer had started the *Hyde Telegraph* in 1891. I have been able to turn up only a fragment of the first issue in February, with a manifesto attuned to the style of the new journalism; non-political and non-sectarian, the new paper would print items of political and religious news if they were original, brief, and to the point: 'We want *many*, not *much*. Life is short; time is short; patience is short.' It seems likely that Rylett was not present at the creation, but he was certainly involved when the ownership of the paper passed to some local Liberal leaders, who in 1894 merged it with the *Hyde, Marple, and Glossop Reporter*, a unified voice for Liberalism in the district. In 1896 Rylett became minister at Bermondsey and the manager of a school; he also, it appears, joined the staff of the *New Age*, increasing his role in the paper after 1899. The paper (and its associated New Age Press) was firmly in the anti-War camp, led by J. A. Hobson in hard-hitting (and often unattractively racist) editorials. During 1902, however, Hobson had disappeared from its pages, and the publishing arrangements, as indicated in the notices to subscribers and advertisers, were gradually shifted: by the year's end, all cheques were payable to Rylett. There was a steady Unitarian bent in the contents throughout the year, and, indeed, John Page Hopps, a regular contributor on South African matters, had referred to it early in the year in his magazine *The Coming Day*: the *New Age*, he said, was 'that splendid fighting weekly . . . . There is nothing like it in the country — so thorough-going, so alert, so brilliant, so audacious, and so absolutely clean. We recommend every good Liberal give it a three months' trial.'

Rylett's involvement in South African matters continued: he had been secretary of the Stop the War Committee, and in 1905 was still advertising the publications of the South African Press Bureau, the London representative of the leading Afrikaaner press, with himself as managing editor. He also saw himself politically as firmly in the Campbell-Bannerman camp. September of 1906 saw another gradual transition in publishing arrangements; at the beginning of the month Rylett was still the recipient of cheques, but on September 20 readers were instructed to pay the New Age Press, and the next week new editorial arrangements were announced, in a note signed by Joseph Clayton, who was listed as editor from October 4. It was Clayton who sold the paper to A. R. Orage through the good offices of George Bernard Shaw, to begin a period of immense cultural influence. From 1905 to 1907, Rylett, by then minister at Tenterden, was also involved in editorial work on the *Tribune* and was a celebrated figure among Unitarians when he returned to a meeting in Manchester in 1922, and obituaries recalled his long career of political and journalistic advocacy.[14]

No minister-journalist had a more dramatic or disturbing career than William Linwood. From a London Congregationalist background, he was accepted in 1834 as a divinity student at Homerton College, then headed by the formidable John Pye Smith. But within three months of his arrival at the beginning of 1835 he was asked to leave, his fellow-students having complained of his boasting and equivocation. Then, after a period of study, he went to Glasgow to study with the celebrated Congregationalist preacher Ralph Wardlaw, and he was briefly enrolled in the University until illness forced him to withdraw. In applying to Wardlaw's academy, Linwood suppressed (he said on advice) the unhappy Homerton episode, but it came to light, and in a long self-exculpatory letter to Pye Smith he asked for a recommendation. If Pye Smith's draft reply was ever converted into a formal letter, it would have been damning, and presumably it was, as there is no record that Linwood went further in his Glasgow studies. He next appears as the minister at Ditchling in Sussex, invited on the recommendation of Robert Aspland, secretary of the British and Foreign Unitarian Association; in the interval, Linwood had been profoundly impressed by reading William Ellery Channing, who had so striking an effect on the English Unitarians of that day, but Linwood's lecture on spiritual knowledge, given at Ditchling in July 1840 and dedicated to Aspland, would certainly have distressed his patron with its insistence on the soul independent of matter, though his description of heaven as 'a higher sphere of education, inquiry, and affection', a school where the soul would explore the mysteries of nature and Providence, tracing laws that are now hidden and speculative, would have appealed to Priestleyan minds. Whatever Linwood's doctrinal soundness, there was no doubting the eloquence, of which his boyhood minister had spoken so enthusiastically in a letter to Pye Smith. He moved swiftly to become minister at Brixton and then in 1842 accepted an invitation to the Old Meeting House in Mansfield, determined 'to bring the gospel home to the affections of much-tortured hearts of the sons and daughters of toil', and to identify religion with politics, trade, and literature. So many people came to hear him that the seating capacity of the chapel had to be enlarged. And he soon began to write for the *Nottingham Review*, the most widely circulated paper in the town and dedicated to realizing such radical goals as universal suffrage and free trade. The *Review* was a wonderfully lively paper, but some of the editorials after 1842 display an extravagant brilliance that suggests Linwood's hand. Whether or not he actually became editor-in-chief, as has been said, it is certain that most of the articles in the expanded review department from 1846 are Linwood's; though there is some reviewing, they are really unsigned columns of opinion on passing events.

Linwood's bringing a new element into the congregation and his journalistic activities were causing unease by 1843, when some old families withdrew their support. Linwood still retained the backing of the great cotton-spinner Henry Hollins, but it was perhaps only a matter of time until Hollins too was alienated — by a campaign Linwood launched, with as much naïveté as passion, against a decision of the Improvement Commissioners that he believed had been dictated by Hollins for his own benefit. After the failure of an attempt at mediation, Linwood was ordered to vacate the chapel; the outcome of his suit for possession and back salary is not known. He returned to London for a short, unhappy association with W. J. Fox and tried to get appointed to the chapel in Stamford Street, but he was swiftly moving back to the old evangelical principles he had so handily and so eloquently proclaimed in the essay he was required to write for admission to Homerton. He somehow purchased a Congregationalist magazine but survived as its editor for only three issues, when his Unitarian past became known. The magazine was bought back by its former proprietor, and Linwood vanishes from the historical record.[15]

———————————

Linwood's stormy passage through Unitarianism, like Barker's at the same time, is useful in its exceptionality. Despite their successes in the pulpit, the two men were set apart from their Unitarian contemporaries by a quite different religious or theological cast of mind, not basically altered by the rejection and frustration that made possible their brief dalliance with heterodoxy. By contrast, the other journalists and ministers with whom we have dealt here shared an outlook fundamentally rational and modern, whether it came to them by inheritance or by genuine and often painful intellectual conversion. But Unitarianism was not static in the nineteenth century, and the accommodations that had inevitably to be made to successive discoveries in science and biblical criticism and to the claims of a culture that grew both more national and more monolithic weakened the links between Unitarian theology and the secular world.

Unitarian journalists were ranged almost without exception on one side of the political debate. When George Lee launched the *Rockingham* in 1809, the prospectus assured readers that the paper was not beholden to the family whose name it bore, except as that family helped to maintain the rights of Englishmen and the purity of the constitution. Despite their appeal to the Whig interest, the paper's conductors were determined on impartiality, though that would not prevent their fearlessly (and moderately) revealing political or local truths that needed to be brought out and that might raise the neighbourhood from its 'indifference to politics'. Edward Parry, in his opening leader for the *Kidderminster Shuttle* in 1870, also declared for impartiality and independence on any 'great subject of interest to the human mind and conscience.' The paper's political principles were best embodied in the Gladstone government — where George Lee nailed the colours of Catholic Emancipation to his mast, Parry raised the banner of National Education — but Gladstone would be criticized as freely as Disraeli.[16] Were the Unitarian journalists, then, merely a fortuitous grouping in a Liberalism shared across a broad spectrum of English opinion determined by economic and class interests and sectarian experience? I suggest that that explanation works better at the end of the century than at the beginning and that the liberalism of early and mid-Victorian times was grounded in, and varied accordingly with, competing religious traditions.

To illustrate the case, let us look briefly at the role of politics in the specifically Unitarian newspapers. There were three: the *Inquirer*, founded in 1842 and in sadly reduced form in existence still; the *Unitarian Herald*, published in Manchester from 1861 to 1889, and *Christian Life*, first published in 1876, absorbing the *Unitarian Herald* in 1889 and being itself absorbed by the *Inquirer* in 1929. The *Herald* was established to meet the need for a penny Unitarian paper at a time when the *Inquirer* still sold for five pence, but it also reflected widespread dissatisfaction with the *Inquirer*'s intellectualism and inclination (as many saw it) to favour the positions of James Martineau and his friends, who were far from popular in the denomination as a whole; it also stood for the North in a polarity that has characterized the denomination over the past century. The *Herald*'s founding editors — John Relly Beard, William Gaskell, Brooke Herford, and John Wright — took, with subtle variations, an essentially middle position in the bitter disputes then dividing the denomination, a centrism reinforced when Gaskell and Herford took over sole management of the paper in 1865. *Christian Life* was the creation of Robert Spears, another of the Unitarians' energetic publishers. A former Methodist, he held his first Unitarian pastorate (and kept a school) at Sunderland, where he launched the *Christian Freeman*, a religious monthly, in 1856. Moving to Stockton, he founded the *Stockton Gazette*, and, sensibly enough, the founders of the *Unitarian Herald* invited him to join their paper as subeditor, an offer he refused. Moving to Stamford Street, London, in 1862, he became in 1869 the secretary of the British and Foreign Unitarian Association, resigning in 1876 in a bitter quarrel over his refusal to sanction official republication of the works of Theodore Parker, whose anti-supernaturalist position (rapidly spreading among younger Unitarians) Spears found abhorrent. *Christian Life*, the new outlet for his energies, took up the conservative, biblically-based position (Spears would have said Channingite) in Unitarianism and advanced it steadily and with notable style against the more advanced views (and the often greater elaborateness) of the *Inquirer*.[17]

William Hincks, the founding editor of the *Inquirer* and formerly tutor in natural philosophy at Manchester College, was a thorough-paced Priestleyan who put the case for that all-encompassing system with combative brilliance at just the point when its grounds were being fatally eroded. One of his students recalled that in his college teaching his surpassing interest lay in politics, and the *Inquirer* in its earlier years was a strongly political paper.[18] A little over a quarter of the leading articles in 1842, the paper's first, partial year, dealt with politics, 13.5 per cent with foreign policy, and a fifth with social problems. Unitarian subjects claimed 8.5 per cent of the editorials, denominational matters 9.3 per cent (the same proportion as the Church of England), and general topics only 14.4 per cent; there were no leading articles on biblical or theological questions. In 1846, Hincks's last full year as editor, general topics accounted for a little over 20 per cent, while politics rose above 38 per cent. Under Hincks's successors, politics fell to 15.9 per cent in 1849 and 17.9 per cent in 1851, rising sharply to 33.9 per cent in 1852, when Richard Holt Hutton and Walter Bagehot as editors were cutting a youthful swath through the sensibilities of staid Unitarians. Neither foreign affairs nor social problems could claim anything like the importance Hincks had given to them in 1842, however: not a single leader in 1852 touched on social problems.

The beginning of the long editorship of Thomas Lethbridge Marshall in 1856 marks a startling shift in concern. In that year general articles counted for 56 per cent of the leading articles, Unitarianism for 6.7 per cent, denominational matters for 4.7 per cent, and the Church for 6.7 per cent; the Bible and theology, almost entirely neglected in the earlier sample years, were now noticeably present, at 4.7 and 4 per cent. But political subjects numbered a mere 4 per cent of leaders, social problems less than 1 per cent, and foreign policy (the Crimean War was ending) 8.7 per cent, a level never again reached in my later samples, even in 1876, the year of the Bulgarian agitation. Marshall's political score rose to 12.4 per cent in 1880 and to 14 per cent in 1885 and almost that number in 1886, when the elections came in for considerable comment, but his successors never came close to those levels: even in 1906 politics claimed only 7 per cent of the leaders, followed by 5 per cent in 1910, 6 per cent in 1926, and 3.8 per cent in 1935. No leaders were given over to social problems in 1906, only one in 1910, three in 1926 (6 per cent), and one in 1935 (1.9 per cent), while foreign policy questions accounted for similarly insignificant numbers. The gains were largely in the general category. In both the *Unitarian Herald* and *Christian Life* Unitarian subjects and denominational affairs counted for far larger percentages of leaders than in the *Inquirer*; theology too carried more weight in most years. But politics, foreign policy, and social problems played relatively little part: *Christian Life* had almost nothing to say, editorially, about the Boer War.[19]

To explain these variations on the basis of the interests or judgments of individual editors does not go very far, given the consistencies over changes in editors and the choice of sample years to coincide with elections or major crises. More persuasive is the argument that, after the abolition of the taxes on knowledge in the fifties and sixties and the rapid growth of the cheap daily press, there was no longer a need for a Unitarian newspaper, which was what Hincks and his successors prior to Marshall clearly had in mind. But the conductors of the papers and their audiences held strong views on political and social matters, so one would expect that even a denominational paper would find it essential to comment extensively on events of the day, at home and abroad, or on the social problems that so absorbed Unitarian attention in the last years of Victoria's reign: if the religious newspapers no longer had a primary mission of informing, one would think that they would try to guide and reinforce opinion. To some extent they did, but why was not more done, more consistently over a greater range?

The answer lies, I think, in an increasing dissociation of religion from political and social questions. This must seem a paradoxical, even perverse, contention, given the apparent symbiosis of religion and politics in, say, Harold Rylett's career or the steady flow of rhetoric about the need to infuse Christianity into the world. But let us look more closely. A constant in Unitarian politics from the late eighteenth century to the 1850s was bitter resistance by congregation after congregation to royal proclamations of days of thanksgiving or humiliation for victories or defeats or disasters: on some occasions observances were pointedly refused, on others congregations would meet to hear a sermon on the impropriety of government dictation to churches or the impiety of the suggestion that men bore responsibility for or could remove by mere petition what was clearly part of God's providential scheme: Hincks, as always, offered a wonderful late

26

instance of that outlook in his contemptuous leader on the general fast proclaimed for March 24, 1847, in connection with the famine. But the next round of proclamations, during and after the Crimean War, brought a very different response. In April 1854 the *Inquirer* made an editorial distinction between humiliation and humility; in its reportorial pages, T. L. Marshall's sermon in Hackney was extensively quoted in praise of Christian patriotism, in justification of some wars, and in repudiation of the 'contemptible maxims of the Peace Society'. In 1857, now as editor, Marshall urged compliance with the proclamation of a day of humiliation for the Indian Mutiny and welcomed the identity of the Christian pulpit with the voice of the Christian statesman. In Liverpool, in 1854, J. H. Thom, James Martineau's close friend, was more troubled than Marshall, but he too admitted the case for a just war, provided 'the Conscience of the Nation deliberately approves'.[20]

Conscience was, indeed, a crucial concept in Martineau's ethics and in the social outlook of the 'New School' he headed. Thom and Martineau together shunned large-scale schemes for political or social reconstruction, seeking social salvation in the power of the heightened personal example, of 'heart acting on heart, conscience on conscience, soul on soul, man on man'. It was conscience that Rylett invoked at the welcoming meeting in Dudley, and conscience came, as it were, to exhaust the religious impulse, which no longer offered authoritative grounds for *knowing*: religion was reacting rather than leading. In 1912 Philip Henry Wicksteed insisted that the churches could provide no solutions to the industrial problems of the time; they could only ask for answers, which had to come from sociology.[21] Such an abdication would have been inconceivable to Unitarians seventy or a hundred years earlier.

A final example may support the argument for dissociation and confirm Unitarian distinctiveness. In 1894, Henry Lunn, the Methodist advocate of ecumenism, held one of his conferences on reunion at Grindelwald in Switzerland. The press was the subject of one session. The first speaker, the Rev. A. R. Buckland, morning preacher at the Foundling Hospital in London, argued that newspapers must pay more attention to the churches and less to sport and crime; he worried, too, about Jewish influence on the press and about a lack of sincerity that allowed Jews or unbelievers to write editorials on Christian subjects such as the observance of Good Friday. Buckland was followed by P. W. Clayden, of the *Daily News*, who accused his Anglican predecessor of ignorance of the Press and of setting up straw men like Jewish influence or insincere writers. It was the Church's duty, Clayden maintained, to fill men with the love of God, a spirit that would then pervade the articles written by those who worked for newspapers; indeed, many religious newspapermen regarded their work as serving country, principles, and God. But the Church and the Press were totally different: 'The purpose of the Church is to keep men in mind of unseen

27

things. The Press is of this world, of things of to-day and to-morrow,' and he greatly disliked the sermon in the leading article and even more the leading article in the sermon. Expressing his entire 'abhorrence and detestation' of what Clayden had said, the third speaker, W. T. Stead, boasted that his leading articles had always been sermons and that he welcomed the echoes of what he had written in hundreds of pulpits the following Sunday — but then he was 'a revivalist preacher and not a journalist by nature'.[22]

Unitarians have always taken pride in their role as a vanguard. And so it was in this confrontation. Stead seems a voice from the past, Buckland seems even more remote, but Clayden was arguing for a dispensation with which we are all familiar: the religious press today is just another specialist grouping, and the general newspaper press is scarcely touched by the subtle moral influences that Clayden thought the churches might still exercise. In the world beyond the press we do not live in a wholly secular society: as institutions, as pressure groups, as political bodies, the churches are very much with us, and believers of the most extraordinary variety abound. But, in general, thought is determined in the secular arena and not in the crucible of God's providence, from which so many Unitarian journalists in Victorian England derived their opportunity and mission to form and remould their society.

Notes

The author wishes to thank the many persons who have helped in myriad ways in the preparation of this study when an ocean intervened: Mrs. Barbara Smith and Mrs. Joanna Parker of the library at Manchester College, Oxford; Mr. John Creasey and Mrs. Janet Barnes at Dr. Williams's Library, London; Miss G. A. Matheson and her staff at the John Rylands University Library, Manchester; Mr. Michael Brook of the Nottingham University Library; and the Rev. Neil Gerdes, librarian of the Meadville/Lombard Theological School, Chicago. Professor Michael Dintenfass, Professor and Mrs. Peter Gay, Dr. Alan Seaburg, Mrs. Jean Raymond, Mrs. Mary Wightman, and Ms. Louise B. Williams gave invaluable help in tracking down references and information.

1 Richard Cobb, *A Classical Education* (London, 1985), pp. 98 – 99.

2 *Memories of George Gilbert Armstrong* (London, 1944), pp. 46 – 51.

3 For the many doubtful sources and an interpretation of these figures and those that follow, R. K. Webb, 'Views of Unitarianism from Halley's Comet', *Transactions of the Unitarian Historical Society*, xviii (1986), 180 – 195.

4 *Inquirer*, December 19, 1903.

5 R. K. Webb, 'The Faith of Nineteenth-Century Unitarians: A Curious Incident', in Richard Helmstadter and Bernard Lightman, eds., *Victorian Faith in Crisis*, forthcoming; R. K. Webb, *Harriet Martineau, a Radical Victorian* (London, 1960), pp. 65 – 133.

6 *Inquirer*, July 11, 1846; John Bowring, *The Press . . . and other Poetry* (Wortley, 1846).

7 *Inquirer*, June 26, 1847; *Christian Life*, January 3, 1891, January 9, 1886, July 27, 1889.

8 Francis E. Mineka, *The Dissidence of Dissent: The Monthly Repository, 1806 – 1838* (Chapel Hill, N.C., 1944). Herbert McLachlan, *The Unitarian Movement in the Religious Life of England: Its Contributions to Thought and Learning, 1700 – 1900* (London, 1934), pp. 168 – 233, surveys both magazines and newspapers.

9 Donald Read, *Press and People, 1780 – 1850: Opinion in Three English Cities* (London, 1961); Michael J. Murphy, *Cambridge Newspapers and Opinion, 1780 – 1850* (Cambridge, 1977); Maurice Milne, *Newspapers of Northumberland and Durham* (Newcastle-on-Tyne, 1971); W. H. G. Armytage, 'The Editorial Experiences of Joseph Gales, 1786 – 1794,' *North Carolina Historical Review*, xxviii (1951), 332 – 361.

10 Read, *Press and People*, deals with the *Mercury* and the *Independent*. Clyde Binfield, *So Down to Prayers* (London, 1977) contains a wonderful chapter on the Baineses. Ward's diaries unfortunately contain little on his editorial work, beyond an account of the formation of the company; and there is one touching glimpse, from an uncited source, of his writing a leader in London and complaining about how tired he is (Alexander B. Bell, *Peeps into the Past, being Passages from the Diary of Thomas Asline Ward* (London, 1909)).

11 David Ayerst, *Guardian, Biography of a Newspaper* (London, 1971). J. L. Hammond, *C. P. Scott of the Manchester Guardian* (London, 1934) is particularly helpful on the Portsmouth Scotts. See also Herbert McLachlan, 'The Taylors and Scotts of the *Manchester Guardian*,' in his *Essays and Addresses* (Manchester, 1950), pp. 70 – 93; obituary of Jeremiah Garnett, *Manchester Guardian*, September 28, 1870; Donald Read, 'John Harland: "The Father of Provincial Reporting",' *Manchester Review*, viii (1958), 205 – 212. On the importance of the older universities to Scott, J. B. Atkins, *Incidents and Reflections* (London, 1947), pp. 71 – 72. The Arnolds were

thoroughly at home with Unitarians, and W. T. Arnold's sister, Mrs. Humphry Ward, not only put Robert Elsmere, after his religious crisis, to working in a Unitarian settlement but frequently wrote for or spoke to Unitarian audiences. J. Frederick Smith is described as a leader-writer in Douglas W. Robson, *The Study of Elder Yard Unitarian Chapel, Chesterfield*, revised by Arthur W. Vallance (Chesterfield, 1967), p. 25; obituary in *Inquirer*, December 3, 1898; James Agate, *Ego* (1935), pp. 39 – 44; and the tribute in the *Manchester Guardian*, June 7, 1947.

12 On Briggs, *Inquirer*, November 28, 1874; Gould, *Unitarian Herald*, November 23, 1861; the Lees, *Christian Reformer*, ix (1842), 532 – 534 and n.s. xviii (1862), 405 – 407; Clephan, *Christian Life*, March 3, 1888; Cowen, *Christian Life*, February 24, 1900, and also Milne, *Newspapers of Northumberland and Durham*, pp. 55, 62 – 66. Sir John Robinson, *Fifty Years of Fleet Street* (London, 1904); *Inquirer*, December 5, 1903; and Henry Solly, *These Eighty Years, or, The Story of an Unfinished Life* (London, 2 vols., 1893), ii, 17 – 19. On Clayden, *Christian Life*, February 22, 1902. Mention might also be made of Theophilus Davies, a divinity student at Manchester New College who, his opinions being unsettled, turned to working for the *Daily News* and for the *National Review* (successor to the *Prospective Review*); he died at the early age of thirty-five (*Inquirer*, October 26, 1861).

13 A survey of ministerial salaries for 1850 showed 5 receiving upwards of £300, 7 between £205 and £300, 21 between £145 and £195, 39 between £100 and £145, and 86 below £100 (*Inquirer*, March 13, 1852); the *Unitarian Herald*, May 3, 1862, thought the average below £100 and the legitimate need not less than £400. See also John Seed, 'Unitarian Ministers as Schoolmasters, 1780 – 1850: Some Notes', *Transactions of the Unitarian Historical Society* (1982), 170 – 176. On Harwood, *DNB* and M. M. Bevington, *The Saturday Review, 1855 – 1868: Representative Educated Opinion in Victorian England* (New York, 1941). For Parry, *Inquirer*, December 11, 1926; E. D. Priestley Evans, *A History of the New Meeting House, Kidderminster, 1780 – 1900* (Kidderminster, 1900), pp. 135 – 139; and the centenary supplement to the *Shuttle*, February 13, 1970. On McKean, *Inquirer*, July 2, 1904. Mention might also be made of journalists who became ministers. Among them was William Bennett, who worked on his brother's paper, the *Dumbarton Herald*, in the 1860s before becoming minister at Canterbury, Aberdeen, Paisley, and Heywood, and a regular contributor to the *Unitarian Herald* (*Inquirer*, January 14 and 21, 1882). C. L. Corkran came by way of temperance and anti-corn law work to work for the *League* in the 1840s and the *Norwich Mercury*, where services at the Octagon Chapel led him to abandon his Methodism; from 1848 to 1879 he was domestic missionary in Spicer Street, Spitalfields (*Inquirer*, March 16, 1901). Jeffrey Worthington, from an old-established Manchester Unitarian family, spent seven years on the staff of the *Manchester Guardian* before going to Manchester New College and serving as minister at Bolton, Brixton, and Taunton (*Inquirer*, April 27, 1918).

14 This shadowy reconstruction of Rylett's career rests on obituaries in *Inquirer*, August 22, 1936, and *Manchester Guardian* (by Herbert McLachlan and particularly well informed), August 9, 1936; on the *New Age* for the period of his association with it; on the surviving fragment of the *Hyde Telegraph* and the transitional issues of the *Reporter* in the British Library; on the account of the reception at Dudley, *Unitarian Herald*, April 1, 1887; on the Flowery Fields records, held in the church, which contain an undated, unidentified cutting with an admirable personal description; and on his letter to Campbell-Bannerman, February 9, 1905, British Library Add. MSS 41,238, f. 22. He is simply not mentioned by writers interested in Orage when they discuss the earlier history of the *New Age*.

15 The account of Linwood's ministry in J. Harrop White, *The Story of the Old Meeting House, Mansfield* (London, 1959) is excellent; see also Derek Fraser, 'The Nottingham Press, 1800 – 1850', *Transactions of the Historical Society of Nottinghamshire*, lxvii (1963), 46 – 66; the Homerton College Register and correspondence covering Linwood's brief stay there and his efforts to study in Glasgow are in Dr. Williams's Library. Correspondence and other material relative to the disputes in Mansfield are in the Nottingham University Library, O1C 14 – 66. *Nottingham Review*, 1842 – 1848, *passim* (the last 'Review Office' column appears on

August 11, 1848, presumably the point at which Linwood's connection with the paper ceased); William Linwood, *Our Spiritual Knowledge of Each Other in a Future State* (London, 1840); Leonard J. Maguire, comp., *A Transcription of the Early Records Relating to the Old Meeting House, Ditchling*, i (South Croydon, 1977), 87 – 89.

16 *Rockingham*, January 2, 1808; *Kidderminster Shuttle*, February 12, 1870. Actually, the first issue of the paper appeared on the preceding Tuesday, when the Queen's speech was sent by telegraph and relayed sentence by sentence from the telegraph office to the printing office, so that it was all set in type by the time the last sentence was received.

17 Roger Thomas published an admirable brief centenary history of the *Inquirer* in that journal, May 9 – September 19, 1942. Dr. Williams's Library holds the minute books of the *Unitarian Herald* during the first four years of its existence. No other records exist for the three papers beyond the Tayler papers mentioned in n. 20.

18 Hincks's political enthusiasm is noted in two letters, November 7, 1830, and March 20, 1831, from William Rayner Wood to his parents (Manchester College, Oxford). Compare the theological and political indoctrination of Russell Scott, John Edward Taylor's father-in-law, by his father, Russell Scott, the Portsmouth minister (J. L. Hammond, *C. P. Scott*, pp. 4 – 5).

19 My analysis of the contents of the three papers is based on an unscientific sample of years determined by four considerations: the availability of printed tables of contents, though in some instances I created my own; years in which the papers co-existed; changes in the editorship; and the importance of particular years, e.g., when general elections occurred. The years chosen are 1842, 1846, 1847, 1849, 1851, 1856, 1861, 1862, 1876, 1880, 1885, 1886, 1906, 1910, 1926, and 1935. The classification is to some extent arbitrary (e.g., education was put under 'General' unless it was the subject of legislation, when it became 'Political'). But the scheme done differently would not result, I believe, in a substantially different pattern.

20 *Inquirer*, March 20, 1947, April 29, 1854, October 3 and 10, 1857; J. H. Thom, *The Religious Spirit that Befits this Crisis; not the Spirit of Humiliation* . . . (London, 1854). Support for the Crimean War among Unitarians foreshadows the imperial enthusiasm that affected some of them later in the century. By omitting significant comment on the Boer War, *Christian Life* avoided the crisis produced in the *Inquirer*'s affairs by the critical leaders published by the editor, the Rev. V. D. Davis. Davis was retained but the editorial board and the business arrangements were altered, a passage discussed in Roger Thomas's history and in papers of S. S. Tayler in Dr. Williams's Library. It is hard to imagine that Robert Spears, a wonderfully candid and brave man, was motivated simply by prudential concern for a divided readership. The self-censorship must have arisen from more fundamental judgments about what was appropriate. Compare the limited definition of 'political' leaders that Marshall assigned to Henry Morley (later professor of English literature at University College, London) in 1856; he was to limit himself to 'great social movements and educational questions of the age, not party politics' (Marshall to John Gordon, February 6, 1856, Unitarian College MSS B1[11], John Rylands University Library, Manchester).

21 *Inquirer*, September 7, 1912; R. K. Webb, 'John Hamilton Thom: Intellect and Conscience in Liverpool', in P. T. Phillips, ed., *The View from the Pulpit* (Toronto, 1978), pp. 211 – 243.

22 The discussion which took place on July 18, 1894, is reported in *Review of the Churches*, Toronto, August 15, 1894, vi, 298 – 301.

2

Pledged to India:
The Liberal Experiment, 1885-1909

Ainslie T. Embree

'We are pledged to India . . . and we have no choice but to apply ourselves to . . . the redemption of the pledge.' (Gladstone, 1881)

'Long years ago we made a tryst with destiny, and now the time comes when we shall redeem our pledge.' (Nehru, 1947)

In 1908, John Morley, as Secretary of State for India, wrote to Lord Minto, the Governor-General, that the British ruled India in order 'to implant — slowly, prudently, judiciously — those ideas of justice, law, humanity, which are the foundations of our own civilisation'.[1] Read at the end of the twentieth century, this statement must seem, even in a private letter, to have been self-serving hypocrisy or, at best, pious delusion, but there is no reason to suppose that Morley did not mean exactly what he said or that Minto did not agree with him. What is significant, however, for an understanding of modern India is that many of the most influential of India's nationalist leaders would have accepted Morley's statement as a reasonable summary of the nature of the relationship between the two countries. Why this was so, and the conclusions that the nationalists drew from it, are a singularly important strand in the history of modern India; so also is the less than enthusiastic reaction of British Liberals like Morley to the appropriation of their ideas and programs by Indians.

The issues at stake had to do with the transplantation of ideas and institutions from one culture to another, with the function of values in shaping social structures, and, above all, with interpretations, by both Indians and

British, of Indian civilization. While it is difficult to give specific content to these large generalities, if we look back over the developments in the subcontinent in the past century we can see that they are at the heart of the long and tortured debate over the introduction of representative political institutions into India. Put in the simplest terms, many of the British involved in India, including some who knew it extremely well, were convinced that Indian civilization and western democratic political systems were fundamentally incompatible. Without the stern authoritarianism of British rule, according to Morley, one would hear 'through the dark distances the roar and scream of confusion and carnage in India'.[2] Indian leaders, on the other hand, many of whom had a scholarly knowledge of their own culture, were passionately convinced that British institutions could be transplanted to India, and that this would fulfil the meaning and purpose of British rule in India. Much modern scholarship, both in India and the West, speaks of the imposition of alien institutions by an aggressive imperial power, but the reality in India is far more complex; it is no exaggeration to say that it was the Indians who wanted such an imposition, and the British who questioned both its morality and its practicality.

The formative phase of the Indian nationalist movement can be conveniently located in the period from 1880 to 1909, which begins with the viceroyalty of Lord Ripon (1880 – 1884), who had been sent out by Gladstone to redress what he considered the shame and dishonor of the Indian policies of the Disraeli government. The period includes the founding of the Indian National Congress in 1885, the creative tumult of Lord Curzon's rule (1899 – 1905), the bitterness of the Partition of Bengal in 1905, and concludes with the constitutional landmark of the Morley-Minto reforms of 1909. All of these events provided the framework in which influences from India and Great Britain coalesced to create a distinctive and coherent political ideology for modern India. One of the most significant aspects of this ideology was that the nationalist leaders accepted as the basis for their thinking about the future of India many of the formulations of nineteenth-century British Liberalism. Almost without exception, they believed that the Indian political system could and should be transformed by the British through the introduction of representative government, free speech, constitutionalism, and all the other landmarks of liberty.

In general, the British Liberals, in Morley's phrase, regarded as 'moonshine' the belief that their ideas were translatable into an Indian political vocabulary.[3] That this was the attitude, not just of Englishmen like Lord Curzon who were known for their contempt for nationalist aspirations, but of the very Liberals whom they so much admired, was not much recognized by the early Indian nationalists. The conflicting evaluations of the possibility of the transfer to India of western institutions, which Indians recognized were as much products of western social development

33

as were modern science and technology, were rooted in the way Indians thought about their own society, and, equally important, in the way British Liberals thought about India. Two different levels were involved in both sets of evaluations, one having to do with the value of India to Great Britain in material terms, the other concerned with the nature of India's culture. Somewhat surprisingly it was on this, the second level of cultural evaluation, that discussion was most frequently carried out in both Indian nationalist and British Liberal circles. To a considerable extent, however, it is probably true that the Liberals' sympathetic understanding of nationalist aspirations was colored by their sense that India was not vital to British interests. Gladstone himself once remarked, referring to the strength of the Empire, 'India adds nothing.'[4] Over against that negative evaluation, it must be said, however, that the Liberals were by no means consistent in placing a low material value on the Indian Empire. Morley, for example, warned his constituents in 1907 that they should not make the mistake of supposing that India did not matter to them economically. 'Do not dream,' he told them, 'that you can go on with that programme of social reforms, all costing money and absorbing attention, in the spirit in which you are about to pursue it,' if India should be lost.[5]

From an opposing political position, Lord Curzon, the former governor-general, insisting with great eloquence on the importance of India for Great Britain, was less guarded and more assertive. In the same year as that in which Morley hinted at the connection between India and the ability of Britain to afford social services, Curzon predicted in the bleakest terms the decline of England if India should ever be lost. English industry could not be sustained without imperial demands and, in addition, English character would atrophy without the challenge of conquests to be made and duty to be performed. 'Swallowed up in the whirlpool of American cosmopolitanism', England would become the inglorious playground of wandering tourists.[6] Indian nationalists had much the same belief in the importance of India to Great Britain, which explains in part their faith that Britain would be willing to make large concessions to their demands for greater autonomy and freedom. This was a belief that died hard, for Nehru and the Congress still saw Indian resources as a bargaining card in the summer of 1947.

Given his presuppositions, Curzon could conclude in 1907 that it was impossible that the nationalist demands could ever be met, since they pointed towards self-government, which 'would mean ruin to India and treason to our trust'.[7] The Liberals, having fed the hopes of Indian nationalists, had, by a circuitous route, reached almost exactly the same position. Stephen Koss was surely correct when he argued that, while all the great Liberals had been advocates of constitutional reforms in India, by the end of the century they had come to the conclusion that there was no way in which their ideas of 'justice, law, and humanity' could be translated into political solutions that would satisfy the nationalist demands. In Stephen Koss's words, 'An inexorable belief in the ultimate futility of the British Raj had discouraged the formulators of nineteenth-century Liberal doctrine from applying their talents to a practicable definition of British aims in and for India.' Koss concludes that it was their shortsightedness that kept them from giving constitutional form to their beliefs.[8] But it is hard to imagine what in fact those definitions might have been, given the contradictions between their understanding of the nature of Indian society and the British connection with it, and that of the Indian leaders. The dilemma of the British Liberals at the beginning of the twentieth century was that they were faced by the demands of Indians who had been fed, as one of the nationalist leaders put it, on 'the strong food of English constitutional freedom'.[9] The Liberals had to provide solutions that were consonant with the exercise of imperial power while not denying their fundamental intellectual positions. The dilemma of the Indian nationalists was to argue for the introduction of British political institutions while asserting the integrity and autonomy of Indian civilization.

The early nationalist understanding of the purpose of British rule in India finds frequent statement in their speeches and writings. The fulsome tone of some of these evaluations is embarrassing to later generations, but it is important to note that almost always they are in praise of ideas and institutions, not of men. When, for example, Keshib Chunder Sen, a famous orator much given to over-heated language, spoke in 1877 of British rule in India as providential, with 'Victoria as an instrument in the hands of Providence to elevate this degraded country in the scale of nations',[10] he was not talking about the servants of the East India Company who had engineered the take-over of Bengal. In the metaphor made familiar to his generation by the Scottish educational missionaries in Calcutta, he was thinking of how British institutions could be 'used' for the moral and material regeneration of India. In this borrowed theology, neither Britain nor India had written the parts they were playing.

References to providential design in the Indo-British connection are as common in Indian as in British writing, and undoubtedly it was a significant element in the complex structure Indian intellectuals were creating to explain India's historical experience. From the early years of the nineteenth century when serious intellectual contacts between Indians and the British were beginning, a central problem for Indians was to find a standing-place within their own history that would permit them to maintain self-esteem and self-confidence. The hard facts were the centuries of Muslim domination followed by the new intrusion of western power, and it was Hindu intellectuals who devised a satisfactory way of coming to terms with India's 'degraded' state. This was not a reading of history that could be accepted by Muslim thinkers, since an essential factor in this explanation of India's situation was precisely the Muslim conquest, but it was well-suited to Hindu social and political reformers. It permitted them, on the one hand, to accept western criticisms of Indian society as corrupt, idolatrous, and, above all, stagnant, that most damning of nineteenth-century characterizations, while, on the other hand, to assert the inherent greatness of the Hindu tradition.

The first and one of the most influential exponents in India of what can be thought of as a social philosophy of acceptance and accommodation was Ram Mohan Roy (1772 – 1833). After a successful career as an administrator for the East India Company, Roy devoted himself to projects for social change. For Roy, the necessity for change was obvious in what he regarded as the superstitious and barbarous practices that had deformed Hindu society. Here he was accepting in large part the harsh evaluations that were currently being made by James Mill, Charles Grant, and a host of others, of the corrupting influence of Hinduism as a religious sytem on Indian society. Such critics, despite their unrelenting denigration of Indian culture, were not racists; what was wrong with India was not rooted in the nature of the people, but in their religion. At this point, Roy parted company with them; for, while what they said about the current practices and beliefs of Hinduism was true, these were, he insisted, corrupt aberrations that had crept in through the centuries. Remove them, and what would be left would be the universal monotheism that was at the heart of all religions. Roy's ambition for his countrymen was, as he put it, 'to awaken them from their dream of error . . . to contemplate . . . Nature's God'.[11] The result would be, not just a theological adjustment, but the restoration of Indian society to its original grandeur.

In this intellectual formulation, Britain was crucial to this process of rebuilding the structure of the vanquished society, for it was through the introduction of British institutions that the transformation would take place. A free press, for example, was necessary, not because it had ever been part of the Indian tradition, but because it was integral to the British system which denied 'the political maxim so often acted upon by Asiatic princes that the more the people are kept in darkness, their rulers will derive the greater advantages from them'.[12] This was the same argument that Roy used for the encouragement of the use of English as the medium of higher education. Sanskrit, the classical language of the Hindu tradition, was admirably suited for keeping the people in ignorance of real knowledge, but it was English that would permit the fulfilment of the glorious British tradition 'of planting in Asia the arts and sciences of modern Europe'.[13] It is possible that Roy wrote in this fashion in 1823 in order to gain his ends by flattering the conqueror, but the whole weight of his numerous books and articles is against this interpretation. He had a passionate faith that the way to the renewal of India's greatness was through the same institutions that had raised the British in power and influence above the inhabitants of other parts of the world. Roy, like many other nineteenth-century Indian intellectuals, saw the future in Britain and knew that it worked. A dominating motif of the intellectual history of India in the modern period is the search for a definition of the past that would make plausible the shaping of the future through the adoption of mechanisms that had transformed Great Britain itself, the segment of the western world that Indians knew best. That these mechanisms were associated with the alien ruling power did not make them less desirable; on the contrary, the obvious superiority of the British in their exercise of material and political power validated their ideas and institutions.

Behind Keshub Sen's rhetoric about the providential nature of British rule in India it is possible, therefore, to see logical structures and intellectual concepts that run through much nationalist understanding of India. One of these was that India's historical experience was rooted in internal weaknesses that had made her subjection possible. She was not, however, a society wounded to the death; renewal and reformation were possible. India was great in the past and would be again in the future. It was in this future return to past greatness that British institutions were to play their crucial part. This was not a role often assigned to an occupying imperial power; it is hard, for example, to suppose that when Byron mused that the Greeks might regain their past freedoms, he saw the Turks as providing a life-giving example.

In making this easy contrast between two empires of conquest, a point of fundamental importance must be emphasized: Indian nationalists were making a deliberate choice, based on rational perceptions, when they linked their political hopes for their country with the ideas, values, and institutions of the occupying power. They were doing so, as will be noted later, based on their understanding of their own culture and the political system of Great Britain. They did not argue for a return to India's own political forms in order to restore India's greatness, although that was obviously a possible choice, but for the introduction of British forms. It was not only in the sphere of political ideas that this process of choosing western, or specifically British, patterns was going on, but also in such quite different aspects of culture as art and literature. Western art forms and techniques were seen as keys to what has been called 'the lost language of Indian art', which, once it was re-learned, could lead to a new creativity.[14]

In the adoption of western forms, Indians were selective in their choices, and while there was some mimicry of superficial or unsuitable aspects of western culture, there was far less than contemptuous critics suggested. In their enthusiasm for western political forms, Indians were careful to stress that these new institutions were consonant with the stress lines of Indian culture. In other areas, there was little tendency to accept western cultural artifacts. Two illustrations of different orders of magnitude come to mind: one is music and the other is religion. Western music appears to have made

37

very little impact on Indian taste (compared to its extraordinary success in Japan and Korea), and as for religion, while there is much praise of the ethical norms of Christianity, its actual adoption as a religion was always a minority option. This selectivity in terms of parts of the western value systems had not, incidentally, been foreseen by foreign proponents of a radical transformation of Indian culture. A powerful argument for the founding by the mission societies of schools and colleges that taught essentially a secular curriculum was that the introduction of western learning itself, quite apart from any formal religious instruction, would lead to the destruction of the Indian religious systems. Before the purifying force of European knowledge, as an advocate of religious and social change put it in 1793, 'idolatry, with all its rabble of impure deities . . . its false principles and corrupt practices, would fall', and the people, would rise 'in the scale of human beings'.[15] Things did not work out this way, and the light that broke in on young India was not the gospel, but nineteenth-century British Liberalism.

Corroboration that the vision of India's political future was largely articulated in terms of the introduction of western political institutions into India can be found in the speeches and writings of early nationalist leaders, including the presidential addresses at the annual meetings of the Indian National Congress from 1885 on to the early years of the twentieth century. Thus as president of the Congress in 1886, Dadabhai Naoroji, the Parsi from Bombay who had lived in London for many years engaged in business and Liberal politics (he was elected member for Central Finsbury in 1892), spoke of 'the new light' which had been poured on India through western education. Through it, Indians had been taught 'the new lessons that kings are made for the people, not people for the kings'. His insistence that this lesson was learned amidst the darkness of Asian despotism from knowledge of free English civilization was greeted, according to the record, by loud cheers.[16]

Naoroji was quite explicit, however, that it was from the record of British historical experience, not from relationships with the English as individuals in India, that the new lessons were learned. As far as any personal influence was concerned, the Englishmen in India 'might just as well be living in the moon'. Isolated from the people, they were strangers in the land, without moral influence, and they were not, as they so frequently prided themselves, the natural leaders of the people. 'All they effectually do is to eat the substance of India, material and moral, while living here and when they go, they carry away all they have acquired.'[17] This is a very different reading of the impact of the British as people from the one found in many British writers, where the tendency was to deride the institutions and exalt the individuals by emphasizing the respect the Indians had for personal character. Kipling is, of course, the most articulate spokesman for this attitude, but it is reflected in the work of many less well-known writers. In Indian writing this reading of the imperial experience is almost entirely lacking, replaced by a frequent condemnation, as with Naoroji, of British officials and their practices while praising the values exemplified in the British political system. This understanding of the relationship between India and Great Britain is one of the many complex ironies of the imperial experience in India that make the history of Indian nationalism so radically different from nationalist movements elsewhere, including those in other parts of the British Empire.

Where could Indians find models for courage, devotion, and sacrifice?, Surendranath Banerjea asked the Indian National Congress in his presidential address in 1895. He suggested Greece, Rome, and revolutionary France as possibilities, only to reject them; that he did not mention India reflects both the content of the education he had received in Calcutta and the purpose of his rhetorical question. The answer, of course, was that the most edifying examples of the patriotic virtues were to be found, subsumed under the rubrics of love of country and of God, in the history of the English people's 'stately march towards constitutional freedom'.[18] Yet, more than most people of his class, Banerjea had reason for bitterness and resentment against the British. One of the first Indians to secure admission to the Indian Civil Service, he had been dismissed in 1872 for incompetence, but he believed, probably correctly, that he was a victim of the racism that was beginning to characterize the British in India. Then in 1875 he was denied admission to the Bar, even though he had eaten the requisite number of dinners at the Middle Temple. Among his defenders was Charles Dickens, who in *Good Words* deplored the prejudice of officialdom against Indians.[19] But Banerjea's private grievances against members of the bureaucracy did not alter his faith in the British political system and the need to transplant into India the ideas and values that had shaped it. The nationalist ideology of which he was one of the architects had a large place for such things as the belief that the history of England was the story of the gradual enlargement of liberty, and that this would be replicated in India, with the assistance of the British as rulers of India. Banerjea's persistence in combining praise of British values with attacks on British officials once led Lord Curzon to refer to him as 'that vitriolic windbag', which is an understandable response. But so also, from the other side, is the characterization a nationalist spokesman made of Curzon's failure to respond to Indian demands for British freedoms. In 1904, Dinshaw Wacha, a former President of the Congress, wrote to Gokahle, the great admirer of Gladstone and Morley, 'The person who said that Lord Curzon was an *Asiatic* viceroy will prove true. He has forgotten English methods of governing India and is daily growing in love with *Asiatic* ways of ruling.'[20]

On the surface, their repeated use of 'Asian' as a derogatory term for British officials suggests that the nationalists were repudiating their own past, but this is not really so. Consciously or not, they were separating what they regarded as valid and worthwhile in the Indian tradition from what they identified as Asian, and the implications of the term for them were largely political. They had adopted the western term as a synonym for despotism, and as far as India was concerned, what they had in mind were the Turkish, or, in the familiar nineteenth-century usage, the pre-British Muslim rulers. Historiography is important in all nineteenth-century nationalist movements for validation of claims of legitimacy to rule, but it had a peculiar centrality for the leaders of the Indian National Congress. Almost without exception they were products of the new system of higher education with its curriculum that drew very heavily on western, especially British, literature, history, and political philosophy. Recent studies have argued very persuasively that this literary education had the definite ideological purpose of undermining the values of Indian culture and sacralizing those of the imperial power, and even if this interpretation can be questioned in detail, there can be little doubt of the extraordinary success of the curriculum in imparting admiration for British political values.[21] It is true that, as Curzon said, they were a microscopic minority — there were perhaps not more than fifty thousand graduates at the end of the century — but they were a dominant minority. It was not only the future that belonged to them, but the past as well, for they were drawn from the traditional élites, particularly the Brahmans and other high castes, whose links with the fabric of Indian culture were strong.

These linkages kept the western-educated from being isolated from their own society and from becoming brown Englishmen, as was so often and so erroneously claimed. It was here that their interpretation of India's history functioned in a most creative way. The history of India that was part of the curriculum was written by nineteenth-century western scholars who emphasized above all else the political disunity of India. The ideological purpose of this emphasis is spelled out in the famous foreword to Elliott and Dowson's great collection of translations from the Muslim historians of India, where it speaks of the history of India in the centuries previous to British rule as characterized by an unending procession of 'conspiracies, revolts, intrigues, murders and fratricides'. From this record, the 'bombastic Babus' who ranted against British rule might learn what India was like before it was unified and pacified.[22] In the early twentieth century, in what was probably the most widely used text-book on Indian history, Vincent Smith gave almost canonical status to this view when he declared that without a paramount power the political units of India, 'hundreds in number, might be likened to a swarm of free, mutually repellent molecules in a state of incessant movement, now flying apart, now coalescing'.[23]

Reaction to this reading of the Indian past is a vital element in modern Indian intellectual history, for its acceptance would have undercut the development of a nationalist ideology. Few aspects of that ideology were more fateful for the future than the unquestioned assumption that a free India would be coterminous with the Indian Empire created by the British. Partition was one of the fruits of this commitment, as was the turmoil in the Punjab in the 1980s.

The movement towards political unification in Germany and Italy were of great interest to educated Indians, and Garibaldi and Mazzini were special heroes for young Bengalis. Surendranath Banerjea tells of how in the 1870s he popularized Mazzini's work for Italian unity as a model for Indians, although he was careful to stress his devotion to constitutionalism, not his revolutionary ideals.[24] From the beginning, the emphasis in the nationalist movement was on the unity of India, and to a very considerable extent nationalist history was written in terms of the great moments when India was united. In this reading of the past, India ceased to be a geographic expression, and she was seen, not as a state that was newly created in the nineteenth century, but as one that had been a great nation under the Mauryas, the Guptas, and Akbar. This, it should be noted, is a Hindu view of history. Akbar is there because, in the words of many modern text-books, he was not a fanatical Muslim, but a believer in religious tolerance and other virtues that were regarded as typically Hindu. In contrast, Aurangzeb, who was in fact the greatest unifier of the sub-continent before the British achievement in the nineteenth century, but who did not succeed in preserving his imperial conquests, was seen as the destroyer of unity because of his alleged Islamic fanaticism.

That the periods of unity were separated by hundreds of years' disunity and that India had been ruled by foreigners were not denied by the nationalists; on the contrary, these facts were made to serve their cause as demonstrating the internal weakness of Indian society. It was their analysis of those weakenesses that linked the nationalist understanding of history as found in the periods of national unity with their commitment to the ideas and values of British Liberalism. Indian social reformers had accepted as valid much of the criticism that westerners had made of Indian society, and this in fact did not go against the grain of Indian thought itself, for in the Hindu concept of time and history we live in a decaying and degenerating world. But what was new and exciting was the message that although society was corrupt, through human action it could be renovated and renewed. In the Indian view, progress was built into the universe, but it was movement downward; in this new view, progress was upward. The impact of the European belief in progress on Indian intellectual history has been little explored, but it was one of the genuinely new ideas that made a significant contribution to the articulation of a nationalist ideology. Early in the century a cultivated and perceptive Indian visitor to England had seen the implications of what he regarded as the exotic idea that mankind had progressed from a state of savagery and would move up to even higher levels of achievement. 'If this axiom of theirs be correct,' he pointed out, 'man has yet much to learn, and all his boasted knowledge is but vanity.'[25] The generation that had been brought into contact with such ideas through the new system of western education, with its emphasis on moral and material reform, found in the speeches of Gladstone and the other great Liberals, with their many references to progress and improvement, materials on which to build their expectations for the future of India.

Especially during the Midlothian campaign of 1879 – 80, Gladstone's denunciations of the Indian policies of Disraeli suggested that he had heard the protests of Indians against the Vernacular Press Act and the Arms Act, those measures which educated Indians saw as inspired by racism and fear to prevent social change. When word of Gladstone's triumph reached Calcutta, a reformist journal broke the news with red-bordered headlines: 'Rejoice India! Rejoice all countrymen! . . . Let cries for Mr. Gladstone and his coadjutors rend the skies from the Himalayas to Cape Comorin.'[26] Just as it has been argued that in England there was an affinity between Nonconformity and the Liberals based upon belief in moral progress and in popular control of government,[27] so in India they were seen as having a special role as the guardian of her interests. This relationship, however, went far beyond paternalism. For the nationalists it meant, quite simply, the introduction into India of those political institutions which the Liberals fostered in England. They neither expected nor desired that this change would take place overnight, but they wanted evidence that the Government was willing to listen to those who spoke for India. Given the Liberals' defence of Indian interests and the admiration that the early nationalists expressed for British institutions, this seemed a modest proposal, but it was in fact the most difficult of all issues. 'Who spoke for India?' Curzon once asked, and gave as his answer that it was the rulers, with their concern for 'the Indian peasant, the patient, humble silent millions', who spoke for India.[28] Over against this view, which is, after all, not unique to the British in India but has been widely shared by rulers in all times and places, was the one articulated with increasing clarity after the 1880s by the leaders of the Indian National Congress. People like themselves, who had fulfilled Macaulay's vision of a class which, having been educated in English, was English 'in taste, in opinions, in morals, and in intellect', would be the natural interpreters who would speak for India.[29]

This issue had been put very succinctly by Sir Rameshchandra Mitra, a judge of the Calcutta High Court, when he addressed the Indian National Congress in 1896. The educated people of India, he urged, were the legitimate spokesmen of its illiterate masses. To believe otherwise was to suppose that foreign officials knew them better than their own country-men. He then added a comment to reinforce his case for the Indian educated, rather than, for example, the landlords or the rajas: 'The natural order of things' was 'that those who think must govern those who toil'.[30]

Mitra was speaking in English as he drew upon the great ideas of the nineteenth-century Liberal tradition, but he was very clearly reflecting an Indian, specifically a Brahmanical, world view. Implicit in this statement is that the British have overturned this natural order by denying the educated group their rightful place, not as representatives, but as spokesmen, for India's masses. A very important difference is involved here, and one that often eluded the British when they dismissed the western-educated group as an insignificant minority. Mitra was not talking of a right to act as spokesmen based on numerical plurality but on knowledge, social status, character, in short, on the natural order of things. It is not surprising that the members of this group counted Burke among their chief mentors in formulating their nationalist ideology, for an aspect of the intellectual history of nineteenth-century India is that validation for values and concepts from within the culture was often found by discovering analogues in western thought. Working in the other direction, it was possible to gain acceptance for ideas from the west by arguing that they were identical to those within Brahmanical tradition itself.

Mitra's emphasis that the claim of the educated classes was grounded in the natural order of things says much about the background from which Mitra and many of the others who gained positions of leadership came. They were not aristocrats in the European sense, since political and economic conditions under neither indigenous nor Muslim rulers had been conducive to the creation of such a class, but they were, in the Indian usage of the English word, from 'respectable' families, that is, worthy of respect within the context of the norms of the society itself. They were not new men from classes that had changed their status and position as a result of the intrusion of western political and economic power, but their bases were firmly in the traditional society. This is another one of those factors that give the Indian nationalist movement its distinctive character, and has special relevance to the importance of regionalism within its development. Families like the Tagores and Mitras had certainly aligned themselves with the British in the sense that they found functions for themselves in the new political system, but this was possible because of what they brought with them: the skills of literacy and easy access to the traditional structures of society.

The members of the new professions that had been created in the nineteenth century, such as law, medicine, journalism and college teaching, as well as those who were actually employed in the administration or who were engaged in new forms of trade and commerce, were almost without exception from the groups that had traditionally exercised power and influence in Indian society. They were not necessarily Brahmans, but they were from caste groups that were literate in the languages used by the ruling powers and had performed functions analogous to those of the new professions or to those required by the new government.

A fundamental explanation of the stability of Indian society through the centuries, despite the enormous shocks it suffered from the political dominance of such alien intruders as the Turks and the British, is that the indigenous élites maintained their position within the society. This means that the forebears of many of the nationalist spokesmen in the late nineteenth century had been influential in the former administrative structures. Mitra's father, for example, who belonged to the Kayastha caste, had been a high official in the old legal system in Bengal, and thus knew Persian, the language of the courts of the Muslim rulers, as well as Arabic. Rameshchandra Mitra was the first Indian to act as Chief Justice, and the fact that under the regulations he could not hold the post permanently gives special meaning to his assertion that the natural order had been subverted in India.

Perhaps the most careful analysis of the meaning for Indian society of the ideas of liberal England came from M. G. Ranade (1842 – 1901), who, like Mitra, had achieved great distinction under the new legal system of British India. As a Judge of the Bombay High Court he could not be openly involved in political work, but his ideas had great influence on the leaders of the Indian National Congress, notably G. K. Gokhale (1866 – 1915), who is the pivotal figure in the period before the First World War. This is when the Indian National Congress was transformed from being the loyal opposition, as the first generation of leaders liked to think of themselves, into an organization that denied the legitimacy of British rule. Ranade's ideas, as articulated in Gokhale's political programs, were the basis for the attempt to persuade John Morley at the India Office and the bureaucracy in India that the Congress spoke for India.

Deeply versed in the history and culture of the Marathas, and concerned with social and religious reform, Ranade expressed his views in speeches and in articles, many of them unsigned, in the journal of the Poona Sarvajanik Sabha, an organization founded, according to its constitution, to act as a mediating body with government by 'making a true representation of the real circumstances' of the people of India.[31] Like the other early nationalists, Ranade insisted upon the beneficial results of British rule: laws that applied to everyone, irrespective of civil condition; the subordination of the military to civilian power; the separation of the judiciary from the executive; and the development of trade and commerce.

In emphasizing the blessings of British rule, Ranade was doing more than assuring the rulers of his loyalty — he was also arguing against members of his own particular class, the Chitpavan Brahmans of Poona. Many members of this small group, who had had a dominant place in the old Maratha political system, were intensely conscious of what they had lost through the British conquest and they were regarded with deep suspicion by the Bombay administration. They were also orthodox in religion, and considered themselves the guardians of the Hindu tradition.

By the 1880s, these Brahmans in the Poona area had begun to appeal to the glories of the Hindu past and, as Ranade said, their interest was in revival, not reform. Long before chauvinistic revivalism linked nationalism and religion in the twentieth century, Ranade perceived its peril to societies like India. Advocates of a return to the old ways, to the ancient authorities, to the sanctions of the past, were subverting all the gains that had been made from the enforced contact with the West. The revivalists were in fact revolutionaries, not understanding that usages and customs change through growth and decay, in an organic fashion, and that, when they talked of returning to the past, what they wanted to do was to break the continuities of growth. What was needed was an understanding of how the new ideas and institutions that come from the West could be used to build a better society in India. A congratulatory address to the Queen in 1876 from Ranade's organization, the Poona Sabha, spelled out the expectation of the generation of Indians who founded the Indian National Congress: representative and responsible legislative bodies where spokesmen for the people of India could make contact with their rulers. They recognized that this could not happen suddenly, but there should be gradual development of institutions that would elevate the people to 'the political and social status of the British nation, and teaching them gradually, by examples and encouragement, and by actual exercise of responsible power, to be manly and self-sustained, prepared to welcome their connexion with England as a providential arrangement intended for their welfare'.[32]

Ranade gladly acknowledged, as did many other of the early nationalists, that their understanding of the political system needed for India and its relationship with Great Britain was grounded in their reading of Burke, Macaulay, John Stuart Mill, John Bright, Herbert Spencer, and Gladstone. It seemed reasonable to them, then, having learned their lessons so well, that they would be accepted as spokesmen for India by British Liberals, who would initiate reforms leading to the gradual establishment of representative government. In retrospect, it is possible to argue that this is indeed what happened between the Morley-Minto Reforms of 1909, which gave a measure of representation, if not responsibility, and the transfer of power in 1947, but this reading ignores the reality of political history. While John Morley expressed condescending satisfaction that the grand themes of his own political tradition — gradualism, constitutionalism, liberty, and representative government — had been so enthusiastically accepted by educated Indians, he reminded them that they had not read their own history carefully. Intoxicated with the ideas of freedom, nationality, and self-government which breathe from the pages of the great English writers, they had made the mistake of believing that India was a nation. They were fervent admirers of Burke, but they had not understood his celebrated saying: 'How weary a step do those take who endeavour to make out of a great mass a true political personality.'[33]

45

Morley was making the point that had been made with unwearying insistence by British interpreters for many years, and that would continue to be made up to and beyond 1947: India was not, and never had been, a nation. The task of anyone who cared for India, Morley contended, was to try to persuade educated Indians who had been seduced by the glorious vision of India as a nation that the fundamental basis for such a dream, a true political personality, did not exist. Nowhere in his speeches does he seem to deny the possibility of the growth of an Indian nation, but this would come only through a process of slow development. For any foreseeable future, India must remain an empire, which meant, he told probationers for the Indian Civil Service in 1909, government by foreign rulers.[34] Morley was well aware that there was an alternative, and that was to leave the Indians to manage their own affairs, but, as he said on another occasion, this was not a possibility for a responsible British government. 'Anybody who pictures to himself the anarchy, the bloody chaos, that would follow from any such deplorable step, must shrink from that sinister decision.'[35]

This understanding of the relationship between India and Great Britain as one where the imperial power's first duty was to save India from herself had impeccable credentials in John Stuart Mill's great work on representative government. Mill, with his long experience in the work of the East India Company, undoubtedly had India in mind when he argued that government by an imperial power is as legitimate as any other providing it fulfils its responsibility to the people. This could only be accomplished by the alien power facilitating the transition of the subject people from their existing low state of civilization to a higher stage.[36] The British could do for the people of India all that the previous despotisms had done, which in itself was a form of legitimization, but they could go far beyond this by communicating to them all that the more advanced nations possessed.

This was, of course, precisely what the Indian nationalists had learned from Mill, but they drew very different conclusions from his doctrine than did Morley. For them, England had done her duty in mediating her genius for law and order to India, and the time had come to fulfil the pledges made by Gladstone in 1881. This meant, at the beginning of the twentieth century, that India should move towards the kind of self-government that already existed in Canada. For Morley, this proposition was 'the grossest fallacy in all politics, a thoroughly dangerous fallacy', based on the supposition that institutions were transferable without any regard to historical experience.[37] This was both incontrovertible and platitudinous, since in fact there were probably very few knowledgeable people in either Great Britain or India who believed otherwise, but behind it was an awareness that an impasse had been reached in the dialogue between the two cultures. The most visible symbols of this were acts of sporadic violence, especially in Bengal and western India, including attempted assassinations of officials. By modern standards, this terrorism was extremely modest, but memories of the Mutiny were never far from the surface in government circles, and this is reflected in the frequent reference to sedition and the need for protection from what Morley colorfully referred to as 'the blood-stained havoc of anarchic conspiracy'.[38] While he saw the need to appeal to the self-styled Moderates in the nationalist movement, represented by Gokhale, and to rally them to the side of the Government against the Extremists, represented by B. G. Tilak, one senses that he knew which way the tides of history were running.

In 1774, at the very beginning of British rule, Warren Hastings had declared that 'The dominion exercised by the British Empire in India is fraught with many radical and incurable defects . . . All that the wisest institutions can effect in such a system can only be to improve the advantages of a temporary possession, and to protract that decay which sooner or later must end it.'[39] Very few of those most deeply concerned with British rule in India had any illusion about its permanence, but it was extraordinarily difficult to think beyond its immediate continuance. When Morley made his proposals for Indian constitutional reform in 1908 he quoted what John Bright had said in 1858 as control of India was about to be transferred from the East India Company to the crown: 'We do not know how to leave India, and therefore let us see if we know how to govern it.'[40]

The reasons why Morley thought it impossible to leave India included, as we have seen, the economic importance of the Indian Empire to Great Britain, but the arguments that he most frequently used were based upon his conviction that India would descend once more into the chaos from which she had been rescued by the administrative structure Britain had created. That his was possibly a questionable reading of India's history as well as of her future seems not to have occurred to Morley, and certainly not to the members of Parliament without his erudition and sense of history.

There are, of course, many literary sources for this understanding of Indian history and Britain's role, which may be thought of as the prevailing western, not just British, view, but it was admirably and persuasively summarized for Morley and his generation by Sir Alfred Lyall (1835 – 1911), one of the most thoughtful and knowledgeable students of Indian history and culture. After a distinguished career in the Indian Civil Service, Lyall had been appointed a member of the Council of India, the advisory body intended to provide the Secretary of State for India with assistance based upon first-hand Indian experience. According to Stephen Koss, Lyall exerted a profound influence on Morley's thinking about India, both in terms of policy and general understanding, justifying Morley's description of him as 'friend of a lifetime'.[41] This friendship had begun through Lyall's contributions to the *Fortnightly Review*, of which Morley was then editor, and continued for nearly forty years. Lyall also wrote for the *Edinburgh Review* and the *Quarterly Review*, mainly on aspects of Indian culture and politics.[42]

As an official in India and London, Lyall wrote many carefully reasoned memoranda on Indian political questions, particularly on Russian expansion in Central Asia. Unlike most Indian officials, he did not believe there was any real danger to India from Russia. He once suggested that it would not be a bad thing if the Russians took over Afghanistan; this would rid the Indian government of the need to deal with 'such wretched barbarians as the Afghans'.[43] He saw much more danger to India and to British interests from resurgent Islam, for he believed that a linking of religious obscurantism and nationalism posed the greatest threat to progress. In contrast to most British officials in India, Lyall was far more sympathetic to Hinduism than to Islam or, indeed, than to Christianity. This attitude towards Hindu religion and culture has an important place in his lack of sympathy towards the demand for western political institutions in India. He was convinced that such institutions as representative government were rooted in cultural values that precluded their transference to the Indian cultural environment with its fundamentally different set of assumptions. He was careful to point out that this did not mean that Indian culture was in any way inferior to western, only that it was different. Lyall argued that Indians who spoke of 'reforming' Hinduism to make it a vehicle of social change did not understand that behind 'the puppet show of popular idolatry' was the profound Brahmanic perception of unconditional and unconscious Being, in which there was no differentiation of subject and object. Such a religion could have no true concern with social reformation, and Indian scholars, like Ranade, who sought to find a moral ruler in Brahmanic thought were doomed to failure. He believed that the Indian social system, with its infinite shadings and gradations of hierarchy, made representative institutions impossible, as these were based on the idea of the equality of individuals. He thought that the lack of a monarchical Supreme Being of the kind found in the Semitic religions was reflected in the political fragmentation of Indian society and in the lack of a doctrine of state sovereignty in Indian political thought. The great political ideas of the western world which were so seductively attractive to the western-minded modern Indian were grounded in an entirely different world view. The ordinary Indian was being summoned 'to join a citizenship which he had not inherited . . . His consent has not been asked; he has simply been included within the dominions of a busy, roving, casteless nation, with ideas and habits totally incongruous to his own'.[44]

An explicit statement of Lyall's understanding of the relationship between Indian culture and western political ideas is found in the introduction he wrote in 1909 to Valentine Chirol's very influential account of Indian politics, significantly entitled *Indian Unrest*.[45] For many western readers, including people of such different political opinions as Morley and

48

Lord Curzon, it provided the decisive proof why democratic, representative institutions were an impossible dream for India. Chirol, who had been Director of the Foreign Department of *The Times*, was a freqeuent visitor to India and a confidant of various Governors-General, including Curzon. Both Chirol and Lyall were admirers of Morley, who reciprocated their high regard, and it was to Morley that Chirol owed his knighthood for his support of Morley's Indian policies.[46] All of this is summed up in the book's dedication to Morley with a quotation from him on the title-page referring to 'that vast congeries of people we call India'. Denial of nationhood and insistence that India is a British artifact remained central to the Liberal understanding.

Lyall began, as did so many writers on the British relationship with India, by evoking memories of the great empires of the classical world. A historical generalization sets the tone: at different times in the world's history, the nations foremost in civilization have undertaken the founding of a dominion in Asia, and have met with great success. The Macedonians led the way, followed by the Romans. While it was because of their military superiority and organizing genius that they were able to subdue and govern vast Asiatic populations, their science and literature flourished in the great cities of the East. The educated upper classes, Lyall asserted, willingly accepted the learning from the West as well as foreign rulership because they recognized the alien power was their barrier against relapsing into barbarism.[47] As the legatee of Greece and Rome, Britain in India 'has revived and is pursuing the enterprise of ruling and civilizing a great Asiatic population'. But there were plenty of warning signals on the horizon in 1910 to indicate that, unlike the literate populations of the ancient world, educated Indians were not willing to recognize the necessity of British rule. The good intentions of the British in their educational reforms, in their administration, in their public works, had been perverted by the very group that had profited by them, and were engaged in stirring up revolt against the British. The condition of India at the turn of the century 'illustrates the perils that beset a Government necessarily pledged to moral and material reform'.[48] For Lyall, here was the inherent contradiction of imperialism: the implementation of British ideas of justice, law, and humanity in India had provided the base from which British rule itself could be attacked.

Lyall was not, of course, the first to comment on the dangers inherent in British power in India being used for 'moral and material reform'. From the early debates at the end of the eighteenth century on the wisdom of exporting such British institutions as Christianity and the free press, there had been warnings that these things would work against the necessary authoritarianism of British rule in India. In 1793, a Proprietor of the East India Company had reminded his fellow shareholders that recent events in the American colonies had given clear warning of the fruits of education and that the same errors should not be repeated in India.[49] Sir John Malcolm, one of the architects of princely rule in central India, was certain that opposition to British rule would come not from the masses or the military chieftains. Testifying on the dangers of a free press in India, he told a Parliamentary committee in 1834 that the people who would be affected by education and a free press were the Brahmans and similar classes, who for ages have been 'the nominal servants but real masters of the turbulent and bold, but ignorant and superstitious, military tribes of their fellow countrymen'.[50] At the beginning of the twentieth century it was the same Poona Brahmans whom Malcolm had feared, men like Ranade, Gokhale, and Tilak, who demonstrated quite extraordinary ability to appropriate those aspects of British political culture that could serve their purposes in the renovation of India. They were 'natural leaders' in this process, not, however, because they were 'westernized' but because of their understanding of the dynamics of their own political culture.

For Lyall, Chirol, and Morley, the motivating cause of the unrest and resentment which they saw as the characteristic features of Indian politics in 1909 was the activity of the Brahmans and other high castes who were asserting their traditional role in Indian society. Lyall dismissed as almost unworthy of discussion the argument that the unrest was the product of what western and Indian writers were beginning to call 'the rise of nationalism'. The term itself was a reification of half-understood imported abstractions. The fundamental nature of Indian society, he insisted, with its interlocking hierarchical structures and its lack of centralized authority in either the secular or religious spheres, had, on the one hand, prevented any real fusion between conqueror and conquered, while, on the other, it worked against national unification. 'Each class and rank has its place,' he had once written, 'and the upshot of all is that this state of society is not half as bad as it sounds.'[51] Lyall's studies of Indian culture had given him an understanding of Indian society that was at once scholarly and romantic, and he was convinced that the immemorial power of the Brahmans was being turned against British rule.

The dominance of the Brahmans in the so-called nationalist movement as well as in the new professions led, Lyall insisted, to a fusion of religion and politics that was also certain to explode into violence. This union of religion and politics is a commonplace at the end of the twentieth century, but it was not in the world of Lyall and his friends. As his biographer put it, Lyall was 'by reasoning an advanced Liberal; by temperament he was a Conservative',[52] and both inclinations made him, as they did Morley, regard the union of religion and politics in India with increasing foreboding.

Over against those who believed in the rise of a pan-Indian nationalism, Lyall argued that the various centers of unrest, such as Poona and Calcutta, were widely separated not only in distance but in culture. Quite different

50

causes were at work in the two areas. In the Maratha country, the Brahmans had exercised great secular power through the Peshwa and his successors into the nineteenth century, and they bitterly resented its loss to the British. Now, with their appeal to the glories of the Hindu past, and especially in the revival of the memories of Shivaji's wars against the Mughals, they were headed for violent confrontation with the government. In Bengal, the situation was very different. There the Brahmans and other high castes had made common cause with the British in the destruction of the power of the Nawab of Bengal, but this had been through bribery and financial manipulation, not through war as in the Poona country. The Bengal upper classes took with enthusiasm to the new English education, and soon, according to Lyall, the not very edifying discovery was made that 'a young Bengali can be trained to write almost exactly like a Londoner'.[53] The ready acceptance of the English language was the root of Bengal unrest, for education cannot be haphazardly dispensed, as it had been in Bengal. 'It acts upon the frame of an antique society as a powerful solvent, heating weak brains, stimulating rash ambitions, raising inordinate expectations.'[54] Young men were particularly affected by the new education, and Lyall predicted that everywhere in Asia one would see young men who had received some western education becoming the vanguard of movements of religious violence.

The appeal to religion was the common link between violence in Bengal and Bombay, for, in Lyall's understanding, it was the Brahmans who saw that it was possible to appeal at once to the dark superstitions of Hinduism and the radical notions of western democratic thought. The Liberal dilemma was clear: a reasonable pledge had been made for the material and moral improvement of India, but education, which was at the heart of such reform, seemed to lead inexorably to Brahmanical dominance and violence. The continuance of a strong British administration was the only defence against this return to the past.

Such was the intellectual background for the India Councils Act of 1909, which provided for elections, on a very narrow franchise, to the provincial councils. Muslims were given a number of separate constituencies to ensure their membership, despite the general Hindu majority. When Morley, moving the second reading of the Bill in the House of Lords in 1909, had spoken of 'the baleful forces' that must be repressed, even if they could not be destroyed, the reference was to that alliance of religion and political extremists that haunted Lyall and Chirol. They had, he said, 'fantastic dreams that they will someday drive us out of India'. He identified two other groups in Indian political life who did not need to be repressed. One was made up of those who hoped for a large measure of autonomy and self-government on the Canadian model. This, too, was an unattainable dream, but they could be drawn into alliance with a third group, consisting of those whom the 1909 Act was intended to satisfy. The members of this group had asked to be brought into 'our administration, and to find a free and effective voice in explaining the interests and needs of their people'.[55] Two important issues lie behind this careful phrasing. One is the avoidance of the suggestion that the elected members would actually represent their constituents. In a fragmented society, deeply divided by caste and religion, the only guarantee for what the King's Proclamation on the eve of the Act called 'the fabric of security and order' was the recognition that representative government was not a possibility. Secondly, Morley's pronouns were instructive: 'our administration', 'their people'. There was no hope that the second group could be co-opted by the new Act into joining the administration or that the third group would for long be content with their status. Morley's groups were, in fact, largely fictitious, for the boundary lines between the positions he identified were blurred and meaningless. The educated, articulate classes, to whichever of the three groups they belonged, wanted to be recognized as the natural representatives of their people and they wanted the administration to belong to India.

The great irony of the decisions taken in 1909 is that, despite the well-reasoned arguments against attempting to transfer western political institutions to India, the India Councils Act did precisely that by embodying in the new legislation that most characteristic of western political ideas, namely that the fundamental basis of a state is the aggregation of individuals. However much Morley might protest that such was not his intention, the concept was implicit in the 1909 Act that the will of the majority is the will of the nation, despite the safeguard of reserved seats for Muslims. This was in line with the great formulations of British Liberalism, although John Stuart Mill had wrestled with the problem of the rights of minorities. So had the authors of the great series of Federalist Papers as they thought about a constitutional structure for the new American republic, but both Mill and the Federalists were thinking of minority opinions; in India, something quite different was involved — the rights of minority communities. Very little attention had been given to this problem in modern political thought, and the precedent that is sometimes suggested as having been available, that of the 'millet' system of the Ottoman empire, was not relevant to liberal democratic thinking. Nevertheless, one can imagine the basis of the Indian state being a 'community of communities' instead of a community of individuals.[56] Morley had pointed in this direction when he suggested, although not with as much conviction or clarity, the establishment of some kind of electoral college with proportional representation that would have recognized communal groupings.[57]

The fateful commitment in 1909 was not so much the creation of separate electorates for Muslims, as Indian nationalists have always argued, but rather the commitment to a state based on individuals, not groups.

52

There is no doubt that this was what was wanted by the spokesmen who were voicing Indian opinion, because it reflected both the general liberal political philosophy they had made their own as well as their well-justified sense that they would emerge as the natural leaders in an all-India system founded upon a numerical majority. At the end of the twentieth century, the belief in political power based on a simple all-Indian majority is being challenged in the name of regional autonomy, group identities defined in terms of religion and ethnicity, and, in more abstract theoretical terms, arguments for a loose federal system. There are those, like Prime Minister Gandhi in 1975 when she moved towards an authoritarian centralism, who see behind such demands, as Morley and the others did in 1909, conspiracies that threaten chaos and anarchy. A house takes many years to build, she reminded her people, but a fire can destroy it in a few minutes. It was the same issue as Morley had in mind when he remarked to his constituents in 1907 that people were saying that a democracy cannot govern remote dependencies. His comment was: 'I do not know how; it is a hard question.'[58] It remains a hard question, whether the center of power is London or Delhi.

Notes

1 Morley to Minto, quoted in Stephen Koss, *John Morley at the India Office, 1905 – 1910*, (New Haven, 1969), p. 128. Koss's insights, especially those he did not develop at this time but to which he hoped to return, are frequently used in this essay.

2 Quoted in Koss, *Morley*, p. 177.

3 *Ibid.*, p. 188.

4 Gladstone to Ripon, quoted in Koss, *Morley*, p. 177.

5 John Morley, *Indian Speeches (1907 – 1909)* (London, 1909), p. 30.

6 Lord Curzon. 'The True Imperialism', in *The Nineteenth Century and After*, lxiii (1908), p. 158.

7 *Ibid.*, p. 163.

8 Koss, *Morley*, p. 177.

9 S. N. Banerjea, *The Speeches and Writings of the Hon. Surendranath Banerjea* (Madras, 1927), p. 322.

10 K. C. Sen, *Keshub Chunder Sen's Lectures in India* (London, 1901), p. 132.

11 R. M. Roy, *The English Works of Raja Rammohun Roy* (Allahabad, 1906), p. 5.

12 *Ibid.*, p. 43.

13 *Ibid.*, p. 472.

14 Partha Mitter, unpublished paper, 'Art and Nationalism in India'.

15 Quoted in Ainslie T. Embree, *Charles Grant and British Rule in India* (New York, 1962), p. 145.

16 C. L. Parekh, ed., *Essays, Speeches, Addresses and Writings on Indian Politics by the Hon. Dadabhai Naoroji* (Bombay, 1887), p. 333.

17 *Ibid.*, p. 466

18 Banerjea, *Speeches*, p. 96.

19 S. N. Banerjea, *A Nation in the Making* (ed., Bombay, 1963), p. 190.

20 Quoted in S. Gopal, *British Policy in India, 1858 – 1905* (Cambridge, 1965), p. 298.

21 This theme is treated in Gauri Viswanathan, 'The Ideology of Literary Education in British India, 1813 – 1880', Ph.D dissertation, Columbia University, 1985.

22 Sir H. M. Elliott and John Dowson, eds., *The History of India as Told by its Own Historians*, (Allahabad, n.d.), i, xxii.

23 Vincent A. Smith, *Oxford History of India* (Oxford, 1923), p. ix.

24 Banerjea, *A Nation in the Making*, p. 40.

25 Abu Taleb Khan, quoted in W. T. de Bary *et al.*, *Sources of Indian Tradition* (New York, 1958), p. 565.

26 Quoted in S. R. Mehrotra, *The Emergence of the Indian National Congress* (Delhi, 1971), p. 296.

27 Stephen Koss, *Nonconformity in Modern British Politics*.

28 Quoted in Sir Thomas Raleigh, ed., *Lord Curzon in India* (London, 1906), pp. 486 – 487.

29 Thomas Babington Macaulay, 'Minute on Education', in de Bary, *Sources of Indian Tradition*, pp. 596 – 601.

30 Quoted in Banerjea, *A Nation in the Making*, p. 135.

31 Quoted in Mehrotra, *Indian National Congress*, p. 194.

32 *Ibid.*, pp. 198 – 199.

33 Morley, *Speeches*, p. 135.

34 *Ibid.*, p. 135.

35 *Ibid.*, pp. 27 – 28.

36 *Ibid.*, p. 19.

37 *Ibid.*, p. 35.

38 *Ibid.*, p. 81.

39 Quoted in Embree, *Charles Grant*, p. 142.

40 Quoted in Morley, *Speeches*, p. 95.

41 Quoted in Koss, *Morley*, p. 133.

42 Sir Alfred Lyall, *Asiatic Studies, Religious and Social* (London, 1899) [First and Second series] contains many of the essays. His memoranda, most of which are unpublished, are in the Lyall Collection, India Office Library. His *Rise and Expansion of British Rule in India* (London, 1911) is an important analysis of the nature of British power in the subcontinent.

43 Sir Mortimer Durand, *Life of the Right Hon. Sir Alfred Comyn Lyall* (Edinburgh, 1913), p. 201.

44 Lyall, *Asiatic Studies*, ii, 23.

45 Sir Valentine Chirol, *Indian Unrest*, with an introduction by Sir Alfred Lyall (London, 1910).

46 Sir Valentine Chirol, *Fifty Years in a Changing World* (London, 1927), p. 239.

47 Lyall, introduction to Chirol, *Indian Unrest*, p. vii.

48 *Ibid.*, p. viii.

49 Embree, *Charles Grant*, p. 154.

50 Sir John Malcolm, 'Memorandum', *Parliamentary Papers*, 1834, vii Paper no. 601.

51 Durand, *Lyall*, p. 174.

52 *Ibid.*, p. 174.

53 Lyall, *Asiatic Studies*, ii, 2.

54 Lyall, introduction to Chirol, *Indian Unrest*, p. xiii.

55 Morley, Speeches, p. 115.

56 Lloyd Rudolph, 'India and the Punjab', in *The Asia Society Newsletter* (New York, 1986).

57 Morley, *Speeches*, p. 124.

58 *Ibid.*, p. 34.

3

'A Working Man's Representative': Joseph Chamberlain and the 1874 Election in Sheffield

Peter T. Marsh

Through the many twists and turns of his career Joseph Chamberlain engaged in a dance with labour that made a lasting impression on all observers. The dance was increasingly strenuous, for Chamberlain was a successful metal manufacturer, proud of his accomplishment in industry and that of men like him, and aggressive in his defence of their economic interests. The most remarkable feature of his dance with labour was its duration. But it had early moments of tenderness. Politically the most important of these began in the summer of 1873.

The two dancers reached out to each other in the spring of that year, both of them spurned in their courtship of the Liberal party under Mr. Gladstone. The spirits of all three had soared in the heady days that followed the passage in 1867 of the second Reform Act. The tide of feeling that swept Gladstone into power in 1868 also encouraged Chamberlain and the leaders of labour to expect a victory for their varied causes. Making his debut on the public stage in support of the newly formed National Education League, Chamberlain anticipated the speedy creation of a system of elementary education that would overcome the division of the country by class and religion and enable England to engage ever more profitably in international economic competition.

The leaders of labour were not as euphoric as he.[1] 1867 had been a mixed year for them. While the Reform Act had created a predominantly working-class electorate, organized labour had been tarnished and weakened, first by violent intimidation leading to murder by trade unionists in Sheffield and then through a ruling in the courts that undermined the legality of trade unions and exposed their funds to theft by dishonest officers. These events prompted the Conservative government to set up a royal commission of enquiry. Through the appointment to that commission of Frederic Harrison, a Positivist lawyer devoted to the rights of labour, fear about the commission among labour gave way to hope. Furthermore, instead of producing a demand for punitive measures, the quickening of public concern about labour relations in the wake of the violence at Sheffield led to a Masters and Servants Act designed to make it easier for labour to deploy its strength peacefully. The intent of the Act was frustrated, however, by the courts. Far from easing the pressure of the law on labour, the Act was followed by a doubling of judicial prosecutions and convictions.

The hopes of labour in the early '70s rose largely as a result of the industrial boom from which manufacturers like Chamberlain were also prospering. Membership in trade unions shot up, especially in fields that had been badly organized, as men sought to take advantage of industry's need for labour and ability to pay better wages. The demand for a nine-hour day scored notable successes in the engineering and building trades. The number of trades councils, which provided an often effective forum for organized labour on a town by town basis, doubled between 1866 and 1873. After Gladstone came to power with a large parliamentary majority elected on a pledge of doing justice to Ireland, both Chamberlain and the leaders of labour felt reason to believe that the Liberals would soon go on to enact the educational and legal measures that they required.

In 1870 and '71 Gladstone's ministry did indeed produce momentous education and trade union legislation. But the Acts of those years fell far short of anticipations, so far short as to produce anger rather than gratitude. Though the Education Act of 1870 erected the frame for England's first national network of elementary schools, it included within that network the socially divisive schools that the Church of England had already built, and even increased their number. Similarly, while the Trade Union Act of 1871 placed trade unions on a secure legal foundation, a Criminal Law Amendment Act at the same time all but eliminated the capacity of the unions to take industrial action. To make matters worse, when decisions by the courts narrowed the concession of 1871 to the trade unions, the government declined to take remedial action.

The refusal of Gladstone's government to deal with the deficiencies of the Acts of 1870 and '71 completed the disillusionment of Chamberlain and the leaders of labour. The responsible cabinet ministers in each case, W. E. Forster for education and H. A. Bruce for labour law, became the most determined opponents of the reformers. The National Education League under Chamberlain's direction, exploiting every resource and strategem that he could think of, conducted an impassioned agitation to amend the Education Act, while the Trades Union Congress came to life as the agency through which labour fought for repeal of the Criminal Law

Amendment Act:[2] but to no avail. Refusing concession even on points of little substantial importance, Forster resolutely supported the denominational schools within the national network, while Bruce upheld the principles of laissez-faire economics against any further infringement in favour of organized labour. Conditions appeared ripe for cooperation between the two sets of would-be supporters whom Gladstone's ministry so deeply disappointed.

From its inception the National Education League had sought the support of labour. Chamberlain played a leading part in this effort. He was convinced that the creation of an educated work force would raise both wages and profits, and hence help to reduce the chasm that the growth of large-scale businesses like his own was deepening between industrialists and labour. He was uneasy about the heavily Nonconformist character that the agitation of the League assumed after 1870. In 1872 he committed the League to strictly secular rather than unsectarian schooling partly in order to make the economically beneficial objectives of the League clearer to labour. But this effort, like the League's campaign as a whole, left him disappointed. Labour and the rank and file of the League did not leap wholeheartedly to each other's aid. Ordinary working men proved much less interested than their leaders in an educational system that could deprive them of their children's wages. On the other side the segment of the electorate most enthusiastic in its support for the League was Nonconformity; and the ardour of pious Nonconformists was clouded by the League's adoption of a secular policy, particularly as that change failed to win additional working-class support.

By the spring of 1873 Chamberlain was ready to try a fresh initiative. Perhaps, if he appealed directly to labour's own interests, he could fuse the efforts of the Trades Union Congress and the National Education League in a campaign that would carry both to success. Instead of invidiously subordinating one to the other, each would find fulfilment in an embracing Radical movement under his leadership. Furthermore, if he did not make the most of the opportunity for cooperation, labour might move on threateningly in its own direction. Exasperation with the Liberal party among leaders of labour and of the League reached a peak simultaneously in mid-1873.[3] Both groups sponsored candidates that stood against official Liberal nominees in bye-elections that spring and summer: the Education League most conspicuously at Bath, independent labour at Greenwich and Dundee. These separate challenges raised the possibility of empowering cooperation or enfeebling competition. The Birmingham Liberal Association had recently experienced a good deal of difficulty over local elections with the demand for representation of labour by working men, which it had kept at bay largely through Chamberlain's mediation. A Radical fusion of the two national rebellions could ward off the parallel danger and proceed either to convert or,

58

failing that, to supplant the Liberal party that had resisted their separate assaults.

Chamberlain felt confident that labour and Nonconformity were natural allies in the Radical cause. But his confidence was ill-timed. During the latter half of 1873, particularly in connection with the parliamentary politics of Sheffield, he tried to convince the two groups that their true interests lay in cooperation with each other. But neither group was dependable even on its own, let alone in combination. The day when denominational affiliation dictated political loyalties was passing, and the day when they would be dominated by class had not yet dawned. Meanwhile the relationship between Noncomformity and labour was streaked with suspicion, for the Nonconformists were overwhelmingly middle-class. Chamberlain proved no more successful in combining the two groups under a Radical banner than he had been within the National Education League. He won cordial support from the leaders of labour in Sheffield but not from its rank and file, and he paid for this meagre reward by alienating respectable Noncomformists. The campaign for his nomination and election at Sheffield was further weakened by the running sore of Radicalism, the rival ambitions of individual middle-class politicians, including of course his own. The outcome also demonstrated that Conservatives or their surrogates could combine pious and proletarian support more effectively than their opponents.

I

Chamberlain was invited to Sheffield in May 1873 by a Reform Association recently set up by dissident Radicals at the prompting of a cranky iron-smelter, H. J. Wilson. Wilson was intent on ending the ascendancy of Robert Leader, currently the determining power among the Liberals of Sheffield and owner of the *Sheffield Independent*. Wilson sought an attractive nominee to fill the vacancy that was expected when the senior of Sheffield's two M.P.s, George Hadfield, retired. Sheffield was only one of several constituences that had their eye on Chamberlain. At the time he was more interested in Newcastle. But he welcomed every opportunity to fan the sparks of discontent with the government. Sheffield seemed well suited for the initiative he was contemplating to draw Nonconformists and labour together into an over-arching Radical army. Forster's attempt to enforce the provisions of the Education Act had produced unusually acute bitterness in Sheffield where some Nonconformists, including Wilson, refused to pay rates that could be used to defray fees of children in denominational schools, and hence had their property sequestered. Sheffield was also the site of the violence that prompted the appointment of the 1867 royal commission on trade unions, and trade unionists were strongly represented in the Sheffield Reform Association.

59

In his first address to the association that May, Chamberlain sought common ground between Nonconformity and labour by appealing to them as a democrat committed to the enfranchisement of all adults. Strengthened electorally, they could enforce respect for the wishes of 'the people' upon the government which, as things were, whatever party was in power, was devoted to the propertied classes and vested interests such as the Established Church. However trenchantly Chamberlain expressed it, this kind of argument was not unfamiliar among progressive spokesmen for the National Education League. But with remarkable candour he moved on to new ground:

> I am a manufacturer, and am proud in some respects of the class to which I belong. I believe (that) upon the union between the employers and the employed and upon the identity of sympathy and interests between the middle and the working classes, depend the future progress and the prosperity of the country — but I am bound to admit that the middle classes, having used the numbers and the influence and the power of the working classes to secure for themselves representation, have not been too eager to obtain for their allies the benefits which they have obtained for themselves.[4]

He denounced the Masters and Servants and the Criminal Law Amendment Acts as 'class legislation of the worst kind'. Using abstractions that covered over the tension between Nonconformity and labour he concluded: 'Everywhere the same battle is being fought out — the battle between the classes and the people.'

The labour leaders of Sheffield did not immediately salute when he ran up these colours. He commanded the respect of labour in Birmingham largely because he could convince them from the conduct of industrial relations in his own business that he was genuinely committed to the advancement of their interests. In order to duplicate the achievement on a national scale, he needed to win the confidence of labour leaders who could not have first-hand knowledge of his performance as an employer.

That need helped to shape the manifesto that he issued at the end of the summer in the *Fortnightly Review*.[5] He began by asserting again what he had said so often over the past three years, that Liberal government as it was currently practised was little better than the Tory alternative. To regain the distinction of the Liberal party and restore the spirits of its disheartened would-be supporters, he outlined a fourfold 'programme' which he summed up as *'Free Church, Free Land, Free Schools, and Free Labour'*. *'Free Church'* came first as a bid to rouse Nonconformity; and as an earnest of the uncompromising character of his proposals he proposed to plunge straight for disestablishment. This demand would also be more intelligible to labour than subordinate controversies like the one over prohibition of Nonconformist burial services in parish churchyards; and the accompanying demand for disendowment would appeal to labour economically. '*Free Labour*' enjoyed the conspicuous final position in Chamberlain's quadrilateral. Probing the failure of the government to release labour from the fetters that the courts had placed on collective bargaining, he insisted that the amendments organized labour required in the law were quite modest and need not threaten the interests of property.

Chamberlain's challenge to 'The Liberal Party and Its Leaders' as his article was entitled was more fully defined than anything that the advocates of independent labour had issued. The breadth of his challenge and his prominent incorporation of the legislative demands of labour had the desired effect. John Morley, the editor of the *Fortnightly*, not entirely certain how to handle the article when it first reached him, sought the advice of his close friend Frederic Harrison, who was also the champion of labour. Harrison was pleasantly surprised by Chamberlain's new approach and encouraged Morley to proceed. Harrison's blessing was indicative of the response of other spokesmen for organized labour to the manifesto. It attracted so much attention that Morley had to reprint the issue of the *Fortnightly* that contained it.

Chamberlain was invited back to Sheffield to speak at the end of September. He used the occasion to elaborate his defence of trade unions against middle-class criticism. The growing industrial strength of the unions and the increasingly sympathetic hearing that the Trades Union Congress was receiving among critics of the government, Conservative as well as Liberal, were alarming many employers. In the spring of the year an Employers' Federation had been formed to make their case. Chamberlain responded, confident from his own experience of the current economic boom that industry could afford to be generous.

[The trade unions] have raised the rate of wages, and that, of course, is their primary claim upon the support of the working class. But when I consider the enormous strides which have been made by commerce during the last fifty years; when I know that the profits of trade never were so great as they are at the present time; when I know that enormous fortunes never were so easily or so quickly accumulated, I say it is just and right that the poorer class should also share in this general prosperity. But then it is said that the effect of these unions has been to drive trade out of the country. That is said; but it has never been proved. And when I look at the undoubted evidence of our Government statistics, showing how there is a continuing and enormous increase in the exports of this country, I say that such apprehension is altogether uncalled for.

He even defended the restrictive practices of organized labour, pointing out that the middle-class professions indulged in similar behaviour:

any physician who should presume to do the work of an apothecary by dispensing his own medicines would never again be met in consultation with any member of that learned body. What is that but the rule which forbids masons to do bricklayers' work and bricklayers to do masons' work?

After a detailed examination of the unfair operation of the Masters and Servants and the Criminal Law Amendment Acts, he concluded with a plea for sympathetic justice in place of the harsh rulings that the courts had been handing down:

> Don't let us exert the full force of the law to pluck out the mote from the eye of the workman, while we leave untouched the beam in the eye of the employer.[6]

These were stirring words from a manufacturer who was giving himself to public service. Back in Birmingham, the trades council, led by W. J. Davis of the brassworkers, passed a resolution of thanks and had the speech published. At the school board elections in November, forgetting the tension of past years, labour threw itself wholeheartedly behind the campaign of the Birmingham Liberal Association and then celebrated its triumph with a torchlight procession.

The success of the Birmingham Association in the elections for the town council placed Chamberlain in the mayoralty of the town as well as in the chair of the school board. His new responsibilities did not prompt him to draw in his horns at Sheffield. On the contrary, the Liberal victories in Birmingham encouraged him, after several months of depression, to raise his estimate of Radical prospects on the national stage. Yet, even for a man of boundless energy, there were only twenty-four hours in the day. His responsibilities in Birmingham left him no time to devote to Sheffield for the rest of the year, while the policy of secular education which the Birmingham school board proceeded to introduce alienated Nonconformists in Sheffield.

His absorption in Birmingham misled him about Sheffield at a more fundamental level.[7] Superficially the two towns had a good deal in common. The economies of both were based on metal manufacturing. However, the emergence of large units of production had occurred somewhat earlier in Sheffield. For a variety of reasons the manufacturers of Sheffield tended to ally themselves with the landed élite around the town rather than with the local working class as was the case in Birmingham. Furthermore the civic pride that distinguished Birmingham was weak in Sheffield. One result of these accumulated differences was that the kind of businessmen who formed the inner circle of Chamberlain's confrères in the Birmingham Liberal Association were scarce among the Radicals of Sheffield and also inferior in ability. Though H. J. Wilson was an iron-smelter, he was at odds with most other men of his class in Sheffield. Given moreover to a variety of Radical enthusiasms, particularly to the campaign for repeal of the Contagious Diseases Acts, he did not calculate the chances for electoral success soberly. At the same time, because the tradition of cooperation between masters and employees was weak in Sheffield, labour was more strongly organized and self-reliant there than in Birmingham.

The Sheffield Reform Association derived its strength primarily from labour, and Chamberlain responded accordingly. But that was not the pattern that worked so well for him in Birmingham. The Birmingham Liberal Association was dominated by industrialists like himself together with allies from the middle-class professions and the leading Nonconformist ministers. Such men were conspicuous by their absence from the ranks of Chamberlain's supporters in Sheffield. In contrast to his ally John Jaffray, owner of the *Birmingham Daily Post*, Robert Leader of the *Sheffield Independent* led the opposition to Chamberlain's candidacy. Chamberlain genuinely sought to advance the common interests of labour and business. But the perception of those interests varied from industrial town to town. Mistaking Sheffield for Birmingham, Chamberlain found himself on quicksand.

Some days after the school board elections in Birmingham, unable to size up the situation in Sheffield for himself, he despatched William Harris to do so for him. Harris was another of the civic spirited businessmen who worked together to lay the foundation upon which Chamberlain's public career was based. Harris was the organizing genius behind the Birmingham Liberal Association. But Chamberlain allowed his anxiety for election to Parliament at Sheffield to fetter Harris, and he confined Harris's inquiries to those whom Wilson wished him to see. When Harris returned to report, the new mayor was too deep in civic affairs to find more than five minutes to see him. 'I must,' Chamberlain wrote to Wilson, 'be guided almost entirely by you.'[8] Harris soon sensed the nature of the problem in Sheffield, and he recruited one of the salaried staff from the Education League's Birmingham headquarters, J. Paynter Allen, to deal with it. As Harris pointedly explained to Wilson, 'during our recent Municipal & School Board Elections [Allen] organised & worked one of our most difficult wards, containing many good working-men voters but no leading or active people'.[9] Allen's help did not go down well with Wilson. Blissfully disregarding his lack of support from manufacturers and ministers, Wilson breathed optimism. 'I always try to avoid being sanguine about anything,' he told Chamberlain, 'but really it is very difficult in this case, when we have every element of success on our side.'[10] Yet two days later he confessed that 'We have a little over-estimated the political knowledge & interest of the people'[11], not the sort of mistake that Birmingham organizers would make.

The formal invitation for Chamberlain to become a candidate for the expected parliamentary vacancy came from organized labour, from the executive of the Sheffield Trades Council. Its vote on the invitation was 10 to 2, a small foretaste of the lack of solidarity among the working class that was to trouble his campaign. Other constituencies sounded him out. But the only clear invitation came from Sheffield, and its source among

63

the working class gratified him. So he committed himself ever more deeply there, though the situation was troubled.

There was another candidate for the expected vacancy, Robert Leader's nominee, A. J. Allott. Allott was a local worthy, an alderman and respected Nonconformist. He was not uncritical of Gladstone's government. In fact on most issues Allott differed only in his mildness from Chamberlain. Allott opposed the National Education League in favour of unsectarian religious rather than secular education, but on that issue even Wilson had to admit that Allott was closer to prevailing sentiment in Sheffield than was Chamberlain. Allott was also a generous employer and, though quiet about the rights of trade unions as on most subjects, he was not disliked among labour. Still he was not the least bit forceful or exciting. The contest between Allott and Chamberlain was as much a choice between local esteem and charismatic talent as between moderate and advanced Radicalism.

The working-class base of Chamberlain's candidacy was soon assailed. Within a week of the Trades Council's invitation to him, some trade union secretaries repudiated it. Harris wrote to Wilson in alarm: 'Now, for the last time, I entreat you to re-examine your ground before Chamberlain is asked to commit himself.' [12] Knowing his master's ambition, Harris did not press harder: 'After you have considered the matter,' he assured Wilson, 'you will command our adherence as you deserve to do.' Yet Harris had already discovered another cause for concern that touched close to home. A rumour was circulated in Sheffield that the wire-drawers at Nettlefold and Chamberlain's Imperial Mill were paid sub-standard wages and prohibited from joining a union. Harris raised the matter with Chamberlain as soon as he could see him. Chamberlain was not directly in charge of that mill and had to enquire himself. What he learned was embarrassing though not quite discreditable. His partner Joseph Nettlefold had indeed insisted that the wire-drawers whom he employed must resign from their union, and he paid less per hour for the high quality of wire for screws on which his mill concentrated than was customary in other mills that drew wire of varying grades at corresponding piece-work rates. Nettlefold nonetheless attracted a good work force because his men could count on regular employment with full hours and hence a better weekly wage than they could obtain anywhere else. Informed of the damaging rumour in Sheffield, they readily signed a letter praising Nettlefold and Chamberlain as employers; and Chamberlain made sure immediately that they joined a union. Yet the suspicion that this episode raised never entirely died. Later at one of Chamberlain's rallies in Sheffield a silent heckler made his point by holding aloft a huge screw.

On insecure ground even among labour, Chamberlain failed to fathom the difference between the situation that confronted him in Sheffield and the one he was mastering with spectacular success in Birmingham. He tried to account for the opposition of Robert Leader as a reflection of Leader's hostility to the aspirations of labour. The junior Member of Parliament for Sheffield, A. J. Mundella, who intended to stand for re-election, was arguably the most notable champion of labour in the current House of Commons, though not quite as trenchant as Chamberlain had become. Mundella had been elected in 1868; and Chamberlain contended that the people who opposed his candidacy now had opposed Mundella then. But in fact Leader had been Mundella's chief sponsor in 1868. Leader's ambition essentially was to dominate the politics of his town.[13] He feared that Chamberlain's candidacy would undermine this dominance in one way or another, either by over-extending Sheffield's willingness to elect advocates of labour or, if Chamberlain were successful, by installing a rival power in Sheffield, whether Wilson or Chamberlain himself. Allott might be more electable since less disturbing to the Nonconformists of Sheffield, and would certainly be more deferential.

A further figure lurked threateningly in Leader's calculations. J. A. Roebuck, one of mid-Victorian England's more ferocious Radicals, had served as Member of Parliament for Sheffield for nearly twenty years. But in the 1860s his chauvinism and dislike for Gladstone got the better of his Radicalism, and he became an admirer of Disraeli, though without changing party affiliation. Roebuck was ousted in 1868 in favour of Mundella. But Roebuck still enjoyed a good deal of covert support in Sheffield from Conservatives and also from the lower, less politicized ranks of labour who liked Roebuck's truculent nationalism and disliked the recent efforts of the Liberal government to reduce the availability of beer. If he also managed to win votes from Nonconformists alienated by Chamberlain, Roebuck could quite possibly win.

Like Allott, who was in effect their candidate, the Nonconformist worthies of Sheffield agreed with the familiar Radical planks in Chamberlain's platform and were prepared under the popular pressures of an election to give formal assent to most of his social nostrums. But on those issues, preeminently the use of the Bible in schools and Sunday observance, where the claims of religion ran counter to the demand for full and equitable democracy, these men came down fervently on the side of religion. Chamberlain came down with equal insistence on the other side. Though an advocate of local electoral control of drink traffic, he opposed Sunday closing of public houses, for 'I could not support legislation which would practically affect the poor only'.[14] He gave firm support to the principle of one day's rest in seven but on strictly social grounds; and he insisted on the value of opening museums on Sundays so long as the Sabbatarian scruples of the attendants were respected.

Wilson and Chamberlain were aware of the price they would pay for these policies among the local Nonconformist élite. They were confident that the loss would be more than repaid by the enthusiasm Chamberlain could arouse among the mass of Liberal voters, particularly among labour. 'We never pretended to be great men,' Wilson commented to Chamberlain,

> — we have always regretted the comparative obscurity of most of our associates, & the absence of monied men. But we say we are the Radicals & working men of Sheffield, and that we are essential to any candidate; and that we have got the *votes*, though we have no money; and we say *now* that we have got a candidate whom it is useless to oppose.[15]

Chamberlain's response belied some of the most notorious characteristics of his behaviour in Birmingham:

> I dont think much of smoke room politics — & as to the 'respectables' I neither expect nor want their aid. I am a working man's representative, if I am any thing, & it is to ensure fair consideration for their claims as to all questions, not merely on special labour legislation, that I chiefly care to enter Parliament.[16]

In a more bitter vein, he commented to his friend Admiral Maxse, who was engaged in a similarly vexed contest in Tower Hamlets:

> I am afraid the leading London Dissenters are a nasty, narrow, bigoted lot, from whom no help can be expected. . . . You must win, in spite of them, & without them, by the force of the working class vote; — as I hope to win in Sheffield.[17]

II

On New Year's Day 1874, after an absence of three months, Chamberlain returned to Sheffield and accepted the trades council's invitation to make himself available for election. In order to underscore the popular nature of his candidacy, he delivered his speech out of doors in Paradise Square, close to the centre of the town. Some ten to twelve thousand people pressed in to listen, curious but uncertain about their visitor from Birmingham.

He soon warmed his audience up by proclaiming 'the radical programme of the future'.[18] It put together all the ingredients of the appeal that he had been developing since he first visited Sheffield. The programme began with a demand for universal adult suffrage and equal electoral districts. 'Then,' he proclaimed, 'we can go on to further legislative changes,' which he summed up in his four freedoms: free schools, free labour, free land and a free church. He did not give free labour pride of place this time because he had said so much about it in the autumn; but he extended the concept to include compensation for industrial injuries caused by the neglect or carelessness of employers. The symmetry of his programme was weakened by the attachment of a string of further policies, including repeal of the Contagious Diseases Acts, about which Wilson felt particularly concerned. Still the power of Chamberlain's appeal and the response it evoked were unmistakable.

The New Year's address in Paradise Square made Chamberlain the clear front runner for the Liberal nomination for Sheffield's second parliamentary seat. But he could not spend time in Sheffield to consolidate his achievement. He was obliged as mayor of Birmingham to go back and preside over a string of public meetings. Then in mid-January, just as he was presenting plans to the town council for municipalization of the local gas companies, the Trades Union Council convened in Sheffield for its largest annual meeting to date. The metropolitan press headed by *The Times* lavished attention on the meeting. The conflict in timing not only deprived Chamberlain of a matchless opportunity to make his case nationally as well as in Sheffield. It also opened up another crack in his support from labour. The more timorous souls on the parliamentary committee of the Trades Union Congress were inclined to favour the candidacy of Allott at Sheffield, and they secured an invitation for Allott to attend the annual meeting.

That meeting and Chamberlain's absence from it served to delay a resolution of the contest between the two men, though everyone agreed that it should be settled quickly. The longer the decision was put off, the deeper the emotional division between the two sides, and the greater the danger that Roebuck would intervene. The problem was how to settle the contest. The alternative methods that the two sides put forward reflected their differing notion of what was desirable in the Liberal party. Allott, placing his trust in established élites, wanted arbitration by independent M.P.s of national repute. Chamberlain, and still more his supporters in Sheffield, insisted that the contest be decided according to which candidate had the greater popular support. They might accept arbitration confined to this point, but they much preferred to seek a decision from another meeting of the Liberal populace in Paradise Square.

The contestants might propose, but Gladstone disposed. Negotiators for the two sides were about to break off when they were hit by unexpected news. Gladstone had called a sudden general election. The news made the need for a decision between Chamberlain and Allott urgent, yet cut off the time required for the division between the two camps to heal. The news reached Chamberlain in Birmingham at the deathbed of his father. The dissolution of Parliament, as Chamberlain observed to Wilson, 'could hardly have been worse timed for us'.[19] But it was even worse for Allott. He had no choice but to accept the arbitrament of an immediate mass meeting in Paradise Square. Though naturally distracted and depressed at the moment, Chamberlain looked closely to the arrangements for the meeting. 'It is important,' he told Wilson, that 'both speakers should be pledged to not more than 15 minutes each, or otherwise the working men will leave for dinner before the vote is taken.'[20]

Less than a week after the dissolution, the largest crowd that Sheffield had ever seen, perhaps twice the size of the New Year's assembly, crushed into Paradise Square and the nearby streets to hear the two men and decide between them. The windows of the surrounding offices were filled with the faces of the town's élite, for the moment powerless. Allott tackled his assignment with evident discomfort. His remarks in support of Gladstone provoked so much disorder that he had to stop speaking for a while. Chamberlain's short speech on the other hand was punctuated with cheers that broke wave upon wave when he concluded. Hands would decide the outcome. The first show of hands was for Allott, and so many went up that it seemed to one reporter 'as if the number could not be exceeded; but when the name of Chamberlain was raised, it seemed as if all the Square . . . had uplifted their hands.'[21]

III

Chamberlain's success at this meeting in winning the Liberal nomination for Sheffield's second parliamentary seat marked the high point of his venture as a working men's candidate. His achievement left the local Liberals divided; and he had no time and little inclination to spend his energies bridging the division. The situation was worst at the personal level. The antagonism that divided Wilson and Leader now separated Chamberlain and Allott. Allott took his defeat in Paradise Square badly. He told the crowd to its face that he found such a forum 'distasteful'. Though he expressed the hope that Sheffield would present an unbroken Liberal front come election day, he could not bring himself to mention Chamberlain by name; and Chamberlain repaid his ungracious behaviour with contempt. Allott's sentiments were shared by his supporters. The pious and respectable Nonconformists whom he represented sat the election out.

Their decision would not have been so serious if the working-class electors had given Chamberlain solid support. But the unhealed contest between Allott and Chamberlain encouraged Roebuck to enter the field. The appeal that he issued — for 'The Briton's Bible and the Briton's Beer: our National Church and our National Beverage' — with enviable ease put together a combination of religious and working-class forces that also hastened the disintegration of his opponents' strength. While 'our National Church' won solid Conservative support, 'our National Beverage' possessed a heady appeal for the common working man and turned the public houses of Sheffield into recruiting centres for Roebuck. His talk of 'the Briton's Bible' also exploited the dismay of otherwise staunchly Liberal Nonconformists in Sheffield at the decision of the Birmingham school board to exclude the Bible from its schools. Roebuck's camp made subterranean use of Allott's candidacy. Some of Roebuck's men may have attended the meeting in Paradise Square to vote for Allott and thus make the result look uncertain. Afterwards they nominated Allott anyway in order to draw support from Chamberlain; and though Allott declined to make the requisite deposit, his name stayed on the ballot.

The campaign between the nomination and the election was brief and nasty. When Chamberlain and his fellow Liberal candidate Mundella tried to hold another rally in Paradise Square, supporters of Roebuck, some reputed to be prize fighters from Nottingham, massed themselves on the steps of the platform. Though driven off, they created enough uproar to make the speakers inaudible. Mundella was later struck with half a brick, Chamberlain with a red herring. The public houses pumped out generous inducement to vote for Roebuck. Between meetings, twenty-two for Chamberlain within five days, he and Mundella walked arm in arm through the streets, sometimes as much for physical support as to demonstrate their solidarity. Yet there was strain between them. The extent of Chamberlain's Radicalism made Mundella uneasy. Beginning to sense the strength of party loyalty, Chamberlain toned down his criticism of the Liberal government. Seeking nevertheless to make the most of his particular supporters, he put posters out on the eve of the election asking Liberals to plump for him.[22]

In the country at large as well as in Sheffield, Gladstone's sudden dissolution of Parliament caught his Radical critics unprepared. Neither the Education League nor organized labour was ready for a general election on its own or in cooperation with each other. The National Education League had been dormant since August, set aside while Chamberlain sought to unite its forces with those of organized labour. Jerked out of sleep, the League managed to induce 300 of the 425 Liberal candidates in Britain to pledge themselves for repeal of the Education Act's 25th clause which required local authorities to pay the fees of poor children in denominational schools. But the League did not oppose those who rejected this minimal demand. Only a small fraction of the Liberal candidates came out in support of the League's full set of policies. In the emergency, the Nonconformist instinct of loyalty to the Liberal party overrode concern about particular grievances. The Trades Union Congress seemed a little better prepared and more determined to force its point. In the preliminary notice for its annual meeting at Sheffield, the Congress had urged its members to press candidates for election, regardless of their party, to agree to vote for the needed changes in labour law. But like Nonconformist supporters of the Education League, when it came to the point of a general election with the risk of a Conservative victory, the leaders and spokesmen for organized labour tended to allow their Liberal loyalties to override their special interests. Meanwhile the relationship between the League and organized labour was far from settled. Attempts by organizations of Nonconformity and labour to subordinate each other during the election, for example at

Halifax,[23] exacerbated tension. Some working men liked the Education Act's 25th clause because it gave poor families a choice between denominational and board school education for their children.[24]

Except for the placing of Allott's name on the ballot, the campaign at Sheffield kept Chamberlain in good spirits. He was stunned by his defeat. Roebuck topped the poll with 14,193 votes, over 4,000 more than he had received in 1868. Mundella, with 12,858, secured the second place. Chamberlain was well back with 11,053, saved from the bottom of the poll only by the 621 votes for Allott, too few in themselves to account for Chamberlain's failure. A good many Liberals had stayed at home: the total vote was markedly smaller than in 1868. Roebuck had won back some of the working-class support he lost in 1868. More than 1,500 Liberals, whether Nonconformist or working-class, had either split their votes between Mundella and Roebuck or plumped for Roebuck.

IV

Chamberlain was indeed beaten by the Bible and beer. There were lesser contributing factors to his defeat. Some of Sheffield's electors may have resented Chamberlain as an interloper; but neither Roebuck nor Mundella were local sons. The hasty calling of the general election deprived Chamberlain of time to heal the division among Sheffield's Liberals; but he was never blessed as a peacemaker. The root reasons for his defeat were clear: the secular brand of his Radicalism alienated local Nonconformity, while Roebuck's alliance with the brewers cut into Chamberlain's working-class support. Comments on Allott's side as soon as the results were announced rubbed the message in. Allott claimed that if he had refused the test vote and stood for election he would have won. Unctuously he offered to place his services at the disposal of his fellow townsmen whenever their next parliamentary vacancy should occur. Letters from his supporters documented the defection of Nonconformists from Chamberlain. But the cruellest blow came from a metropolitan leader of skilled labour,[25] Robert Applegarth of the carpenters and joiners union, who told a post-election crowd in Sheffield that he hoped they would take Allott at the next opportunity.

Chamberlain lashed back at Allott. 'There is only one thing which will ever bring me to Sheffield again as a candidate,' he declared to Wilson, '— & that is Mr. Allott's offering himself. He has behaved like a "cad" all through, without a spark of nobleness or generosity.'[26] Chamberlain made sure that this resolve became common knowledge in Sheffield. He found little comfort from the fact that his defeat was part of a countrywide trend. For the first time in a generation the Conservatives swept into power with a solid majority. The outcome in the country seemed to magnify Chamberlain's folly in resisting the moderate drift in the Liberal party over the past four years. Defections among the Liberal electorate probably occurred more on its right flank disconcerted by what Gladstone had done than on the left offended by what he had left undone.[27] *The Times* crowed over Chamberlain's defeat as proving the wisdom of the governing élite. Before the election Chamberlain had gloried in the hostility of *The Times* as useful advertising. He had also expected and even looked forward to a spell of Conservative government as good medicine for the Liberals. But his own defeat, coupled with the victory of his archenemy the education minister, W. E. Forster, in a similar contest at Bradford, furnished evidence to discredit his entire enterprise in national politics, first with the Education League and now as a working men's candidate. He winced at the evidence and sought to publicize an alternative explanation, one that would put his defeat down to local circumstances.

But he did not accept these excuses himself. With remarkable speed he learned much of the lesson that underlay his defeat. He recognized immediately that he had misinterpreted the balance of strength between Nonconformity and labour and had underestimated the importance of party unity. 'The best thing for Sheffd. Liberals,' he advised Wilson, 'would be to unite at once on some new man, in case of Roebuck's death';[28] and he suggested Alfred Illingworth of Bradford as someone who would appeal to all Nonconformists but would need warming up to working-class demands. To help mobilize and bind both sources of support together, Chamberlain urged Wilson to adopt the organizational techniques perfected at Birmingham.

He distanced himself from Sheffield, plunging deeper than ever into the civic life of Birmingham. He did not, however, disengage himself from Sheffield abruptly. He still wanted to enter Parliament; and the insistent loyalty of Wilson and the Sheffield Trades Council together with his own anger at Allott kept him from severing the connection for another two years. During his periodic return engagements at Sheffield he kept on trying to reduce the suspicion that divided Nonconformity and labour. 'The first condition of success,' he told a post-election rally of his supporters, 'is a more cordial and thorough union between the Nonconformists as a body and the working classes.'[29] Accordingly he tightened up his Radical programme, reducing his four freedoms to the two dearest to each side: Free Church and Free Labour.

One feature of the working-class scene that Chamberlain discovered in the election at Sheffield continued to puzzle him: the Roebuck supporter, the local form of that national phenomenon, the Conservative working man. 'Even now,' he confessed, 'when the evidence of his existence has been forced upon me in a way which cannot be mistaken, I am bound to say that [the Conservative working man] is a monstrous anomaly and abortion.'[30] He tried to use the monstrosity as grist for his mill. Apparently a

71

good many working men, particularly in Lancashire and Yorkshire, had voted Conservative because Conservative candidates had been more responsive than Liberal devotees of laissez-faire economics to the demand for reform in the law governing trade unions. Chamberlain pleaded with Liberals to regain the loyalty of the working class by acceding to that demand. He had, however, a premonition that the Conservatives would beat them to the draw.

Chamberlain's bid for the support of labour was by no means a complete failure. His manifesto in the early autumn of 1873, his outspoken sympathy in ensuing months for trade unions and his support for their legislative demands helped at a critical juncture to retard the emergence of organized labour as an independent force in politics. In 1875, when the Conservative Home Secretary gave the trade union movement most of the legal rights and protection it desired, the Liberals in Parliament took note of the threat to their political interest by supporting and extending the concessions. Together these actions removed the main bone of contention between labour and the Liberals. In 1876, when Gladstone raised the banner of party conflict in the field of foreign policy that disguised class conflict, labour leaders leapt to his colours.

Even so, Chamberlain would never again put himself forward primarily as 'a working man's representative' whose chief interest in seeking election to the House of Commons was 'to ensure fair consideration for their claims as to all questions'. His experience at Sheffield restored balance in his calculations between Nonconformity and labour. He also began to rely more heavily upon party organization than upon reformulated programmes to unite the two contingents in the Radical army that he sought to lead. This shift in his focus deepened his hostility to representation of labour on its own. Preaching his organizational message to the rival liberal chieftains of Sheffield, Chamberlain implicitly abandoned the notion of standing as a working man's candidate. He wooed Robert Leader by indicating how a Sheffield association formed on the model of the one in Birmingham could serve to suppress any candidacies like that, whether by middle-class spokesmen for the working man or by the genuine article. 'Tell Mr. Leader from me,' he wrote Wilson,

that a Liberal Ass[ociatio]n. such as ours is the most magnificent machine ever invented for social, philanthropic, educational & political work. . . .

With this organisation we have beaten the Tories till they dare not show their heads . . . we have beaten the publicans . . . we have beaten the priests in the Wards in which the Irish Catholics chiefly live; & now we are going to beat the so called 'Working men's candidates' — a little knot of idle vagabonds who raise this cry in the hope of foisting themselves into notice against the wishes of all the intelligent portion of the working class.[31]

Notes

1 See P. S. Bagwell, *Industrial Relations: Government and Society in Nineteenth-century Britain: Commentaries on British parliamentary papers* (Dublin, 1974), pp. 40ff.; D. D. Woods, 'The operation of the Master and Servants Act in the Black Country, 1858 – 1875,' *Midland History* vii (1982), 95ff.; and H. C. G. Matthew, ed., *The Gladstone Diaries* vii (Oxford, 1982), lxxvi – lxxvii.

2 For an excellent account of this campaign, see W. H. McCready, 'British labour's lobby, 1867 – 1875,' *Canadian Journal of Economics and Political Science*, xxii (1956), 141 – 160.

3 Royden Harrison, *Before the Socialists* (London, 1965), p. 299; also W. H. Fraser, *Trade Unions and Society: The struggle for acceptance, 1850 – 1880* (London, 1974), p. 144.

4 Speech to the Sheffield Reform Association, 14 May 1873 (Chamberlain papers [University of Birmingham], JC4/1/74). All quotations from the Chamberlain papers are by kind permission of the University of Birmingham.

5 xiv, n.s. (1 Sept. 1873).

6 23 Sept. 1873, in C. W. Boyd, *Mr. Chamberlain's Speeches* (London, 1914), i. 28ff.

7 See Dennis Smith, *Conflict and Compromse: Class formation in English society, 1830 – 1914: A comparative study of Birmingham and Sheffield* (London, 1982).

8 Chamberlain to Wilson, 13 Dec. 1873 (Wilson papers [University of Sheffield]).

9 Harris to Wilson, 12 Dec. 1873 (Wilson papers).

10 Wilson to Chamberlain, 14 Dec. 1873 (Chamberlain papers, JC6/5/2/7).

11 Wilson to Chamberlain, 16 Dec. 1873 (Chamberlain papers, JC6/5/2/10).

12 Harris to Wilson, 17 Dec. 1873 (Wilson papers).

13 J. L. Kitze, 'To dare and to lead: Partisanship and independence in the nineteenth-century Anglo-American press' (Syracuse University Honors thesis, 1985).

14 Chamberlain to Wilson, 23 Dec. 1873 (Wilson papers).

15 Wilson to Chamberlain, 24 Dec. 1873 (Chamberlain papers, JC6/5/2/22).

16 Chamberlain to Wilson, 25 Dec. 1873 (Wilson papers).

17 Chamberlain to Maxse, ? Dec. 1873 (Maxse papers 205, p. 14 [West Sussex Record Office], quoted by kind permission of Mrs. Maxse).

18 Speech at Sheffield, 1 Jan. 1874 (Chamberlain papers, JC4/3/23 – 31).

19 Chamberlain to Wilson, 24 Jan. 1874 (Wilson papers).

20 Chamberlain to Wilson, 26 Jan. 1874 (Wilson papers).

21 *Sheffield Post*, 31 Jan. 1874.

22 W. H. G. Armytage, *A. J. Mundella, 1825 – 1897* (London, 1951), p. 366, n. 46.

23 H. W. McCready, 'The British election of 1874: Frederic Harrison and the Liberal-labour dilemma', *Canadian Journal of Economics and Political Science*, xx (1954), 172.

24 See Morley to Harrison, 11 Feb. 1874, in F. W. Hirst, *Early Life & Letters of John Morley* (London, 1927), i. 297.

25 Cf. Zygmunt Bauman, *Between Class and Elite: The evolution of the British labour movement* (Manchester, 1972), p. 109: 'The stratum of skilled workers . . . regarded the liberal radicals as disturbers of the social order in which it was vitally interested.'

26 Chamberlain to Wilson, 9 Feb. 1874 (Wilson papers).

27 D. A. Hamer, *The Politics of Electoral Pressure* (Atlantic Highlands, N.J., 1977), pp. 137 – 8.

28 Chamberlain to Wilson, 9 Feb. 1874, *loc. cit.*

29 *Sheffield Post*, 19 Mar. 1874.

30 *Ibid.*

31 Chamberlain to Wilson, ?15 Oct. 1875 (Wilson papers [Sheffield City Library collection]).

4

The Diagnosis and Treatment of Nervous Breakdown: A Dilemma for Victorian and Edwardian Psychiatry

Janet Oppenheim

Early in 1882 Karl Marx's daughter Eleanor, depressed and exhausted from nursing her sick parents, confessed to her sister that she 'was terribly afraid of breaking down altogether, . . .' 'What I most dread,' Eleanor explained, 'is the consulting of doctors. They cannot and will not see that mental worry is as much an illness as any physical ailment could be.'[1] In that outburst of frustration, Eleanor Marx virtually summarized the history of psychological medicine in nineteenth- and early twentieth-century Britain. Throughout those decades members of the British medical profession sought to establish the somatic foundations of psychological disturbances. They attempted to ignore, or at least to minimize, the role of mind in a field of inquiry permeated with mentalist assumptions.

The physiological orientation of Victorian and Edwardian psychiatry has been amply illustrated in a range of recent studies that examine the treatment of insanity. The related, but distinct, problem of nervous disorders in British culture before the First World War has, however, remained comparatively neglected. The subject has not yet attracted the sociological, institutional, or legal analyses that enrich modern research into nineteenth-century asylums, for the very designation of nervous disorder as a disease category is unsatisfactory. Its imprecise label appears to cover both specific physical illness, like epilepsy, and such vague traits of temperament as melancholy. Physicians were obliged to employ that loose category of ailment until growing knowledge of toxins, microbes, and cerebral anatomy allowed them to make finer etiological distinctions. The annals of Victorian medicine abound with the records of patients whose baffling disabilities could only be attributed to some indescribable malfunction of the nervous system. Their treatment reflected the ambivalence of the medical profession in analyzing the complex relationship of mind and body.

The nervous breakdown feared by Eleanor Marx belonged among the 'functional nervous disorders' frequently invoked by British doctors before the First World War. Under that heading they crammed a strange assortment of maladies, indeed all the diseases 'in which *no anatomical changes can be found after death, either with the naked eye or with the microscope*, which can account for the symptoms during life'.[2] Accordingly, hysteria, migraine, vertigo, neuralgia, hypochondriasis, nervous exhaustion or neurasthenia, chorea, epilepsy, infantile paralysis, and insanity, among others, figured on the list of functional nervous disorders during the nineteenth and early twentieth centuries. They were also dubbed neuroses, a term first used in the second half of the eighteenth century by William Cullen, the highly influential Scottish physician, to designate those diseases that bore no trace of physical lesion or structural alteration. Despite their acknowledgment of temporary ignorance, Victorian and Edwardian doctors were confident that physiological causes for the diverse forms of functional nervous disorder would in time be revealed.

The Victorians themselves scarcely used the phrase 'nervous breakdown' until the end of the century. The puzzling array of symptoms that characterized this condition were more often described as 'shattered nerves' or 'broken health'. 'Nervous exhaustion' likewise found a place in medical parlance, particularly after George Beard, an American neurologist, advocated neurasthenia as a separate disease entity and thus brought the concept of nervous prostration more prominently to British medical attention in the 1870s and 1880s. By the 1880s, however, physicians also spoke of breakdowns, and biographers soon followed suit. Silvanus Thompson, for example, in his 1898 biography of Michael Faraday mentioned the scientist's 'serious breakdown' during the early 1840s, whereas an earlier biography, published in 1870, had referred only to Faraday's 'loss of memory and giddiness', and his pressing need to rest from overwork.[3] In 1903, Sir James Crichton-Browne, Lord Chancellor's Visitor in Lunacy, disparagingly described Jane Welsh Carlyle as 'the very woman in whom the physician would expect a nervous breakdown at a critical epoch of life', while by 1913 G. M. Trevelyan could explain that John Bright's illness in 1856 would 'in our day . . . popularly be called a "nervous breakdown"'.[4]

As these examples demonstrate, nervous breakdown was not exclusively a female medical problem in the Victorian and Edwardian eras. Although doctors assumed that the female sex was inherently more subject to nervous excitement and less able to bear nervous strain than the male, they never assigned to women any monopoly on nervous collapse, for their own casebooks told them otherwise. In addition to Faraday and Bright, they might have cited the painter Edwin Landseer, Charles Kingsley, Herbert Spencer, John Stuart Mill, Joseph Lister, Francis Galton, the diarist and writer A. C. Benson, and John Tulloch, Principal of St. Andrews, among many other men. At differing stages in their lives, all these examples endured periods of profound depression and intense anxiety that rendered them incapable of focusing their attention or pursuing their customary activities. Yet so much work in recent years has highlighted the psychological and social uses of illness for Victorian women, on both sides of the Atlantic, that the subject of illness in their husbands, fathers, sons, and brothers has been substantially overlooked. The unfortunate result is that historians have come to interpret women's nervous ailments as passive-aggressive means of protesting against socially, economically, and professionally limited lives. Through this interpretation, Victorian and Edwardian women cannot help but appear manipulative, to our way of thinking, whenever they complained of nervous illness, particularly if they manifested hysterical symptoms. These psychosocial generalizations disregard the fact that, for every woman who languished in invalidism, there were scores that soldiered on against the same conditions that broke their sisters' health, just as the generalizations fail to account for valetudinarianism in Victorian men. With an illness so variable and so personal as nervous breakdown, no facile generalization sheds much light on the reasons why one person, male or female, proves vulnerable, while another does not, or why someone succumbs at one time of life and resists at another.

If the assumption that nervous prostration was the creation of Victorian women is misleading, even more so is the belief that it primarily befell ladies of leisure. Nervous breakdown in the nineteenth century, as in the twentieth, knew no class barriers. It is true that one school of medical thought in Britain, viewing the prevalence of nervous disorders as a sign that the pace and competition of modern life was more than the human nervous system could easily sustain, argued that the burden fell most heavily on those in the vanguard of civilization — 'the cultured classes'.[5] Once neurasthenia became the fashionable name for all the symptoms previously implied by 'shattered nerves', this school of thought derived support from Beard's own assertion that neurasthenia largely affected the affluent members of society.[6] Another point of view that attracted a wider following among British doctors in the Victorian and Edwardian periods took its lead from the great French specialist in nervous disorders, Jean-Martin Charcot. As a reviewer in the *Journal of Mental Science* pointed out in 1891, Charcot counted neurasthenics not only in the 'upper classes, enervated by over-civilization', but also 'on a large scale amongst the work-a-day classes'.[7] Thomas Dixon Savill, a London physician affiliated with the West End Hospital for Diseases of the Nervous System, published a textbook in which he drew many of his clinical examples from male workers. He described, for example, a policeman whose 'condition of nervousness and inaptitude for work' was 'pitiable', a professional cook 'subject to attacks of complete helplessness and prostration', and an engine-fitter who likewise suffered from miserable 'sensations of bodily illness, depression, helplessness, and weariness'.[8] If overwork could cause nervous exhaustion, as was commonly believed, the majority of British medical opinion before the First World War recognized physical as well as intellectual labor as a causative agent.

Doctors concurred that no two cases of nervous prostration were identical, but a number of symptoms appeared frequently enough to serve as the characteristic features of the disorder. They included a sense of inadequacy and profound pessimism, inability to concentrate on intellectual tasks or to assume responsibility, physical lethargy, insomnia, lack of appetite, nameless dreads, painfully acute or abnormally dull sense perceptions, intense self-consciousness, assorted bodily pains like excruciating headache, palpitations, indigestion, and neuralgia.[9] The superficial reasons summoned to explain these incapacitating conditions presented as great a mixture of physical and psychological factors as did the symptoms themselves. Victorian and Edwardian physicians attributed nervous breakdown to intense mental anxiety, emotional shock, overwork of muscles or brain, physical trauma such as railroad accidents, malnutrition, or sexual excess. With women, doctors assumed that the life cycle played a critically important role, inseparably linking women's nerves with biological functions. The medical profession expected that its female patients would prove more susceptible to shock, strain, and fatigue at the time of menarche, or as a result of menstrual malfunctions, during pregnancy and just after childbirth, while nursing infants and, finally, at the time of menopause. Nervous collapse in men was not specifically affiliated with the life cycle, and doctors customarily perceived male sufferers as victims of professional pressures, tensions arising from financial or intellectual responsibilities, and various forms of sexual indulgence. While physicians diagnosed differently the secondary causes of nervous breakdown in men and women, there was widespread agreement that the primary cause was always somatic. Indeed, the very term 'nervous breakdown' implied the destruction of something physical.

The fundamental physiological explanation that Victorian and Edwardian medical theory applied to nervous breakdown was the exhaustion of nerve force. This was not a metaphorical concept but an indubitably material substance. If it could not be precisely measured, it could certainly be depleted, thereby causing weakness, lethargy, depression, and all the associated symptoms of shattered health. The essential nature of nerve force was the subject of considerable controversy in the nineteenth century, as it had been since the second century A.D., when Galen explained the impact of nerves on muscles in terms of animal spirits that might or might not be fluid. Although one school of thought had persisted in viewing animal spirits as immaterial forces, the material interpretation gained ground during the seventeenth and eighteenth centuries, in keeping with the development of scientific thought at that time. When investigators of the nervous system encountered processes that eluded physical explanation, they joined researchers in many other fields of biology and physics alike and sought recourse to subtle, imponderable fluids. These superfine, invisible fluids had no weight or other quantifiable properties, yet they were deemed to be material substances possessing physical extension. Thus the imponderable fluid known as nerve force could escape instruments of investigation as it coursed along the nerves, but its advocates could nonetheless insist upon its bodily existence. In the early modern period, Borelli, Boerhaave, Haller, and Cullen were among the leading physiologists who maintained that the nerve force operated as a liquid.[10]

The fluidist explanation of nervous action exerted a wide and understandable appeal, for it required no special expertise to comprehend the movement of liquid through tiny tubes. The notion, furthermore, that supplies of this liquid could fall behind demand was easily conceived by anyone who had seen wells, public conduits, or irrigation ditches run dry. The lack of evidence to reveal any channel in the nerves through which the nervous fluid might flow posed no serious obstacle in the case of a subtle fluid, and the liquid theory of nerve force continued to find support among British physicians in the nineteenth century.

By the start of the Victorian period, however, it was gradually losing its dominant position among explanations for the functioning of the nervous system. Anatomical investigations, by such men as Charles Bell in England and François Magendie in France, had helped to reveal the complexities of that system, showing how nerve fibers that stimulate muscular movement differ from those conveying sensation. Some physicians sought a less simplistic explanatory theory in light of these new discoveries, and one was ready to hand in the hypothesis first proposed by the French physiologist Xavier Bichat around the year 1800. Bichat's doctrine of 'specific nerve energies' was far from simple for it posited that 'the nervous conductions subserving the various elements, sensory and motor, were of different quality. This difference in quality of 'energy' was then supposed to be the basis for the variety of qualitative modes of consciousness.' With refinement by German physiologists — especially Müller and Helmholtz — a belief in specific nerve energies became integrated into physiological and neurological theory by the middle of the nineteenth century and was not discredited until the start of the twentieth.[11] It provided a link with the magnificent work of Victorian physics: energy and force became the prevailing modes of expression in the sciences of matter, whether organic or inorganic.

The influence of contemporary physics was even more evident in the growing conviction that electrical activity underlay the workings of the nervous system. When the mysteries of electricity were yielding to scientific probe and electricity was being harnessed for human purposes, it is scarcely surprising that it appealed to physicians and scientists as the form of energy most applicable to the nerves. The association of nerve force with electricity was not new to the Victorian age, but had first emerged in the eighteenth century and received strong confirmation in Galvani's work during the 1790s. As research into the transmission of the nervous impulse advanced, it became increasingly plausible to conceive of that impulse as a kind of electrical conduction. Laboratory experiments in the second half of the nineteenth century amply demonstrated that electricity could provoke muscular contractions, so that late Victorian and Edwardian doctors felt justified in asserting the close similarity of nerve force and electricity. Although final proof that the nerve impulse consists of an electric current was not forthcoming until the 1930s, by the end of the nineteenth century the ancient enigma surrounding the nature of nerve force appeared to have been resolved in favor of some form of electricity.

Whatever physical properties doctors assigned to the nerve force, they were unanimous in warning that supplies of it were limited. Heedless over-taxation of nerve force could result in an exhausted nervous system incapable of all endeavour. The phrase 'nervous prostration' was no figure of speech in Victorian and Edwardian medical vocabulary, but expressed the collapsed state of a person's nerves when lacking adequate quantities of the dynamic nerve force. 'Nervous lethargy' or 'nervous debility' similarly designated what physicians assumed to be a real physiological condition of utter weakness. Doctors believed that some people under stress more easily depleted their nervous power than others, thanks to a hereditary nervous temperament or constitution.[12] Without knowledge of genetic transmission, yet certain from studies of insanity in successive generations of families that instability of the nervous system was inheritable, the medical profession found temperament and constitution indispensable for explanatory purposes. When patients began life with an inherent nervous diathesis, or constitutional predisposition to disorders of the nervous system, the attending doctor had no trouble elucidating the causes of ill health. Furthermore, the doctor's own responsibility was diminished in such a case, for a successful treatment redounded to his credit, but failure could be ascribed to an unfortunate inheritance. Whether nervous prostration arose from a hereditary condition or was acquired through over-exertion, anxiety, or trauma, depletion of nerve force served as a protean concept capable of surviving successive discoveries in neurology. Just as nervous fluid could run dry, the nerve cell that operated like a faradic battery could run down, if used without respite. Thus doctors throughout the Victorian and Edwardian periods treated patients in the belief that nervous power was something

80

to be carefully husbanded, for if once lost, the price might be chronic helplessness.[13]

The treatments designed to cure, or at least to mitigate, the crippling symptoms of nervous exhaustion all addressed the paramount need to replenish supplies of nerve force. Doctors practised a variety of different therapies in the Victorian and Edwardian periods, but all required the patient's removal from whatever strain, pressure, or excessive activity had drained power from the nervous system. Since there was wide agreement within the medical profession that the tensions and tempo of contemporary civilization placed too heavy a burden on delicate nervous systems, affluent patients were generally sent away from urban homes into a peaceful, rural environment. Others went to the seaside, or the fashionable hydropathic spas, at Malvern, Cheltenham, or Ben Rhydding, Yorkshire, for example. Still others pursued such gentle forms of outdoor exercise as golf and fishing. (After John Bright found no relief at Ben Rhydding in 1856, he tried salmon fishing in Scotland, with greater effect.)[14] Short country walks were also recommended for patients with sufficient strength. The purpose of mild exercise was to induce just enough physical fatigue to promote sleep, for a good night's rest was an essential part of the therapy. Exercise, however, was never allowed to become strenuous, lest it endanger the quantity of nerve force which the patient was sedulously accumulating through prolonged rest. What physicians did invariably insist upon for nervous disorders was exposure to the open air. They fervently believed that clean country air purged the body of poisons infesting the polluted urban atmosphere that most of their patients habitually inhaled.

As many doctors prized fresh air and sunshine for restoring exhausted nerves, so others recommended particular climates as uniquely suited to nervous sufferers. After an initial period of complete rest, numerous patients were packed off to seek renewed health in various corners of Europe and North Africa. Although medical opinion differed enormously on the subject, a large portion of it assumed that patients benefited from the dry, cold, bracing climate of the Alps, and in the summer months it was not unusual to find British neurasthenics strolling along the mountain paths of Switzerland. Not a few British doctors, however, warned that all forms of travel could be upsetting to fragile nerves and kept patients safely on their side of the Channel.

In extreme cases, absolute bed-rest had to be prescribed. From the 1880s on, the 'rest cure' devised by Silas Weir Mitchell, an eminent neurologist from Philadelphia, attracted attention among British doctors as appropriate in these cases. They particularly applied it to female patients whose nervous prostration was exacerbated by anorexia, for Weir Mitchell advocated both prolonged bed-rest (a month or longer) and enforced overfeeding to counter 'the malnutrition, the emaciation, and the anaemia

81

which is so frequent an accompaniment . . . in pronounced cases of neurasthenia'.[15] He also insisted that patients be isolated from family influences and that they receive regular stimulation of their muscles, by massage and electricity, to avoid muscular atrophy. British doctors had begun recommending electrotherapy before Weir Mitchell's ideas circulated in England, but the literature on electricity as a form of treatment in neurasthenia increased as his rest cure became better known and gained a powerful supporter in W. S. Playfair, professor of obstetric medicine at King's College, London. At a time when nerve force was being identified with electricity, electrotherapy made great sense for patients suffering from depletion of nervous energy. Applied to spine, neck, limbs, pelvic region, or wherever, mild electric currents could not, it seemed, fail to revitalize an exhausted nervous system. Nonetheless, British doctors rarely applied the Weir Mitchell treatment in its full rigor for fear that patients might 'contract the "bed habit"', if allowed to remain recumbent too long.[16]

Long before Weir Mitchell developed his therapy, nutrition had played a major role in the treatment of neurasthenic patients, for many Victorian doctors considered the connection between digestive tract and nervous system to be of paramount importance. James Manby Gully, the best known of Victorian hydropaths, claimed that numerous nervous disorders arose from visceral disturbances affecting the circulation of blood to the brain.[17] Without espousing the water cure that Gully deemed medicine's most effective response to this organic link, more orthodox physicians likewise sought access to the nerves through the stomach. Dyspepsia, they were sure, could prompt nervous irritability, and, under unfavorable circumstances, prolonged dyspepsia could contribute to the onset of nervous prostration. A broad range of diets was prescribed throughout the Victorian and Edwardian years, with few elements in common besides a warning against spicy and highly seasoned fare for the nervous patient. One opinion advised total abstinence from tea, coffee, wine, and spirits; another found all four beneficial in moderate amounts. One point of view labelled red meat too rich for a faulty digestive system; another pronounced it essential for regaining strength. Still others urged a diet heavy in fats, or protein, or fruit, vegetables, and bread. While vigorously arguing the merits of their preferred system, physicians agreed that no general rule was possible for patients whose nervous ailments exhibited strikingly individual differences.

The somatic assumptions behind medical concern for diet in the treatment of nervous collapse also supported a heavy reliance on drugs. Throughout the Victorian era, doctors blithely prescribed strong medications for patients suffering from functional nervous disorders, and while the first half of the nineteenth century witnessed the heyday of promiscuous drugging and 'heroic' doses, even at the end of the period physicians ordered sedatives, tonics, and laxatives in liberal quantities. Among the drugs freely dispensed were acetate of lead, calomel (mercurous chloride), arsenic, and antimony, which some Edwardian doctors came to recognize as 'nerve poisons'.[18] Strychnine, quinine, and iron enjoyed particular popularity as nerve tonics, or strengtheners, but there was less agreement about other drugs used in treating nervous exhaustion. Opium (or morphine), bromide of potassium, sulphonal, bromide of ammonium, and chloral, for example, all had advocates and opponents. Indeed, there was scarcely a drug on the market that did not inspire extravagant praise or dire warning from a reputable medical spokesman. Warnings seem to have had scant effect, however, for it was only by the late Victorian period that the impact of chemicals on the body began to attract systematic scrutiny. The one substantial advantage of medicines over retirement in the country, change of climate, hydropathy, and the rest cure was their availability to the poor in infirmaries and dispensaries across the country, but one can only suspect that working-class neurasthenics reaped little benefit from them. Regardless of the patient's social class, medication prescribed to fortify shattered nerves doubtless contributed, in many cases, to chronic ill health.

However resolutely the Victorian and Edwardian medical profession emphasized physiological conditions underlying nervous breakdown and designed therapies addressed to somatic deficiencies, they could not ignore the critically important non-physical will. British psychiatrists practised medicine in a culture that placed a high social and moral value on individual self-control, and all theories of mental health in the nineteenth and early twentieth centuries stressed the role of the will in governing instincts and imagination — in achieving a well-balanced, socially responsible personality.[19] While doctors argued that neurological disorders had definite physical bases, none ever claimed that the mind's role was inconsequential. As Daniel Noble, a Manchester physician, explained in mid-century: 'Practically, it is always difficult to draw the boundary line between what are commonly considered purely Nervous maladies, and diseases of the Mind, on account of the connection subsisting amongst all the nervous centres and the correlated psychical states.' About the same time, Sir Henry Holland, physician in ordinary to the Queen, concluded that questions concerning the nature and action of the nervous power lay 'on that obscure boundary between the mental and material functions, over which it has been the perpetual but fruitless aim of philosophy to pass'.[20] Clearly the nervous system, connected with mind through the brain and with body through muscles and sensory organs, occupied a place of central significance in the age-old philosophical puzzle of mind-body interaction.

Before the First World War, the concept of will entered into the diagnosis of nervous breakdown by the very absence of will-power. It is easy to see how failure of nervous energy came to be associated with failure of will.

83

Since nerve force was believed to join the commanding brain to the obedient muscles, inadequate amounts of such force must render the patient incapable of action. Holland described a typical case of deficient nervous power in which 'all the voluntary movements of walking, speaking, eating, &c., were in a sort of abeyance — the mind inert, as if unable to force itself into any effort of thought or feeling'.[21] A patient thus handicapped could equally be described as lacking the will to act. In such a state, the patient also lacked the moral capacity to choose right over wrong. In the eyes of the Victorian and Edwardian medical profession, he or she was no longer an autonomous, self-directed individual, and the doctor's primary duty became obvious. 'What we want to secure,' asserted David Drummond, a Newcastle physician, 'is a central will, reassured, instructed, strengthened, and set free from worrying trammels to play its proper part as director-general of the personality.'[22]

There was an inherent contradiction between a somatic theory of nervous breakdown and what have been called the 'moral-pastoral responsibilities' of the physician[23] for the mental health of his patients. Doctors recognized that their own personality and authority played a considerable part in restoring vigor to the patient's will. Combining the power of positive thinking with the influence of a father confessor, the doctor had to stimulate the patient's own involvement in recovery. He had to nurture in the victim of nervous collapse the will to be whole and strong. In so doing, doctors deviated substantially from a strictly physiological interpretation of the medical problem. One way to avoid the mentalist implications inherent in any discussion of the will was simply to assert that the will possessed a physical basis. Henry Maudsley boldly adopted this course in *Body and Will* (1883), while an article that appeared in D. H. Tuke's authoritative *Dictionary of Psychological Medicine* in 1892 actually referred to 'lesions' of the will.[24] Most Victorian and Edwardian psychiatrists, however, were uneasy about an overtly materialist approach to the will that threatened to eliminate free choice from the realm of human behaviour. A few, like Crichton-Browne, clung to phrenological concepts long after phrenology had been discredited, precisely because they allowed one to talk simultaneously of mental states and of the physical arrangement of the cerebral hemispheres.[25] Most commonly, British medical psychologists in these years applied forms of treatment that, ostensibly catering to an exhausted nerve force, also stimulated the will to resume its governing and coordinating activities. Breathing country air, relaxing at hydropathic spas, or wading in salmon streams carried the psychological advantage of a change of scene. Physicians fully realized that to remove a patient from a place associated with anxiety, sorrow, or tension was often the first step towards recovery.

It was one thing to acknowledge that mind influenced body in countless direct and indirect ways, but quite another to design a treatment that accorded priority to the mind in the healing process. In fact, specific forms of psychotherapy found few advocates because they appeared both to obstruct the goal of reinvigorating the will and to undermine the physician's exalted role. The failure of hypnosis to attract a significant following in Great Britain provides a case in point, as does the largely hostile response to Freudian psychoanalysis before the First World War. Hypnosis, for all its demonstrable efficacy and despite prestigious support from Hack Tuke, was too closely associated with the mumbo-jumbo of mesmerism to appeal to professionally ambitious physicians. More serious, however, was the conviction that susceptibility to hypnosis was in itself the mark of disorder in the patient, for it meant that the patient's own will was too feeble to exert a desirable degree of control. As Drummond observed, hypnotic suggestion had the considerable 'drawback of substituting the will of another person instead of reinforcing the patient's own intelligent will and self-government . . .'[26] Freud's version of psychotherapy, when it became known in England during the 1890s and early 1900s, similarly appeared to promote the pathological over the normal. British doctors had long since identified sexual excess as a cause of nervous exhaustion, and they had little need for Freud's refinement of that hypothesis, with its focus on masturbation to the virtual exclusion of heterosexual coitus. Here was excellent proof that Freud's theories merely underscored, and even elicited, morbid desires, leaving the patient's will all the less able to exercise supervision over a healthy, integrated personality.[27]

Even more important in determining the British reaction to these psychotherapies before the First World War was the belief that they challenged the physiological assumptions about mental and nervous illness that offered scientific status and professional prestige to Victorian and Edwardian psychiatrists. The highly proclaimed scientific method, although far less rigorous than its admirers supposed, appeared to offer a sure path to incontrovertible knowledge. Empirical research and the careful study of controlled experiments were leading science in the nineteenth century to impressive discoveries about the biological, chemical, and physical structure of the universe. In the emerging medical field of neurology, clinical observation and laboratory tests were beginning to chart the regions of the brain and consequently to unravel some mysteries of the nervous system. Whether in the investigation of cerebral localization, of paralysis and convulsions, or of the possibly microbic causes of so-called functional nervous disorders, the methods of laboratory research and experiment were paying large dividends by the end of Victoria's reign. Psychiatry, too, aspired to rank as a science based on regular, observable, predictable physiological laws. Such rank, it was assumed, would not result from concentration on the shadowy regions of mind, about which psychiatrists could articulate no irrefutable theory of illness, but rather from objective inquiry into the substantial tissue of the brain.

85

In its professional development during the second half of the nineteenth century, psychiatry in Great Britain was torn between the German model of physiological psychology and the native tradition of philosophical speculation about mind. As many scholars have argued, it was the former that became the dominant mode in British psychiatry before the First World War, or at least the majority of scientists and medical pyschologists gave enthusiastic lip-service to it. It would be a mistake, however, to underestimate the enduring strength of the philosophical approach in British psychiatry. Although young British doctors intending to specialize in psychological medicine customarily studied in Germany during the last quarter of the nineteenth century — many at Leipzig where Wilhelm Wundt had founded the first pyschological laboratory in 1879 — comparatively little work in experimental psychology was undertaken in England and Scotland at this time. Instead some of the most important names in late Victorian and Edwardian psychology — Maudsley, Alexander Bain, W. B. Carpenter, James Ward, G. F. Stout, and James Sully, for example — continued to ponder such concepts as volition and purpose, and still found moral problems an appropriate area of inquiry. Indeed, in Ward's hands, a fundamentally unsympathetic attitude towards neurophysiological psychology and a refusal to strip humanity of non-material moral attributes became a distinctive British contribution to psychology at the turn of the century.[28]

Wundt and Ward are, in a sense, representative of the two poles between which British diagnosis and treatment of nervous breakdown hung suspended before the First World War. Even in the earlier Victorian period, although the contrast between the two viewpoints was less pronounced than in subsequent decades, medical attitudes towards shattered nerves were rendered more complex by the intrusion of moral issues into a presumably physiological problem. In this respect, the questions raised by nervous prostration were very similar to those provoked by insanity. The moral treatment of insane people, for example, had no more convincing a scientific rationale behind it than did the application of psychotherapy in the treatment of nervous prostration, although both occasionally produced positive results. British psychiatrists, therefore, could no more construct a plausible interpretation of insanity on the basis of moral treatment than they could elucidate nervous collapse by reference to hypnosis. (The fact that both hypnotist and humane asylum attendant needed no medical expertise to work successfully also antagonized British physicians, needless to say.) Furthermore, just as the concept of will complicated theories of nervous exhaustion, so the undeniable element of mind in mental illness involved psychiatrists in elaborate theoretical evasions.[29]

It has, indeed, been argued that, in late Victorian psychiatry, 'much the same framework of interpretative ideas' was applied to the treatment of functional nervous complaints as to severe mental unsoundness.[30] This is

86

scarcely surprising since insanity was actually categorized as a functional nervous disorder for much of the Victorian period, and nervous exhaustion was widely regarded as an intermediate stage between madness and mental health. Although Victorian and Edwardian doctors agreed that victims of nervous collapse were usually capable of lucid thought, they also warned that loss of nerve force might prove the first step towards the loss of reason. Forbes Winslow, a leading figure in psychological medicine in the middle of the century, was one of many physicians to believe that 'an incapacity to control and direct the faculty of attention', to perform one's customary mental work, could signal incipient disease of the brain.[31]

Nevertheless, by the last quarter of the nineteenth century, a significant difference was developing between British medical attitudes towards insanity, on the one hand, and nervous breakdown on the other. At the center of this divergence of opinion was the issue of moral blame. As the Victorian era progressed, psychiatry came to view lunacy ever more firmly as an illness whose victims were not responsible for their own behaviour. Even if cerebral lesions could not be identified in all cases, the British medical profession grew increasingly confident that pathological conditions of the brain's structure caused insanity. The celebrated neurologist John Hughlings Jackson formulated a physiological theory of nervous degeneration that offered a reasonable explanation of insanity in evolutionary terms. According to his hypothesis, those parts of the human nervous system that had evolved last — the portions of the cerebral cortex that controlled intellectual activities — were the first whose functions broke down under the strain of modern life and succumbed to disease. This so-called "dissolution" of the highest cortical centers not only was consistent with the prevailing evolutionary perspective in the biological sciences, but also struck the theme of degeneration that figured prominently in late Victorian and Edwardian socio-biological thought. It was certainly not the lunatic's own fault if the brain's intellectual center ceased to operate.

At the same time, however, doctors could not rid themselves of the belief that victims of nervous breakdown were somehow guilty of moral weakness. Many such sufferers maintained unquestionably sound judgment throughout their periods of illness and, if they felt sufficiently energetic, could write or talk about their condition rationally and calmly. During his breakdown in 1841, Faraday's letters were 'free from the slightest sign of mental disease', while A. C. Benson described his state of mind during his breakdown of 1907 – 09 as 'perfectly unclouded'.[32] It was, accordingly, very difficult to deny that the patient's condition could improve, if only he or she would exert an effort of will. If the mind were not affected, surely the will, after the necessary period of rest and renewal, could reassert its supervision of the personality. The physiological inadequacy that led a person to 'break down', one prominent psychiatrist remarked in 1906, was 'closely related to will power and moral capacity'.

A few years later, Ernest Jones, Freud's loyal disciple, complained about the lack of sympathy shown towards patients with neurotic illnesses, observing that 'a neurotic illness is vaguely felt to have something essentially unreal about it, to contain something of a pose, for instance a "craving for sympathy", and to be much more under the control of the patient's will than he can be got to admit'.[33]

However reverently British psychiatry might celebrate a morally neutral experimental psychology, it remained an elusive goal before the First World War, and in their investigation of nervous breakdown medical psychologists faced a formidable dilemma. If they compromised their commitment to a physiological explanation of the disorder, they jeopardized their scientific reputation. Yet somaticism carried to its furthest conclusion necessarily undermined the existence of free will, which was central to the Victorian ethos, both in its theological and its social aspects. The denial of free will was, of course, devastating for spiritual reasons, but for physicians it also brought damaging professional repercussions. Without will, they had no morally elevated part to play in restoring their nervous patients to health. Thus they were forced to choose between the status of objective scientist and the values of voluntarism, autonomy, and self-help. In order to preserve the latter, Victorian and Edwardian psychiatrists sacrificed something of the former and refrained from taking their physical interpretation of mind as far as it could logically extend.

Notes

1 Eleanor Marx to Jenny Marx Longuet, 8 January 1882, in *The Daughters of Karl Marx: Family Correspondence 1866 – 1898*, tr. Faith Evans, with commentary and notes by Olga Meier (Harmondsworth, 1984), pp. 145 – 6.

2 Thomas Dixon Savill, *Clinical Lectures on Neurasthenia* (3rd ed., rev., London, 1906), pp. 11 – 12 (Savill's italics).

3 Silvanus Thompson, *Michael Faraday: His Life and Work* (London, 1898), p. 170; Bence Jones, *The Life and Letters of Faraday* (2 vols., London, 1870), ii. 126.

4 James Crichton-Browne, Introduction to *New Letters and Memorials of Jane Welsh Carlyle*, ed. Alexander Carlyle (2 vols., London, 1903), i, lvii; G. M. Trevelyan, *The Life of John Bright* (London, 1913), pp. 254 – 5.

5 W. S. Playfair, 'Some Observations Concerning What is Called Neurasthenia', *British Medical Journal* (1886, pt. 2), 854.

6 Throughout this essay I shall use the term 'neurasthenia' — literally 'nerve weakness' — as synonymous with other expressions for nervous breakdown, although Beard erroneously claimed that he had discovered a new disease.

7 Anonymous review of F. Levillain, *La Neurasthénie, maladie de Beard*, in *Journal of Mental Science*, xxxvii (1891), pp. 587 – 8.

8 Savill, *Clinical Lectures on Neurasthenia*, pp. 27 – 30.

9 Victorian medical psychologists expended considerable energy trying to distinguish shattered nerves from other forms of neurosis, such as hysteria, hypochondria and melancholia, which shared the same, or similar, symptoms. Although those efforts filled columns of print, they were largely fruitless.

10 Roderick W. Home, 'Electricity and the Nervous Fluid', *Journal of the History of Biology*, iii (1970), 235 – 41, explains the development of the theory of a nervous fluid and discusses the alternative mechanical explanations — based on vibrations — espoused in the eighteenth century.

11 Roger Smith, 'The Background of Physiological Psychology in Natural Philosophy', *History of Science*, xi (1973), pp. 87 – 8.

12 In the late eighteenth century, James Gregory, a disciple of Cullen, had added 'nervous' as a fifth temperament to the other four — phlegmatic, sanguine, bilious, and melancholic — associated for centuries with the Galenic humours. Although the humoral theory of illness had long since retired from medical philosophy, Victorian and Edwardian doctors were sure that temperament played a major role in determining health.

13 In the first half of the ninetenth century, another physical explanation offered for many of the symptoms of nervous prostration, if not for the totality of the condition itself, was spinal irritation. See Francis Schiller, 'Spinal Irritation and Osteopathy', *Bulletin of the History of Medicine*, xlv (1971), 250 – 60.

14 R. A. J. Walling, ed., *The Diaries of John Bright* (London, 1930), pp. 204 – 5, 229; Keith Robbins, *John Bright* (London, 1979), pp. 120 – 2.

15 David Drummond, 'Neurasthenia: Its Nature and Treatment', *British Medical Journal* (1906, pt. 2), 13.

16 W. H. B. Stoddart, *Mind and Its Disorders* (London, 1908), pp. 366 – 7.

17 James Manby Gully, *The Water Cure in Chronic Disease* (London, 1846), pp. 274 – 9, 282 – 3.

18 Alfred T. Schofield, *Functional Nerve Diseases* (London, 1908), p. 60.

19 Michael J. Clark, 'The Rejection of Psychological Approaches to Mental Disorder in Late Nineteenth-Century British Psychiatry', in Andrew Scull, ed., *Madhouses, Mad-Doctors, and Madmen: The Social History of Psychiatry in the Victorian Era* (London and Philadelphia, 1981), p. 275.

20 Daniel Noble, *Elements of Psychological Medicine* (London, 1853), p. xii; Henry Holland, *Chapters on Mental Physiology* (2nd ed., rev., London, 1858), pp. 261 – 2).

21 Holland, *Chapters on Mental Physiology*, p. 303.

22 Drummond, 'Neurasthenia', p. 14.

23 Clark, 'Rejection of Psychological Approaches', pp. 292 – 3.

24 Henry Maudsley, *Body and Will, Being an Essay Concerning Will in its Metaphysical, Physiological and Pathological Aspects* (London, 1883), pp. 99 – 123; Th. Ribot 'Will, Disorders of', in Hack Tuke, ed., *A Dictionary of Psychological Medicine* (2 vols., London, 1892), ii. 1366.

25 James Crichton-Browne, *The Story of the Brain* (Edinburgh, 1924), pp. 1 – 10. Also see William F. Bynum, Jr., 'Rationales for Therapy in British Psychiatry, 1780 – 1835', in Scull, ed., *Madhouses,* pp. 51 – 2.

26 Drummond, 'Neurasthenia', p. 13.

27 This paragraph is much indebted to Clark, 'Rejection of Psychological Approaches', pp. 278 – 83, 288 – 92, 298 – 300.

28 See Lorraine J. Daston, 'British Responses to Psycho-Physiology, 1860 – 1900', *Isis,* lxix (1978), 192 – 208; and Janet Oppenheim, *The Other World: Spiritualism and Psychical Research in England, 1850 – 1914* (Cambridge and New York, 1985), pp. 236 – 49.

29 Bynum, 'Rationales for Therapy', pp. 38 – 40, discusses how British medical psychologists in the late eighteenth and early nineteenth centuries developed a physiological parallelism by which they could attribute mental disorders to diseases of the underlying (parallel, not intersecting) cerebral structure, thereby leaving the mind free from taint. This was important, since the immaterial mind was widely interpreted as synonymous with the immortal soul. Also see Andrew Scull, *Museums of Madness: The Social Organization of Insanity in Nineteenth-Century England* (New York, 1979), pp. 158 – 61.

30 Clark, 'Rejection of Psychological Approaches', p. 304 n.10.

31 Forbes Winslow, *On Obscure Diseases of the Brain, and Disorders of the Mind* (London, 1860), p. 335.

32 Bence Jones, *Faraday,* ii, 126; Arthur Christopher Benson, *Thy Rod and Thy Staff* (London, 1912), p. 1.

33 T. S. Clouston, *The Hygiene of Mind* (London, 1906), p. 36; Ernest Jones, 'The Treatment of the Neuroses, including the Psychoneuroses', in William A. White and Smith Ely Jelliffe, eds., *The Modern Treatment of Nervous and Mental Diseases* (London, 1913), i. 331 – 2.

5

Anglo-Irish Literature, Gaelic Nationalism and Irish Politics in the 1890s

Roy F. Foster

Macaulay, in his *History of England*, postulated an appropriately mechanical 'explanation' for the scientific revolution of the late seventeenth century: 'The torrent which had been dammed up in one channel rushed violently into another. The revolutionary spirit, ceasing to operate in politics, began to exert itself with unprecedented vigour and hardihood in every department of physics.'[1] It is the sort of analysis whose ingenuousness raises an indulgent smile now. But an analogous process of reasoning has dominated commentaries on Ireland after the fall of Parnell. The torrent of 'politics' was seen suddenly to run into the channel of 'culture', in a curiously unquestioned way, creating a ferment which is automatically assumed to have been the necessary precondition of the 1916 Rising.

Thus Nicholas Mansergh sees post-1891 as

> a shift of interest from Westminster to Ireland, from the source of constitutional reform to the breeding-ground of rebellion . . . Encouraged in their romanticism by the poetry of Yeats and his circle, dreaming of the regeneration of Ireland with Douglas Hyde, the young men marked out as their goal, not the pedestrian Home Rule haven of the Nationalist party, but the independent Ireland of the Fenians.[2]

This led Mansergh on to a suggestive treatment of 'The Influence of the Romantic ideal in Irish politics', which fundamentally presented the contemporary argument of Yeats's friend John Eglinton. 'Yeats, and the literary movement in which he was a commanding figure, may be said to have conjured up the armed bands of 1916.'[3] F. S. L. Lyons endorsed this, though with characteristic (and increasing) caution,[4] and so did Conor

Cruise O'Brien, Richard Ellmann, and George Dangerfield.[5] The 1890s were presented as the seedbed of cultural revolution, absorbing energy that had somehow diverted itself from political to intellectual agitation, as with Macaulay's physicists. The question of what — or whose — energy was thus diverted tended to be left aside; so was the question of whether the energies that produced the cultural efflorescence of the 1890s would ever have found their way into political channels. The idea was too potent, and too inspirational, for questions as mundane as that.

This was largely because the thesis was so well expressed by the generation who lived through the upheavals of the early twentieth century. In fact, even as the 1890s drew to a close, in a celebrated lecture to the Gaelic League in September 1899 Father Peter Yorke of San Francisco denounced the passing decade. It had been a time of disastrous apathy, a 'lull' in politics while the Gaelic League alone kept the faith. In relating his lecture directly to the progress of proselytising on behalf of the Irish language, and mounting an onslaught on supposed organs of Anglicisation, he advanced the idea that anything productive in Irish life since Parnell's fall had been cultural.

Yorke would not have looked to the revolution in local government of 1898, nor to the mass movement of land agitation which was at that very time galvanizing the west. Nor, as an extremely bigoted Irish-American, would he have been an admirer of the already celebrated W. B. Yeats. But in fact Yeats was already outlining a similar analysis in public letters at this time, and later (in 1924) gave classic form to the Yorke thesis during a lecture delivered to the Royal Academy of Sweden:

> The modern literature of Ireland, and indeed all that stir of thought which prepared for the Anglo-Irish War, began when Parnell fell from power in 1891. A disillusioned and embittered Ireland turned from parliamentary politics; an event was conceived; and the race began, as I think, to be troubled by that event's long gestation.[6]

The 'event' mentioned was, of course, the 1916 Rising. Thus, just like the luckless Chief Secretary Augustine Birrell, Yeats saw the Rising as inevitably looming up from the debris of post-Parnellite politics, and inevitably brought about by the cultural events which started twenty-five years before.

Birrell, whose political career was destroyed by 1916, had his reasons for laying this emphasis. But it is essentially a very Whiggish version of history, telescoping a quarter-century and viewing it retrospectively through the prism of 1916. Whig history might be forgiven in a Liberal *littérateur*; it is less expected from that firm irrationalist and devotee of catastrophe theory, W. B. Yeats. And the analysis must provoke some questions.

What happened, first, to Irish politics after 1891? The supposed 'lull' in politics should not be taken as read. An assumption that literary activity took over politics leaves out not only the Irish Parliamentary Party (both wings), which continued to hegemonize the world of Irish politics, but also the agrarian mobilizing of the United Irish League, which towards the end of the 1890s set the terms for a major political initiative. Both the IPP and the UIL had little to do with literature, but they were no less politically energetic and productive for that. 'Productivity' need not necessarily take in the second Home Rule bill of 1893, which showed Gladstone sustaining a classic fudge by stating that he was 'requesting full equality' for Ireland and in the same breath accurately defining the bill as 'a wide extension of the privileges of local self-government'.[7] But real local government reform five years later was another matter; as, indeed, was the record of reforming Unionism in the 1890s. Recent work has emphasized this, not so much as an effort to kill Home Rule by kindness, but as a series of measures contingent upon immediate political pressures, which sometimes led their devisers further than expected.[8] Local government in 1898, for instance, was a vital step in entrenching nationalist influence on county councils; and the extension of land purchase provided similarly concrete gains, as — potentially — did the plethora of schemes for agrarian investment and experimentation.

All this provided a solid sub-stratum for nationalist advance. The ideas and atmosphere of the 1890s are well profiled in the pages of the *New Ireland Review*, an important forum, which first printed D. P. Moran's celebrated onslaught on 'shoneenism' and cultural Anglicisation, later published as *The Philosophy of Irish Ireland*. There too can be found regular bilingual pieces by Douglas Hyde on the religious poetry of Connacht, or more unequivocal pieces dealing with 'The race type in Celtic literature'.[9] Hungary also occurs early on, as a model for Irish aspirations.[10] But the periodical is equally notable for articles with titles like 'Where does Ireland stand?' which analyse current politics in the tones of hard-headed constitutionalism, and advocate tactical alliances with the Conservatives; and for floating influential ideas on land tenure, the forestry question, the work of the Recess Committee, the Financial Relations issue, and the perennial education question.[11] Mixed in with all this are pieces eulogising any radical separatists just so long as they are dead. The whole thing is an odd compound of Gaelicism and constitutional reformism, linked by unstinting criticism of Britain if not of the British connection.

This brings us rather nearer to the ethos of the Irish Parliamentary Party, a curious blend of Trollopian fixers, political journalists, respectable ex-Fenians and closet imperialists. They excelled in the politics of sleight of hand, and rested on the powerful local machinery inherited from the 1880s. Their backing from the Catholic clergy dated from the same era, ever since Parnell's concordat over education in 1885. The Catholic ethos also influenced them in their critical stance regarding welfarist fads.

93

Despite the split over Parnell, the party retained vitality; despite the lack of detailed sources (and of a proper biography of John Redmond), they should not be consigned to the dust-heap of history before their time. And several of them were conscious of the need for a high political profile, especially given the revived land agitation in the west.[12]

For the land question had not been taken out of Irish politics after Gladstone's 1881 Land Act, or even the 1886 Plan of Campaign. And the late 1890s sees the last stage of the uncompleted land war, beginning with the concerted agitation mounted by western farmers against the large-scale stock-grazing interests. This mobilised political energy in the shape of the United Irish League, which spread at such a rate, and posed such a political threat, that by 1900 it provided the means of reunifying the Irish Parliamentary Party (which then subsumed it). It is a movement curiously written out of Irish history, despite a number of important theses. (The same is true of its successor, the All-for-Ireland League.)[13] This was partly because it failed (the UIL, starting out as a movement against the graziers, ended by co-opting them into the leadership of the movement), and partly because later developments in Irish history followed a different tack. Vampirized by the IPP, it dropped from sight; though its leaders had a firmer idea than Redmond and Dillon about the possibilities of land purchase, and the unsatisfied interests it represented would crop up again in the war of independence, greatly alarming the conservative leaders of the Irish revolution.

What should be emphasized is the power of what began as (so to speak) a grass-roots movement against graziers in the west, but spread across the country, claiming 33,000 members by 1899 and mustering 60,000 to 80,000 by 1900.[14] The politics of boycott and trade war had taken over in certain areas: there was a National Directory, with offices in Dublin; a newspaper, the *Irish People*, started in September 1899, calling for a public movement 'wide enough to give free play to every school of honest Nationalist conviction from the believer in a Gladstonian parliament to the believer in an Irish Republic'. It mobilized anti-Parnellites and Parnellites alike; it entered urban politics, to considerable effect; it fought the new local elections with conspicuous success (more success, in fact, than it showed in altering traditional rural power-structures).[15] The issue was politically galvanic: all the more so as the UIL agitators were preaching Home Rule as part of their message. If the IPP had not taken steps to subsume it, the UIL might very well have subsumed them. And even after the reunion in 1900, and the ostensible defusing of the land issue by Wyndham's Land Purchase Act of 1903, a core of radicalism remained, articulated by the volatile William O'Brien.

For those involved in cultural revivalism, all this was irrelevant. Yeats gives the accepted, withering view of the politicians from the Land War era on:

And so was founded an agitation where some men pretended to national passion for the land's sake; some men to agrarian passion for the nation's sake; some men to both for their own advancement . . . they had grown up amid make-believe, and now because their practical grievance was too near settlement to blind and to excite, their make-believe was visible to all . . .[16]

Faced with the necessary venality of contemporary politics, both Yeatsian and Fenian iconography preferred the image of the dead Parnell as an icy, aristocratic Anglophobe. Thus Yeats, again:

I had seen Ireland in my own time turn from the bragging rhetoric and gregarious humour of O'Connell's generation and school, and offer herself to the solitary and proud Parnell as to her anti-self, buskin followed hard on sock, and I had begun to hope, or to half-hope, that we might be the first in Europe to seek unity as deliberately as it had been sought by theologian, poet, sculptor, architect, from the eleventh to the thirteenth century.[17]

A more visceral tone enters his memory of Sir Charles Gavan Duffy, Young Irelander turned imperial constitutionalist:

One imagined his youth in some little gaunt Irish town, where no building or custom is revered for its antiquity; and there speaking a language where no word, even in solitude, is ever spoken slowly and carefully, because of emotional implication; and of his manhood of practical politics, of the dirty piece of orange-peel in the corner of the stairs as one climbs up to some newspaper office; of public meetings where it would be treacherous amid so much geniality to speak or even to think of anything that might cause a moment's misunderstanding in one's own party. No argument of mine was intelligible to him . . .[18]

Elsewhere, too, he appears to indict the parliamentary politicians more on the grounds of excessive clubbability than anything else. It is probably relevant to remember Yeats's own social insecurity and marginalization at this stage of his life; and, for all his contempt of the bourgeois, his mentors in nationalism — John O'Leary and Standish O'Grady — were anything but radical, despite Yeats's claims to the contrary.

Parnell's image, even a decade after his death, was more important than his record. It is characteristic that R. M. Henry, writing *The Evolution of Sinn Fein* from first-hand knowledge in 1920, presents Parnell as the usual 'strong, romantic and mysterious personality', who held the future of Irish politics in his hand. This is contrasted with 'the story of small intrigue, base personalities, divided counsels and despairing expedients' after his death, presided over by the flunkey Redmond. However, Henry adds, à propos Redmond's call for Home Rule within the Empire: 'It is true that Parnell would have obtained little more than this, if he had lived; but he would have obtained it in a different way, and would have accepted the concession with a gesture of independence.'[19] In other words, the difference was simply one of rhetoric and style. Yeats himself unguardedly implied as much elsewhere, admitting that in the 1890s few wanted separation from England, and that he himself viewed the actuality with some misgivings.[20] Talking about it, in the right tone, was apparently something else.

In the light of this, Redmond's strategy of accepting what reforming unionism had to offer does not appear quite so pusillanimous. Land tenure reform, the Congested Districts Board, a Department of Agriculture, the achievement of Sir Horace Plunkett's influential Recess Committee (which lay behind this step), and revolutionised local government were decent payments on account — not to mention the Childers Financial Relations committee reassessing Ireland's dues to imperial revenue, in which Redmond had been extremely influential. In retrospect, this may look like settling for half a loaf; contemporarily, it had a different resonance. Unduly optimistic though he was, Horace Plunkett had some reason for remarking that 'the decade of dissension which followed the fall of Parnell will, perhaps, some day be recognised as a most fruitful epoch in modern Ireland's history'.[21]

From certain points of view, then, by the time Redmond succeeded to the leadership of a united party in 1900 constitutional politics could be seen to be working. Conventional rhetoric might not have allowed the case to be stated. But, as has been well remarked of an earlier period, 'popular Irish nationalism was a matter of the self-assertiveness of the Catholic community and of a search for material benefits rather than a question of yearning for constitutional reforms'.[22] And much of the rhetorical criticism even at the time came, not from the cultural nationalists (who held themselves above the detail of material benefits) but from Young Turks within the constitutional movement like the Young Ireland branch of the UIL. Vacuum theories notwithstanding, politics went on happening.

By 1907, Redmond was even receiving letters from the veteran Fenian Patrick Ford, couched in glowing terms:

> You are of course aware that the bitterest enemies of the Irish cause are those of our own household. They iterate and reiterate that Ireland will never get Home Rule except by fighting for it. These men can take care to make no allusion to the victories won by the Irish Parliamentary Party.[23]

Such indulgence is surprising, coming from someone always suspicious even of Parnell's nationalist probity, who had only supported the UIL in the hopes that they would 'invite the constabulary to shoot the people down in an eviction campaign inaugurated for the purpose'.[24] Perhaps equally significant, for the present purposes, is the fact that when Standish O'Grady wrote excitedly in 1897 of 'a new Irish movement which has risen with the suddenness and power of a tidal wave', letting loose 'forces whose play no man can predict', he did not mean the Gaelic League; he was referring to the Financial Relations Committee and the co-operative constitutional agitation that lay behind it.[25] The cultural movement of these years only replaces 'politics' when viewed strictly in retrospect.

II

When considering to whom cultural revivalism appealed, and how it related to political agitation, it is interesting to revert to the archetypal organ of Gaelic revivalism in a Catholic, Irish-speaking sense: *The Celt*, a weekly periodical of 1857 – 8 edited by a committee of the Celtic Union. It produced the usual exhortation to the youth of the country to read up on dead heroes, and the usual vague calls to action ('not only, in our judgement, does the history of this country remain to be written — it requires to be acted'). But it also invariably looked back rather than forward; and, despite coinciding with the founding of Fenianism, it emphasized that the evils caused by the British connection 'may be remedied in a manner within what is called the constitution, and not outside the law'.[26] It even threw up, in July 1858, a leader under the title 'Home Rule', emphasizing Australian and Canadian parallels and adding 'we do not view this question at all as a physical force question . . . we look for Ireland's rights by moral and constitutional means and will dream of and listen to none other, until these have failed. And if properly used, they cannot fail, and must win.' All this, twelve years before the foundation of Butt's Home Government Association, went with calls to revive the language as 'a vehicle for national thought', and fulminations against degrading English influence. 'To be Anglicised is to lose our national and characteristic identity, to merge everything Irish and Celtic in, not a British union, but a British supremacy.' The point here is that a violent predisposition against 'Anglicisation' was not incompatible with a realistic commitment to constitutional reform. And similarly, the amateur poets and antiquarians who shortly began recycling the most bloodthirsty pieces of ancient mythology in order to draw apparent parallels for contemporary separatist heroics do not themselves appear to have adhered to anything like revolutionary beliefs: a mild collection of vegetarians, theosophists, India Office civil servants, and so on, whose glorification of fighting was literary trope rather than political exhortation to anything more radical than Home Rule.[27]

Similarly, in the 1890s Gaelic zealotry happened, and mattered, at a different level from that of politics; nor were the cultural ideologues those who would ever have taken part in politics under the previous dispensation, as the Yeats thesis seems to imply. The Gaelic Revival is, reasonably enough, approached through key texts like Douglas Hyde's 'The Necessity for De-Anglicising Ireland', a presidential address delivered to the

97

National Literary Society on 25 November 1892 and subsequently published. It is too often forgotten, though, that Hyde's lecture began by presenting de-Anglicisation as a strategy that should appeal to Unionists as much as to Nationalists, while emphasizing — rather innocently — Anglophobia as the motive power of a movement that still need not be separatist.

> It is the curious certainty that come what may Irishmen will continue to resist English rule, even though it should be for their good, which prevents many of our nation from becoming Unionists upon the spot. It is a fact, and we must face it as a fact, that although they adopt English habits and copy England in every way, the great bulk of Irishmen and Irishwomen over the whole world are known to be filled with a dull, ever-abiding animosity against her, and — right or wrong — to grieve when she prospers, and joy when she is hurt. Such movements as Young Irelanders, Fenianism, Land Leaguism, and Parliamentary obstruction seem always to gain their sympathy and support. It is just because there appears no earthly chance of their becoming good members of the Empire that I urge that they should not remain in the anomalous position they are in, but since they absolutely refuse to become the one thing, that they become the other; cultivate what they have rejected, and build up an Irish nation on Irish lines.[28]

In the end, however, Hyde presents the priority of poetry over politics, and casts his argument entirely in a Home Ruler context. 'We can, however, insist, and we *shall* insist, if Home Rule be carried, that the Irish language, which so many foreign scholars of the first calibre find so worthy of study, shall be placed on a par with — or even above — Greek, Latin and modern languages in all examinations held under the Irish government.'

That was to be the real revolution (and that is what worried the English-speaking Yeats).[29] Like all Gaelicists, Hyde was anti-O'Connell because of his Anglophone policy; but that was one of his few political stances. Costume and place-names remained his chief preoccupations, outside his own beautiful translations. Nor was he alone; Eoin MacNeill, for one, thought the early Gaelic League exhibited a strong streak of cautious Home Rulerism.[30]

What then of the strong subseqent tradition of Fenianism within the League: and the traditional identification of John O'Leary, veteran Fenian leader, as *cicerone* to the Yeats generation in cultural and separatist politics alike? It should be remembered that by now O'Leary was seen by his IRB colleagues as (according to police reports) a 'fossil',[31] or 'an old crank full of whine and honesty'. He had become the classic armchair Fenian, incensed by the revival of land agitation which decimated his rentier income, and endlessly writing the history of the movement for publication in the *Weekly Independent*. (When Yeats reviewed it as a book, it was a severe blow to their intimate association.) Fenianism overlapped with cultural associations; four out of the original seven founders of the Gaelic Athletic Association were Fenians; the IRB organization was behind the famous guard of honour carrying draped hurley sticks after Parnell's coffin. But at the same time, by the early 1890s the number of members in good standing was falling.[32] Assistant police commissioner Mallon believed in October 1892 that there were only fifty active IRB men, and he could put his hand on every one of them; he may well have been right.

What, however, was an 'active' Fenian? The image of a pledge-bound, conspiratorial, Malatesta-influenced group, dedicated to revolutionary separatist action by means of violence, was technically true of the leadership cadres in Paris and America. But recent work has given us a picture of Fenianism in Ireland which was casual, public and recreational in a way that suggests the Oddfellows or the Foresters. In late nineteenth-century Ireland, the same large crowds reported at nationalist demonstrations apparently turned up cheerfully again for royal visits: the play was the thing. Fenianism was as much a verbal (and social) commitment as an ideological one.

If this was the case, it is easier to see how even Redmond could be fingered as a 'Fenian';[33] it could be as political a gesture as joining the Ancient Order of Hibernians. The word was being widely used to mean *any* kind of nationalist as early as the 1860s. To see it as the ideological counter-pole of the Irish Parliamentary Party is an over-simplification (even leaving aside the fact that the movement had itself splintered into the Invincibles, the Irish National Brotherhood and so on; the latter being joined by Yeats, who remained rather vague about their antecedents).

Fenianism had its own tradition of cultural nationalism from the late 1850s, when many Fenians were involved in the Society for Promotion and Cultivation of the Irish Language, dominated by A. M. Sullivan (who could not himself speak Irish, but was no less anti-English for that). The rhetoric of Fenian-influenced literary journals like the *Shan Van Vocht* tended to portray Home Rulers as cringing royalists; but rhetoric it was. And the great Anglophobic outburst of the 1798 centenary celebrations should be seen as therapeutic Anglophobia as much as an endorsement of separatism. Going back to the 1860s, strident Catholic nationalism had not meant the same thing as a commitment to republican values; Fenian cadres throughout the country had worked readily for Home Rule candidates in by-elections. Fenianism reflected the variousness and sophistication of Irish nationalism: 'the concept of a pure Fenianism incapable of compromise with a corrupt political world is largely an invention of the 1870s; it had as a corollary a cult of physical force and that alone, which for many was, unconsciously, a cult of inaction.'[34] More generally, it attracted the 'joiners' of Irish society at certain quite well-defined levels, many of whom joined other associations as well (Yeats had a Fenian acquaintance who was also a member of the Primrose League). To quote Dr. Comerford again, 'From the 1860s being a Fenian was a mode of life in Ireland in the same way as being anti-clerical or republican was in provincial France.'[35] One might

99

add that being a Parnellite after 1891 was to subscribe to a cult of safely romantic leader-worship which was rather analogous to Bonapartism.

This idea of Fenianism should be borne in mind when considering how far the cultural revivalists thought of themselves as 'Fenians'. When Eoin MacNeill's biographer finds it 'surprising' that the unpolitical and pacific Hyde used a Fenian analogy for the Gaelic League in its work of revivification, he misses the point: it was not as dangerous as it retrospectively sounded.[36] The Catholic identification of the League should be noted, which took over so quickly that by 1900 people like T. W. Rolleston were proposing a parallel Gaelic League for Protestants. In both the League and the Fenians, Anglophobia and confessionalism were provided for; but revolutionary separatism need not necessarily be inferred.

And though Hyde emphasized the non-sectarian and unpolitical nature of the League, he himself passionately declaimed against 'the creeping Saxon'; the message was quickly read in a climate where organizations like the Celtic Literary Society demanded that members be of Irish descent. But though Pearse would in 1913 claim the League as a nursery of practical revolution, it did not look like it in 1900.[37]

Another 'classic' example of Fenian infiltration is provided by Arthur Griffith, the influential Gaelicist ideologue who later founded Sinn Féin. His Fenian connection supposedly led to his becoming Chief Organizer of the INB. But this was part of an ideological 'package', not an all-consuming involvement. Griffith was pro-Boer, anti-British, the moving spirit behind the Transvaal Committee; the flavour of the organisations which he inspired is epitomised by Cumann na nGaedhal, an anti-English (but not a separatist) organization founded in 1900, which met in premises owned by the Celtic Literary Society. A hilarious police report on the first meeting profiles the committee: two habitual drunkards, two 'corporation scavengers', two schoolboys, and a car-driver who was also bandmaster of the Milltown Band. Yet one of their number produced a very impressive account of the meeting for newspaper publication, giving a long list of distinguished but imaginary attenders; if this stood alone as source-material, it would lead historians to much more portentous conclusions. (The police spy later watched impassively as the author, after a long evening's drinking, set off to deliver the article and 'spent a quarter of an hour trying to find the letter-box in the door of the publishing office of the *United Irishman*'.)[38]

According to police reports, the most active associations in Dublin in 1901 were the Celtic Literary Society, the Gaelic League and the Gaelic Athletic Association. The 1897 Centenary Committee had fizzled out, and embezzlement had put paid to the funds of the Wolfe Tone Memorial Bazaar. The tiny clubs of extremists were seen as negligible, and probably were. The whole scene is strongly reminiscent of the atmosphere delineated in James Joyce's *Dubliners*, rather than the ferment of cultural revivalism and revolutionary politics recalled in the disillusioned tranquillity of the Free State. It is worth remembering Joyce's vitriolic picture of the genteel Gaelic Revivalists in 'A Mother', and the appalled Ascendancy reactions of Synge, Yeats and Moore to the petit-bourgeois bigotries of Gaelic League society; Moore saw Hyde as having crossed over to become 'the archetype of the Catholic Protestant, cunning, subtle, cajoling, superficial and affable'.[39]

The relationship of any of these attitudes to practical planning towards revolutionary separatism is hard to assess. Clerical influence militated against it (as well as against romantic Parnellism: Eoin MacNeill, visiting the Aran islands to commune with the pure Gaelic spirit, found the islanders firmly anti-Parnellite on strict moral grounds). The ill-starred Sir Antony MacDonnell probably got it about right when he wrote in a memorandum: 'The information I receive . . . does not invest the Gaelic movement at all events with malign and disloyal objects, though the objects are certainly "national".'[40] Cultural nationalism was of course Anglophobic, as Yeats nostalgically remembered:

New from the influence, mainly the personal influence, of William Morris, I had dreamed of enlarging Irish hate, till we had come to hate with a passion of patriotism what Morris and Ruskin hated. Mitchel had already poured some of that hate drawn from Carlyle, who had it of an earlier and, as I think, cruder sort, into the blood of Ireland, and were we not a poorer nation with an ancient courage, unblackened fields and a barbarous gift of self-sacrifice?[41]

The de Valera vision of Ireland was also anticipated, defined against English materialism:

We Irish do not desire, like the English, to build up a nation where there shall be a very rich class, a very poor class . . . I think the best ideal for our people, an ideal very generally accepted among us, is that Ireland is going to become a country where, if there are a few rich, there shall be nobody very poor. Wherever men have tried to imagine a perfect life, they have imagined a place where men plow and sow and reap, not a place where there are great wheels turning and great chimneys vomiting smoke. Ireland will always be a place where men plow and sow and reap.[42]

Yeats, unlike many extreme nationalists, maintained a warm support for Horace Plunkett and the Irish Agricultural Organization Society, whose strategy was to make the Union work in economic terms. At the same time, he could declare (at the Pan-Celtic Congress in 1901) that the Gaelic movement 'would soon be shaking governments'. But this was like Hyde remarking that 'every speech we make throughout the country makes bullets to fire at the enemy'. Violent metaphors were employed without any necessary thought of revolution.

There is a strong case for saying that Yeats's approach to politics had become more serious, more realistic and more committed by the time he was writing his memoirs in the 1920s: whereas in youth, he remarked grandly, 'one can grow impassioned and fanatical about opinions which one has chosen as one might choose a side upon a football field'.[43] In the 1890s and 1900s he was demonstrably disingenuous about thorny issues like speaking Irish;[44] and even at his most committed there was always the congenital ambivalence of the Protestant bourgeois. For all his identification with the Gaelic ethos, a wistful hope remained for leadership from a regenerated landlord class. Thus writing to Katharine Tynan in 1895 from Sligo, about the fashion for things Celtic among the local gentry:

> These people are much better educated than our people, & have a better instinct for excellence. It is very curious how the dying out of party fealing [sic] has nationalized the more thoughtful Unionists. Parnellism has greatly help[ed] also, & the expectation of Balfour's threatened emmense [sic] local Government scheme. However, this is to[o] big a subject to get into at the end of my second sheet.

This is of a piece with his remarks to Alice Milligan the previous September: 'My experience of Ireland, during the last three years, has changed my views very greatly, & I now feel that the work of an Irish man of letters must be not so much to awaken or quicken or preserve the national idea among the mass of the people but to convert the educated classes to it on the one hand to the best of his ability; & on the other — & this is the most important — to fight for moderation, dignity & the rights of the intellect among his fellow nationalists.'[45]

Occultism predisposed him to expect a revolution, but that was something else. Stuart Merrill, talking to him a year later, recorded their conversation:

> Yeats, who has a very clear idea of social questions and who sees them from a lofty level, favours a union of superior forces for revolutionary action. He envisages revolution after an impending European war, like us all. He has even collected the prophecies of various countries on this subject, and all are agreed that the war will be unleashed in these next few years.[46]

Playing with prophecy and rejecting English materialism, however, did not lead to any very specific pronouncement on separation from Britain. Malcolm Brown noted some time ago what John Kelly's definitive edition of Yeats's letters has recently made very clear: that his references to Parnellite or nationalist politics in correspondence during the 1880s and early 1890s are extremely scarce and vague.[47]

Even his nationalist poetry for The Gael was expressed in conventionally backward-looking balladry about the Cromwellian period, rather reminiscent of Fanny Parnell:[48] far less bloodthirsty and more tentative than even the gentle Hyde. With all three, one senses the tensions and

102

overcompensations of cultural deracination, as much as a specifically political commitment.

Even before Parnell's death, Yeats had been prophesying 'an intellectual movement at the first lull of politics'; his desire to fulfil the prophecy encouraged him to define the post-1891 period as the expected lull, when 'Ireland was to be like soft wax for years to come'.[49] But it is not surprising that his efforts to mould the wax were brutally abused as fey and half-hearted posturing in the 1898–9 *New Ireland Review* articles by D. P. Moran, later published as *The Philosophy of Irish Ireland*.

Moran's brilliant and vitriolic journalism has been taken as the text for exclusivist Irish nationalism from that day to this; certainly, his hatred and contempt for Anglicisation and for Anglo-Ireland still burn off the page. But what comes across nearly as strongly, on a careful reading, is his ambivalence about separatism. There is an attractively robust line on the 'nonsense' of complaints about 'England stealing our woollen industries some hundreds of years ago', and he is very hard indeed on 'prating mock-rebels'.

> A great many people in Ireland, unfortunately, live from hand to mouth; most of them, apparently, think after that fashion also. They not only think in that unsatisfactory way, but they impose arbitrary limits on their thinking. There are certain things which the average Irish mind will never allow as debatable. The spirit of nationality is eternal — that is a fine-flowing Irish maxim. No-one ever thinks of asking himself — Is it? We nearly won in '98; we may win another time. Another undisputed view. No-one ever dares to ask himself — Can we?[50]

Moran remained realistic about the necessity for economic initiative rather than 'rebel clap-trap'. Economic opportunities and language revival were at least as important as Home Rule (though he also expressed a distaste for gombeen commercialism — 'the greasy draper rubs his hands and dilates on "the circulation of money"' — which curiously anticipates the Yeats of 'September 1913'). Irish nationality should recognise its limitations: 'We can never beat England, can't even remain long in a fight with her, on her own terms. All we can do, and it should be enough for us, is remain Irish in spite of her, and work out our own destiny in the very many fields in which we are free to do so.'[51] Even his famous and chilling dictum that 'the Gael must be the element that absorbs' is prefaced by a much less often quoted passage:

> No-one wants to fall out with Davis's comprehensive idea of the Irish people as a composite race drawn from various sources, and professing any creed they like, nor would an attempt to rake up racial prejudices be tolerated by anyone. We are proud of Grattan, Flood, Tone, Emmet and all the rest who dreamt and worked for an independent country, even though they had no conception of an Irish nation; but it is necessary that they should be put in their place, and that place is not on top as the only beacon lights to succeeding generations. The foundation of Ireland is the Gael, and the Gael must be the element that absorbs.[52]

103

Moran objects to 'racial hatred' of England as a bogus strategem: 'Privately, some of the hillside men will tell you that all the wild rebellion talk is nonsense, but that it is necessary to keep up the national spirit.' And a surprising degree of his contempt is reserved for, of all things, Fenianism. He draws a brilliant picture of the career of an Irish snob: in which his hero begins by joining the Fenians as a necessary but harmless involvement.

> He joined a revolutionary society, where they talked wisely of foreign complications and held a picturesque midnight drill occasionally. He tried to persuade himself as long as he could that a few of the members were not drunkards, and he exhausted his ingenuity in attempting to square his youthful idea of a revolutionary hero with the characters of several of his comrades. He held on to the society for a few years, but it did nothing. There was one informer; two suspected of informing; one who bolted with the funds; and the great body of members — mostly honest, enthusiastic youths like himself — were getting sick of all the boasting and lip-rebellion that went on. He dropped out of it after a while and attended to his business, but still held extreme opinions.[53]

Of course, he ends up 'fat and comfortable in a mansion in Rathmines, the butt of every young Nationalist politician who little suspects that, unless conditions alter, a similar ending awaits him should he prosper in life'.

What Moran is preaching, like Hyde, is language revival and a plague on politics. 'The fact of being a sound political nationalist of any stamp, from a constitutional Home Ruler to a fire-eating revolutionist, does not necessarily mean that one is Irish at all'; he is more scathing about separatism and revolutionary 'desperadoes' than anything else.[54]

III

In some ways this general picture holds good for the period after the 1890s. There is a case for saying that by 1900, when Moran's last article appeared, there was little ground for expecting political separatism to be practically encouraged by cultural revivalism; and, moreover, to see the Irish Parliamentary Party as morally bankrupted by a decade of sterile bickering is equally to miss the point. Looking briefly ahead, the Sinn Féin movement founded by Griffith seems similarly unimpressive if judged at this stage as an avatar of independence. It began by calling for a restoration of the 1782 Constitution, and how far it proceeded from this before its effective reconstruction during the First World War is a moot point. It tried to square circles from Parnellism to Fenianism, following the rhetorical tradition of Irish nationalism, and was always careful to emphasize that it would not reject Home Rule.[55] From 1910 to 1913 it had sunk to a low ebb, before its traumatic reformation by the Young Republicans and the Independent Labour Party of Ireland. Though allegedly permeated by the IRB, this

104

should be modified by a realization of what Fenianism actually meant, and by remembering that the historian of the IRB sees it as practically moribund in 1905, though it was entering upon its revitalisation. By about 1910, the name 'Sinn Féin' had come to stand for a combination of various policies rather than a 'movement'. (In this sense, the much-derided contemporary British view of 1916 as a 'Sinn Féin rebellion' may have something to be said for it after all.)

What flourished after the 1890s, as before, was Anglophobia and confessional identification, both well established for good historical reasons, and epitomised by Devlin's Ancient Order of Hibernians — one of the chief elements that dissipated O'Brienism, the All-for-Ireland League, and the initial impetus of the United Irish League. Looking ahead even as far as 1910, one should still be cautious about assuming that cultural revivalism had produced an implicit revolution in politics. Not many Dubliners were reading the new literature.[56] In some ways, their energies had flagged; even Pearse, virulent in 1899 about Yeats ('a mere English poet of the third or fourth rank') and the Irish Literary Theatre ('more dangerous, because less glaringly anti-national, than Trinity College'), was by 1905 praising Yeats's opinions on nationalism and literature and sending honeyed letters to Lady Gregory.[57]

It is possible that the real seeds of the separatist crisis were sown only in the Volunteer movements of 1913, with the formation of the UVF and the National Volunteers: a reaction sparked off by the Home Rule impasse. MacNeill's odd idea that Carson could march his Volunteers to Cork and receive a tumultuous welcome from their Nationalist counterparts in joint defiance of Britain may have marked a new level of self-delusion.[58] But the events of the next few years moved with bewildering speed; and Pearse's graveside speeches of 1913 to 1915 mattered more, in the end, than Yeats's *Cathleen Ni Houlihan*.

Moreover, the vital conditions of germination were provided by the First World War. The greatest military cataclysm of the modern era affected Ireland too, though in post-1921 historiography it was somehow hived off as an English involvement.[59] 1916 depended on the European war scenario. Reactions to the subsequent government repression, and the anti-conscription movement, may have mobilised more Irish people politically than the Gaelic League or the Irish Parliamentary Party or Sinn Féin or the IRB ever dreamt of. The support of the Catholic church was equally important: Anglophobia and confessionalism again.

Both these reactions seemed amply justified by British policies in Ireland over the next six years. Still, when it was all apparently over in 1922, a significant remark was made in the Free State Senate. Proposing the unlikely figure of Lord Glenavy as chairman of the assembly, John McLoughlin superbly quoted Léon Gambetta: 'I refuse to ask the date on which any man became a republican.'[60] Given the realities of Irish history over the previous thirty years, this was just as well.

In all this, the Yeatsian view of the 1890s as the stirring of the bones, and the race being troubled by the long gestation of the 1916 Rising, seems rather at odds. So does the idea that political energy was 'diverted' into culture. Yeats astutely saw the confusion at the time; in a public letter of December 1893 he attacked the 'stupefying' effect of oratory which led the Irish 'headlong into unreality'.[61] But this did not stop him from drawing out his own artful patterns. When Richard Ellmann was discussing Yeats with his shrewd widow, she pointed out to him that 'one quality of her husband never ceased to astonish her . . . This was his extraordinary sense of the way things would look to people later on.'[62] To which must be added his extraordinary ability to impose his view of how things *should* look to people later on. 'Man can embody truth but cannot know it.' In Yeats's terms, this gave the poet of revelations, the interpreter of unconscious manifestations, a dual identity as the ideal historian.[63] This is nearly as risky as making him an unacknowledged legislator. Perhaps our tendency to accept the poetic version of that quarter-century from 1891 to 1916 arises, not so much from ideological inflexibility, as from simple suggestibility: 'thinking from hand to mouth' again.

Notes

1 *History of England* (Albany ed., 1898), i, ch. 3, p. 425.

2 *The Irish Question* (3rd ed., London, 1975), pp. 243, 246.

3 John Eglinton, *Irish Literary Portraits* (London, 1935), p. 20.

4 See especially his *Culture and Anarchy in Ireland 1890 – 1939* (Oxford, 1979), pp. 51ff.

5 See especially O'Brien's brilliant and seminal 'Passion and cunning: an essay on the politics of W. B. Yeats' in A. N. Jeffares and K. G. W. Cross (eds.), *In Excited Reverie: a centenary tribute to William Butler Yeats 1865 – 1939* (London, 1965). 'In the nineties and in the early years of the new century ''the literary side of the movement'' was the only side that was moving and its leader was Yeats . . . the politician Yeats was about the poetry business, using for the ends of poetry the political energy diverted by the fall of Parnell' (p. 220). The same theme of diversion is to be found in Richard Ellmann, *Yeats: the man and the masks* (2nd ed., Oxford, 1979), p. 100: 'All the patriotism which Parnell's earlier successes had encouraged was now ready to be diverted elsewhere.' George Dangerfield also adopted it in *The Damnable Question: a study in Anglo-Irish relations* (London, 1977), though it is Standish O'Grady's *History of Ireland: Heroic Period* (1878) that Dangerfield places 'somewhere at the heart of the Easter Rising of 1916' (p. 30).

6 Reprinted in *Autobiographies* (London, 1955), p. 559.

7 *Hansard*, 4th ser., viii. 1250 – 51; 12 Feb. 1893.

8 See Andrew Gailey, 'Unionist rhetoric and Irish local government reform, 1895 – 9', *Irish Historical Studies*, xxiv no. 93 (1984), 52 – 68.

9 By James L. McLoughlin; see vol. 5 (1896), pp. 26 – 38, 81 – 94.

10 *Ibid.*, vi (Oct. 1896), 109 – 12.

11 See e.g. vol. v, May 1896, 129 – 41; Aug. 1896, 729 – 38.

12 Thus Alfred Webb to J. F. X. O'Brien in 1897: 'What is going on is *talk* about the past and in-activity regarding the present. We went to war for Home Rule and should continue that war each in our own way as best we may . . . We have the evicted with us and we are letting them starve . . . in fact Horse Racing, cycling and other amusements is what the country is most eager about at present.' In which he probably also included collecting faery lore, playing hurley, and reviving the Irish language. J. V. O'Brien, *William O'Brien and the Course of Irish Politics 1881 – 1918* (London, 1976), p. 10.

13 See Paul Bew, *Parnellites and Radical Agrarians in Ireland 1898 – 1910* (Oxford, forthcoming); Sally Warwick-Haller, 'William O'Brien and the Land War in Ireland 1877 – 1903' (Ph.D., University of Kent, 1980); Philip Bull, 'The reconstruction of the Irish parliamentary movement 1895 – 1903' (Ph.D., Cambridge, 1972). Also, for the All-for-Ireland League, Brendan Clifford, *Reprints from the Cork Free Press 1910 – 16: an account of Ireland's only democratic anti-partition movement* (Cork and Belfast, 1984).

14 J. V. O'Brien, *op. cit.*, p. 112.

15 See Michael D. Higgins and John P. Gibbons, 'Shopkeeper-graziers and land agitation in Ireland, 1895 – 1900' in P. J. Drudy (ed.), *Ireland: land, politics and people* (Cambridge, 1982), esp. pp. 100 – 101.

16 *Autobiographies*, pp. 358 – 59.

17 *Ibid.*, p. 195.

18 *Ibid.*, p. 225.

19 R. M. Henry, *The Evolution of Sinn Fein* (Dublin, n.d. but probably 1920), pp. 36 – 7.

20 See *Autobiographies*, pp. 361 – 2. 'I dreaded some wild Fenian movement, and with literature perhaps more in my mind than politics, dreamed of that unity of culture which might begin with some few men controlling some form of administration.'

21 *Ireland in the New Century* (1905 edition), p. 79. Plunkett, of course, had his reasons for taking this view, as he had to present agricultural and industrial co-operation as unpolitical and therefore unthreatening. Thus he saw the 1890s as repudiating political sterility: 'In practical England the Irish Question became the great political issue, while in sentimental Ireland there set in a reaction from politics and an inclination to be practical' (pp. 2 – 3).

22 R. V. Comerford, *The Fenians in Context* (Dublin, 1984), p. 194.

23 D. Gwynn, *The Life of John Redmond* (London, 1932), p. 152. It should be said that Redmond had to play the nationalist card in order to ensure such support: see Plunkett, *op. cit.*, pp. 310 – 11, for Redmond's public letter declaring that Home Rule had to come before the revival of industry and attacking Plunkett's book.

24 According to Michael Davitt; see J. V. O'Brien, *op. cit.*, p. 111.

25 *New Review*, Feb. 1897.

26 *The Celt*, 1 Aug. 1857, p. 5, and leader in *ibid.*, June 1858.

27 As with A. P. Graves, J. H. Cousins, William Larminie, Shane Leslie — and for that matter Standish O'Grady. A point missed by Martin Williams in his interesting 'Ancient mythology and revolutionary ideology in Ireland 1878 – 1916', *Historical Journal*, xxvi (1983), 307 – 28.

28 *The Revival of Irish Literature: addresses by Sir Charles Gavan Duffy, K.C.M.G., Dr George Sigerson, and Dr Douglas Hyde* (London, 1894), p. 120.

29 John Kelly and Eric Domville (eds.), *The Collected Letters of W. B. Yeats, volume I 1856 – 1895* (Oxford, 1986), p. 338: W. B. Yeats to the Editor of *United Ireland*, 17 December 1892.

30 See Michael Tierney, *Eoin MacNeill: Scholar and Man of Action, 1867 – 1945*, edited by F. X. Martin (Oxford, 1980), p. 19.

31 L. Ō Broin, *Revolutionary Underground: the story of the Irish Republican Brotherhood 1858 – 1924* (Dublin, 1976), p. 88.

32 *Ibid.*, p. 49.

33 *Ibid.*, p. 50.

34 Comerford, *op. cit.*, p. 204.

35 *Ibid.*, pp. 212 – 3.

36 Tierney, *op. cit.*, pp. 22 – 3.

37 The nature of Irish Anglophobia has rarely been examined systematically, much as the Catholic confessionalism of Irish nationalism has not often been analysed. Comerford puts it with characteristic forcefulness: 'The creators and custodians of mainstream Irish mythology have succeeded over a period of generations in blurring recognition of a salient fact about Irish nationalism, namely, that since the early nineteenth century at least it has been essentially an expression of the felt needs, social and psychological, of the Irish Catholic body, including their apparent need to challenge other Christians on the island in various ways' (*op. cit.*, p. 30). This is refreshing, but demands some examination of the extent to which this challenge was itself a historical response.

38 Ō Broin, *op. cit.*, p. 117.

39 George Moore, *Hail and Farewell* (1976 edition of the 1933 version, edited by Richard Cave, Gerrard's Cross), p. 587.

40 Ō Broin, *op. cit.*, p. 125.

41 *Essays and Introductions* (London, 1961), p. 248.

42 Speech in New York, 1903 – 4, quoted in E. Cullingford, *Yeats, Ireland and Fascism* (London, 1981), p. 25. Ironically, Parnell would not have agreed; his great ambition was to link the coalmines of Kilkenny with the iron-ore of Wicklow by means of railways, and create something like the 'Black Country' of Pennsylvania, which he greatly admired. See my *Charles Stewart Parnell: the man and his family* (Hassocks, 1976), p. 165.

43 *Autobiographies*, p. 233.

44 Referring to a play in Irish in *Samhain*, October 1901, he tempered his judgement: 'although I had not Irish enough to follow it when I saw it played . . .' Subsequently he passed judgement on Father Dineen's *Creideamh agus gorta* as 'the best Gaelic play after Dr Hyde's'. In a letter to the editor of *The Gael* of November 1899, he remarked how well he was getting on with learning Irish. But it seems to have remained at the level of intention.

45 Kelly, *op. cit.*, pp. 455 and 399.

46 Ellmann, *op. cit.*, p. 97.

47 Malcolm Brown, *The Politics of Irish Literature from Thomas Davis to W. B. Yeats* (London, 1972), pp. 374ff.

48 J. S. Kelly, 'Aesthete among the athletes: Yeats's contributions to *The Gael*' in *Yeats: an annual of critical and textual studies* ii (1984), 128 – 9.

49 *Autobiographies*, p. 120. He wrote at the time, in a letter of 27 January 1899 to the editor of the *Daily Chronicle*, that 'the lull in the political life of Ireland has been followed, among the few, by an intellectual excitement so remarkable that a learned German is writing a book about it; and among the many, by that strange sense of something going to happen which has always in all countries given the few their opportunity.' But the opportunity is an artistic one, and the whole letter is about art, not politics.

50 D. P. Moran, *The Philosophy of Irish Ireland* (Dublin, 1905), p. 11.

51 *Ibid.*, p. 48.

52 *Ibid.*, p. 36.

53 *Ibid.*, p. 57.

54 Cf., ironically, Synge's nationalism as interpreted by Stephen McKenna. 'I judged Synge intensely, though not practically, national. He couldn't endure the lies that gathered round all the political movement, flamed or rather turned a filthy yellow with rage over them, gently hated Miss Gonne for those she launched or tolerated, loathed the Gaelic League for ever on the score of one pamphlet in which someone, speaking really a half truth, had urged the youth of Ireland to learn modern Irish because it would give them access to the grand old saga literature: I have never forgotten the bale in his eyes when he read this and told me "That's a bloody lie: long after they know modern Irish, which they'll never know, they'll still be miles and years from any power over the saga."' E. R. Dodds (ed.), *Journals and Letters of Stephen McKenna* (London, 1936), p. 39.

55 See R. M. Henry, *op. cit.*, p. 86.

56 See Declan Kiberd, 'The perils of nostalgia: a critique of the Revival' in P. Connolly (ed.), *Literature and the Changing Ireland: Irish literary studies 9* (Gerrard's Cross, 1982), pp. 3 – 4.

57 'I have been trying in *An Claideamh Soluis* to promote a closer comradeship between the Gaelic League and the Irish National Theatre and Anglo-Irish writers generally. After all we are all allies.' S. Ō Buachalla, *The Letters of P. H. Pearse* (Gerrard's Cross, 1980), p. 94. For the earlier references, see his letter to the editor of *An Claideamh Soluis*, 13 May 1889, *ibid.*, pp. 8 – 9.

58 Oddly, this vision would have been shared by Parnell, according to his widow. See interview in *Daily Express*, 18 May 1914: she told a reporter that 'Sir Edward Carson's little army would have appealed greatly to him — only he would have tipped the Ulster rebellion into the Home Rule cauldron and directed the resulting explosion at England.'

59 Cf. R. M. Henry, writing before hindsight in 1920. 'The months before the European War broke out saw Nationalist Ireland practically unanimous in its support of the Home Rule legislation of the Liberal Government, ready to be reckoned as a part of the British Empire, prepared to acknowledge the supremacy of the Imperial Parliament, content with an Irish parliament charged only with the control of a number of matters of domestic concern' (*op. cit.*, p. 279).

60 Seanad Eireann debates, i, 8–20 (12 Dec. 1922); quoted in M. O'Callaghan, 'Language, nationality and cultural identity in the Irish Free State 1922–27: the *Irish Statesman* and the *Catholic Bulletin* reappraised', *Irish Historical Studies* xxiv (1984), p. 231.

61 Letter to the editor of *United Ireland*, 30 Dec. 1893; Kelly, *op. cit.*, p. 372.

62 1978 preface to 2nd ed. of *Yeats: the man and the masks* (Oxford, 1979).

63 A point well made in Malcolm Brown, *op. cit.*, p. 362.

6

Lord Northcliffe Befriends the Wright Brothers: A Chapter in Aviation History

Alfred Gollin

The achievement of the Wright brothers was so stupendous that we tend, at times, to forget its significance. Their invention of the airplane changed the nature of human life. Nevertheless, controversy has always been associated with their names. Some of those who have written about the Wrights have praised them as few figures in history have been praised; but others have condemned them in the harshest terms.

A contemporary who observed one of their early flights compared the brothers to Columbus and another who saw them flying at Kitty Hawk in May 1908 wrote: 'Here on this lonely beach was being formed the greatest act of the ages . . .'[1] A recent writer declared of their creation of the airplane that it was 'the most remarkable achievement in the history of invention';[2] and when the Acting director of the National Air and Space Museum, in Washington, D. C., wrote a Foreword to a book commemorating the seventy-fifth anniversary of their first flight, he asked: 'What can we say here? . . . How, on this anniversary of flight, can we add to the general perception of the grandeur and brilliance of the Wrights' insight? . . . Obviously we cannot. We can only restate . . . the story that we know so well . . . By their triumph they changed . . . our world and us . . . and for all time.'[3]

Negative critics have been equally forceful in the expression of their views of the Wright brothers. Although the Wrights impressed many people with their genius, bravery, quiet charm, and modesty, others developed a curious and remarkable antipathy to them, or to their memory. Some of their French contemporaries, for example, were envious of their achievements and all that chauvinism which characterised

111

the Third French Republic found a place in French comments about Wilbur and Orville Wright. These Frenchmen, for a period of several years, would not believe that the Wrights had flown successfully and referred to them regularly as 'bluffers'. The great British aviation historian, C. H. Gibbs-Smith, has written of an 'anti-Wright faction' with its 'chauvinistic bias' and 'emotional antipathy to the Wrights themselves . . .'[4] One of these French pioneers, Gabriel Voisin, refused to admit the validity of the Wright achievement as late as 1961 when he wrote in his autobiography: 'America, with unbelievable insolence, claims to have been the birthplace of aviation. It is inconceivable that France should bow before so naive a claim. Aviation was born in France, and not one of our . . . pioneers of the air, borrowed anything at all from the men of Dayton.'[5]

The hostility the Wrights aroused was more complex even than this negative attitude of the Frenchmen. Some historians praised Wilbur and denigrated the quality of Orville's work while others expressed admiration for Orville but made the most serious charges against the name and memory of Wilbur Wright. For example, in 1974, a distinguished British authority, Percy B. Walker, wrote an authorised history of the Royal Air-craft Establishment at Farnborough. The book was a tremendous and powerful contribution to British aviation history. It dealt with the Wright brothers in very considerable detail because 'for some years' the Wrights 'dominated' British thinking about aviation.[6] However, in his treatment of Wilbur Wright the author denounced him regularly, and in the most disagreeable terms. According to Walker, Wilbur Wright, in his dealings with the British Government, was 'slippery';[7] his attitude assumed 'paranoic proportions';[8] his correspondence revealed 'indications of incipient paranoia';[9] and he showed also 'the most distressing symptom of neurotic imbalance'.[10] This author's analysis of the character of Orville Wright was much kinder. Of him Walker wrote: 'Orville shows none of the peculiar psychological traits of his elder brother. He is seen as one of the most level-headed of men . . .'[11] In the very next year after Walker's history appeared, an American, John Evangelist Walsh, published a brilliant and fascinating book about the Wrights entitled *One Day at Kitty Hawk*. The themes and arguments of this work were quite opposed to many of the conclusions set out in Percy Walker's book. According to Walsh it should be obvious that Wilbur Wright was the radiant genius who was responsible for the invention of the airplane, and that Orville contributed very little to the grand achievement of the brothers. Walsh wrote with respect to the publication of their papers, a two-volume work entitled *The Papers of Wilbur and Orville Wright*, that: 'While the editor of the volumes in his commentary continued to bracket Wilbur and Orville as equals, it was, or should have been, fairly clear that the older brother had been, at the very least, the controlling intelligence and had exercised

112

absolute dominance over all the work . . .'[12] Walsh also argued that Orville selfishly and deliberately sought to enhance the quality of his own contribution to the invention of the airplane while denigrating that of his brother Wilbur, who died prematurely in 1912, and was therefore no longer able to defend the record of his own accomplishments.[13]

One contemporary who came to know the Wrights well, and to respect them, was Lord Northcliffe, the great British newspaper-owner. He reached the zenith of his power at exactly the time the Wright brothers began to attract worldwide attention. Northcliffe, throughout his life, was always interested in new technical and scientific inventions. He was particularly and especially fascinated by developments in the field of early aeronautics because he grasped, before most of his contemporaries, the significance for England of successful mechanical flight. He realised that Britain's insularity, her defence for ages and generations past, would disappear as soon as men could fly through the air. As early as 1906, Lord Northcliffe was proclaiming in his newspapers that the time was not far off when air power would become more important for Britain's defences than sea power.[14]

As a journalist, Northcliffe kept a careful watch on the activities of all the early aviation pioneers, including the Wright brothers. He eventually became personally involved in their affairs when they tried to sell their invention to the British Government, in 1907. A few years earlier, in 1905, when the Wrights first decided to sell their airplane to the British War Office and to the United States War Department, they fixed upon a curious and peculiar stipulation in order to protect themselves from unscrupulous competitors and from the power of Governments. They decided they would not show their machines to anyone until the prospective purchaser had signed a contract with them. As they put it: 'By the terms of the contract not one cent need be paid out by the government until after the machine has fulfilled certain stipulated requirements in a trial trip in the presence of the government's representatives.'[15]

The Wrights fixed upon this 'contingency contract' idea because they were afraid of two developments. Firstly, if someone was allowed to see their airplane before a contract were signed, he might be able to divine some of their secrets. Secondly, they feared their own or another Government might simply appropriate their invention without rewarding them for it in any way. As Orville Wright once wrote: 'Our course . . . has been based upon an impression that governments often appropriate inventions useful in warfare, and tell the inventor to prosecute a claim under law . . .'[16]

This insistence upon secrecy resulted in a series of classic charges against the Wright brothers which must now be dispelled. Percy Walker called their 'contingency' idea a 'rigmarole' and claimed that Wilbur, in adducing it, was 'shifting his ground, and in a rather slippery way'.[17]

113

Another British aviation authority, Oliver Stewart, made an even more grotesque charge in this connection. He wrote of the Wright attitude in 1905: 'To the doubter this attempt to sell something without allowing the buyer to see it in action suggests that the Wrights could not at that time make a powered flight . . .'[18]

These comments were ridiculous since they neglected contemporary evidence of the most significant kind. The Wrights, after their return from Kitty Hawk in December 1903, had made plenty of powered flights in a field known as Huffman Prairie, near their home in Dayton, Ohio. These experiments of 1904 and 1905 at the Huffman Prairie were carried out so that they could improve the primitive machine they had flown at Kitty Hawk and, after much labour and practice, they were entirely successful in this object. In June 1906, the British Military Attaché in Washington, Lieutenant-Colonel Count Gleichen, was ordered by the War Office to communicate with the Wright brothers in order to try to ascertain exactly what they had accomplished. Accordingly, Gleichen went to interview the Wrights in Dayton. Although they would not permit him to see their airplane, he was tremendously impressed by them and by accounts of their powered flights which had been witnessed by plenty of people who lived in the vicinity. Indeed, Gleichen was so excited by what he learned in the course of his visit that, in addition to reporting back to the War Office, he also wrote a detailed letter about the Wrights to Sir Mortimer Durand, the British Ambassador in Washington. Count Gleichen, a cool, aloof, experienced and professional military observer wrote to the Ambassador on 17 August 1906. His letter is an important document in the early history of aviation since, among its other accomplishments, it makes nonsense of the charges levelled against the Wrights by Percy Walker and Oliver Stewart. Gleichen wrote:[19]

In order to elucidate certain points connected with some previous correspondence between the War Office and Messrs. Wright Brothers of Dayton, Ohio, about their flying machine, I stopped on the 8th instant at Dayton . . . and had a couple of hours' most interesting conversation with the brothers . . .

The brothers Wright are two young men of about 30, intelligent looking, not 'cranks', apparently honest . . . and with little or none of the usual braggadocio of the Yankee inventor. Strange to say, they are modest in demeanour, and even shy.

They have been at work for 10 years now on flying-machines, and consider that it is only during the last 2 or 3 months that they have finally succeeded. During the first 4 years they invented and perfected their 'glider', and took out several patents over this . . . The experience . . . which they gained over this was invaluable, and they took to inventing a 'power-flyer', i.e. a flying-machine driven by an engine . . .

This aeroplane can go up to 40 miles an hour, even against a head-wind. It appears that the stronger the headwind the better it goes. Downwind it can go at a rate of 40 miles an hour + the velocity of the wind. These figures seem almost incredible: but I subsequently interviewed two independent witnesses, a banker and a chemist, who assured me that the machine went 'like a train' and turned very handily . . .

They have taken out no patent for their flyer, for, in the first place the Government would be entitled to use their patent and in the second, everybody would be entitled to read its terms and descriptions . . .

To turn to the military aspect: they expect the flyer to be used chiefly for scouting. It can fly at any height, would not be visible till fairly close, on account of its thin wooden framework and white wings (canvas), and could fly at such a rate that it would be practically invulnerable . . . Messrs. Wright . . . assured me that after a few trials it came as natural and easy as riding a bicycle!

As above remarked, they have not flown since last autumn; they are now employed in perfecting their motors and constructing others and different parts of the aeroplanes, so as to have a supply handy when the demand comes . . .

Despite Colonel Gleichen's keen interest and advocacy, the British War Office, for its own reasons, decided not to purchase the Wright airplane in 1906. Later on in the year, therefore, the Wrights began to negotiate with Charles R. Flint, a wealthy New York banker and promoter. Flint's company dealt extensively in the sale of armaments to foreign governments in every part of the world. Eventually, it was arranged that Flint's firm would act as the Wrights' business representatives, on a commission basis, in all countries except the United States. Charles Flint, who was known as 'the father of trusts' because of his many and lucrative business activities, was naturally anxious to check up on the veracity and reliability of the Wrights, at the very start of his dealings with them. In order to find out if he could trust the brothers he wrote to Octave Chanute, at that time the most respected and famous aeronautical authority in the whole world. Chanute's reply is a further refutation of the charges levelled against the Wrights by such writers as Walker and Stewart. He clearly told Flint of the Wrights:[20]

I may say . . . that I have followed their work since 1900, have seen all their machines and witnessed a short flight of one quarter mile in 1904 with their power machine. The long flights of 1905 I did not see, being then in the East, but had abundant information of their length (about 24 miles) from eye witnesses in Dayton.

From somewhat intimate acquaintance I can say that in addition to their great mechanical abilities, I have ever found the Wright brothers trustworthy. They tell the exact truth and are conscientious, so that I credit fully any statement which they make.

As soon as the deal worked out between Flint and the Wrights was completed, Flint and his assistants at once alerted their colleagues and associates in various foreign countries. In Britain, Flint selected Lady Jane Taylor, a highly placed aristocrat and the widow of a distinguished General, as his agent. Early in 1907, he urged her to approach R. B. Haldane, the Secretary of State for War, and Lord Tweedmouth, the First Lord of the Admiralty, in order to offer to sell the Wright invention to them. When these officials refused to act upon her suggestions, Lady Jane Taylor turned to Lord Northcliffe, well known in Britain as the nation's foremost aviation enthusiast, and begged him, in the national interest, to press the Ministers to comply with her requests.[21]

For some unknown reason, the official British history, Sir Walter Raleigh's *The War in the Air*, neglected to make any prominent mention of these negotiations of 1907. Instead, Raleigh wrote of the Wrights: 'The American Government would not touch their invention. When it was thrice offered to the British Government, betweeen the years 1906 and 1908, it was thrice refused, twice by the War Office and once by the Admiralty.' [22] This lapse formed the basis for one of Percy Walker's severest charges against the Wrights. In his history, Walker pointed out that when the British authorities refused to purchase their airplane in 1906 the Wrights '. . . did not, in fact, approach the British War Office again until nearly two years later — in April 1908 . . . the universality of unsuccessful negotiation does bear out the belief that subconsciously the Wright brothers did not want to sell their aeroplane; and especially does this appear to have been so in the course of the negotiations with Britain.' [23] Far more accurate was the comment of Charles R. Flint. He wrote of the 1907 negotiations in his *Memoirs*: 'The Wrights . . . without any reservations whatsoever gave England the opportunity to be the first to establish a navy of the air.' [24]

Charles R. Flint was concerned with making money. Indeed, Wilbur Wright once called Flint and one of his colleagues mere 'hustlers'. [25] Flint and his employees and associates were hard-headed business men, experienced in selling inventions to all kinds of purchasers. They were not men prepared to pander to the self-esteem of the Wright brothers for no purpose nor would they involve themselves with an airplane that was incapable of a powered flight, as Oliver Stewart suggests in his book. [26] In fact, in 1907 they did not believe the Wrights were too secretive or that they were mentally unbalanced or that they really did not want to sell their airplane. On the contrary, they entirely agreed with the prudence, caution, and business acumen of the Wright brothers; in effect, they disagreed with historical critics like Percy Walker, Oliver Stewart and others who, over the years, have condemned the Wrights for their 'excessive secrecy'. In the course of the 1907 negotiations, Flint, Lord Northcliffe, and the British War Office authorities all urged the Wrights to allow them the opportunity to see the Wright airplane in flight, before any contract was signed. The brothers refused to comply with these requests; and the firm of Flint & Co., with years of experience in such transactions, upheld them in this decision. On 14 February 1907, Flint himself wrote to the Wrights: 'I see there is a strong desire on the part of parties to get information regarding your machine and as it is not fully covered by patents and you expect to deal to a considerable extent with Governments, I see the soundness of your policy of withholding information . . .' [27] Later, when the British War Office wanted Colonel J. E. Capper, one of their aviation experts, to witness a flight before they would sign a contract, Flint's associate wrote to the Wrights: [28]

It seemed to us that we were justified in interpreting the suggestion of Capper witnessing a flight before a contract as a 'Walk into my parlor said the spider to the fly' proposition and we therefore cabled immediately that we were not able to show to Capper as he is a competitor . . .

If you think . . . that it is desirable that we should cable that we are willing to have Capper present in the event that the contract precedes the flight, we will do so, but we think our advices to that effect by letter are sufficient. From what we have written they should certainly appreciate that we are willing that all or any experts they desire should be present provided the contract precedes the flight. . . .

Lord Northcliffe, owing to his great interest in aviation, was intrigued by these developments of 1907 but he was also annoyed by the obstinacy and recalcitrance shown by the Wright brothers. In exasperation he told Lady Jane Taylor of them: 'They are always going to do, and do nothing that can be seen or appreciated . . . they are never ready to talk business . . .'[29] Lady Jane Taylor, however, like so many others of her class, was not easily thwarted when she sought the gratification of her wishes or desires. She arranged to see Northcliffe again, in May 1907, and she then reported to Flint: 'Lord Northcliffe . . . now requires a full statement of the proposals of the Wrights, which you will have to send in type, signed by them, stating what they can do, will do, where they will do it, and what remuneration they demand and in what form . . . This letter shall be given to Lord Northcliffe, who says that he will then present it to Mr. Haldane, and that Mr. Haldane's answer shall be the final answer.'[30] No such letter of the kind Lord Northcliffe required was sent to him in 1907 and his scepticism about the Wrights' achievements continued to dominate his attitude towards them.

This situation was changed with dramatic suddenness on 8 August 1908. On that day Wilbur Wright flew in public for the first time at the small race-course of Hunaudières, near Le Mans, in France. His aerial performance there thrilled, shocked, and startled the entire civilised world. He stunned all those who saw him by the quality and calibre of his flying. Wilbur's mastery of manoeuvre had not even been dreamt of by his French rivals who, until that moment, had been considered the most advanced fliers in the world. Men realised, for the first time, that the air had been truly conquered at last. No one was more alive to these developments than Lord Northcliffe. *The Times*, which he owned, declared of Wilbur that he 'had just won for his brother and himself the title of the real creator of aeroplanes . . .'[31] His *Daily Mail* remarked: 'The scoffer and the sceptic are confounded. Mr. Wilbur Wright last evening made the most marvellous aeroplane flight ever witnessed on this side of the Atlantic . . . A bird could not have shown a more complete mastery of flight.'[32] His *Daily Mirror* referred to 'the most wonderful flying-machine that has ever been made . . . No such perfect control over a flying-machine has ever been shown as that exercised by Mr. Wilbur Wright . . . In the words of a spectator . . .

117

other aeronauts are "babies by comparison; the American is their master" . . .'[33]

Lord Northcliffe appreciated the significance of Wilbur Wright's achievement in a way that many of his contemporaries did not. For example, Octave Chanute, the friend of the Wright brothers, a man who had devoted much of his life to the study of aeronautics, failed to understand the nature of their accomplishment. In January 1904, shortly after he learned of the initial triumph of the Wrights at Kitty Hawk, Chanute wrote to the famous British aviation pioneer, Francis Herbert Wenham, that: 'To you, who first called attention to the possibility of artificial flight, thirty eight years ago, I send the first correct account which has been published of the achievements of the Wright brothers. It is a beginning, and if no accident occurs it may lead to practical results; but the uses will be limited.'[34] Lord Northcliffe's attitude was completely different. Once he was convinced of the Wright brothers' abilities he saw to it that news of them and their invention appeared regularly in his newspapers, especially in the *Daily Mail*. In September 1908, the *Daily Mail* began to publish an entire series of articles entitled 'Man In The Air'. The series started by pointing out that the science of aviation was still in an experimental stage but that great progress in it had been made recently, and that the time had now come to survey 'the immense social changes' that were bound to follow as a result of the further development of the new technology. This *Daily Mail* series surveyed the nature of flying machines; it predicted the eventual appearance of a passenger-carrying 'aero-liner' of the future, an international organisation to control air traffic as it increased and significant developments in aerial commerce and sport.[35] By 5 October 1908, the *Daily Mail*, which had already offered a huge prize, the sum of £10,000, for a flight from London to Manchester, now announced the offer of yet another generous prize to the first person who flew across the English Channel in an airplane. In particular, the *Daily Mail* emphasised that the success of practical aviation would forever change the nature of the defences Britain required, in order to ensure her national safety; on 14 October, the paper announced that the British War Office was at last showing interest in the Wright invention.

Lord Northcliffe was convinced that the British future would be changed more significantly than that of any other country, as a result of the successful development of the airplane. In these circumstances, early in 1909, he decided to see for himself; he arranged to visit the Wright brothers at their new base of operations at Pau, in Southern France. In addition, he asked Arthur Balfour, the former Tory Prime Minister, to accompany him to Pau, as his guest. Balfour, who was always intrigued by the problems of national defence, eagerly accepted Northcliffe's invitation.[36] The *Daily Mail* made much of the Tory leader's visit to the Wright camp at Pau. On 19 February, the paper quoted the aloof aristocrat as follows: 'It is a wonderful sight . . . It is worth coming far to see. I wish I could be flying with him.' In the following month, King Edward VII adorned the scene at Pau. According to the *Daily Mail*, 'the King exclaimed in admiration as the flight proceeded'.[37] Northcliffe did far more than emphasize the mere novelty of flying. From the beginning of his visit to Pau, he became alarmed by the military potential of aircraft and also by the fact that the British authorities seemed to be neglecting a development that might, eventually, help to determine the very fate of the nation and empire. He agreed with Balfour that it was now their duty to press Haldane, at the War Office, to look into the matter of aircraft more carefully than he had done. Where Lady Jane Taylor's advocacy had failed entirely in 1907, Wilbur Wright's performances in the field now had their effect, in 1909. On 19 February, Northcliffe wrote to the Secretary of State for War: 'I notice that the Germans and French have both military representatives here watching the Wrights' machine, which Mr. Balfour came to see, and of which he will speak to you . . . it occurs to me that if it is worth the while of Germany and France to be on the spot, one of your young men might be down here . . .'[38]

In the *Daily Mail*, Northcliffe now launched a campaign to force the War Office to purchase a Wright plane. On 11 March, the first leading article in the paper reported that Wilbur Wright was planning a visit to London. The editorial continued: 'France and Germany require no visit to awaken them to the importance of this art. For ten years they have spared neither money nor effort to lay the foundation of aerial fleets. We have much leeway to make up . . .' Northcliffe, of course, called particular attention to the activity of the German authorities in these aerial spheres. On 7 April 1909, the paper printed an article from its Berlin Correspondent which described the developing German airship fleet: 'Germany is sparing no effort to keep the lead in the realm of aerial navigation. I am able to state that plans for the aerial fleet include the construction of enough vessels of the Zeppelin, Gross, or Parseval type to permit of the stationing of at least one in every fort of the country, including those on the land frontiers as well as on the coast . . .' Northcliffe, throughout his career, was always accused of promoting 'scares' of various kinds[39] in order to increase the circulation of his newspapers, despite the deplorable effects and consequences of these journalistic alarms and excursions. When he began to warn his countrymen about the danger that might come to them from the air the charge was made that he meant to exploit the situation, not from motives of vigilant patriotism, but only because he wanted to sell more newspapers. Lord Northcliffe, of course, would do all that he could to enhance his circulation figures but there can be no doubt that he was keenly and genuinely alert to the dangers and the significance of the arrival of the air age for his country. He must have been gratified to receive a letter of support for his new course, at this time, from Sidney Low, later Sir

Sidney, a former editor of the *St. James's Gazette*, and one of the most respected practitioners of the 'old journalism' in England. Low wrote to Northcliffe:[40]

> You have no doubt more papers than you or any man can reasonably want; but can you not add to them by giving us a first-rate aviation journal? I am not suggesting that I could help you in this, as I am not an expert; but I have been watching the subject for some years past . . . A journal of this kind would do much to assist England in gaining the position which she has so deplorably lost in connection with this momentous development . . .

Early in May 1909 the Wright brothers arrived in London, with their sister Katharine. They were at once hailed as heroes. At successive formal banquets they were presented with gold medals by the Aeronautical Society of Great Britain, and by the Aero Club. Their British contemporaries were delighted to acclaim Wilbur and Orville Wright for their great achievements; but they also looked upon the visit as an opportunity to be used to alert their Government to the requirements of the new aerial age. The technical publication *Flight* in welcoming the brothers to London pointed out that foreign countries had sought to develop air forces but that Britain had failed to do so. In its first article for 8 May 1909 which reported the Wrights' activities in Britain *Flight* also stated: 'Highly important and very practical results have been arrived at already by foreign countries, while the construction of aerial fleets has been in rapid progress abroad for some time, but with no appreciable response from this country.' When the Wrights paid a visit to R. B. Haldane at the War Office on 3 May, *Flight* came to the conclusion that 'It may be taken as assured that our Government will duly acquire Wright aeroplanes . . .'[41] Lord Northcliffe played a great part in urging the British authorities to purchase a Wright machine. The *Daily Mail* for 3 May announced in a bold headline that the Wrights, the 'Air-Kings', were in London at last. Northcliffe, who had become very friendly with Wilbur, Orville and Katharine during his French visit now placed his automobile at their disposal in London. He also invited them to stay with him and Lady Northcliffe at their great country home, Sutton Place, near Guildford in Surrey.[42]

Northcliffe, at the time of this visit to London, was particulary distressed by Haldane's failure to reveal any concern whatsoever about the Wright invention. The *Daily Mail* for 4 May 1909 predicted, in reporting the Wright interview at the War Office, that 'the Government intends at last to take a tangible interest in the Wright machine . . .' Although Northcliffe did not know it at the time, this was not the case. Earlier in the year the Committee of Imperial Defence had secretly undertaken a review of Britain's aerial arrangements and had adopted a policy for the future, with respect to them. The Committee decided in January 1909 that it would not recommend the purchase of a Wright airplane;[43] but it was eventually agreed that there should be established a board or panel of expert scientists to advise the Army and the Navy on aerial matters. In these circumstances Haldane had no technical reason for inviting the Wrights to see him at the War Office. He acquiesced in meeting them only out of courtesy and in order to mollify British public opinion which had been genuinely upset by the Government's failure to act decisively in the sphere of aeronautics. Although they had expected an entirely different result the Wright brothers now departed from Britain for the United States, laden with honours and distinctions, but without having secured an arrangement of any kind with the British Government for the sale of their machines or their technical knowledge. Northcliffe's campaign on their behalf had produced no positive result at the War Office, or anywhere else.

The Wrights returned home in triumph. In Europe, princes, kings, and statesmen had competed to do them honour. Now their own countrymen were determined to add their portion. In New York, the Aero Club of America awarded them gold medals and these were formally presented in June, by President Taft, in a ceremony at the White House. Later, in further ceremonies in Dayton the brothers were given medals voted by the Congress of the United States, by the state of Ohio, and by the city of Dayton itself. These developments marked a high point in the career of Wilbur and Orville Wright because, later in 1909, significant changes began to take place in their lives. By that time competitors started to produce airplanes that, in their construction, impinged upon the Wright brothers' patents. Glenn Curtiss and Louis Paulhan, the Frenchman, were early in this lucrative field but others followed in regular order until the Wrights were involved in a dozen different suits in the United States in addition to legal actions in various foreign countries. The most important of these was the case against the Herring-Curtiss Company and Glenn H. Curtiss. This suit was begun by the Wright brothers late in the year 1909 but it was carried on for a considerable period of time thereafter. The Wrights in offering such defiance to Curtiss sought to protect their pecuniary interest in aviation, but insofar as they were concerned much more was involved. They would permit no one to challenge the fact that they, and they alone, had been the first to invent a successful and practical flying machine. It has been well said of them in this connection: 'In determining the attitude of the Wrights, puritanical conscience, economic self-interest, and the desire for recognition as pioneer inventors played important roles. As the first men to solve the problem of flight with a heavier-than-air machine, they deeply resented the doubts, aspersions, and disputes to which their claims had been subjected. This made them the more eager to establish their claims juridically. Besides, they had a strong sense of duty to their invention, especially to its future scientific and utilitarian development . . . They were puritans, committed to making the right prevail. They were also better business men than they were willing to acknowledge.'[44]

Nevertheless, significant sections of American and foreign opinion now began to turn against the Wright brothers. They won their legal actions against Curtiss but they, and their company, were condemned as aspiring monopolists while Curtiss, for his part, eventually attracted a good deal of public sympathy.[45] This general attitude was well reflected in an older aviation story: 'The vigorous action of the Wright brothers in prosecuting their patent claims is easy to understand. The Wrights were not, as was once thought, fighting against Glenn Curtiss or any other individual. They were fighting against nothing less than the stream of science itself. Having created the successful airplane, it seemed a bitter thing to them that they could not indissolubly tie up its future with themselves. But . . . it is easier to see that a machine providing man with a great new means of communication was bound, by its own very grandeur, to escape the bonds set for it by any two men.'[46]

This alteration in the public attitude to the Wright brothers was also responsible, in part, for a bitter quarrel between them and their old friend Octave Chanute. The causes of this dispute had been rankling for a long time but they only became patent and obvious early in 1910.

Years before, in 1903, Chanute had visited Paris where, at that time, he lectured and also wrote on the development of aviation in the United States. During this stay in France, Chanute, an acknowledged expert and authority of world-wide pre-eminence, encouraged the idea that the Wright brothers had taken up the study of aviation at his suggestion; and he also permitted people in France to believe that the Wrights were his pupils. The brothers soon learned of these falsehoods from published accounts of Chanute's activities in France; and, naturally enough, they were very annoyed as a result.[47] As time passed, such is the nature of man, Chanute convinced himself that he had contributed substantially to the Wrights' success, and that they were lacking in gratitude, or even appreciation, for the help that had been afforded them. He once wrote to George Spratt, a former colleague, of the Wrights: 'I think myself that they have unduly ignored the assistance which has been rendered them by others, but that is natural in men who want to make a fortune . . .'[48]

By the end of 1909 a number of interviews with Chanute were published in the newspaper press. In these articles Chanute allowed himself to criticise that conduct of the Wright brothers, and he also questioned the originality of their invention. In January 1910, Wilbur Wright challenged the validity of Chanute's remarks in a long and very frank letter to him; and a most unpleasant correspondence between the two followed. On 29 January 1910, Wilbur wrote to Chanute: 'One of the . . . articles said that you had felt hurt because we had been silent regarding our indebtedness to you. I confess that I have found it most difficult to formulate a precise statement of what you contributed to our success.' When Chanute was invited to prepare such a statement he could make no reply but he admitted later that 'I have sometimes thought that you did not give me as much credit as I deserved.'[49] As a result of this quarrel, Chanute joined the Curtiss camp and by March 1910 he was actively helping Curtiss in his legal battle with the Wright brothers, publicly and also in private.[50]

In these unpleasant circumstances one contemporary of the Wright brothers stood fast in their defence. This was Lord Northcliffe, who followed the development of these events from his headquarters in London. Northcliffe had carefully taken the measure of the Wrights when he met them in France. As one of his colleagues once wrote of him: 'He reads character at a glance, with an insight that borders on the uncanny.'[51] His reading in this instance convinced him of the genius, decency, modesty, charm, intelligence and absolute honesty of the Wright brothers. Moreover, he had checked up on the validity of their various patents and had convinced himself of their soundness.[52] Often criticised as a man who exploited talented people and then dropped them when they had served his purpose,[53] Northcliffe, now on his own initiative, came to the support of the Wright brothers when they could benefit him in no way, and when they would appreciate aid and assistance from wherever they could obtain it. On 26 May 1910, he wrote to Katharine Wright from his office in *The Times*:[54]

> I have never made any statement other than that your brothers, the absolute inventors of all that is going on today in aviation, have, by their natural instinct of American gentle folk and by the lofty nature of great minds, stood aside while others have exploited the fruits of their genius. This attitude is very well understood in England, where, with many faults, we yet remain a simple people with considerable horror of self-advertisement.
>
> I have always two fears with regard to your brothers: firstly, that they will be robbed of the proper pecuniary reward of their many years of achievement under restraint; secondly, that dishonest men . . . so confuse the original issue that in the future there might be the same sort of doubt as exists today about the originator of the steam-boat (which, as you know, Fulton was by no means the first to invent), the electric telegraph, the photograph, and the bicycle. So far as England is concerned, I am resolved that that doubt shall never exist as to the aeroplane, and, on the occasion of the Manchester flight, I at once telegraphed to London from the Mediterranean, where I was, that in every reference to the flight credit to your brothers, as it was due, should be given in all my papers, editorially and in the reporting.
>
> . . . Peary spent twenty-seven of the best years of his life getting to the North Pole, and got there, as assuredly as your brothers were the first persons to leave the earth in a mechanically propelled plane and to invent the means of controlling that plane. I did not find many Americans who realized what your brothers had done. I must except Mr. & Mrs. Roosevelt . . .
>
> . . . This is a long letter, but it is a matter on which I feel very strongly.
>
> With our kind regards and respectful homage to you and your brothers.

In the years after 1910, Wilbur Wright took the lead in the various patent actions that plagued the life of the Wright brothers in this period.

In May 1912, however, Wilbur contracted typhoid fever and after an illness of a few weeks he died. The Wright family always believed he had exhausted himself in these legal battles and was therefore without the resources he needed to fight the disease successfully.[55]

After his death, the court actions continued, unabated, but there was a new development in 1914, one of the famous incidents of early aviation history. Glenn Curtiss believed he had at last discovered a way to set upon one side the prior claims of the Wright brothers. One of their early rivals was the famous professor Samuel Pierpont Langley, of the Smithsonian Institution. Langley, a most distinguished scientist, was an early believer in the possibility of mechanical flight. Despite his devoted efforts, however, and after a minor success or two, he was unable to produce a successful heavier-than-air flying machine. His last failure in these protracted attempts occurred in December 1903 shortly before the Wright triumph at Kitty Hawk. In 1914, Glenn Curtiss proposed that he should again test the Langley flying machine of 1903 in order to see if it was capable of flight. The authorities of the Smithsonian Institution who controlled Langley's 'aerodrome', as it was called, were loyal to their colleague's memory, and they agreed to this proposal. Furthermore, they appointed as their official observer Dr. A. F. Zahm, even though Zahm had acted as a technical expert witness for Curtiss in his recent lawsuits with the Wright company. The Langley machine of 1903 was taken to Curtiss's workshops at Hammondsport, New York, where certain changes in its construction were made; and it was then flown briefly over Lake Keuka, near Hammondsport, in May and June 1914. This 'Hammondsport hoax'[56] cast a pall over the achievements of the Wrights, and was most probably designed, in the first place, to buttress up Curtiss's weak and even desperate legal position. Katharine Wright was so upset by Curtiss's actions that she appealed to Lord Northcliffe for help:[57]

I am writing to ask if you have any objections to my using your letter to me, of 26th May 1910 . . . You doubtless know what a flurry was caused by the Curtiss attempt to fly the Curtiss-Zahm-Langley machine to prove that Langley was the real inventor of the flying machine.

Your letter to me contains such strong statements in regard to the invention of the aeroplane that I am sure it would have great weight with American editors of magazines[58] who have been fooled by a clever trick but who wish to be fair and just . . .

Orville refuses to pay any attention to this whole effort on the part of Curtiss, aided naturally by Langley's friends. He says the whole scheme must fall of its own weight and that he has seen too many of these efforts to prove some new 'real inventor of the aeroplane' to be very much excited over it. He thinks history will take care of things fairly. No one in the world knows better than you do the power of the daily and weekly press and all our papers and magazines have been full of these reports, vague but giving the impression that Curtiss is most eager and anxious to create. I do not think it safe to ignore it at all . . .

124

I am sorry to say that Orville is far from well. In fact, I am convinced that he will go like Wilbur unless we find some relief for him. That is why I am writing to you without consulting him. He would not wish me to trouble you. But I realise that you are, in this matter, the most powerful friend we have in the world and I have confidence that you and Lady Northcliffe will understand my great concern for the reputation of both of my brothers and for the health and life of the one who is still with us . . .

Northcliffe's reply to this appeal was clear and succinct:[59]

By all means use my letter . . .
Please give my warm regards to Orville and tell him it is his duty to see that he is not robbed of his fame by these rogues.

On 6 June 1916, Lord Northcliffe was given an opportunity to speak about the Wright brothers at a formal public meeting. His remarks on this occasion, before a most distinguished company of technical experts, could in no way benefit himself or any of his newspapers. Owing to the generous support he had given aviation over the years he was asked to second the vote of thanks to Griffith Brewer, a London patent attorney and a great friend of the Wright brothers, who had just delivered the Fourth Wilbur Wright Memorial Lecture at the Annual General Meeting of the prestigious Aeronautical Society of Great Britain. Northcliffe turned his remarks into a tribute to the Wrights that attracted the attention of contemporaries and merits our attention, even now. He said:[60]

. . . The fact remains . . . that after a hundred years of experiment with aeroplanes, these two brothers were the first people in the world who made a machine to fly, and flew it.
I make that remark emphatically, because there is one point to which Mr Griffith Brewer did not call attention, and that is the attempt that has been made to rob the Wright brothers of the credit of their invention . . . in the United States there have been long and persistent attempts to belittle the work of Wilbur and Orville Wright. I have closely read and followed the history of the hundred years of aeroplane experiments, and I am convinced that the credit of the first flying aeroplane is due to the Wright Brothers, and from the point of practical flying to nobody else. As an Englishman, I am in an independent position, and I know that these words of mine will go across the Atlantic, and I believe they will assist in stopping the spread of the insidious suggestion that the Wrights did not invent the aeroplane.

Notes

1 Amos I. Root watched Wilbur Wright fly in September 1904 and when he wrote an account of the incident he compared the Wrights to Columbus. Root's article is reproduced in Richard P. Hallion, ed., *The Wright Brothers, Heirs of Prometheus* (Washington, D.C., 1978), pp. 110 – 115. The witness at Kitty Hawk was Byron R. Newton, a correspondent of the New York *Herald*. His account appears in Mark Sullivan, *Our Times*, vol. II, *America Finding Herself* (New York, 1935), pp. 607ff.

2 John Evangelist Walsh, *One Day at Kitty Hawk* (New York, 1975), p. 9.

3 Melvin B. Zisfein, 'Foreword' in Richard P. Hallion, *Wright Brothers*, p. ix.

4 Charles Harvard Gibbs-Smith, *The Rebirth of European Aviation, 1902 – 1908* (London; 1974), p. 6.

5 Gabriel Voisin, *Men, Women and 10,000 Kites* (London, 1963), p. 160. The original French edition of this work under the title *Mes dix mille cerfs volants* was published in Paris in 1961.

6 Percy B. Walker, *Early Aviation at Farnborough*, vol. II (London, 1974), p. xvi.

7 *Ibid.*, p. 39.

8 *Ibid.*, p. xv.

9 *Ibid.*, p. 62.

10 *Ibid.*, p. 63.

11 *Ibid.*, p. xvi.

12 Walsh, *One Day*, p. 7.

13 *Ibid.*, pp. 6 – 7, 252 – 3, and *passim*.

14 See the *Daily Mail*, 15 November 1906. As early as that month Northcliffe was planning to launch a campaign to 'make the nation aeroplane-minded.' See Graham Wallas, *Flying Witness* (London, 1958), p. 44.

15 For their point see Walker, *Early Aviation*, ii, p. 38.

16 See Marvin McFarland, ed., *The Papers of Wilbur and Orville Wright* (New York, 1953), vol. II, p. 826. See also the strong support for this attitude of the Wrights in J. H. Parkin, *Bell and Baldwin* (Toronto, 1964), where it is stated at p. 170 that 'The Wrights . . . operated in secrecy, in the understandable belief that . . . in dealing with government secrets were more valuable than patents.' Even their enemy Gabriel Voisin agreed with this attitude of the Wrights. See Voisin, *Men, Women*, p. 214.

17 Walker, *Early Aviation*, ii, p. 39.

18 Oliver Stewart, *Aviation: The Creative Ideas* (New York, 1966), p. 25.

19 P.R.O., W.O. 32/8595. Gleichen, Lieutenant-Colonel, Military Attaché, to His Excellency Sir Mortimer Durand, His Britannic Majesty's Ambassador, Washington, August 17th 1906, and marked 'Very Confidential'. Although Walker, *op. cit.*, vol. II, p. 60 mentions Colonel Gleichen's letter to Sir M. Durant and quotes a bit of it, he neglects most of the significant details contained in it. See also in this connection Alfred Gollin, *No Longer An Island, Britain and the Wright Brothers, 1902 – 1909* (London, 1984), pp. 174ff., hereafter cited as *No Longer An Island*.

20 Octave Chanute Papers (Library of Congress) O. Chanute to Flint, 26 December 1906. See also Gollin, *No Longer An Island*, p. 200.

21 For an account of these developments see Alfred Gollin, 'The Mystery of Lord Haldane and Early British Military Aviation' in *Albion*, xi. pp.46ff

22 Sir Walter Raleigh, *The War in the Air* (Oxford, 1922) vol. I, pp. 70–71.

23 Walker, *Early Aviation*, ii, pp. 62–63.

24 Charles R. Flint, *Memories of an Active Life* (New York, 1923), p. 246.

25 See Fred C. Kelly, ed., *Miracle at Kitty Hawk* (New York, 1951), p. 223.

26 See Stewart, *Aviation*, p. 25.

27 Wright Brothers Papers (Library of Congress) Charles R. Flint to Messrs. Wright Brothers, 14 February 1907.

28 Wright Brothers Papers (Library of Congress) Flint & Co., to Messrs. Wright Brothers, 19 April 1907. In his comment about Colonel Capper, Flint was entirely correct. Capper was trying desperately to build a British Army airplane in this period, in direct competition with the Wrights. For these points see also *No Longer An Island*, p. 240.

29 Wright Brothers Papers (Library of Congress) Lady Jane Taylor to Flint, 17 April 1907, Copy.

30 Wright Brothers Papers (Library of Congress) Lady Jane Taylor to Flint, 13 May 1907, Copy; and *No Longer An Island*, p. 238.

31 *The Times*, 10 August 1908.

32 The *Daily Mail*, 10 August 1908.

33 *Daily Mirror*, 13 August 1908.

34 Octave Chanute Papers (Library of Congress) O. Chanute to Mr. Wenham, 9 January 1904. See also Gollin, *No Longer An Island*, p. 34.

35 For the 'Man In The Air' series see the *Daily Mail*, 28 September 1908; 29 September 1908; 30 September 1908; and 1 October 1908.

36 B.M.Add.MSS. (Northcliffe Papers) Arthur James Balfour to Northcliffe, 7 January 1909; and 6 February 1909.

37 *Daily Mail*, 18 March 1909.

38 B.M.Add.MSS. (Northcliffe Papers) Northcliffe to Haldane, 19 February 1909. Northcliffe's letter identified the military representatives for Haldane as 'Capt. Girardville & Capt. Hildebrandt'. Captain Paul-Nicolas Luca-Girardville was a pupil of Wilbur Wright's who was trained to fly by him at Pau. Captain Alfred Hildebrandt of the German Army visited the United States in 1907 in order to check up on the Wrights' accomplishments. In 1909 he flew with Orville Wright in Berlin. See also Gollin, *No Longer An Island*, p. 442.

39 For a recent example of this kind of criticism see Zara S. Steiner, *Britain and the Origins of the First World War* (New York, 1977), pp. 168ff.

40 B.M.Add.MSS. (Northcliffe Papers) Sidney Low to Northcliffe, 7 April 1909. Lord Northcliffe, as might be expected, understood the political power of his various journals. He once wrote to T. Gibson Bowles, the M.P., that: 'After all, if a newspaper that goes every day into one household in every six in this country cannot move the people, nothing can.' See B.M.Add.MSS. (Northcliffe Papers) Northcliffe to T. Gibson Bowles, 14 December 1911. See also *No Longer An Island*, p. 445.

41 *Flight*, 8 May 1909, p. 257.

42 For the incident of Northcliffe's motor car see B.M.Add.MSS. (Northcliffe Papers) Harold Perrin to Northcliffe, 12 May 1909. Perrin, Secretary of the Aero Club, thanked Northcliffe for loaning his car to the Wrights. For his invitation to the Wrights to stay at his home see B.M.Add.MSS. (Northcliffe Papers) Katharine Wright to Northcliffe, 28 March 1909.

43 See P.R.O. Cab.2/2. 'Committee of Imperial Defence. Minutes of 101st Meeting, February 25, 1909.' Marked 'Secret'.

44 For these comments see the excellent work Lloyd Morris and Kendall Smith, *Ceiling Unlimited* (New York, 1953), pp. 111–112.

45 The names of stockholders in the Wright Company, incorporated in 1909, included, in addition to the Wrights, those of August Belmont, the international banker; and Cornelius Vanderbilt, Morton F. Plant, and Howard Gould, all railroad magnates. Many Americans concluded the Wright brothers had sold out to the monopolists. For a full account of this attitude see *ibid.*, pp. 113ff. where it is stated (p. 115) 'In the popular view the Wrights had sold out to Wall Street.'

46 F. Alexander Magoun and Eric Hodgins, *A History of Aircraft* (New York, 1931), p. 338.

47 See the excellent analysis of Chanute's false claims in Charles Harvard Gibbs-Smith, *Rebirth*, pp. 23ff., 57ff., and 71ff. Chanute did not confine his boasting about the Wrights to his visit in France. He also went to England during this European tour and clearly told the English lady balloonist, Gertrude Bacon, that the Wrights flew in a glider of his design. In her diary for 1903, Gertrude Bacon wrote that Chanute told her 'of a gliding machine of his own design, on which two young men were even then accomplishing most successful flights . . . He said they were brothers of the names of Orville and Wilbur Wright.' See Gertrude Bacon, *Memories of Land and Sky* (London, 1928), p. 129. Of course the Wright glider was the design of their own genius and not Chanute's.

48 Octave Chanute Papers (Library of Congress) O. Chanute to George Spratt, 12 April 1909.

49 For these painful exchanges between the two old friends see Marvin McFarland, ed., *Wright Papers*, pp. 979ff.

50 See Octave Chanute Papers (Library of Congress) Chanute to Curtiss, 19 March 1910. With his great knowledge of aviation history Chanute was sending Curtiss information about old patents that he might exploit in his defence. He also complained about the Wrights to a former assistant, C. H. Lamson. See Octave Chanute Papers (Library of Congress) Chanute to Lamson, 25 March 1910.

51 Hamilton Fyfe, *Northcliffe, An Intimate Biography* (London, 1930), pp. 74 – 5. Northcliffe recognised one fault in the attitude of the Wrights. They believed that their machine was 'the last as well as the first word in flying.' Northcliffe realised progress beyond the Wright achievement was certain to come. For these points see *ibid.*, pp. 146 – 7.

52 Northcliffe was in communication with Hart O. Berg, the Wrights' business representative in Europe. He wrote to Northcliffe about the Wright patents. See. B.M.Add.MSS. (Northcliffe Papers) Hart O. Berg to Northcliffe, 26 April 1909, who wrote: 'I feel perfectly convinced that the Wright patents are beyond attack. Our patent lawyer in Paris has made a most exhaustive search and his conclusion is as I state above.'

53 See Tom Clarke, *My Northcliffe Diary* (London, 1931), p. 26.

54 B.M.Add.MSS. (Northcliffe Papers) Northcliffe to Miss K. Wright, 27 May 1910.

55 See the emphasis on this point in the authorised biography, Fred. C. Kelly, *The Wright Brothers* (London, 1944), p. 227.

56 For details of these developments see Marvin McFarland, ed., *Wright Papers*, pp. 1087 – 8, and *f.n.* 10; and Kelly, *Wright Brothers*, pp. 248ff.

57 B.M.Add.MSS. (Northcliffe Papers) Katharine Wright to Northcliffe, 21 July 1914.

58 For Northcliffe's powerful position in the minds of American editors and journalists see Reginald Pound and Geoffrey Harmsworth, *Northcliffe* (London, 1959) p. 268.

59 B.M.Add.MSS. (Northcliffe Papers) Northcliffe to Katharine Wright, 25 August 1914.

60 Northcliffe's speech was published in *The Aeronautical Journal*, *xx* (1916). 81 – 82. Griffith Brewer responded to the efforts made to rob the Wrights of the credit of their invention. A few years later he travelled to the United States and carefully investigated the details of the 'Hammondsport hoax', perpetrated by Curtiss. On 20 October 1921 he lectured to the Royal Aeronautical Society on this subject. His lecture, together with counter-comments by Glenn Curtiss, Dr. Zahm, and others is printed in *ibid.*, *xxv* (1921).24.

7

'Nature's Pruning Hook': War, Race and Evolution, 1914-18

Nancy Leys Stepan

Historians of science generally recognize that most scientists of the late Victorian and Edwardian period took for granted the validity of 'biosocial' argument — the validity, that is, of applying biology to society and thus making 'nature' the touchstone of social understanding and policy.

How that 'nature' was defined, however, and what kinds of social ideas and policies could be derived from it, are still matters of considerable debate. After Hofstadter published his *Social Darwinism and American Thought* in 1944, historians tended to assume that the 'nature' that pre-occupied scientists in the late nineteenth century was Darwinian in character, and that the social ideas that flowed from Darwinism were conservative and emphasized individual struggle. The phrase called up the image of human society gripped by conflict, with the inference that Darwinists welcome such struggle as the price of progress.

In recent years, historians have revised this view very considerably. First, Darwinism has been shown to have been associated with no single political message; at some time or another, Darwin's name was appropriated by conservatives, liberals, socialists, anarchists and communists, because Darwinism seemed to provide sanction for their social views. Many Darwinians of different political persuasions also refused to associate evolution with naked struggle. Darwin himself had said he used the expression 'struggle for existence' in a large metaphorical sense, and there was much in his own writings to suggest that cooperation and mutual dependency were as much part of evolution as struggle. The analogy between a cooperative nature and cooperative society was frequently drawn by Darwinians. The label 'reform Darwinists' has even been introduced,

129

to distinguish them from the 'social Darwinists' who emphasized struggle.[1]

Even the Darwinian basis of social Darwinism has been called into question. Many scientists, in Britain and on the continent, sought alternative explanations of social evolution, based on quite different models of biology than Darwin's. Inasmuch as neo-Lamarckism remained a common feature of biosocial thought well into the twentieth century, for example, many biological and social scientists stressed the importance of purposeful and teleological change in nature and society, rather than straightforward struggle and selection.[2] Whether the labels 'social Lamarckism' or even 'reform Lamarckism' should be introduced into historical analysis bears thinking about.

Enough has been said to suggest that Hofstadter's original definition of social Darwinism has been shown to be inadequate for capturing the complexity of the unions that could occur between biological and social thought in the late nineteenth and early twentieth centuries. In fact, the whole matter of biosocial analysis, particularly in the first decades of the twentieth century, needs to be explored in much greater depth than it has, both in relation to the changing fortunes of biology, and to political culture. Did one style of biosocial analysis dominate in a particular period, and if so why? When did old-style social Darwinism, in Hofstadter's sense, disappear from science and social thought?

It is these latter questions that this essay addresses. In the new studies that have appeared on social Darwinism, the relation between political experience itself and the claims of social Darwinism as a style of biosocial analysis is often given little attention. In this regard, World War I, as a truly overwhelming political experience, would seem to be particularly appropriate for the study of the history of social Darwinism. Oddly enough, however, the Great War has usually been given only passing or cursory attention as a theme; in British studies, in fact, the year 1914 is very often taken as a useful termination point for the analysis. It is the argument of this paper that World War I was in fact a key factor in defining the meaning of social Darwinism and establishing the legitimacy and illegitimacy of different kinds of biosocial analysis.

That the war of 1914–18 would have provoked biosocial debate was virtually inevitable. As the psychologist Havelock Ellis said, 'The Great War of to-day has rendered acute the question of the place of warfare in Nature, and the effect on the human race.'[3] This was because the war brought to the fore the problem of human conflict on a scale unprecedented in the modern era. Moreover, it was the first large-scale war to involve the British since Darwinism had been absorbed into national consciousness and become the common vocabulary of social and scientific discourse. Since the Darwinian model of evolution was based on struggle, the war of 1914–18 inevitably provoked the question: Was what people were witnessing in Europe Darwinian evolution in all its harshness and savagery? Was it a 'struggle for survival' driven by natural means? Would a victory for the British signal the 'survival of the fittest'? Or did the shock and uncertainty of the war help break the analogy between war in nature and war in society — and thus the power of old-style social Darwinism?

The large number of books written by scientists on the subject of science and war suggests the immediacy of the war's impact. These books included Benjamin Kidd's *The Science of Power*, which Kidd had completed on the eve of the war and then had felt compelled to rewrite in order to take into account the conflict; Whetham's *The War and the Nation*; P. Chalmers Mitchell's *Evolution and the War*, and Ellis's own *Essays in Wartime*, to name only a few of the more biologically oriented ones. The question is, how far did war figure in these works? Was war in society taken to be analogous to evolution in action, thus confirming social Darwinistic expectations? Or did the war lead to a rejection of such analogies? What significance, if any, did the Great War really have for biosocial debate?

These questions are answered in part by a study of the life and work of the anthropologist, anatomist and pioneer human paleontologist, Sir Arthur Keith (1866 – 1955). Keith merits examination for several reasons. First, he was one of the more intellectually flamboyant social Darwinists of the pre- and post-war periods. Second, though his life and work have been largely neglected by historians of science, he played a prominent if controversial role in British science in a formative phase of human paleontology and anthropology. And third, Keith is interesting because it can be shown that the Great War of 1914 – 18, as a political phenomenon, played a decisive part in the development of his ideas. It was responsible for turning Keith the Darwinist into a particular kind of social Darwinist intent on applying Darwinian ideas about struggle to not only the war, but to all manifestations of racial and national hostility in the modern world. Keith argued that the intense nationalism demonstrated by the European powers was a reflection of an instinct deeply embedded in human nature whose function was to bring about evolution and progress via racial and national struggle. Weeding out war and nationalism, Keith maintained, would emasculate mankind, 'bringing it the kind of peace which is to be found in a cabbage-patch'.[4]

How typical was Keith's reaction to the war? To answer this question I examine some scientists with whom Keith ostensibly had much in common and who are indeed usually classified as social Darwinists par excellence. These were the eugenists, Darwinists who argued that evolution by natural selection provided a sound foundation for a social programme of 'better breeding'. Analysis shows that the war was equally important to them as to Keith, but that its effects were in the opposite direction. When it became time for the eugenists to assess the relation of human warfare to Darwinism they discovered that the real war being fought in the mud in France had little to do with either evolution or progress. Few were prepared to see any biological good in the war, or justify it in Darwin's name. If anything, the war crystallized the limitations of the older tradition of analogical Darwinism represented by Keith.

This paper, therefore, explores the ways in which the actual experience of human warfare in 1914 – 18 was a defining experience for science as it was for so many other aspects of British culture, and assesses the way war can help clarify that important and elusive subject, social Darwinism.

1 The Making of a Darwinist

Sir Arthur Keith provides an appropriate entry-point into the history of Darwinism and social Darwinism in the first three decades of the twentieth century on several grounds. He was a leading interpreter of human evolution, taking part in all the most interesting debates of the period, such as those about Piltdown Man. He occupied a commanding position within the medical and anatomical scientific establishment. He played a prominent part in public debates about the meaning of science for social and political interpretation. And lastly, his extensive personal notes, correspondence and publications allow the historian to trace the process by which political events lying apparently 'outside' science can nevertheless become constituent elements of that science.[5]

Keith's personal life suggests a truly Darwinian tale of struggle and survival. Born in 1866 to a poor farming family in Aberdeenshire, Keith managed by dint of sheer hard work and ambition to rise to the heights of British science — Curator of the Royal College of Surgeons by 1908, Fellow of the Royal Society in 1913, President of the Royal Anthropological Institute from 1914 to 1917, knighted in 1921, President of the British Association for the Advancement of Science for the Leeds meeting in 1927, Fullerian Professor of Physiology at the Royal Institution 1917 – 19 (where Keith later served as Secretary in 1922 and then Treasurer in 1926), and Rector of Aberdeen University in 1930.[6]

If Darwinian evolution provides an appropriate metaphor for understanding Keith's life, actual 'Darwinism', as a theory of the evolution of organic forms, gave unity to a long career spanning the opening Darwinian decades to the period of the final triumph of Darwin in the 'new synthesis' of the 1940s (Keith died in 1955). All his life Keith took pride in his 'Darwinian' stance. It was Keith's professor of anatomy at Marischal College in Aberdeen who 'opened the Darwinian gates' for the young medical student in the winter of 1884 – 85, by giving him a copy of The Origin of Species in the sixth edition. Three years spent as a medical officer for a mining company in Siam between 1889 and 1891 provided Keith with further opportunities for reading the evolutionary literature, such as

Haeckel, for applying evolutionary ideas to the anatomical study of primates, man's nearest animal relatives, and for speculating about human racial differences. Keith's evolutionary interests were somewhat interrupted during his eight busy years as Senior Demonstrator in Anatomy at the London Hospital between 1895 and 1908; but they were renewed in 1908 when he was appointed to the Royal College of Surgeons to serve as the Curator of the Anatomical Museum. In many respects, all of Keith's future ideas as an anthropologist and Darwinian racialist lay in the period between his arrival at the Museum and the end of the First World War, with the war itself having a large impact. After the war, he merely extended, consolidated — and defended — them.

These ideas centered on three inter-related fields — human paleontology, race, and pathology. As Curator of the most important museum of anatomy in Britain, Keith had access to a large collection of prehistoric human skulls. He quickly made himself expert in the reconstruction of fossil remains, and an important figure in the rapidly developing field of human paleontology, becoming first a friend, and later often an enemy, of many of the important paleontologists of the period.

The subject of human evolution is by its very nature subject to controversy, since broad conclusions have often to be drawn from material — fossilized bones — that are usually in a very fragmentary state. In Keith's day, certainly, the subject of human ancestry offered every opportunity for speculative interpretation, as evidenced by the impassioned debates over Piltdown Man, over the antiquity of modern man (Keith's particular interest), and related subjects.[7] Human evolution, in short, helped make Keith a controversialist, a role he came to relish.

Nowhere was Keith's special role as provocative interpreter of human evolution more in evidence than in his writing on race. A friend once suggested that Keith's fascination with racial evolution and competition could be explained by the fact that Keith was 'raised in a tribal society and grew to manhood in a competitive one', and so saw the world in those terms.[8] It was an interest that manifested itself early, during his days as a medical student, when the work of Owen, Darwin, and Huxley led him to the question, 'How, why and where did the races of man arise?' His racial ideas took a new direction after his move to the Royal College of Surgeons in 1908, when he began to reconstruct ancient human racial types from fossils and to work out what the path of human descent had been.

Race was, of course, a central concept in physical anthropology in Keith's day. Racial types, however, were usually thought of as static elements lying somehow outside or beyond evolution, with race formation a distant and closed episode belonging to the ancient past. Keith's novelty as a theorist was to argue instead that racial evolution was a continuous process of the past and the present — to make race formation in a sense the very mechanism of evolution itself.

133

The first element of Keith's pre-war model of human racial evolution derived from the study of Neanderthal man, a human-like ancient type which seemed like and yet very unlike modern man. The questions posed by Neanderthal man were several: How did this ancient type fit into the general scheme of human evolution? What had its fate been? Had it evolved into *Homo sapiens*, or was it off to one side of the direct path, one of nature's experiments that had 'failed'?

By 1913, Keith had become convinced that Neanderthal man was sufficiently different from us in type to have formed no part of our own evolution. Neanderthal man was, therefore, a truly extinct pre-sapiens form whom superior modern man, invading Europe from the outside, had succeeded in exterminating.[9]

This model of human races was extended by Keith's realization that the human past contained not one, but many extinct racial types, all of which had evolved locally, without freely mixing. This suggested that racial hybridization was not, as most anthropologists believed, the mechanism of racial change. Instead, Keith emphasized the slow evolution of racial types *in situ*, the antiquity of modern man, and the importance of a series of racial exterminations and replacements. 'So I perceived,' wrote Keith, 'that man's evolution . . . had been made by a series of zigzags, one progressive local type encroaching on, and ultimately exterminating, a neighbouring less progressive type.'[10] Here, then, in incipient form, was a conflict model of racial evolution based on the study of man's ancient past.

Connecting the human past with the human present in Keith's work was a very different set of preoccupations derived from medical pathology. One of his tasks as Curator was to prepare pathological anatomical specimens for the surgeons in the Royal College. Among the specimens that Keith studied were some curious deformations of the human skull and body, such as acrogemaly, which were associated with disturbances of the recently discovered 'internal secretions' or hormones of the body. Since Neanderthal man was, at the time, typically portrayed as an ape-like creature with almost pathological deformations of the skull, far different from refined modern man, Keith seized hold of the idea that perhaps racial features, in the past and present, were caused by hormonal changes in evolution.[11]

By the time World War I broke out, Keith was in possession of a set of notions and preconceptions which, while only remotely Darwinian in our modern sense, provided him with a relatively satisfactory (if highly debatable) explanation of human racial evolution. It required, however, the experience of the Great War itself to add the component of contemporary human struggle to his view of racial evolution. The result was to turn Keith the 'Darwinist' into Keith the 'social Darwinist'.

134

Like most of his contemporaries, Keith had taken only a patriotic and personal interest in warfare in modern society before 1914. The Boer War had stirred his nationalism, without suggesting that contemporary human struggles had much to do with evolution. If anything, he believed that war played no part in the evolution of a nation, 'for a calamity which deprives a nation of the best and bravest of its manhood must render that nation less fit to carry on its struggle for existence in the world'.[12]

Indeed, in 1914, Keith was working on a problem seemingly only tangentially related to the current crisis. This was a difficulty that arose from his model of racial evolution in the past — namely, how a race which had acquired, through hormonal changes, a distinctive countenance, would have been kept from cross-breeding with other tribes, so as to prevent a merger of its traits with other groups and to allow it to evolve as an independent unit. Prehistory showed Keith that distinct tribes had existed, had lived out their lives and become extinct, without losing their special characteristics. What had kept them from crossing? This puzzle led Keith to read the scientific literature on primitive tribes, modern 'equivalents' of extinct races, for evidence of tribal hostility. He read Darwin on the Tierra del Fuego Indians and Baldwin Spencer on the Australian aborigines. Later he came across Francis Galton's idea of 'the herd instinct' in animals, the psychologist McDougall's notion of the human instinct of 'gregariousness', and the sociologist Gidding's discussion of the concept of 'consciousness of kind'. These readings suggested to Keith that in primitive times human beings had been divided into tribal units that were hostile to each other. Generalizing to the entire sweep of human evolution, Keith proposed that there had evolved in the human species a deep-seated instinct of 'clannishness' which inclined members of the same tribe towards each other and made them averse to other tribes. This allowed tribes and races to keep their identities intact, so that the tribe, race — and later, Keith would add, the modern nation — served as a natural evolutionary unit. Isolation — a topic being discussed at the time by evolutionists as a mechanism of speciation — thus became in the human species not geographical but mental — it was lodged in the human brain and was nature's way of evolving new races.

Note that struggle between races *per se* was not yet emphasized by Keith. Rather it was isolation that interested him, as a means of keeping racial distinctions. Admittedly, the instinct of clannishness had a dual aspect — on one side it encouraged a spirit of fraternity and cooperation in a tribe, and on the other a spirit of isolation and defense of the tribe. He would later make much of this distinction, but in 1915 his interest lay in finding a mechanism that would keep races apart. As a mechanism, it did not arouse much criticism or indeed interest.[13]

It was at this point in the development of Keith's thought that the war in Europe broke out. Everything suggests that it took the experience of contemporary nationalistic struggle on a vast scale to make Keith's implicitly conflictual model of human evolution explicit — to make struggle between races seem, to Keith, an inevitable result of the tribal instinct for isolation and self-preservation.[14]

This interpretation of the impact of the war on Keith's thought is suggested by the fact that the concept of struggle in warfare figured prominently in his work for the first time during the war. Keith was forty-eight when the war broke out in 1914, too old to serve at the front, but the effects of the war were made vivid to him when officers engaged in training recruits for the Army Medical Service brought their men to the Museum to be instructed by Keith in the elements of human anatomy. In the last two years of the war, Keith became even more directly involved in the war effort when he began to work on the problem of how to restore movement to men disabled in the war. The point is that Keith was less removed from the reality of the war than some intellectuals, such as Havelock Ellis himself.

The impact of the war was clear in a talk Keith gave in October 1915 to the Medical Society of St. Thomas's Hospital. The purpose of his talk was, Keith said, to answer the question, 'What has war to do with the evolution of human races?', a question he said was on everyone's mind at the time. He began by going backwards from the current crisis to the Franco-Prussian war of 1870 – 71. Isolation, he argued, was a deep-seated instinct in human beings, binding the people of Germany into one unit and the people of France into another, and pitting them against each other. Thus 'statesmen . . . accepted as a truth that the essential factor in the evolution of a new race was that of isolation'. The fact that the war cost Germany 28,000 lives and 100,000 wounded or disabled 'is a detail as far as racial evolution is concerned'. The conclusion? That statesmen who conduct war are race-builders 'in a true Darwinian sense', and that war, far from being an isolated event in human history, was 'part of the real biological processes which shape the future of living races'. Turning then to the current conflict in Europe, Keith predicted: 'The Allies will win, and when they have won they will have spilled their best blood, emptied their purses — and for what — to safeguard the future of their stock and ward off a German racial domination of Europe.'[15]

This view of war and evolution was reiterated and elaborated in Keith's annual Address to the Royal Anthropological Institute in January 1916, the third of four such addresses he gave during his tenure as President between 1914 and 1917; in his lecture as President of the section of Anthropology of the British Association for the Advancement of Science in 1919;

136

and in his Boyle Lecture to the Oxford University Junior Scientific Club also in 1919.[16] Two years later, in 1921, the press cuttings of yet another talk by Keith on nationalism and war led the novelist and advocate of 'universalism', H. G. Wells, to furious reply. Wells had learned his biology from Darwin's bulldog, Huxley, but as a Darwinist would have no truck with Keith's war-mongering. 'God damn you, Sir,' he wrote to Keith.[17]

With war, it was clear, Keith had found his theme, a provocative, 'Darwinian' theme after his own heart. It was also a theme capable of arousing the passions and so Keith found himself much in demand by daily and weekly newspapers eager to increase their sales. Keith's clever use of the popular press, which began during the war, gave him a platform for his biopolitical views in the inter-war years; he had a fluent and attractive writing style, was never averse to controversy, rarely lost his temper, and was a gift to editors.[18]

Keith's theme was the competitive and racialist basis of human society. Just as varieties were constantly forming in animal nature, so in man, Keith argued, new varieties were forming which, if isolated, would become new species. Admittedly, the old tribalism was being constantly frustrated by statesmen. Nevertheless, races and racial competition were to be seen as basic parts of the evolution of man. The political implications of such a view were clearly spelled out — war and the nationalism which drove it were real, if muffled, expressions of nature's old ways, and any attempt to interfere with them could only lead to disaster. Such ideas pitted Keith against all those like H. G. Wells who, after the war, dreamed of a new and peaceful order in which nationalism and racialism had been eradicated and replaced with true internationalism. As Keith himself said in 1919, 'You can see I am not preaching a doctrine likely to help on the League of Nations very much . . .'[19]

The idea of the evolutionary naturalness and necessity of war was one he maintained for the rest of his life and elaborated in a series of talks, newspaper articles, papers, books and addresses. These included *Nationality and Race from the Anthropologist's Point of View* (1919), *Ethnos or The Problem of Race from a New Point of View* (1930), *The Place of Prejudice in Modern Civilization* (1931), his *Essays on Human Evolution* (1946) and *A New Theory of Evolution* (1948), the last purporting to be a major new contribution to evolutionary thought but actually consisting of a reiteration of views which had become only too familiar to his critics. Perhaps Keith's greatest notoriety occurred in the summer of 1931, when in his lecture to the students of Aberdeen University as their newly elected Rector he proposed that 'Nature keeps her human orchard healthy by pruning; war is her pruning-hook', an unfortunate phrase for which he later expressed his regret.[20] But, however he said it, Keith's ideas kept him in the news — when he warned that 'de-racialization' of the world would result in disaster for humankind, when he proposed that the statesman, not the zoologist, had got the definition of 'race' right, when he spoke of Hitler as an 'evolutionist'.[21]

It was Keith's role to keep alive this 'conflict' model of evolution in the inter-war years and to try to appropriate Darwinism for his own view of war and evolution. As a social Darwinist he fits uneasily into the classic Hofstadter mold, since he saw struggle in group or racial terms, rather than individual ones, and tended to balance cooperative nature with competitive nature. Yet it is as a social Darwinist that he is probably best categorized. As a leader of British anthropology, Keith was no lightweight or crank. But though his ideas won him some admirers — his racialism was shared, secretly and not so secretly, by a wide variety of scientists — Keith's effort to link Darwin's name unequivocally to the model of warfare failed. What is interesting about Keith's life is that right at the moment he 'discovered' modern warfare in evolution, so many Darwinists were ready to abandon it. The question is why?

3 The Eugenists and the Great War

To answer this I look briefly at the eugenists. The eugenists are doubly interesting because they have invariably been labelled social Darwinists by historians, and because their growth as a social movement coincided with the Great War.[22] By focussing on the eugenists, one can learn a great deal about the differential impact of World War I on biopolitical discourse and some of the reasons for the changes that were occurring in Darwinism and social Darwinism by the second decade of the century.

The origins of Darwinian 'eugenics' go back to the 1860s, when Francis Galton, Charles Darwin's cousin, first proposed the possibility of artificial selection as a way of improving the human breed. Institutionally, however, the growth of eugenics coincided rather precisely with the growing economic and military rivalry of the European countries, with the preparation for actual war, and with the outbreak of war itself. In 1907 the Eugenics Laboratory was established under Pearson's leadership. In 1911, the year Galton died, a chair of eugenics was established in his name, with Karl Pearson as its first professor. Meanwhile, the Eugenics Education Society had been organized in 1907–08 to popularize eugenics, and the *Eugenics Review* founded in 1910. The first legislative success claimed by the Society occurred in 1913 with the passage of the Mental Deficiency Act. The previous year, in 1912, the first International Congress of Eugenics was held in London, under the leadership of Major Leonard Darwin, Darwin's son. Eugenists from all the major countries of Europe attended, as well as from the United States.

As a group, the eugenists apparently shared much with Keith. Galton's most important eugenic disciple, Karl Pearson, for example, is remembered as an ardent eugenist and social Darwinist who glorified the struggle between races and nations as the spur to national efficiency and the means to social progress.[23]

Scientifically, the whole argument of the eugenists — that, in contemporary life, we should carry out an artificial form of human selection of the fittest individuals — was based on Darwinian natural selection. Since, according to evolutionary biology, natural selection was a mechanism of progress because it weeded out the unfit and selected the fit, the eugenists argued that the introduction of an artificial form of selection to eliminate the unfit and encourage the breeding of the fit had its justification in Darwinian nature. As Halliday says, 'The eugenists were true Darwinians in assimilating the biological problem of survival to the social problem of reproduction.'[24] Many social as well as scientific ties also united Keith with the eugenists, especially his friendship with Leonard Darwin, the President of the Eugenics Education Society, whom Keith met during the war and with whom he corresponded when they were both old men. Keith was an honorary member of the Eugenics Society, though he declined to participate on the grounds that all his energies were absorbed by the many other scientific societies in which he was active. He did, however, address the Eugenics Education Society on several occasions.[25] Keith and the eugenists, in short, shared a commitment to Darwinism and a fondness for Darwinian metaphors, especially the metaphor of the world as an unweeded garden requiring some kind of pruning. The question was — was war itself a natural pruning-hook, necessary and progressive in its effects?

The answer is that the majority of eugenists, once actual war was before them, found they did not share Keith's view of the evolutionary significance of war at all. (Pearson's views on struggle, which coincided with Keith's, were untypical of eugenics as a whole, as several historians have realized.) Many eugenists were in fact liberals who had rejected the grimmer social ideology of struggle.[26] Almost without exception, the British eugenists argued that war was a dreadful evil whose effects on society could only be dysgenic and harmful. Far from revealing to them Darwinian struggle at work, the world war was the defining historical event that led them to speak out against the damage that could come to 'nature' by man-made conflict and to deepen their resolve to design eugenic policies to protect the nation's germ plasm. Even a British victory was viewed as a pyrrhic one as far as eugenical goals were concerned.

The British eugenists, of course, had long been concerned with factors in the modern world that seemed to them to reduce the efficiency of natural selection as a biological process eliminating the unfit. But, like the majority of scientists, before 1914 they had reflected relatively little on the problem of actual human warfare in the contemporary world as an evolutionary or anti-evolutionary agent. The Boer War, it is true, sparked alarm at the degenerate condition of the British people, but as Searle notes, in his short book on eugenics between 1900 and 1914, most eugenists, if they thought about it at all, believed that militarism could be a useful aid to eugenics, in that it would encourage human preparedness and fitness. In Searle's account of eugenics before the war, where the issue of war and eugenics is discussed, the ideas of some of the eugenic 'militarists', if we can call them that, are mentioned. Searle cites Colonel Melville, Professor of Hygiene at the Royal Medical College, for instance, as arguing in an article in the *Eugenics Review* for 1910 – 11 that 'it may be that an occasional war is of service by reason of the fact that in times of danger the nation attends to the virility of its citizens'.[27]

On the dissenting side, however, some eugenists could point to Charles Darwin himself on the negative or *dysgenic* effect of war and militarism. In the second edition of the *Descent of Man*, Darwin, in response to suggestions by Greg and Galton, had added a paragraph on war:

> In every country in which a large standing army is kept up, the finest young men are taken by the conscription or are enlisted. They are thus exposed to early death during the war, are often tempted into vice, or are prevented from marrying during the prime of their life. On the other hand the shorter and feebler men, with poorer constitutions, are left at home, and consequently have a much better chance of marrying and propagating their kind.[28]

It took the Great War really to bring home the force of this argument. The war immediately stimulated a series of addresses and papers on a diversity of topics such as war and evolution, the differential impact of war on conscript and volunteer armies, the sex imbalance caused by the war, and the need for eugenic programmes to combat the negative effects of the war.

Let us examine how ambivalence about war and evolution expressed by eugenists at the start of war increasingly gave way to the conviction that warfare was genetically disastrous.

The ambivalence is neatly captured in an address given to the Eugenics Education Society on 8 October 1914 by Theodore G. Chambers. Chambers began by citing the psychologist McDougall on the instinct of war: 'The instinct of pugnacity has played a part second to none in the evolution of social organization.' McDougall also warned that, while international law would in the long run reduce hostility, it would also end 'what has been an important, probably the most important, factor of progressive evolution of human nature, namely the selection of the fit and the extermination of the less fit (among both individuals and societies) resulting from their conflicts with one another'. The author himself suggested that, whatever the horrors of war in the present age, 'the world has not yet reached a stage of development in which it can be dispensed with'. On the other hand, the author wanted to dissociate himself from any endorsement of Germany. The militarists there, he said, were fighting for the wrong reasons, as though war in itself was a good. This was a false conception of Darwinan evolution, of 'might as right', which the Bishop of Down in a letter to *The Times* had called 'simply Darwinism turned into an ethical principle'.

Having muddled his way through this problem, Chambers then gave an equally confused account of the eugenic and dysgenic effects of the war. On the one hand, there were those who, like the American Starr Jordan, thought war was a reverse selection eliminating the best germ plasm. On the other hand, there was the opinion of Sir Ronald Ross, that the 'magnificent physique of the Scottish clans' was evidence of the eugenic results of warfare. 'I am afraid my conclusions are somewhat indefinite', confessed Mr. Chambers.[29]

Four months later, the biologist J. Arthur Thomson, Professor at Aberdeen University, was very much more definite. In the Second Galton Lecture to the Eugenics Education Society on 16 February 1915 Thomson acknowledged, as many eugenists did, that in ancient times tribal warfare had probably been nature's way of raising racial standards. That is, he acknowledged struggle as a vehicle of social evolution in the past. He then went on, however, to distinguish the human past from the present. In modern times, said Thomson, other social habits had replaced naked struggle, such that, biologically speaking, war could only be regarded as dysgenic, not eugenic. As a Darwinist, Thomson then proceeded to defend this view by arguing that, when Darwin used the term struggle, he often meant struggle 'in a metaphorical sense', which included much dependence and cooperation, so that the mode of struggle was not always competitive and did not always eliminate the unfit. The only struggle that made for evolution, in Thomson's opinion, was one involving discriminating selection. Since the current war in no way resulted in such discriminating selection, it could not be thought of as part of evolution. To this scientific argument, Thomson added the moral point that man was not anyway bound to follow nature, and that to depend on struggle was to 'slide down to barbarism'.[30]

This view of war and eugenics was endorsed by Leonard Darwin, in his Presidential address to the Annual General Meeting of the Society on 1 July 1915, thus giving it the status of semi-official eugenic policy. Like Thomson, Darwin argued that, while war might have been eugenical in the past, modern civilized life reduced the selective effect of conflict. For instance, success in war was no test of the highest eugenical traits, but only of brute strength. In addition war, as his father, Charles Darwin, had pointed out, eliminated the finest representatives of Europe's manhood. To the eugenist, therefore, the only remedy was complete abolition of war. Since Darwin believed the chances of this were slight, the next best solution was to try to mitigate its effects by caring for the wounded, encouraging the fit to marry before going to the front, and by rewarding

141

middle-class families with large numbers of children — by a eugenic programme, in short.[31]

Havelock Ellis, who was much more radical than other eugenists on any number of subjects, was prepared to go even further than Leonard Darwin. In an essay on 'Evolution and War' he maintained that warfare was characteristic of neither human nor even animal life. He concluded that 'War is not a permanent factor of national evolution, but for the most part has no place in Nature at all.'[32] If this is social Darwinism, it is a Darwinism in which struggle has been all but eliminated.

Ellis also put his finger on one aspect of the debate about war that was to tarnish further the old social Darwinists in the minds of many of the British eugenists, namely the association between evolution and German militarism. Ellis claimed that the Germans believed in war 'as a religious dogma'. An editorial in the *Eugenics Review* dismissed the 'war philosophy' of Germans such as Treitschke and Nietzsche as a 'reversion to savagery'.[33] Thus tarred with the Prussian brush, war lost its appeal in Britain as an agent of evolution.

One of the most interesting, because most convincing, contributions to the entire British debate on war and eugenics came from the geneticist F. A. E. Crew in 1919, just after the end of the war. Convincing because, as he had reminded his audience at the Eugenics Education Society, he had been trained by Britain's own 'militarists', such as Spencer, Galton, Pearson and Bateson, and because his actual participation in trench warfare changed his mind. Like the Germans, said Crew, many British biologists before the war had maintained that war in human society was biologically predestined and therefore justified. Since the British 'militarists' were his own scientific masters, these had been his views — until he experienced war at first hand. By the end of that experience he had become convinced that they and he were wrong. He was now certain that the Darwinian theory of the evolution of the individual was not the science of evolution of society, that the mental and moral qualities of human beings were acquired and not inborn, and that one could change the psyche of a nation in a short time. He therefore looked for 'the final rejection of the Darwinian conception of the fittest animal as the standard of the individual as a member of society . . .'[34]

4 Conclusion: The War and Social Darwinism

Enough has been said to show that Keith and the eugenists had really very different ideas about how to apply Darwinian evolution to the contemporary world. Their differences encompassed more than the fact that Keith believed war was natural and evolutionarily progressive while the eugenists believed war to be unnatural and evolutionarily retrogressive;

they extended to a series of subtle differences in the interpretation of 'nature' and 'society' which clearly showed they were very different kinds of social Darwinists.[35]

Keith, for instance, insisted that Darwinian evolution continually operated in the animal and human world, in the present as it had in the past, even if in distorted or thwarted form. From this derived Keith's peculiar form of racialism and nationalism. To Keith, all expressions of racialism or nationalism, however deplored on moral grounds, could not be deplored on evolutionary grounds. They were seen to be necessary and ultimately to have their own evolutionary justification. It was nature working her way for the good of the species.

The eugenists certainly had their own brand of racialism. Race was in fact the subject most uniting them with Keith, his notion of race form-ation coming close to a notion of racial purity, while the eugenists in turn often depicted eugenic fitness in racial terms.[36] Nevertheless, on the ques-tion of how Darwinian evolution operated in the modern world, the British eugenists disagreed with Keith rather sharply. Indeed, the whole eugenic imperative was to a large extent based on the belief that Darwinian struggle and elimination of the unfit no longer operated with the force it once had. Civilization itself interrupted the process of natural selection to such an extent, the eugenists often argued, that evolution by natural means had almost come to an end.

These differing views of the operation of Darwinian evolution help explain the very different attitudes taken by Keith and the eugenists to the problem of social intervention. Keith was essentially satisfied that evolu-tion would express itself in the modern world if left alone; he had a negative view of political and social intervention in the natural process. To him, therefore, efforts to overcome nationalistic struggle via new inter-national organizations, or to suppress racialism by moral or political means, were not only doomed to failure but ultimately harmful, since evolution worked in the long run through nationalism and racialism for the good of the human species.[37] Though at times he gave eugenics his ap-proval because it seemed to him a programme to strengthen racial identity, his very real reservations about eugenics were based in part on his fear that eugenists might try to 'breed out' the racial instinct, something he be-lieved would affect progress adversely.[38] To the eugenists, on the other hand, some kind of intervention in nature was seen as necessary, to put right a nature no longer properly regulated by nature herself.

In making a distinction between Darwinian struggle in nature and struggle in modern human life, the eugenists cast doubt on the simple and direct analogy between nature and society dear to Keith and typical of social Darwinists like him. The rejection of the 'old' analogical Darwinism did not, of course, mean an end to biosocial argument — the use, that is, of the biological to explicate the social. The persistence of eugenics as a scientific and social movement after the war, with its emphasis on the importance of hereditary nature in human society, attests to this. But the divide between Keith and the eugenists did indicate that the war had helped change Darwinists' minds about what kind of argument from nature could count as legitimate.

That most Darwinists agreed with the eugenists that grand analogies from struggle in nature to society were illegitimate (even when not agreeing with eugenical ideas *per se*) is suggested by Keith's increasing isolation as a biosocial thinker after the war. Even though many of his professional successes still lay in the future in 1918, these successes were based on his painstaking work in anatomy and paleontology, rather than on his views on war and race. These latter views appeared more and more extreme as time went on. His continued emphasis on enmity did not recommend itself to the internationally minded scientists, many of whom had become pacifists during and after the war. His idea that nations should be thought of as incipient 'races' and that statesmen who equated race with nation had grasped the essentials of racial definition (rather than the zoologists who wanted to separate the two terms) seemed perverse to most scientists.[39] By the 1930s, very few scientists could be found who shared Keith's view that the growing nationalism of the period was the predictable outcome of Darwinian evolution, or that Hitler's racism made Hitler a true 'evolutionary' statesman.[40]

Only Keith's kindly personal qualities, his well-known patriotism, and his distance from the mainstream of biosocial thought kept him from being more savagely attacked for his views than he was. By the 1920s, he was already a heretic who much enjoyed his heresies.[41] But heresy was what his Darwinism had become to the average British Darwinist by then. By the time of his death in 1955, ten years after the second, even more fateful and devastating world war, a war which saw a basic reassessment of the science of race as well as the final triumph of Darwinian evolution in the 'modern synthesis', Keith's racial and evolutionary ideas made him seem a Darwinian of a truly bygone age.

In conclusion, this study of war, evolution and social Darwinism provides further evidence that 'social Darwinism' as a term needs considerable refining. This paper also indicates that, among the many causes of the eventual eclipse of the old kind of analogical social Darwinism represented by scientists like Keith, with its simple transferral of struggle from nature to society, the Great War itself played a significant part. It heightened awareness among scientists that the interactions between biology and human life were of a different order altogether than the kind Keith claimed.[42] That the eugenists, with their simple dichotomy between nature and nurture, were no closer to the truth than Keith took many years to grasp. Eventually, as Darwinism became established as the foundation stone of biology, a more sophisticated, 'interactionist' model of the relations of biology to human social life began to emerge in which neither Keith's social Darwinism nor eugenics found a comfortable place.

Notes

1 The new literature on social Darwinism is now quite extensive. On Britain, see Greta Jones, *Social Darwinism and English Thought: The Interaction between Biological and Social Theory* (Hassocks, 1980); D. P. Crook, 'Darwinism — The Political Implications', *History of European Ideas*, ii (1981) 19 – 34, and his *Benjamin Kidd: Portrait of a Social Darwinist* (Cambridge, 1984); for America, see Roger Bannister, *Social Darwinism, Science and Myth in Anglo-American Thought* (Philadelphia, 1979); for France, Linda L. Clark, *Social Darwinism in France* (University, Alabama, 1984); and for Germany, Ted Benton, 'Social Darwinism and Socialist Darwinism in Germany, 1860 – 1900', *Rivista di Filosofia*, lxxiii (1982), 79 – 121.

2 Even eugenics, normally seen as classically Darwinian and social Darwinian, could be based on neo-Lamarckian ideas. For an example, see Nancy Leys Stepan, 'Eugenesia, genética y salud publica: el movimiento eugenésico brasileño y mundial', *Quipu: Revista Latinoamericana de Historia de las Ciencias y la Tecnología*, ii (1985), 351 – 384; Peter J. Bowler, in *The Eclipse of Darwinism: Anti-Darwinian Evolution Theories in the Decades Around 1900* (Baltimore, 1983), comments that the term 'social Lamarckism', has never gained the popularity of 'social Darwinism', though he provides considerable evidence of the existence of social analogies based on neo-Lamarckism foundations, p. 18.

3 Havelock Ellis, *Essays in War-Time. Further Studies in the Task of Social Hygiene* (1917: edn. cited, Freeport, N.Y., 1969).

4 Sir Arthur Keith, *An Autobiography* (New York, 1950), p. 436.

5 Keith's notes, letters, typescripts and reprints are in the library of the Royal College of Surgeons. At the time I examined them they were not catalogued, but were kept in boxes. I have indicated sources to letters and other unpublished materials as Keith Collections, RCS.

6 Brief acounts of Keith's life and work are found in: Sir Wilfred Le Gros Clark, 'Arthur Keith', *Biographical Memoirs of the Fellows of the Royal Society*, i (1955), 145 – 161, and J. C. Brash and A. J. E. Cave, 'In Piam Memoriam: Sir Arthur Keith, FRS', *Journal of Anatomy*, lxxxix (1955), 403 – 418. Both of these were written at the time of Keith's death and both downplay his more controversial stands on war, evolution and race. Since 1955 there have been relatively few references to him, though Peter J. Bowler's forthcoming study, *Theories of Human Evolution: A Century of Debate, 1844 – 1914* (Stanford University Press) gives due emphasis to Keith's role in human paleontology. Along very different lines is Misia Landau, 'Human Evolution as Narrative', *American Scientist*, lxxii (1984), 262 – 268. The best available published source on Keith's life is Keith's unusually frank autobiography, cited in n. 4 above.

7 Keith's major work was *The Antiquity of Man* (London, 1915), which was a classic of its kind. It appeared in a new edition in two volumes in 1925. Keith's claims for the great antiquity of modern man, in the form of Galley Hill man, were not subsequently substantiated.

8 Letter from the anthropologist Ashley Montagu, quoting a mutual friend, September 8, 1951. See Keith Collections, RCS, Box of Letters A-M.

9 See Keith, 'Certain Phases in the Evolution of Man', *British Medical Journal* (1912), 734 – 736. In his *Autobiography*, note 4, p. 347, Keith claimed evolution had been carried out via the production of races.

10 Sir Arthur Keith, *Evolution and Ethics* (New York, 1946), p. 141. This was the American edition of Keith's 1946 *Essays on Human Evolution*.

11 Though Keith was already convinced of this by 1912, the clearest statements of his ideas are found in: 'The Differentiation of Mankind into Racial Types', *Annual Report of the Smithsonian Institution*, 1919, pp. 443 – 453, and 'The Evolution of Human Races in the Light of the Hormone Theory', *Bulletin of the John Hopkins Hospital*, xxxiii (1922), 155 – 159.

12 Keith, *Evolution and Ethics*, p. 140, n. 19; *Autobiography*, p. 228.

13 Arthur Keith, 'On Certain Factors Concerned in the Evolution of Human Races', *Journal of the Royal Anthropological Institute*, xlvi (1916), 10 – 34; *Evolution and Ethics*, pp. 142 – 143, n. 10. Keith apparently did not read Galton's essay of 1863 on the 'herd instinct' until 1915.

14 Bowler, *Theories of Human Evolution*, ch. 7, suggests that the growing nationalism before and during the war may have led Keith to emphasize the importance of conflict in prehistory and the sudden disappearance of Neanderthal man. Certainly the model of struggle drawn from the current war could be turned back onto the prehistoric human past, making prehistory also more explicitly one of struggle.

15 Arthur Keith, 'War as a Factor in Racial Evolution', *St. Thomas's Hospital Gazette* (Croydon, 1915), esp. pp. 7 – 9; see also Keith, *Autobiography*, pp. 396 – 397.

16 His most important statement during the war was that cited in n. 13 above. See also his 'The Differentiation of Mankind into Racial Types', *Nature*, mciv (1919). 301 – 305; the Boyle lecture appeared as *Nationality and Race from an Anthropologist's Point of View* (Oxford, 1919).

17 *Autobiography*, p. 436.

18 Keith also very much enjoyed the additional income writing for the popular press gave him.

19 Keith, in the debate on 'Eugenics and Imperial Development', under the chairmanship of Leonard Darwin, as reported in *Eugenics Review*, xi (1919 – 1920), 129.

20 Sir Arthur Keith, *The Place of Prejudice in Modern Civilization: Prejudice and Politics* (London, 1931), p. 49. Though Keith's fellow paleontologist, Elliot Smith, savagely attacked Keith's views in the London press, Keith notes his little book met with no demand. The metaphor of a garden requiring pruning was an old one in evolutionary debates, dating back at least to Thomas Henry Huxley's Romanes lecture of 1893, 'Prolegomena to Evolution and Ethics', *Collected Essays* (London, 1894 – 1895), ix. This essay Keith certainly knew, since he was a great admirer of Huxley's and did much to elevate Huxley's modern reputation as an anthropologist; see Mario A. de Gregorio, *T. H. Huxley's Place in Natural Science* (New Haven, Conn., 1984), p. 157.

21 Keith also engaged in lively controversies over Darwinism and religion, defending Darwin's essential materialism. Keith published several Darwinian books along these lines, such as *Darwinism and What it Implies* (London, 1928), and *The Religion of a Darwinist* (London, 1925). An account of his battles with Sir Arthur Conan Doyle and Sir Oliver Lodge over spiritualism can be found in Keith's *Autobiography*, pp. 484, 518 – 520.

22 See, for example, Daniel Kevles, *In the Name of Eugenics: Genetics and the Uses of Human Heredity* (New York, 1985), pp. 20 – 21, 70.

23 Nancy Stepan, *The Idea of Race in Science: Great Britain, 1800 – 1960* (London, 1982), p. 129.

24 R. J. Halliday, 'Social Darwinism: A Definition', *Victorian Studies*, xiv (1971), 400.

25 Some letters from Leonard Darwin to Keith are found in Keith Collections, RCS, Box of Letters, A-M. See also Keith in his *Autobiography*, pp. 522 – 523, 525. On Keith's connection with the Eugenics Education Society, see his lecture on the founding father of eugenics, Francis Galton: 'Galton among the Anthropologists', *Eugenics Review*, xii (1920), 14; and Keith's contribution to the debate cited in n. 19 above.

26 G. R. Searle, *Eugenics and Politics in Britain, 1900 – 1914* (Leyden, 1976), p. 38; and Michael Freeden, 'Eugenics and Progressive Thought', *The Historical Journal*, xxii (1979), 645 – 671.

27 Searle, pp. 36 – 37, n. 26. Searle shows clearly that by 1914 most eugenists had changed their minds.

28 Charles Darwin, *The Descent of Man and Selection in Relation to Sex* (2nd ed., London, 1890), p. 134.

29 *Eugenics Review*, vi (1914 – 1915), 272, 274, 277 and 281.

30 'Eugenics and the War', *Eugenics Review*, vii (1915 – 1916), 1 – 14.

31 'Eugenics During and After the War', *ibid.*, pp. 91 – 106. This did not mean that all British eugenists agreed; see the dissenting address by Prof. W. Ridgeway, in 'The Problem of our Racial and National Safety', *ibid.*, pp. 122 – 130, and Coulton's negative view of the American pacifist Jordan's book, *War and the Breed*, in the same volume, pp. 187 – 292. Nevertheless, in the *Notes and Comments* of the volume, it was made clear that the majority of eugenics lectures argued war was disastrous to eugenical aims.

32 Ellis, n. 3, ch. 2 on 'Evolution and War', quotation from p. 26. Bannister and Clarke, n. 1, comment on the same association drawn by scientists between German militarism and evolutionism in America and France.

33 'Eugenics and the War', *Eugenics Review*, vi. (1914 – 1915), 197.

34 F. E. A. Crew, 'A Biologist in a New Environment', *ibid.*, xi (1919 – 1920), 119 – 123, quotation on p. 122.

35 Several British writers commented directly on Keith, rejecting his interpretation. See Prof. J. A. Lindsay, 'The Eugenic and Social Influence of the War', *ibid.*, x (1918 – 1919), 133, and E. P. Poulton, 'Eugenics Problems After the Great War', *ibid.*, viii (1916 – 1917), 34 – 49, the latter attacking Keith's *Pall Mall Gazette* article of February 19, 1916, in which Keith had disputed Leonard Darwin's conclusions. Keith had said it was 'nonsense to talk of war being the cause of the catastrophe of eliminating the best men'.

36 See Stepan, *The Idea of Race*, pp. 124 – 134, n. 23.

37 See typescript in Keith Collections, RCS, 'Can Race Be Rationalized?' Address to the National Union of Students, Oxford, April 5, 1932.

38 Keith's views on eugenics vacillated between approval and disapproval. He wrote a preface to the eugenist George Pitt-Rivers's *Weeds in the Garden of Marriage* (London, 1931), but noted his disagreements with Pitt-Rivers's more extreme ideas on compulsory sterilization. Later Pitt-Rivers joined Mosley's party. Keith also wrote positively about eugenics for the press, as in his 'The Greatest Test for Mankind', *The New York Times Magazine*, 8 February 1931, where he wrote about the need to breed 'higher types'. On the other hand, an addendum written in Keith's hand, and dated 16 January 1942, to the typescript cited in n. 37 above, shows Keith to have become much more dubious about eugenics by the 1940s.

39 The question of 'race' and 'nationality' was one of the few subjects over which Keith took issue with his hero Huxley: see Keith's Huxley Memorial Lecture, 'The Evolution of the Human Races', *J. Anth. R. Inst.*, lvii (1928), 305 – 321.

40 *Evolution and Ethics*, p. 10, n. 10. Keith never lost faith in the efficacy of modern struggle and warfare for the progress of the species. See his 'The Evolutionary Interpretation of the Second World War', in his *Essays on Human Evolution* (London, 1946), ch. 7.

41 Keith, 'A History of Some of My Heresies', *The Rationalist Annual*, 1939, pp. 3 – 13.

42 Hamilton Cravens, in *The Triumph of Evolution: American Scientists and the Heredity-Environment Controversy, 1900 – 1941* (Philadelphia, 1978), suggests that eugenics itself, in America at least, helped bring to an end loose analogies and hastened the end of social Darwinism, by providing biologists and social scientists with much more precise definitions of nature and nurture. See p. 291.

8

Asquith and Lloyd George Revisited

Peter Clarke

Some historians maintain that the First World War was more the occasion than the cause of the downfall of the Liberal party; but few would deny that it was one cause. During the war, politics at the top turned peculiarly upon personal considerations, and the Liberal party was ultimately split between the followers of Asquith and Lloyd George. In this power struggle, moreover, the press played a prominent role. With his penchant for exploring the vicissitudes of British Liberalism, his biographer's eye for the cut and thrust of political manoeuvre, and his unrivalled understanding of the links between journalism and politics, Stephen Koss was persistently drawn to write about the political crisis which encompassed the fall of the last Liberal Government. Indeed his first essay upon this theme advanced what was dubbed — to his irritation — 'the Koss thesis'.[1] Such an approach, in fact, was as uncharacteristic of his historical work as the subject itself was characteristic.

At the time Stephen Koss initially addressed this problem, it was still swathed in the layers of retrospective mythology and selective documentation in which Lord Beaverbrook and Lady Asquith of Yarnbury had helped to swaddle it. Custodians alike of rival interpretations and of important documents, their longevity not only kept alive the embers of a heated partisanship but also restricted research upon sources of which they held the copyright. In particular, neither the diary of Frances Stevenson, with its intimate observation of Lloyd George, nor the letters with which Asquith bombarded Venetia Stanley had entered the domain of scholarship, though garbled extracts from both had at times been published. Now that reputable editions of these important texts are to hand,[2] a less speculative and more intimate view of both Asquith and Lloyd George can be obtained. Their individual characteristics and their mutual relations can be reassessed from the perspective of 1915, a year which proved to be the beginning of the end for British Liberalism.

Lord Beaverbrook, who for many years had privileged access to the Stevenson diary, called it 'a startling political document'.[3] It is certainly, as its editor has claimed, unique. 'Where else have we the detached picture of a British prime minister by one who was at once his devoted mistress and his confidential secretary?' (Taylor, p. ix). The published diary consists of a more or less continuous section running from 1914 to 1922, with some entries for later years, notably the mid-1930s, when Lloyd George was mounting his last bid for power. It is his first and more fruitful bid for power during the First World War which is illuminated best. It is especially useful in Lloyd George's case to have a record of this kind since he was notorious for not writing letters, and he rarely put himself into what he put down on paper. What picture of Lloyd George, then, do we gain from the Stevenson diary?

Frances Stevenson's own position was never easy. An educated and independent-minded young woman, she was first engaged to teach Lloyd George's daughter. Like the heroine of a Wells novel, she fell for a man twice her age; and when he offered her a post as his secretary in 1912 it was, as she later put it, 'on his own terms, which were in direct conflict with my essentially Victorian upbringing'. She made one effort to break away and, staying in Scotland at Christmas 1912, considered a proposal of marriage from a young man whom she had met on holiday. Lloyd George responded first by saying that he would not stand in her way, then, almost immediately, by doing so. He summoned her to London, something terrible had happened, he needed her, she returned. 'It was the Marconi scandal which was about to break,' she recalled — as indeed it was, though not for some weeks.[4] In the meantime Lloyd George's terms were accepted and Frances Stevenson became his 'darling Pussy'. Her affair upset her parents, who later tried to separate them — 'they think I am his plaything, and that he will fling me aside when he has finished with me — or else they think that there will be a scandal and that we shall all be disgraced' (Taylor, p. 33). Frances Stevenson's confidence that the relationship would last triumphed on the first point. But the fear of scandal is a thread that runs through the story. Even in later years, they always had to be careful: careful not to go about in the government car, nor to dine together in public; careful not to travel back and forth together too often between London and the Versailles Conference; careful not to be 'too reckless' in going about together in July 1921. Lloyd George believed that it was possible to defy respectability provided a certain homage was paid to conventions. 'There is much satisfaction in "doing" the world!' (p. 69). So he shamelessly helped propagate a picture of himself as a conventional family man, despite Frances Stevenson's unease.

That Lloyd George felt a deep and lifelong attachment to Margaret, his wife for over fifty years, is the intriguing counterpoint to this theme. True, he was not faithful to her and lived flagrantly with his mistress for more than half the time. Despite all this, the marriage never really broke down and it may come as a surprise how often he was to be found in the house at Criccieth which Margaret maintained in later years and which was still in a sense his home. It was she who kept the Carnarvon Boroughs seat warm for him in his absences and he never contested it without her at this side, choosing to take his earldom after her death instead.

Lloyd George and Frances Stevenson could spend weekends together only when Mrs Lloyd George was away at Criccieth: a predicament which would set Lloyd George 'scheming . . . to get Mrs Lloyd George back to Wales again' (p. 217). The problem was to shuttle the Lloyd George family between Downing Street, Walton Heath, Criccieth and Chequers, with Frances Stevenson enjoying only a residual claim. 'I cannot go down to Chequers today as the family are there . . .' '. . . I left in the afternoon, as the arrival of the family would have made things unpleasant' (pp. 220, 227). These arrangements, though far from ideal, avoided an overt domestic crisis. There was always the latent threat that Lloyd George's career, like Parnell's before it, would end in the divorce courts. By January 1916 Lloyd George claimed that he could face disgrace. 'I can understand Parnell now for the first time' (p. 92). But Frances Stevenson remained happier that the issue should not be put to the test, recording twenty years later that 'he is always inclined to blame the woman when it is a question of a man choosing her and his career — he is always for the immolation of the woman' (p. 322). This tallies with a later comment by Lloyd George's daughter Olwen, recognising that Pussy did not have all the cream: 'Frances had to wait on him like a servant, as I am sure she had to most of the time they were together, for Father was always one of the most demanding of men.'[5]

Frances Stevenson, of course, was more than 'the other woman'. She saw Lloyd George at work as well as at play, and scrutinised his methods closely. She noted the thoroughness and resource with which he tackled problems; she observed his indefatigable efforts as he probed away; she watched him 'adopting flanking movements, so to speak, when a frontal attack is not likely to prove successful, "roping in" persons whose influence is likely to prove helpful or whose opinion counts for something, seeking out those who are "on the fence" and whose opposition would be dangerous, and then talking them round, using all the arts of which he is a pastmaster' (p. 21). She saw that charm was 'essential to a Lloyd George'

(p. 11); that he was hardly so innocent of craft as he claimed. She recalled him as saying on one occasion that 'No one ever convinced anyone by an argument' (pp. 323 – 4); and using all his personal wiles instead to gain the point at issue. Once he had seen his way ahead, he would follow it with absolute disinterestedness and never give in. 'When once D. fastens his teeth, he never lets go' (p. 80). These comments go to the heart of Lloyd George's effectiveness in politics. Equally, Frances Stevenson came to see a concomitant failing in his inability to admit mistakes: 'he seems to be incapable of doing this — possibly because he is able always to make out such a completely good case for everything — the instinct of the clever lawyer at all times' (p. 261). She analysed the way Lloyd George would exhaust all those around him — 'he *distributes* his own nerves in a crisis' — and fortify himself in the process (p. 264). She too saw how he would relax off duty: how he would go 'quite mad', improvising mock sermons, reciting Welsh poetry, all 'like some wild boy broken loose from school' (pp. 45 – 6, 74).

Lloyd George would talk sometimes, especially in these early years, of his basic sense of purpose in politics in ways that created a further bond of sympathy. He described in February 1915 'this job I have taken up of bettering the lives of the poor' (p. 31) and the intense emotional commitment — maybe inspired by his hearer as much as by the subject — comes through in several similar remarks. Frances Stevenson was moved to write that: 'This horror of all the needless suffering which human beings are called upon to endure, is the keynote to his career, and if anyone attempts to portray his character without realising this, then they are ignorant of the man himself and all that he stands for' (p. 78).

The earliest letters from Asquith to Venetia Stanley, a daughter of the Liberal peer Lord Sheffield, date from 1910, but only in 1912 did the correspondence pick up, and the bulk of it comprises the virtually daily series from December 1913 to May 1915. The letters are altogether fuller and freer than any official correspondence. By the time the First World War broke out, Asquith's commitment to writing had become an act of faith by which this outwardly undemonstrative man of sixty-two set great store. At the end of July 1914 he mentioned 'calculating in bed last night that, roughly speaking, since the first week in December I must have written you not less than 70 letters . . .' (Brock, p. 128). The schedule of more than 560 surviving letters in fact shows 133 in these eight months, with another 151 to follow before the end of 1914, an average of more than one a day. In January 1915 the total rose to 45 and to 48 in February. The climax came with 58 in March, dropping back to a mere 35 in April, then roughly one a day in May, until, on the 12th, there came an abrupt end to the intimacy. 'As you know well, *this* breaks my heart,' Asquith wrote curtly in response to the shattering news of Venetia's engagement to Edwin Montagu, a member of his own cabinet (p. 593).

The letters have been known about, in one way or another, for quite a long time. After the First World War, Venetia Montagu was induced to show many of them to Lord Beaverbrook — she was said to be his mistress — and he used them for his own distinctly non-Asquithian purposes. Asquith himself drew upon them restyled as his 'diary' or 'notes', in compiling his memoirs, a euphemism sustained by his daughter Violet in her book *Winston Churchill As I Knew Him* (1965). Not until the biography of Asquith by Roy Jenkins the previous year had explicit use been made of the originals, as it was in Stephen Koss's *Asquith* (1976), with fewer inhibitions. The difference it makes to have a text which is properly identified and free from corruption is more than just a technical scholarly improvement. In his memoirs Asquith wrote disingenuously that 'I have been in the habit of jotting down irregularly my impressions of noteworthy persons and incidents while they were still fresh in my memory.' And added: 'I believe this to be an innocent and even a useful practice.'[6]

A good example is the extract for 25 March 1915, where one visualises 'the last of the Romans' impassively setting down his judgements on the foibles of his colleagues. When it is revealed as a letter to Venetia, however, with the omitted words (in italics below) restored to the text, there is a change of tone which subtly transforms the whole impression.[7]

Thurs. 25 March, 1915 [i]

My darling — it was sweet of you to send your little letter of last night this morning: it makes all the difference to me not to have to wait in suspense for it. It is sad to think that you are not visible even for a moment all day to-day. But I count on to-morrow & shall pick you up at the Admiralty soon after 3.

Massingham *told Margot yesterday* a 'horrible tale', which he swears can be proved true on the best authority. It is that Winston is 'intriguing hard' to supplant E. Grey at the Foreign Office & to put A.J.B. in his place. *I gave you the other day a milder version of the same story, which the suspicious mind of the Assyrian had treasured up.* There is no doubt that Winston is at the moment a complete victim to B's *superficial* charm; *he has him at the Admiralty night & day, and I am afraid tells him a lot of things which he ought to keep to himself, or at any rate to his colleagues. Since I began the last sentence,* Ll. George has been here for his favourite morning indulgence (*it corresponds in him to the dram drinking of the Clyde workmen*) — a 10 minutes discursive discussion of things in general. I asked him what he thought of the Massingham story, & rather to my surprise he said he believed it was substantially true. He thinks that Winston has for the time at any rate allowed himself to be 'swallowed whole' by A.J.B., on whom he, L.G., after working with him for a week or two, is now disposed to be very severe. It is a pity *isn't it?* that Winston hasn't a better sense of proportion, *and also a larger endowment of the instinct of loyalty. As you know, like you,* I am really fond of him: but I regard his future with many misgivings. *Your little Indian plan for him commands I am afraid no favour in any quarter: the mere mention of it makes the Assyrian foam at the mouth, and is received with less demonstrative but equally emphatic disapproval by the 2 or 3 others to whom I have casually hinted at it.* He will never

153

get to the top in English politics, with all his wonderful gifts; *to speak with the tongues of men & angels, and to spend laborious days & nights in administration, is no good, if a man does not inspire trust.*

Two revisions are necessary here. One is of our view of the author, with his over-agitated propensity to sublimate political tension into the sort of gossip which fuelled romantic fantasy. The other revision concerns his pro-tégé Churchill, raising a jarring doubt about their mutual confidence in the spring of 1915 for which readers of Lady Asquith's *Winston Churchill As I Knew Him* would be unprepared. It is a point with obvious relevance to any interpretation of the fall of the Government and must be considered later.

There were two notable changes of gear in the relationship between Asquith and Venetia Stanley. The first came at the beginning of 1912 when Venetia really emerged from her schoolgirl role as his daughter Violet's friend and appeared in a new light to the prime minister. 'Suddenly, in a single instant, without premonition on my part or any challenge on hers, the scales dropped from my eyes,' he wrote three years later (Brock, p. 532). It was a moment on which he looked back both fondly and frequently — it was when 'I made my great discovery of the *real* you' (p. 185). This is a sug-gestive phrase, to be sure, and one which Edwardian fiction could endow with explicit connotations. But Asquith seems only to have been playing with it in such references as 'such a sweet and characteristic expression and revelation of your *real* self' (p. 309), or the saccharine tribute: 'You were (as you always are) your *real* self today: sweet, resolute, undeceiving' (p. 490).

It is notable, all the same, that one of these phrases dates from August 1914, coinciding with another statement which lends itself to an obvious construction: 'I would give more than I can put down on paper to be able to — some sentences are better left unfinished' (p. 182). Obvious or not, the idea that Asquith was in any position to consummate his passion for Venetia at this juncture — busy man as he was — must be discounted on contextual evidence. A further contemporary comment provides confirmation of the proportion of physical to emotional involvement. On 29 July there comes Asquith's thrilling assurance: 'I shall never forget a week ago to-night' (p. 133). This tempestuous occasion, however, is later identified from his pocket diary as 'a most divine hour I spent with you at Mansfield St late on July 22nd' — that is, at her own parents' house, on terms tolerated by them. It needs only Asquith's forlorn parenthesis: ('I wonder if you have for-gotten it?'), to set the scene (p. 245). There was undoubtedly a second change of gear in the relationship in July – August 1914, but the intensity of the verbal bombardment is pretty certainly how it expressed itself.

Considered intimately, therefore, the liaison was probably not carried as

154

far as might initially be supposed. But there was clearly much more in it than was apparent to members of Asquith's circle, for all their ready acceptance that the prime minister, as he put it himself, manifested '(perhaps) a slight weakness for the companionship of clever and attractive women' (p. 471). This served as his cover. It meant that his contacts with Venetia needed no apology provided nothing happened to flout the indulgence they were accorded by the two families and friends alike. Only when Venetia started her course at the London Hospital did the arrival of a messenger, delivering letters from the prime minister to a trainee nurse, in itself cause eyebrows to be raised (p. 476). Though the existence of the letters generally aroused no suspicion, their substance would undoubtedly have done so: a point to which Asquith was not oblivious, as his effusions began to transgress the borders of convention. 'Don't leave this on your table or in someone else's envelope,' he warned at one point (p. 68), and later professed himself 'rather alarmed at the family curiosity as to the contents of my letters . . .' (p. 150).

The fact is that the correspondence cannot possibly be regarded as merely sentimental, and its erotic charge clearly signalled a threat to Margot Asquith. The more innocent gloss which she at times put upon it was, to say the least, innocent on her part. Her contention that 'he shows me *all* his letters & all Venetia's' (p. 547) does not ring true as a literal account, whatever the admirable canons of liberality observed in the Asquith household. Any single letter might be easily explained away, but the cumulative import was something which Asquith took pains to conceal. It is pretty clear from internal evidence that he did not rely upon the official arrangements for mail in 10 Downing Street, nor was it simply left to Margot to post the letters she happened to find in the front hall — her subsequent recollection notwithstanding (p. 12). In practice, the prime minister made a point of seeing that his letters to Venetia were correctly stamped and often put them into the box himself, probably on his walks across to the Athenaeum (pp. 150, 270).

At the Athenaeum — 'the only place where I am free' (p. 363) — he was, of course, safe from Margot, whose régime he undoubtedly found taxing, especially when he sought respite from public affairs. In Margot he had a loyal, vivacious, outspoken supporter; but cooped up with her, rehearsing in an impetuous, undisciplined way the disputes of the day, was not the way he wished to spend his nights. When he had married her in 1892, as his second wife, she had opened doors for him in creating a stylish social life which he certainly enjoyed. By 1915 she was adopting a more tragic aspect, brooding on 'the knowledge alas! that I am no longer young & I daresay — in fact I always observe — as men get older they like different kinds of women . . .' (p. 547) Asquith was not unfaithful to Margot. He regarded marriage, in nineteen cases out of twenty, as exhibiting 'all the many shaded gradations between serfdom, colourless acquiescence and habit, a more or less workable *modus vivendi*, and hunger and mutiny' (p. 424). His own marriage was sustained until his death, providing the framework for vigorous and varied family life: evidence in itself that some *modus vivendi* had been found.

It is not very mysterious what Venetia had to offer Asquith. Aged twenty-seven in 1914, presentable, well-connected, good-natured and trustworthy, she was well qualified for an *amitié amoureuse*. What Asquith had to offer was a flattering degree of attention from a man of great eminence who was ready, indeed eager, to cut through the veils of discretion and formality with which he was customarily surrounded. It was an implicit trade-off between sex and power, mutually titillating in the way that each fed off the other. Thus the phases of the affair had a private and public synchronisation. It was no accident that it began at a time of political tension in March 1912 — 'I remember it was on the eve of the Coal Strike, which gave me one of the most trying experiences — up to then — of my public life,' Asquith recalled (p. 532). Thereafter, the emotional level was commensurate with the trying problems in British politics from which Asquith sought relief. 'Bless you beloved' was the affectionate conclusion to his letters. But, as the crisis over Irish Home Rule impinged more sharply in July 1914, the note intensified: 'My darling — you are dearer to me than I can tell you' (p. 97). Moreover, Venetia was now told, for example, of an interview ('which is most secret') between Asquith and Northcliffe (pp. 100 – 01), with none of the prevarication over mentioning actual names in which allusions to earlier meetings with Carson had been shrouded (pp. 40, 52).

When Ireland itself came to be eclipsed by the imminent threat of European war, Asquith's endearments and indiscretions scaled new heights. He claimed that 'I want you to keep au courant with what is going on step by step in these anxious days', and laced his letters with the latest information (p. 101). The disposition of British troops in France — 'all this is *most secret*' — was revealed (p. 209). His only regret was the lack of 'something like a code that we could use by telegraph' so as to cut out postal delays. 'Do you think it is impossible to invent something of the kind?' he asked Venetia (p. 191). The bright idea of the prime minister sending telegrams full of hot military secrets to his girlfriend in an amateur code of her own devising is surely beyond the reach of satire. Asquith in fact had to make do without this refinement in his indecent urge to spill the beans. On 27 October 1914 he wrote under some check of 'a terrible calamity on the sea, which I *dare* not describe, lest by chance my letter should go wrong' (p. 287). Yet, on 28 October, this information, kept from the Germans for another five weeks, was given fully as 'the sinking of the *Audacious* — one of the best & newest of the super Dreadnoughts, with a crew of about 1000 and 10 13.5 inch guns, off the North coast of Ireland' (p. 290). Name, armour, crew, position — what more would German intelligence have wanted? The Dardanelles produced the same effect a few months later. 'This as I said is supposed to be a secret . . .' (p. 423).

The parallels between the private lives of Asquith and Lloyd George are not exact. Whereas Asquith made Venetia Stanley his confidante for a couple of years before she decided to marry another man, Lloyd George made Frances Stevenson his mistress in a virtually bigamous lifelong relationship. In both cases, however, they found a release from political tension in these dangerous liaisons with women half their age. Their sentimental anniversaries were dated by political crises — the Coal Strike, the Marconi Affair — and the outbreak of war, by intensifying the pressure of public life, seems to have forced the pace in their private life. Asquith told his wife Margot in April 1915: 'These last three years I have lived under a perpetual strain, the like of which has I suppose been experienced by very few men living or dead' (Brock, p. 548). His way of coping with it was likewise out of the ordinary. Frances Stevenson and Venetia Stanley in different ways absorbed stresses which flowed from the heart of government. Did nothing flow from the heart in the other direction? The political careers of Asquith and Lloyd George are chronicled in intimate detail in the letters and in the diary, but it is easier to infer how public life fed into private concerns than vice versa.

Asquith's letters offer some useful *aperçus* upon his premiership, and on the whole do credit to his percipience and self-knowledge. On 1 August 1914 he wrote that 'if it comes to war I feel sure (this is entirely between you and me) that we shall have *some* split in the Cabinet', preparing himself for the loss of Morley 'and possibly (tho' I don't think it) of the Impeccable' (p. 140). The latter was Asquith's soubriquet for John Simon — about whose pusillanimity he was exactly right. Morley duly resigned; so Asquith's only surprise (not a big one) was the resignation of John Burns. He knew his cabinet well, and knew well too how to handle it, making it all look deceptively easy. He reported that 'not for the first (or perhaps the last) time I was able to devise a form of face-saving words which pleased everybody' over Welsh Disestablishment in August 1914 (p. 163). Looking back, in a fictive second person, on his record in March 1915, he claimed: 'You had, or acquired, a rather specialised faculty of insight and manipulation in dealing with diversities of character and temperament' (p. 471).

As a peacemaker and political broker, Asquith moved with a sure instinct, rarely allowing personal feelings to divert him from the main chance. Much turned on his relations with Lloyd George, and he showed a tactful appreciation of the fact. In peacetime they had established a fund of mutual respect and good faith. In Lloyd George's later reminiscences to

157

Frances Stevenson, the tone towards Asquith is generally cordial. Asquith's support had, he would recall, been invaluable in getting the Budget policy adopted in 1909. The Marconi Affair was hardly something to look back upon with pride, but it had likewise served to bind the two men together. It was not Asquith but Reginald McKenna whom Lloyd George saw as his real rival and antagonist. Asquith's letters show, however, that during the period of the Liberal Government he did not allow his friendship for McKenna to compromise his relations with Lloyd George. Hence the extraordinary episode at the end of March 1915, corroborated also in Lord Riddell's diary, when Lloyd George scouted anti-Asquithian gossip about a coalitionist plot by affirming his absolute loyalty to Asquith.[8] According to Frances Stevenson, Lloyd George 'went to have a talk with the P.M. about it, & found the old boy in tears' (Taylor, p. 42). His 'most bitter onslaught on McKenna' at this encounter on 29 March was confirmed by Asquith, who told Venetia Stanley that Lloyd George then 'declared that he owed everything to me; that I had stuck to him & protected him & defended him when every man's hand was against him' and that 'his eyes were wet with tears' (Brock, p. 519).

Asquith's highly personalised account ('Darling, does that interest you?') was composed for effect, but its substance does not seem exaggerated. Lloyd George's demonstrative nature made his behaviour seem in character, but what Asquith did not know was that his colleague had spent the previous month under considerable personal anxiety. In the authoritative opinion of John Grigg, Frances Stevenson almost certainly had an abortion in March 1915, accounting for her convalescent condition at this juncture.[9] She wrote appreciatively that Lloyd George 'watched and waited on me devotedly, until I cursed myself for being ill & causing him all this worry. There was no little thing that he did not think of for my comfort, no tenderness that he did not lavish on me' (Taylor, pp. 33 – 4). She was concerned that 'through it all he has been immersed in great decisions appertaining to this great crisis', as well as delivering his oratorical tour de force, 'Through Terror to Triumph'. There is no suggestion that he fell below his best as a result — indeed he maintained that 'the anxiety and trouble helped him to make a great speech, for when his mind is disturbed his whole nature is upheaved and it stimulates him to greater power of expression' (p. 34). Even so, his lack of composure in the interview with Asquith on 29 March may be attributable to his unusually fraught emotional state; and perhaps the prime minister's tears, in a month when Venetia Stanley was receiving two letters a day on average, deserve a similar explanation.

That neither man was incapacitated is shown by their actions. Asquith's lack of rancour enabled him to exert his emollient skills in mediating between Lloyd George and McKenna the following day. Asquith was 'glad to say that in the end I not only lowered the temperature, but got them

158

into first an accommodating & in the end an almost friendly mood' (Brock, p. 522). His letter of 1 April showed his gratification at the results, for 'the same pair have just been and spent over ½ an hour with me, cooing like sucking doves in a concerted chorus of agreement and apeal . . .' (p. 527). It was not to last, but while it lasted this political equilibrium undoubtedly depended upon the exertion of Asquith's peculiar gifts.

Within a couple of months of these events, Asquith's equanimity had suffered two rude shocks: privately from the engagement of Venetia Stanley to Edwin Montagu, publicly from a sudden threat to the existence of the Liberal Government. The 'Koss thesis' postulated that the crisis of May 1915 occurred because Churchill entered a conspiracy with Balfour and Lloyd George to bring the Government down, leaking information about the shell shortage in France to Colonel Repington of *The Times* with this end in view.[10] Churchill had indeed met Repington at British head-quarters and *The Times* duly carried a leader which proved highly embar-rassing to the Government which in turn was replaced within a matter of days by a coalition. *Post hoc ergo propter hoc?* In order to be persuasive, a case such as this needs evidence both as to circumstances and motive. Stephen Koss had to rely upon six documents, written by Charles Hobhouse, Arnold Bennett, Margot Asquith, H. A. Gwynne, W. M. R. Pringle and the King. In scholarly controversy there have been efforts to discredit the first; to show that possibly the second, and certainly the third and fourth, have been misconstrued; and to suggest that the fifth and sixth carry little weight. This casts some doubt upon the wider conspiracy theory. Even its most strident critic, however, has acknowledged that 'Churchill might well have been tempted to stir up controversy over the munitions issue, and even to instigate an assault on Kitchener'.[11] At the least, there remains suspicion as to Churchill's discretion when he met Repington, even if he were activated only by frustration at Kitchener's incompetence. Maybe the biographer of Haldane went too far while breaking new ground, but the biographer of Asquith, with all the available sources before him, was surely justified in claiming that 'the fact remains that there was a widespread suspicion that clandestine forces were at work'.[12] If anyone was rocking the boat, however, the finger points not to Lloyd George but to Churchill.

The fall of the Liberal Government was in effect a critical stage in the decline of Asquith and the elevation of Lloyd George in his place. At the time, however, Asquith still appeared in control of events — or rather, as adroit as ever in responding to them. The man whose heart Venetia Stanley had broken on 12 May had, within a week, moved decisively to pre-empt a challenge to his position. Taking Lloyd George into his confidence, he reconstructed his administration upon a broad basis, seeking to implicate the Unionists in its policies without surrendering vital posts to them. His old friend Haldane was sacrificed without apology, his young colleague Churchill demoted without explanation. As Churchill expostulated twenty years later: 'Not "all done by kindness"'! Not all by rosewater! These were the convulsive struggles of a man of action and of ambition at death-grips with events.'[13] Nor do these appear, at first sight, as the actions of a man prostrated by an emotional upheaval with which he could not cope.

It is, however, after the crisis, not during it, that people often go to pieces: not when the pressure is on, but when it is removed. The ending of Asquith's relationship with Venetia Stanley may not provide a short-term explanation of his behaviour during the political struggle of May 1915; but it may still point to a longer-term contrast between the confident statesman who shared his triumphs with her and the increasingly woebegone figure cut by Asquith thereafter. The relationship with Venetia was doubtless more a symptom than a cause of Asquith's inner tensions, as his febrile dependence upon it up to May 1915 illustrates. But its termination is nonetheless a significant date in political history, albeit one more apparent in retrospect than at the time.

Whether Lloyd George's loss of confidence in Asquith should be regarded as coincidental or consequential is a moot point. At any rate, May 1915 once more seems to mark an epoch. Lloyd George's later comments suggest that he did not regard the breach as predestined; and until the formation of the First Coalition there were no signs that it was impending. Indeed, having formed his new administration, Asquith wrote Lloyd George an eloquent letter of appreciation for his support, saying that his 'self-forgetfulness' brought 'to this drabness the lightning streak of nobility'. Both at the time and subsequently (when the irony became more piquant) Lloyd George took this as a remarkable tribute 'from the man who had been my colleague for ten years, and to whom I had been principal Parliamentary lieutenant for seven years', commenting later: 'The black squad of envy had not yet succeeded in poisoning the wells of confidence between captain and second officer.'[14]

One of the tantalising gaps in the Stevenson diary is the summer of 1915, following the formation of the Coalition in May. From the time it resumes in September there is a distinct change of tone. Lloyd George may not be intriguing against the Prime Minister but his support has become perceptibly more grudging — 'D. has always upheld him most loyally, whenever it came to the point' (Taylor, p. 60). The missing link can be supplied from Riddell's record of Lloyd George's growing doubts during July and August: in particular in the development of the theme that 'Asquith will not face inconvenient facts'.[15] This squares too with the timbre of Lloyd George's remarks about Asquith that autumn to C. P. Scott:[16] 'Like Palmerston in his later days, nothing to him matters so much as that he

160

should stay where he is, and quite unlike Gladstone he is never seized with a sudden impression that "something must be done".'

The Stevenson diary gives an account of an encounter between Asquith and Lloyd George which produced a friendly understanding in October 1915. Asquith is reported as saying: 'There are only two men in this Cabinet who count at all, and we are those two. If we quarrel, it will mean disaster' (p. 63). But Lloyd George's dissatisfaction with the Asquithian régime was continually fed by a sense of its inability to meet the peculiar demands of war. The 'wait-and-see' policy, he maintained later the same month, 'is all right in peace time, and often answers admirably, but in war it leads straight to disaster' (p. 67). This is the point he made a few days afterwards to Riddell: 'The P.M. is a great man, but his methods are not suited to war.'[17] The origins and nature of Lloyd George's disaffection are confirmed in all three accounts. By the end of 1915 Asquith could no longer draw on the bond of respect which had previously held the Liberal leaders together. It became a question of trying to bully him into taking a more vigorous line. At this stage the Stevenson diary confirms the impression of some passages recorded by Riddell,[18] that Lloyd George is now waiting for the right opportunity to bring about the reconstruction of the Government. Finally, in November 1916, he is steeled to act and press the issue, and, after his previous uncertainties, finds himself steady and content when the die has been cast. As the story unfolds in Frances Stevenson's transparently uncritical record, Lloyd George's rise to the premiership is a triumph for duty over inclination.

There is also a sub-plot. For at a personal level the real villains are Mrs. Asquith, with her emotional propensity to maintain a vendetta, and Reginald McKenna, who 'between them were the ruin of the late P.M.' (p. 144). McKenna, now installed as Lloyd George's successor at the Treasury, emerges in a most unflattering light, as a petty-minded and inflexible obstacle to full mobilisation for war. Other sources, not least Lloyd George's *War Memoirs*, attest to the friction between McKenna and Lloyd George. In November 1915, for instance, Lloyd George was speaking about him to Scott 'with great bitterness'.[19] But the Stevenson diary gives fullest evidence of the extent to which Lloyd George was consumed with a hearty loathing for McKenna. McKenna is blamed for virtually all the trouble within the Government. By the end of October 1916 the antagonism is reaching a climax: 'I think McKenna is the only person whom D. really detests' (p. 120). Three weeks later, words were issuing in the threat of action: 'D. literally hates him, & I do not think he will rest till he has utterly broken him' (p. 226). Lloyd George saw McKenna as Asquith's malevolent *éminence grise*: disastrous alike from the point of view of the national interest, party unity, or Asquith's own career. The tensions caused by Asquith's determination to hold on to power were thus exacerbated, and the conflict was invested with personal overtones otherwise lacking.

161

When Lloyd George ultimately sent Asquith his resignation in December 1916, he wrote: 'As you yourself said on Sunday, we have acted together for ten years and never had a quarrel, although we have had many a grave difference on questions of policy.' [20] This was a theme of which he had become fond and one which finds a good deal of corroboration. It was not a personal friendship but a partnership buoyed up by its manifest political effectiveness, as the Master of Elibank ruefully recognised in the months after it broke down: 'Theirs has been the most formidable political combination that this country has ever known. Look what has been achieved within the last ten years.' [21] Once their serious quarrel began, it engulfed the Government and the Liberal party alike; and the last phase of their relations constitutes another and more dispiriting story.[22] Even in 1923, however, Lloyd George could still remark: 'The old boy and I get on well together always when mischief makers are kept out.' [23]

Lloyd George's accession to the premiership may stand as a landmark for the conduct of the war, just as it stands also as a tombstone for the Liberal party. The consequences of the split in the party, however, need a longer-term appraisal than its causes, which, though not trivial, can be placed fairly firmly within the short unhappy lifetime of the First Coalition. Before its formation in May 1915, the Liberal party could look to its leaders as a focus of unity, not a source of division. Until then, Asquith and Lloyd George stood together as an impressively formidable partnership, their dissimilar qualities often mutually reinforcing — two strong men who shared '(perhaps) a slight weakness for the companionship of clever and attractive women'.

Notes

1 Stephen Koss, 'The destruction of Britain's last Liberal Government', *Journal of Modern History*, xl (1968). 257 – 77; substantially reprinted as 'The May Crisis', ch. v of *Lord Haldane: Scapegoat for Liberalism* (Columbia U.P., 1969).

2 A. J. P. Taylor (ed.), *Lloyd George. A diary by Frances Stevenson* (London, 1971); Michael and Eleanor Brock (eds.), *H. H. Asquith. Letters to Venetia Stanley* (Oxford, 1982). I am under a heavy debt to these editions, upon which I draw copiously below, using simply the editors' names for identification in my text, with the page reference alone for citations from the same source. Publication of these letters to Venetia Stanley was authorised by the copyright owner, the Hon. Mark Bonham Carter.

3 Lord Beaverbrook, *The Decline and Fall of Lloyd George* (London, 1963), p. 26n. Both this work and *Men and Power: 1917. 1918* (London, 1956) drew upon the diary; but *Politicians and the War, 1914 – 16* (London, 1928) was written before Beaverbrook had acquired it. The frailties of his account are painstakingly exposed in Peter Fraser, 'Lord Beaverbrook's fabrications in *Politicians and the War, 1914 – 16*', *Historical Journal*, xxv (1982), 147 – 66.

4 See Frances Lloyd George, *The Years that are Past* (London, 1967), pp. 52 – 3; the discrepancy between this date and the real peak of the Marconi Affair is brought out by A. J. P. Taylor (ed.), *My Darling Pussy. The letters of Lloyd George and Frances Stevenson, 1913 – 41* (London, 1975), p. 2.

5 Olwen Carey Evans, *Lloyd George Was My Father* (Llandysul, 1985), p. 166.

6 The Earl of Oxford and Asquith, *Memories and Reflections, 1852 – 1927* (2 vols., London, 1928), ii. 2.

7 The text of the first two paragraphs of this letter is from Brock, p. 508. The version in *Memories and Reflections*, ii. 68, begins: 'Massingham came here with a horrible tale' etc. Otherwise the only changes are omissions of the italicised words. There is a valuable appendix dealing with previous use of the letters in Brock, pp. 615 – 17. H. W. Massingham was the editor of the *Nation*; 'A.J.B.' is Balfour; 'the Assyrian' is Edwin Montagu.

8 *Lord Riddell's War Diary, 1914 – 1918* (London, 1933), p. 70.

9 John Grigg, *Lloyd George: from Peace to War, 1912 – 1916* (London, 1985), pp. 223 – 5.

10 Koss, *Lord Haldane*, pp. 192 – 4.

11 Cameron Hazlehurst, *Politicians at War, July 1914 to May 1915* (London, 1971), p. 254.

12 Stephen Koss, *Asquith* (London, 1976), p. 194; cf. the dismissive assertions in Martin Gilbert, *Winston S. Churchill*, vol. iii (London, 1971), pp. 454, 460. Stephen Koss restated his position in *The Rise and Fall of the Political Press in Britain* (2 vols, London, 1981 – 4), ii. 276 – 7.

13 Winston S. Churchill, *Great Contemporaries* (1937; Fontana edn. 1959), pp. 122 – 3.

14 David Lloyd George, *War Memoirs*, 2 vol. edn. (London, 1938), i. 145; the letter is reproduced in facsimile on pp. 140 – 1. It was enclosed in Lloyd George's letter to his wife, 26 May 1915, in Kenneth O. Morgan (ed.), *Lloyd George: family letters, 1885 – 1936* (Cardiff and London, 1973), p. 178.

15 *Riddell's War Diary*, p. 109.

16 Trevor Wilson (ed.), *The Political Diaries of C. P. Scott, 1911 – 1928* (London, 1970), p. 132.

17 *Riddell's War Diary*, p. 126.

18 *Ibid.*, p. 142. See also Lloyd George's letter to his wife, 27 December 1915: 'P.M. and his gang trying to sneak out of their pledges. If they do I wash my hands of the poltroons and come out. I have made up my mind.' Morgan (ed.), *Lloyd George: family letters*, p. 180.

19 Wilson (ed.), *Scott Diaries*, p. 158.

20 Grigg, *Lloyd George*, p. 462; cf. p. 339.

21 Arthur C. Murray, *Master and Brother. Murrays of Elibank* (London, 1945), p. 173.

22 One well told by Stephen Koss, 'Asquith versus Lloyd George: the last phase and beyond', in Alan Sked and Chris Cook (eds.), *Crisis and Controversy. Essays in honour of A. J. P. Taylor* (London, 1976), pp. 66 – 89.

23 Morgan (ed.), *Lloyd George: family letters*, p. 202.

9

Lloyd George and Electoral Reform

John Grigg

The term 'electoral reform' is sometimes used to mean the reform of every aspect of the democratic process, including the franchise, but more often perhaps, in a relatively limited sense, to mean just reform of the system of voting. In this essay the second meaning will apply, and an attempt will be made to describe David Lloyd George's attitude towards the voting system in Britain, which had an increasingly important and baleful effect on the latter stages of his career.

Practical politicians seldom take much interest in political theory, and Lloyd George took no interest in it at all. One of the many ironies of his career is that, despite leaving (as I have ventured to suggest) 'a more decisive mark upon the British State than any man since Oliver Cromwell',[1] he never gave any systematic thought to the better ordering of the State as such. In a general way he wanted it to be more democratic, and he also wanted it to be more efficient; but at no time did he devote his mind to a detailed and thorough consideration of all that true democracy might imply, or to weighing the rival claims of democracy and efficiency where the two might conflict. In all that he did to change the Constitution, both on the Parliamentary side and in the machinery of government, he acted empirically and in a spirit of improvisation. He was no philosopher-king.

This is not to say that his changes were of an ephemeral or merely tinkering kind. Many of them have not only lasted (*ce n'est que le provisoire qui dure*) but have proved their worth over many decades. When he brought them in he may have been acting under the stimulus of an immediate challenge, or in response to an immediate need, but we can now

165

acknowledge that his instinct was often sound for the future as well as for his own time. What Winston Churchill saw as his greatest quality — his 'power of living in the present without taking short views'[2] — was on the whole no less evident in his approach to constitutional problems than to all the others that he had to tackle.

Unfortunately, intuitive vision is not always an adequate substitute for reflection, and on those occasions when Lloyd George's instinct let him down he was apt to go very badly astray, because he had no reserve of well-thought-out ideas to correct and guide him. Moreover, after the end of 1905, when he began his almost seventeen-year continuous stint in high office, he tended to be more of a 'government man' than a Parliamentarian, and his flair for administrative change became correspondingly more reliable than his flair for Parliamentary reform. It is no coincidence that his two most serious mistakes, so far as the State and its institutions were concerned, both related to Parliament rather than to government.

The first was his failure to evolve a consistent and coherent policy on the Second Chamber. From his earliest years he had, of course, a deep prejudice against the House of Lords and a desire to assert the supremacy of the people's elect. In the crisis over his 1909 Budget he successfully defied the peers and to that extent achieved a major triumph for the democratic principle. But he never made up his mind what should be done about the Second Chamber. Should it be abolished, should it be reformed, or should its composition be left unchanged while its powers were either eliminated or drastically reduced? The result of this indecision and mental confusion — shared by the prime minister of the day, H. H. Asquith — was a disastrously botched measure, the 1911 Parliament Act, which in effect was more damaging to the Liberal government that introduced it than to the hereditary Chamber whose power it was supposed to curb. Neither then nor subsequently did Lloyd George clarify his thoughts on the Second Chamber question.

The other constitutional issue on which he erred most grievously was that of electoral reform. At the end of January 1917 — less than two months after he became prime minister — an all-party conference of M.P.s and peers under the chairmanship of the Speaker of the House of Commons, James Lowther, delivered a far-reaching and comprehensive report on electoral reform in the wider sense. But among its many recommendations were two on electoral reform in the more restricted sense in which the term is being used in this essay. The conference recommended unanimously that all boroughs returning three or more members should be formed into three-, four- or five-member seats using the single transferable vote (STV) method of proportional representation (PR). It was also recommended, though not unanimously, that in all elections in single-member seats where more than two candidates were nominated the method of election should be the alternative vote (AV).

166

The 1917 Speaker's conference report was an astonishing document, embodying a very large measure of agreement, even unanimity, on issues that had been — and were still generally assumed to be — among the most contentious in British politics. Lowther's achievement as chairman was by any standards impressive, but even he could not have secured the result he did at any other time. While the conference was sitting the need for reconciliation and cooperation between individuals, parties and classes became supremely evident, if the war was to be won and the nation saved. For a brief moment it could almost be said that none was for a party, all for the State; and the mood of the conference reflected the national mood. 'In the third bitter winter of trench warfare this group of thirty-two middle-aged and elderly politicians found in the conference one of the few ways open to them of making a personal contribution to the cause of national unity; at the least they were sparing the Lloyd George government a disruptive distraction from the war, and at best they might conjure all-party unity out of a dismal and perennial controversy.'[3]

There was a widespread feeling that all the recommendations of the report — which included extension of the franchise to virtually all adult males (compared with the existing barely 60 per cent) and votes for women at an unspecified age, as well as the proposed changes to the voting system — should be treated as a single indivisible package: what might nowadays be called an historic compromise. This was very much the view of Walter Long, squirearchical Tory, former candidate for the party leadership, and Colonial Secretary in the Lloyd George government, who advised his colleagues to 'take advantage of an opportunity which may never recur and decide to legislate on the lines of the report'.[4] Many Conservatives, it is true, did not agree with Long, and there was soon considerable evidence of rank-and-file opposition to the report, or at any rate to particular aspects of it, with which some Conservative leaders, notably Carson and Curzon, were in sympathy. But Bonar Law, the party leader, Austen Chamberlain and A. J. Balfour were of the same mind as Long, and their combined authority was likely to prevail with most Conservatives.

The initiative, however, lay with Lloyd George, who was not only head of the Government but also the politician who seemed to represent, in a unique degree, the patriotic and progressive spirit of the hour, by which even former opponents of his were strongly influenced. If he had acted at once, as Long advised, proposing to the Cabinet that a government bill should be introduced without delay to give effect to all the recommendations of the Speaker's conference, the whole package would probably have gone through with relative ease. But he hesitated, partly because he knew that a Parliamentary reform bill would deny him the chance of holding a snap election on the old register — an option that he was reluctant to lose. Talking to C. P. Scott the day after receiving the Speaker's report he betrayed his uncertainty, first saying that the Government would introduce 'a bill embodying the recommendations of the report', but then going on to say that 'if the bill were carried he would be morally estopped from dissolving till it could come into operation, which would take some time'. As for PR, he said that 'he would apply the principle all round or not at all'.[5]

For two months, therefore, the report was in the public domain (because it was decided to publish it at once) but without any pledge of action by the Government, or even a Parliamentary debate on its recommendations. On 28 March the Commons at last held a debate on a resolution, moved by Asquith, thanking the Speaker for his services and calling upon the Government to legislate on the lines of the report — to which a wrecking amendment was moved by a Conservative back-bencher, A. C. Salter. Lloyd George, making one of his rare Commons appearances in 1917, intervened in the debate. He had very little time, he said, for preparing speeches, so he hoped the House would allow him to 'indulge in a little plain talk', in which he would 'try to make the mind of the Government as clear as possible on a very complicated topic'. He argued against Salter and broadly in favour of Asquith's resolution. But there was one recommendation of the Speaker's conference that he went out of his way to discredit.

> I do not put the proposals about proportional representation in quite the same category as the others. I express no personal opinion upon it. I have not got any. I never made up my mind, and I really have no time to make up my mind upon it. Unless I am really forced to do so, I do not propose even to study it during the War. It is an entirely novel suggestion; it is not an essential part of the scheme. I think that the feeling of the members of Mr. Speaker's conference . . . is that they would not imperil the rest of their plan by pressing this. I cannot imagine their doing so. The common sense they have shown generally in their conclusions proves to me that they are sensible enough not to press this at the expense of the whole of their scheme, and I earnestly trust that it will not be regarded as an integral part of the proposals, because if it is it will undoubtedly make it much more difficult for the Government to find the necessary time to carry this into effect.

Thus he dismissed one of the conference's unanimous recommendations, and in so doing showed that the package was not to be treated as an integral whole, so far as the Government was concerned. He said nothing at all about the other proposed reform of the voting system (that there should be AV in single-member seats where more than two candidates were nominated), which was a majority, though not a unanimous, recommendation. To another majority recommendation, however — that the franchise should be extended to women — he gave the strongest support consistent with leaving it to a free vote of the House. To deny women a voice in the future would be 'an outrage . . . ungrateful, unjust, inequitable', and he had 'not the faintest doubt' what the decision of the House would be.[6]

The line taken by Lloyd George effectively destroyed the best chance of electoral reform in his own lifetime or for many years to come. If he had backed PR, using the argument that conference recommendations had to be implemented in full, the Commons would almost certainly have voted for it — as in due course they did for women's franchise, however reluctantly in the case of some Members. 'There can be no doubt,' Vernon Bogdanor has written, 'that proportional representation would have been carried if the Government had supported it.'[7] This judgment seems all the more convincing in view of the fact that the Commons very nearly carried PR despite Lloyd George's withering comments. When the matter was first voted on there, on 12 June 1917, the majority against it was only seven (150 to 143), and it is surely inconceivable that the sort of moral endorsement that Lloyd George gave to women's franchise — a cause in which, admittedly, he had always believed — would not have been more than enough to turn the scale in favour of PR.

His attitude not only killed electoral reform at that time; it also delayed the passage of the whole bill, because the issue was thereafter contested over many months between the two Houses of Parliament. PR appealed to many Conservatives as a means of guarding against the Left-wing extremism which, they feared, might well result from the adoption of universal manhood suffrage. It was therefore taken up by the House of Lords, only to be rejected on four subsequent occasions by the House of Commons, by majorities always substantially larger than that of 12 June 1917. At the same time people on the Left tended to feel that the alternative vote would work to their advantage in the Tory-dominated country seats: so attempts were made by the Commons to insert AV into the bill. But these were rejected by the Lords as firmly as the Commons rejected PR. Eventually, in February 1919, the bill passed into law without any serious provision for changing the voting system — with consequences that Lloyd George was to rue very bitterly a few years later.

We must return, however, to his crucial speech on 28 March 1917. If it was true that PR was, as he said, 'an entirely novel suggestion', his refusal to countenance it would be easier to understand. But the idea was not new at all; it had been in circulation for some time. At the theoretical level it became, at the very least, respectable when J. S. Mill gave it his blessing in *Thoughts on Parliamentary Reform* (1859); and Mill was by no means the only eminent person who, at about the same time, was converted to the idea (brainchild of Thomas Hare, 1806 – 91). Before long it was making itself a little felt even at the level of practical politics. In 1885 Leonard Courtney — described by F. W. Hirst as 'perhaps the greatest British statesman, since Cobden, of those who have never held Cabinet office'[8] — tried to inset PR into the redistribution bill of that year, and a similar attempt was made when new local authorities were set up in 1888. In 1908 Asquith agreed, at Courtney's request, to establish a royal commission on electoral systems, which reported in 1910 with an almost unanimous recommendation in favour of AV, though the evidence contained in the report seemed to point more logicaly to PR. Either way, the commission gave further publicity and credibility to the principle of electoral reform, which could already be seen in action, in the form of PR, in three foreign countries (Belgium, Finland and Sweden).

Like other British politicians, Lloyd George had had ample opportunity to familiarise himself with the arguments for changing the voting system, but, like most of them, had not bothered to do so, relying instead upon sheer prejudice. It was not true that he had 'no opinion' on the subject. He had an all too robust opinion, rooted in ignorance, which he expressed to C. P. Scott on 3 April 1917. PR was, he said, 'a device for defeating democracy' (whose principle was 'that the majority should rule') and 'for bringing faddists of all kinds into Parliament'.[9] Eight years later, when circumstances had transformed his outlook, he complained of inadequate briefing at the time. 'Someone ought to have come to me . . . and gone into the whole matter. I was not converted then. I could have carried it then when I was prime minister.'[10]

But the truth was that he did not want to hear what the advocates of PR were only too willing to tell him. Though he was, indeed, desperately busy, he could find time to receive a deputation of women suffragists, but not one from the Proportional Representation Society. Courtney tried very hard to see him before the reform bill was framed, but in vain. (With resigned good nature, Courtney wrote to the secretary of the PR Society: 'The P.M. may well have urgent business; but he is very slippery in engagements. He has a little virtue in trying to avoid making them.')[11] It was really nobody's fault but his own that he missed the opportunity presented to him in 1917.

The distorting effect of the existing system of voting had been made very apparent in the first two general elections of the century. In 1900 the Conservatives had a majority over the Liberals, in the popular vote, of about 230,000 in a total poll of 3½ million; yet they won 402 seats compared with the Liberals' 184. In 1906 the distortion favoured the Liberals in almost equal measure. Their popular majority over the Conservatives was about 300,000 in a total poll of 5½ million (the turn-out being up from 74 per cent to 82 per cent in 1906); yet their Parliamentary strength was 400 compared with the Conservatives' 157.

These results could be justified on the commonsensical, if also slightly casuistical, grounds put forward by Bagehot:

The judgment of Parliament ought always to be coincident with the opinion of the nation; but there is no objection to its being more decided . . . It is therefore no disadvantage, but the contrary, that a diffused minority in the country is in general rather inadequately represented. A strong conviction in the ruling power will give it strength of volition. The House of Commons should think as the nation thinks; but it should think so rather more strongly, and with somewhat less wavering.[12]

The results were also in accordance with Lloyd George's simple require-
ment for democracy, 'that the majority should rule', and he had reason
to be grateful for the moral advantage that the disproportionately large
Liberal majority in Parliament gave him during the first stage of his fight
with the Lords over his 1909 Budget.

But the two elections of 1910 showed that the first-past-the-post
system did not ensure a clear-cut Parliamentary majority for a single
party. From 1910 onwards the last Liberal government was dependent
upon the support of Labour and, more especially, of the Irish Party, since
it had no majority at all over the Tories in Parliament (and in the country
had, in fact, polled fewer votes than they in both 1910 elections). The
supposed virtues of the traditional voting system were not much in
evidence during the period immediately preceding the First World War.

Yet for Lloyd George to perceive the vices of the system it was
necessary for him to become its victim, as he did after 1922. Though in
1918 his own Liberal faction won only 1½ million votes and 133 seats,
compared with 3½ million votes and 335 seats for the Conservatives, he
remained prime minister of a coalition and the weakness of his underlying
political position was temporarily masked. Moreover the underlying
strength of Labour, now outside his coalition, was also masked, because
although the party won nearly 2.4 million votes it had only 63 seats. But
in 1922 the new pattern of politics began to appear, when the Conservatives won 5½ million votes and 345 seats, Labour 4¼ million votes
and 142 seats, while both the Liberal factions (Lloyd George and
Asquithite) combined won fewer than 3¼ million votes and only 116
seats.

'It was not yet certain, however, that Labour would replace the
Liberals in the power-sharing duopoly that the traditional voting system
has tended, however imperfectly and intermittently, to sustain. For the
time being three major parties were in contention, since the Liberals
fought again as a single party after 1922; and Lloyd George's first complaint, after the election result of that year, was that the country was
being governed by a minority.

> The most notable feature of the elections is the return of a decisive majority of
> Members by a very definite minority of the electors . . . A minority of three millions
> in a national referendum could hardly be claimed as a vote of confidence . . . It
> would be idle to pretend that in a democratic country like ours, thoroughly imbued
> with a spirit of representative government, this does not weaken the moral authority
> of the government of the day.[13]

He was now on the way to becoming an electoral reformer, and in
April 1924 he appealed to the first Labour Government to undertake a
reform of the system. 'Why can they not . . . have an immediate reform
of the electoral system which would be just? You have a system at the

present moment by which a minority of the electorate may get a majority in Parliament. That is unjust. Why cannot you reform that?'[14]

But what sort of reform did he have in mind? In September 1924, only a month before another general election (the third in three years), he was asked how far it would be desirable to make PR a substantial election issue, and replied:

> That is a stunner. It is quite clear that something should be done to put things right. Personally I am a believer in the old Radical scheme of a Second Ballot. My simple mind is entirely free from subtleties; it does not rise to the appreciation, even if it rises to the comprehension, of the intricacies of Proportional Representation . . . but I would prefer any plan to the present one. The present system might at any moment give you a Socialist majority in spite of the fact that only a minority of the people are voting for the present government. I am not an Alternative Vote man; I don't like there to be a second man when I am fighting for first place. I would prefer either a Second Ballot or Proportional Representation.[15]

This extraordinarily muddled answer, given off the cuff, shows how ignorant Lloyd George still was of the detailed implications of electoral reform, though converted to it in principle. If the two systems were to be bracketed together for the purposes of argument, it should have been the Second Ballot and AV rather than the Second Ballot and PR, because AV, like the Second Ballot, is not a proportional system. His comments on PR are still rather reminiscent, indeed, of what he said about it in his 1917 Commons speech: patronising and facetiously dismissive. His prejudice against PR had been reinforced by the experience of Holland and France where, he alleges, 'it has led to the formation of endless groups' (more justly attributable, in fact, to the state of politics in those countries than to the system itself). Yet he has reached the point of saying that any system, even PR, would be preferable to the one that actually exists in Britain.

The general election of 1924 brought about a further evolution in his attitude, because the Conservatives and Labour emerged clearly as duopolists, with the Liberals polling fewer than 3 million votes compared with 5½ million for Labour and 8 million for the Conservatives, while winning only 40 seats compared with Labour's 151 and the Conservatives' 419. Now, at last, he was concerned not only with saving democracy from the scandal of minority government, but with ensuring proper and fair representation for minorities. In a speech at Oxford in June 1926 he said that the task of political emancipation would not be complete 'until you have some method of securing that electors can be represented even though they do not constitute a majority in any particular constituency'.[16]

The following year he sent a message to be read out at the annual meeting of the Proportional Representation Society — for him almost the equivalent of going to Canossa — in which he said:

The franchise is the stamp of citizenship, but it is an empty privilege unless it enables the citizens to make their voices heard in Parliament. At the last election millions of citizens had votes that were of no value. The responsibility for remedying this defect rests with the Government, and it will be a crime against the nation and against all that representative government stands for if legislation is not introduced in time for the next general election, guaranteeing just representation for all sections of enfranchised citizens. I wish every success to the cause for which your Society stands.[17]

But of course the Baldwin government then in office had no intention of making life easier for Lloyd George, and the next election gave the Liberals under his leadership 2½ million more votes in the country but only 59 seats in Parliament.

Since Labour's majority over the Conservatives was, however, only 28, the Liberals held the balance of power, and it seemed that they should be able to use their position to secure electoral reform. Ramsay MacDonald was as hostile to Lloyd George as Baldwin, and as reluctant to forfeit the advantage that an unjust voting system had recently begun to confer upon his party. To PR, moreover, he had been almost consistently opposed, even when others in his party supported it. All the same, he had to make some concession to the Liberals in order to stay in office, and in the 1929 King's Speech another inquiry into electoral reform was promised.

This was set up in December under Lord Ullswater, none other than the James Lowther of 1917 fame, now ennobled. But the atmosphere in 1929 was very different from that which had enabled him to achieve such a miracle of political ecumenism on the earlier occasion. Partisanship was now the order of the day, and the Ullswater conference was marked by a conflict between rival voting systems similar to that which had occurred between the two Houses of Parliament in 1917, and similarly motivated. Liberals and Tories demanded that any change should include PR, while Labour would only consider AV. The conference therefore broke up in July 1930 with no agreement between the parties.

Faced with Labour's implacable opposition to PR, and insistence upon AV, if there had to be reform at all, Lloyd George began to argue that even AV would be better than nothing — as in 1924 he had argued that even PR would be better than nothing. The King's Speech in October 1930 contained an unspecified commitment to electoral reform, and in December Lloyd George told a meeting of Liberal candidates:

We must, before the election, secure that the decision [of the election] shall at any rate be a majority decision. How? There is no doubt at all how it can be done, and that is by the system of electoral reform that would secure representation in proportion to the numbers of each party in the country. The question which you and ourselves have to consider is that, if we cannot achieve Proportional Representation, is it worth-while to get the second best? [Cries of 'No' and 'Yes'] I do not want you to say yes or no until you hear my argument. Then you can judge. It is always the most difficult thing in life to make up your mind, if you cannot get the best, whether it is worth-while going

173

for the second best. The Alternative Vote — I am not for it ['hear, hear'] — but the thing I have to consider is, if that is all I can get, is it worth-while? There are two things you would achieve by means of it. The Liberal Party at any rate would secure a representation which would be nearer, I do not want to say much nearer, what it ought to secure in proportion to its numbers . . . The second thing, which is more important, is that AV, with all its defects, would secure the defeat of Protection in the absence of a [national] majority [in favour of it].[18]

In the event a reform bill was introduced incorporating AV, but before it could be carried into law the Labour government was overwhelmed by economic circumstances beyond its control. 1931 put an end to any chance of electoral reform for at least half a century. It also put an end to Lloyd George's chances of returning to power in peace-time. He thus shared the fate of the cause that he had failed, disastrously, to champion when he was at the zenith of his power.

Looking back to that earlier time, we should of course make every allowance for the extreme pressure under which he was living and working so soon after becoming leader of the country during one of the biggest crises in its history. It was no time for him to be taking a crash course in J. S. Mill, even if such an exercise had been in his nature, nor could he be expected to give his mind in detail even to important practical questions that had no direct bearing on the war. But there was no need for him to do anything of the sort, so far as the report of the Speaker's conference was concerned. Definite recommendations had been made as part of an agreed package, and it was only necessary for him to give the package his general support on behalf of the government. If there were items in it that he knew or cared relatively little about, then he was quite free to say nothing about them in his speech, reserving his comments for those items, such as votes for women, that he wished positively and personally to endorse.

His negative remarks about PR were quite gratuitous, and had the effect not only of excluding electoral reform from the bill but also of delaying the bill's passage. Why was he so prejudiced? It was unfortunate that he and Leonard Courtney, PR's leading advocate, had drifted apart on other issues. They had been at one in opposing the Boer War, but Courtney lost his seat in the 1900 election, so there was little time for them to develop a close association as opponents of that war in Parliament. Later, after he became a peer (in 1906), Courtney's views on foreign policy evolved on lines very different from Lloyd George's. In 1911 he was so horrified by Lloyd George's Agadir speech that he rebuffed a friendly overture at the time,[19] and in 1914 he was against British intervention. Soon he became identified in Lloyd George's mind with other dangerous cranks (as he saw them) favouring a negotiated peace before the Germans had been defeated in the field, and it is fair to suggest that Lloyd George's prejudice against PR, as a cranky notion, may have been correspondingly increased.

He was by no means alone, indeed he was typical, in connecting the idea of PR with 'faddists'. H. G. Wells deplored this connection.

> Proportional representation is not a faddist proposal, not a perplexing ingenious complication of a simple business; it is the carefully worked out right way to do something that hitherto we have been doing in the wrong way. It is no more an eccentricity than the running of trains to their destinations instead of running them without notice into casually selected sidings and branch lines.

But he suggested a reason for the misunderstanding: 'Perhaps it is because of that hideous mouthful of words for a thing which would be far more properly named *Sane Voting*.' [20]

To Lloyd George, as no doubt to many others, the mathematical character of PR made it seem too subtle by half and, in a way, un-British (even though invented by an Englishman). Always more literate than numerate — Lewis Harcourt said that he used figures as adjectives — he was instinctively repelled by a system that involved more than simple addition and subtraction. Yet his inability to deal with figures was at least partly a pose. As a child he had first become conscious of superior intellectual powers while reading Euclid in an oak-tree, and in August 1914 he astonished experts by the rapidity of his grasp of financial technicalities which, until then, he had not bothered to master. If he had ever felt the urge to understand the workings of PR, he could have understood them quickly enough.

His attitude to electoral reform was cavalier rather than unprincipled. His belief in democracy was genuine, though his credentials as a democrat were often impugned, as, for instance, in a savage passage quoted by Stephen Koss from an article by A. G. Gardiner: 'He plays with democracy . . . he is the antithesis of a democrat; he is a demagogue . . . His method is to break up the organised forces of society and to create a mob opinion — fluid, fluctuating, blown about by every wind of doctrine.' [21] Most of those who have achieved success in democratic politics have been capable, at times guilty, of demagoguery; and Lloyd George was certainly no exception. But when he said that democracy meant, to him, majority rule, he meant what he said, and his changing attitude to electoral reform was throughout consistent with that proclaimed belief.

Far from wishing to create mob rule, he was essentially a man of the Centre (though Left Centre), soon bored, even disgusted, by excesses of partisanship and always willing, after stating his own case with the utmost vigour, to settle a dispute by compromise. He felt that the traditional ding-dong of parties often misrepresented majority opinion in the country, which tended to be more moderate and less doctrinaire than that of party activists. Hence his desire to promote coalition government even before the First World War, and his ready participation in it from 1915 onwards.

175

A logical corollary of his rejection of the traditional party system was that the traditional voting system should be changed. Yet he was slow to perceive this link — too slow for his own or the country's good. In 1917 he was too much of a conservative, in one respect, to support a change that many who, in other respects, were far more conservative than he ever was were willing to face. Such are the vagaries of great men, and so unpredictable is their influence on the course of history.

Notes

1 *The Young Lloyd George* (London, 1973). In his foreword to Kenneth Morgan's *Lloyd George* (London, 1974) A. J. P. Taylor writes: 'It is difficult to resist the feeling that Lloyd George was the greatest ruler of England since Oliver Cromwell' — a slightly different, and perhaps rather more debatable, proposition.

2 *The World Crisis*, chap XV.

3 Martin Pugh, *Electoral Reform in War and Peace, 1916 – 18* (London, 1978), pp. 75 – 6.

4 Memorandum for the Cabinet, 2 February 1917.

5 *The Political Diaries of C. P. Scott, 1911 – 1928*, ed. Trevor Wilson (London, 1934), entry for 28 January 1917, pp. 258 – 9.

6 *Hansard*, Fifth Series, cii, L.G.'s speech, cols. 486 – 496.

7 V. Bogdanor, *The People and the Party System* (Cambridge, 1981), p. 129.

8 *D.N.B.*, vol. covering 1912 – 21, p. 128.

9 C. P. Scott, *Diaries*, p. 274.

10 *Ibid.*, entry for 13 – 14 November 1925, pp. 484 – 5.

11 Courtney to John Humphreys, 10 April 1917 (archive of the Electoral Reform Society).

12 W. Bagehot, 'Parliamentary Reform', *Collected Works*, ed., N. St. John-Stevas, vi (quoted in Bogdanor, *op. cit.*, pp. 142 – 3).

13 Article in *Daily Chronicle*, 22 November 1922.

14 Speech at Llanfairfechan, 22 April 1924.

15 Answer to question at social gathering of League of Young Liberals, Bangor, 12 September 1924, where instead of making a speech L.G. 'submitted himself to cross-examination'.

16 Speech at Oxford Univ. Lib. Club, 15 June 1926.

17 Message to P.R. Society, 25 May 1927.

18 Speech at Nat. Lib. Club, 5 December 1930.

19 G. P. Gooch, *Life of Lord Courtney* (London, 1920), p. 566.

20 *An Englishman Looks at the World* (London, 1914).

21 Stephen Koss, *Fleet Street Radical*, p. 249 (quoting A. G. Gardiner, 23 November 1918).

10

British Liberalism and India, 1917-45

Hugh Tinker

An examination of 'the Indian problem' reveals in typical fashion the Liberal drift into the margin of British politics in the 1920s and '30s.[1] The reforms of 1917 – 19, which first recognised that the political destiny of India would culminate in full self-government, were entirely a Liberal innovation. In the tortuous process whereby, between 1929 and 1935, another major advance towards that goal was laboriously fabricated, individual Liberals played important roles in putting the package together but did not make the central decisions. The Liberal Edwin Montagu made the initial dynamic forward move, though its importance was severely damaged by opposition both in Britain and India. Two other Liberals influenced the direction of events at critical moments — Lord Reading and Sir John Simon; while a third, Lord Lothian, contributed significantly to implementing policy. The Liberal point of view was cogently expressed in parliamentary debate during the critical years 1929 – 35 by Sir Herbert Samuel and Isaac Foot. But apart from Samuel, successive Liberal Party leaders — Asquith, Lloyd George, Archibald Sinclair — had only the most superficial acquaintance with India, and of these only Lloyd George made any contribution whatever — in ways which were as opportunistic and unpredictable as any in his latter-day interventions. In the final dénouement, 1945 – 47, the Liberal Party remained on the sidelines, denied any active part.

Individual Liberals reflected the fissiparous tendencies in the party overall. Two Liberal politicians genuinely devoted to India, Josiah Wedgwood and Wedgwood Benn, moved over to the Left; Simon, Churchill, and to some extent Lothian shifted Right. Others disappeared from the parliamentary scene, as did Montagu and Foot. Throughout the thirty years under review, the Liberal Party was not diverted from a long-term policy of preparing India for self-government, which, it was hoped, would come about within the British Commonwealth as a partnership between West and East. Yet, having accepted the principle, Liberals were not sufficiently alert to the need to take time by the forelock.[2]

The Liberal Party's inadequacy was compounded by what seemed to be a continuing situation within British politics from 1919 onwards: namely that 'We are all Liberals now.' Concerning India this might not seem easy to substantiate in view of the Diehard revolt against Montagu, 1921 – 22, and the Diehard rearguard fight from 1931 against the Act eventually passed in 1935. Yet underneath this surface ferment Montagu's implementation of the Declaration of August 1917 proved to be irreversible. That started India on the long road to independence, and this was accepted by mainstream leaders in both Labour and Conservative governments throughout the period. Sam Hoare, that orthodox Tory, was accused of 'becoming dangerously radical' by Reading on one occasion and was extolled by Sir Malcolm Hailey for following in Montagu's footsteps.[3]

There was a weakness within the widely accepted Liberal philosophy: this was the fallacy that freedom and equality could be conceded by stages. This had been the accepted policy of Liberals (and even some Conservatives) in Britain between 1832 and 1918 in admitting the masses into the electoral process. But self-government on the instalment plan was perceived as a denial of liberty and equality by almost all politically-conscious Indians. It was Montagu's flash of genius that he came to recognise this. In 1920, he wrote:

> As soon as the Indians were told that . . . they were to become partners with us it instilled in their minds an increased feeling of existing subordination and a realisation of everything by which this subordination was expressed . . . I am convinced in my own mind that that has been the fatal mistake of our policy in India. We ought to have let Indians run their own show from the beginning with all its inefficiency and imperfections.[4]

Operating from within a Coalition government moving steadily to the Right, while confronted with a mass movement of protest in India, Montagu endeavoured to ease his dilemma by emphasising that India was now acquiring an accepted place among the family of nations. He tried to assert this new status independently of his Cabinet colleagues — and he fell. The Conservative Viceroy, Lord Irwin, glimpsed the same truth — that India's new status must be recognised — for just a fleeting moment. Unlike Montagu he had not worked out the implications of his moment of revelation.

Edwin Montagu was a loner, in politics and in life: emotional, easily wounded, theatrical at times, he believed that he possessed a special

179

empathy with the Orient. One is reminded of the young Disraeli, also a marginal man on the fringe of the British political Establishment. Montagu, a follower of Asquith, was nevertheless drawn into the orbit of Lloyd George in the great internecine rift. When Austen Chamberlain resigned over the Mesopotamia scandal, the India Office was too tempting to refuse. He arrived at a critical moment in the war when Russian collapse and the mutinies in the French army seemed to threaten defeat before the Americans could help to turn the tide. At this moment of crisis Montagu gave India the assurance that imperial rule must be succeeded by Home Rule, full self-government. The famous Declaration of August 1917 was issued, as Sir John Simon stated later with uncharacteristic candour, 'When we had our backs to the wall, when the Indian war effort on the side of the British was of great importance.'

Securing Cabinet approval for the Declaration was relatively easy: even Curzon was prepared to help with its drafting. But what did it mean? What commitment was being assumed? In the same year of crisis the Foreign Secretary, Balfour, announced that Britain would recognise a Jewish 'National Home' in Palestine, a declaration which secured the support of American Jewry but was without any precise meaning. Montagu intended that his Declaration would be implemented in very definite terms and without delay. And what did this portend? An author generally inimical to Montagu acknowledges that because of the Declaration it was settled 'that India should advance down the path of parliamentary democracy on the Westminster model . . . And it was inevitable that the decision should be what it was.'[5]

Montagu decided that the next stage was to visit India. No Secretary of State had done this before (it was supposed to impinge on the Viceroy's authority) but Montagu seized the opportunity to demonstrate that a new era had opened. He intended to ascertain how Indian expectation concerning 'the realization of responsible government' could best be satisfied. He proposed to draft the new constitution in partnership with Lord Chelmsford, the Viceroy, but he also wanted British and Indian public opinion to be associated with his initiative. So he was accompanied by Lord Donoughmore, an Irish Tory Peer, and on arrival in November 1917 he recruited a leading Indian politician to work with them: Bupendranath Basu, a former President of the Indian National Congress.

The ground had been prepared. Lionel Curtis, 'the Prophet' of the *Round Table* group, had a scheme for *Dyarchy* ('government by two rulers') which transferred power at the provincial level for the 'nation-building' functions of government to Ministers who would be elected Indian politicians. Montagu adapted the Curtis scheme, giving it more political input, taking the cold, withdrawn Viceroy along with him.[6] The outcome was the Montagu-Chelmsford Report, devised 'to give the people of India some responsibility for their own government'.

Back at home, even before the Armistice was signed, Lloyd George was planning to call a General Election in which he would ask the country to elect a new Coalition government. He met Montagu, H. A. L. Fisher, and the other Liberal Ministers on 6 November, 1918 and a major factor in their decision to go along with this departure from the old party politics was the Prime Minister's undertaking to back the Indian reforms, exerting the necessary pressure on the Tories.[7]

The new Coalition government was very different from the one before: out of the 472 new Coalition M.P.s only 127 were Liberals, or 'National Liberals' as they were named in contrast to the 'Wee Free' Asquithian Liberals, reduced to 36 in number. Lloyd George had delivered himself over to the Conservatives, though this was not immediately perceived by 'the Man who Won the War'.

Montagu went ahead with draft legislation, but this was by no means his only strategy. He was determined to demonstrate that India had already attained parity with the White Dominions. India had been accepted into the 'Imperial Cabinet' which Lloyd George, the erstwhile anti-imperialist,[8] established. Montagu insisted that, as the Dominions had secured separate representation at the Versailles Peace Conference, India must be treated the same. India's representatives at Versailles were the Maharaja of Bikanir and S. P. Sinha, a moderate Congress leader. India was a signatory of the Peace Treaty and a founder member of the League of Nations. Also, Sinha was created a Peer and appointed Under Secretary of State, responsible for piloting the reform legislation through the House of Lords.

Montagu's legislation was well received. It went through all its stages in the House of Commons as an agreed, all-party measure, without a division. From the Wee Free benches there was some attempt to enlarge the scope of the Bill. Montagu realised, however, that to retain Conservative goodwill demanded an exercise in tightrope walking and he declined to go further. He maintained that the measure demonstrated that Parliament was ready 'to grant with enthusiasm to India, as soon as may be, the stages of the surrender of her trusteeship to a well-qualified Indian government'. He told the radicals that Dyarchy could be reviewed well in advance of the ten-year period laid down in the Act, though the system *must* be reviewed after ten years.

None of this appeared to upset the Conservatives: Sir Henry Craik praised Montagu's statesmanship and promised that the whole House would 'do all it can . . . to make this advance successful'. Earl Winterton and Ormsby Gore struck a similar note, and only Walter Elliot was captious, calling the measure 'Whiggish'. From the opposition Liberal front bench Sir Donald Maclean hailed 'this great Liberal measure' and a little wickedly surmised that its author might soon find himself among their number. Replying to all this praise, Montagu declared that this was the proudest moment of his life.

Montagu was exceptionally lucky in getting his reforms through then, for already the situation in India had been dramatically reversed. The Government of India, fearful of Bolshevism (undefined) had forced through repressive laws (the so-called Rowlatt Acts) over the combined votes of all the Indian non-official legislators. Gandhi aroused India with a Day of Prayer which escalated into violence. A mob in Amritsar attacked random Europeans and the local army commander, General Dyer, marched a contingent into an enclosed square, Jalianwala Bagh, and fired indiscriminately, killing numbers variously computed between 200 and 400.[9] Details of this massacre were slow to emerge. Not till late in 1919 was the full horror revealed, when a Committee of Inquiry was appointed, headed by a Scottish Judge. The evidence before this committee discredited General Dyer, and the Army Council informed Dyer that he could expect no further employment.

Dyer suffered litttle (he was due to retire shortly) but his 'punishment' unleashed primitive forces among the Conservatives. Led by Carson, their demand for Dyer's vindication became a venomous attack upon the Secretary of State. Unwisely, Montagu responded to the raw emotionalism of his assailants by his own brand of emotion. He accused Brigadier Dyer of a 'doctrine of terrorism', of inflicting 'racial humiliation' on innocent Indians. An incident where an Indian wedding party had been flogged he described as 'frightfulness' (a word much used about alleged German wartime atrocities). 'Are you,' he asked the bellowing Tories, 'going to keep your hold upon India by terrorism, racial humiliation and subordination and frightfulness or are you going to rest it upon the goodwill, and the growing goodwill of the people of the Indian Empire?'

Those who came to his rescue were mainly opposition Liberals, such as Commander Kenworthy and Wedgwood Benn. Among his own colleagues Montagu received greatest support from Winston Churchill, Secretary of State for War, directly responsible for Dyer's early retirement. He employed arguments similar to those of Montagu but without the wild language, observing 'frightfulness is not a remedy known to the British pharmacopeia'.

In view of his later record on India it is instructive to read his verdict in 1920: 'What we want is cooperation and goodwill . . . to look at the whole of this vast question and not merely at one point.' He insisted that the relative calm in India (compared with what was happening in Ireland and Egypt) was 'largely due to the constructive policy' of reform to which Montagu had made 'a great personal contribution'.

When they had all finished and the last cry of Bolshevism had been uttered, 129 Diehards voted against Montagu (they included the swindler Horatio Bottomley) while among the 250 who supported him were many Tories later associated with India such as Samuel Hoare and Edward Wood (to become Lord Irwin, and eventually Lord Halifax) together with all the opposition members.

Having successfully asserted India's right to a separate voice at Versailles, Montagu tried to gain a similar position in the negotiations over the future of Turkey. The Muslims of India identified strongly with the maintenance of the Caliphate or Khalifat, and Gandhi took this up as an issue to bind them more closely to the Congress. Lloyd George was an ardent Hellenist: he pressed the claims of Greece against Turkey. Montagu bombarded him with memoranda, bringing a retort from the Prime Minister: 'Throughout the conference [then in progress at San Remo] your attitude has often struck me as being not so much that of a member of the British Cabinet but of a successor on the throne of Aurangzeb' (25 April 1920).[10]

Storm signals were clearly visible, but at least Montagu acquired a new Viceroy, much more receptive to his ideas than Chelmsford. Lord Reading, who took over on 2 April 1921, shared the vision of a self-governing India. Montagu wrote to the new Viceroy, 'I am quite sure now that we have got to go in for Indianization. We have got to realise that self-government does not merely mean political reform but the substitution of an indigenous administration for a foreign administration.' Reading replied, 'I am in entire agreement with you. I think it useless to make pronouncements of our policy to give India . . . full Dominion Status and yet at the same time to hesitate to put her in a position to manage her affairs when they have been entrusted to her.'[11]

Within the Coalition government the Liberal Ministers were becoming isolated. The backbench Tories were increasingly at odds with Lloyd George's policies. In Ireland he had backed a campaign of repression, yet it became clear that southern Ireland could now only be held down by an army of occupation. At last, in December 1921, a Treaty was signed with the Sinn Fein leaders (excepting DeValera) whereby Ireland, without six of the Ulster counties, was conceded Dominion Status. Ties with the United Kingdom were effectively severed. It was a bitter pill for the Coalition Tories to swallow: the triumph of all that they had opposed for forty years, and their resentment increased when it became clear that the settlement had yielded not peace but further civil war. Their fury was focussed on Montagu. His attempt to introduce a new era in Indian politics, and to neutralise Gandhi's campaign without turning him into a martyr were seen as a betrayal similar to that in Ireland. In February 1922, the extremist Tory Joynson-Hicks took advantage of the debate on the Speech from the Throne to censure Montagu under whom, he alleged, there was 'unrest and lawlessness', 'the direct result of the administration of the Secretary of State during the last three years' in which he had 'used his position as a Liberal Minister in a Coalition Government to govern India in accordance with Liberal and Home Rule ideas'.

Lloyd George came to his colleague's defence by claiming that he had actually been 'trying to walk a moderate path': there was 'no cause for panic'. British rule was not coming to an end: that would create chaos: 'We cannot divest ourselves of that trust.' The censure motion was defeated by 249 votes to 64 votes, a better result than after the Dyer debate. Montagu must have felt reassured. Perhaps that was the reason he now plunged. Lloyd George persisted in his pro-Greek policy, although almost on his own. Reading was increasingly worried by the impact upon the Indian Muslims. Mindful of India's new international status he telegraphed London (1 March 1922) listing the revisions to the Turkish peace proposals which the Government of India considered essential, starting with the evacuation of Constantinople. The telegram ended: 'We press for permission to publish the foregoing . . . forthwith.'

Montagu circulated the text to the Cabinet, but before receiving any comment he authorised Reading to go ahead with publication. As Foreign Secretary, Curzon took umbrage, but was content to insist that this must not happen again. At this time, Lloyd George was absent from London. On his return he at once demanded Montagu's resignation.[12] On 15 March, Montagu delivered his explanation to the House: 'I cannot cure myself of the belief that this reason [breach of Cabinet solidarity] for my resignation was a pretext', devised by the Prime Minister to placate the Diehards. To have occupied the India Office 'was the proudest title an Englishman can hold'. He ended abruptly: 'This is the unhappiest day of my life,' and walked from the Chamber, never to speak there again.

Lloyd George did not find it easy to replace Montagu. Two Conservative grandees turned him down — the Earl of Derby and the Duke of Devonshire; Baldwin's name was considered and rejected (a decision Lloyd George may later have regretted) and the post went to an amiable Tory peer, Lord Peel.[13] His Under Secretary in the House of Commons was another Tory, Lord Winterton, increasingly noted for Diehard views.

The last occasion on which India was debated in the summer of 1922 demonstrated how far the Coalition had edged to the Right. Hoare initiated a debate expressing the 'grave anxiety and discontent in the ranks of the [Indian] Civil Service'. Lloyd George was defiant. Dyarchy was 'a great and important experiment, but still an experiment'. Remembering Ireland he affirmed 'Britain will in no circumstances relinquish her responsibility for India . . . If Britain withdrew her strong hand nothing would ensue except division, strife, conflict and anarchy.' They had to honour a trust: 'Which I hope we shall transmit to our descendants in generations to come.' He went on to produce his celebrated aphorism that the ICS was 'the steel frame of the whole structure'.

The Diehards were not impressed. They were already planning to leave LG. The Liberals were appalled. Maclean asked, did the Prime Minister threaten the people of India? Josiah Wedgwood demanded: 'What evil genius inspired the Prime Minister with the necessity to make this speech today?' Montagu had laid down a 'perfectly steadfast, settled policy'. This was not replaced by 'alternate threats and concessions'. It would prove fatal in India as it had in Ireland.

The Conservative Party at last ended the Coalition and at the subsequent election in October 1922 they were handsomely rewarded with 344 seats. The Liberals, still divided between Lloyd Georgeites and Asquithians, could only muster 113: Montagu was not among them.[14]

Unexpectedly, Baldwin offered the divided Liberals the perfect opportunity to reunite by announcing his conversion to Protection (i.e. Tariffs). He called another election for December 1923, and Asquith and LG hastily patched up their differences. Montagu was still left out in the cold. One year later he was dead.

In the December election the Liberals won 158 seats. Combining with Labour, they turned out the Conservatives. The King invited Ramsay MacDonald to form a government. He passed over the obvious choice of Wedgwood for the India Office to install Lord Olivier, a former civil servant, who took no initiative during his brief period of office. Reading at once wrote to Olivier to suggest that constitutional progress should be advanced.[15] The Statutory Commission laid down under the 1919 Act might be set to work without waiting until ten years had elapsed. Olivier was 'perturbed' at this suggestion, and nothing was done.

When MacDonald had to call another election in October 1924, Labour's representation fell from 191 to 151; the Tories won 412 seats, and the Liberals were left with a rump of forty M.P.s. The party was never after this to recover any respectable parliamentary strength.

Under these conditions the future of Liberalism in Britain depended considerably upon the effectiveness of the Liberal Press. So far as India was concerned, the *Manchester Guardian* was most important. Its circulation was largely concentrated in the cotton belt (where Gandhi's boycott of British textiles had bitten deep) yet the *Guardian* held to its 'Progressivist' policy. C. P. Scott invited C. F. Andrews, the intimate friend of Gandhi and Tagore, to become their correspondent in India. He assured Andrews: 'It is only through men like you . . . that we shall ever do our duty in India . . . Respect and affection must be at the root of policy' (16 October 1926).[16]

The new Tory Secretary for India was Lord Birkenhead. Geoffrey Dawson, editor of *The Times*, wrote of his 'utter neglect of his work . . . Careful inquiries . . . suggest that the number of hours which he devotes to India per week is about three'.[17] In December 1925, Reading renewed his proposal that the Statutory Commission should be brought forward but Birkenhead merely procrastinated.

The new Viceroy, Lord Irwin, was a High Churchman and a High Tory. In his first year in India, the political direction which had become somewhat more encouraging under Reading deteriorated. Hindu-Muslim conflict was a sinister feature. In the summer of 1926 the question of advancing the Statutory Commission was raised again. Irwin insisted that it must be composed only of British parliamentarians: if Indians were included they would press their own policies and a unanimous report would be impossible. Mischievously, Birkenhead suggested that by including both Hindu and Muslim members they could guarantee disagreement and thus prevent the Commission from recommending any 'very considerable advance'.[18] Irwin's view prevailed, and in the spring of 1927 Sir John Simon was invited to become Chairman of the all-British Commission.

Simon was becalmed in his long and tortuous political voyage. A lieutenant of Asquith, he was out of parliament following the 1918 election but returned in 1922. Tipped as Asquith's successor he now had nothing much to succeed. He shared his master's aversion to LG, though he was a close friend of Reading, who might have been counted as a Georgeite. With no clear political future as one of the scanty band uncertainly following the Pied Piper of Politics, the prospect of an important cross-bench assignment was attractive. But it was not so easy to provide him with colleagues. Before their names had been released, Geoffrey Dawson informed Irwin: 'I have succeeded by purely Socratic methods in discovering the whole personnel of the Commission, and here I am bound to say that I am just a little shocked. The Chairman may be very good indeed, but he has a terribly weak team behind him . . . The best that can be said . . . is that they may be tame and harmless. It is really a one man show.'[19]

The members selected were all political neutrals on India. Josiah Wedgwood was once again passed over by Ramsay MacDonald as too radical, and the Tories chosen were all Baldwinites except for Lord Burnham who tended toward Diehard views. Although Simon was the solitary Liberal member the group was augmented by Walter Layton, a distinguished economist, who was commissioned to compose an extensive report on public finance.

Whatever their merits or demerits the Commission members were anathema to all shades of Indian opinion. No previous investigation into Indian government during the previous half century had failed to include Indian members. There was, temporarily, complete unity amongst almost every shade of Indian poitical opinion: they would have nothing to do with the inquiry. Preparation at the government level was unprecedented: the Government of India and each of the provincial governments submitted memoranda of immense length.[20] The Commission toured India from 3 February to 31 March 1928, and again (also visiting Burma) from 11 October 1928 to 13 April 1929. Everywhere they were met by crowds holding black flags aloft and chanting 'Simon Go Back'. Various devices were introduced to mitigate the initial blunder of excluding Indians: they did not even placate the Indian Moderates, the Liberals. The demonstrations increased in violence while administrative counter-measures also became more violent. The Commission began to feel that *they* were under attack, as when bombs were thrown in the central legislature soon after Simon had paid a visit. They toiled on, but as the end approached Simon informed Dawson: 'I sometimes feel as though I had been asked to spend two years over a gigantic crossword puzzle with the tip whispered into my private ear that the puzzle has *no* solution.' [21]

The Commission returned home to find that another election was in the offing. This time Lloyd George had great hopes with his programme 'We Can Conquer Unemployment', but the result was another disappointment for the Liberals. With 5½ million votes they secured only 59 seats. Labour, with 287 M.P.s, were out in front (the Conservatives retained 260 seats). MacDonald selected Wedgwood Benn for the India Office: he had defected from the Liberal party less than two years before (an Asquithian, he was at odds with LG). Meanwhile in India, Irwin, facing a massive campaign of civil disobedience, had come to realise the need for an alternative to repression. Motilal Nehru had led a committee which drafted a constitution intended as a reply to Simon, demanding Dominion Status, but Jawaharlal Nehru and the younger leaders saw this as out of date. Gandhi hesitated before another struggle. Irwin was under pressure: as later in his foreign policy, he went for appeasement. He arrived in England on leave just as the new Labour government was taking its first steps. He brought a proposal for a new deal, based on the reiteration of Dominion Status as the goal, together with an invitation to political India to attend a Round Table Conference to discuss the way forward. Wedgwood Benn was receptive, while MacDonald was always enthusiastic about lofty sentiment not too precisely spelled out.

The proposition was put to Simon. In order that the Commission would appear to be taking the initiative, he would write to the Prime Minister suggesting convening a conference to consider the future of India (including the Princely states) and the Prime Minister would reply, signifying agreement and indicating that 'India should . . . be enabled to attain in due season the full status of a self-governing Dominion.' [22]

For six weeks Whitehall slumbered while Ministers and officials relaxed. Then, on 17 September Simon was asked to meet the Prime Minister two days later; he was informed that a revised Draft declaration would be sent to him. When received, this strengthened the statement about Dominion Status. Simon called his colleagues together on 24 September to review the situation. By now he realised that what had at first appeared a means of enhancing the role of the Commission, as sponsor of a constitutional get-together, had become a move which would up-stage them, nullifying their efforts.

The meeting on 24 September supported this point of view. All four Conservatives were against a Dominion Status Declaration, with varying degrees of vehemence. For Labour, Hartshorn wanted to be helpful to

187

Irwin but added that such a statement 'would certainly be regarded as surrender to the boycotters.' Attlee went around the question: 'The Commission's original plan in July was not merely to help the Viceroy but also to give the Commission the opportunity of making the gesture. The letter as now altered would remove the latter object. He was strongly in favour of the Government taking action without the Commission coming in.'

We need not pursue the comedy of errors which followed, with the Labour Lord Chancellor, Sankey, indicating that he had accepted the Declaration only because he believed the Commission was in favour and Baldwin giving his assent on the same understanding. Nobody seemed to be quite sure what the intention of the announcement was, anyway; only Reading was insistent in adhering to the formula announced in August 1917.[23] The atmosphere of muddle was compounded when MacDonald went off to America (28 September) and Irwin returned to India (10 October). Because of the Commission's objections, when an exchange of letters took place between Simon and the Prime Minister, though the conference proposal was prominent, there was no reference to Dominion Status.[24]

The Viceroy's statement appeared on 31 October 1929. The nub of what *The Times* called a 'prolix and confused' announcement was: 'It is implicit in the Declaration of 1917 that the natural issue of India's constitutional progress . . . is the attainment of Dominion Status.' Irwin slipped in a proviso that the Princely states would have to be brought into any scheme. This proviso was ignored or minimised and the statement seemed to provide the breakthrough for which Irwin hoped. On 2 November the 'Delhi Manifesto' was issued by a panel of Indian politicians representing all the main parties. They welcomed the announcement while laying down certain conditions of their own (such as the release of all political prisoners). They insisted that the forthcoming 'Conference is to meet not to discuss when Dominion Status is to be established but to frame a Dominion Constitution for India'.[25]

Where was all this heading? Parliament was not slow to press for an answer. In the House of Lords, Reading's demand for enlightenment was haltingly answered by the aged Lord Parmoor and by Lord Passfield (Sidney Webb). In the Commons the questioning was led by Lloyd George. On 1 November he inquired if the Statutory Commission was consulted on Irwin's statement? Benn conceded that they had not been consulted, adding that the goal remained that stated in the 1917 Declaration. Was there no change, 'either in substance or in time', inquired LG? The Indian leaders appeared to believe that there was a 'fundamental change'.

On 7 November the question was raised again. Baldwin made an exculpatory apologia for his role in the muddle, insisting that any forward move must have 'the united support of the people of this country'. Lloyd

George was more belligerent. He had received no intimation that the statement was to be issued though he was leader of the Liberal Party. Between 1917 and 1919 the reforms had the united support of Parliament: but now? He looked forward to 'a partnership of the East and the West in a great community of nations', but there were obstacles. Quoting the Delhi Manifesto he observed that India expected 'a very great deliverance', yet Passfield had declared there was 'no change at all'.

Benn, replying, called LG's speech 'lamentable and mischievous'. Yet LG had his point; if there had been a change, Parliament had the right to know. Benn's explanation was that this was 'a restatement and interpretation of the Montagu policy'. With some justification he stressed the feeling in India that 'the days of Mr Montagu were past'. Yet Congress had spurned Montagu's imaginative innovations! Rather hopefully Benn declared that India awaited the Simon Report 'with eagerness'; this was a move to create a good atmosphere.

Simon followed with a restrained speech. He was not complaining that his Commission had been sold down the river. They were a 'completely united body', and he asked for time to complete the report, free of party controversy. He did complain that Irwin's statement, and these proceedings, 'have added to our difficulties through no fault of our own'. MacDonald wound up the debate with a characteristically meaningless assurance, 'I cannot remember that anybody ever suggested that the Declaration raised a new policy or effected any change.'[26]

Simon had managed remarkably well throughout the disruption caused by Irwin's announcement. Only Burnham threatened resignation, and he was dissuaded by a tactful message sent on behalf of the King.[27] It was astonishing how the Commission remained cocooned from contemporary pressures. Even Attlee, now Chancellor of the Duchy of Lancaster in MacDonald's Cabinet, kept aloof from the controversy into which the Cabinet had been drawn.[28]

The sequel was exactly as Lloyd George had anticipated. On 23 December Irwin had a meeting with Gandhi, Motilal Nehru, Jinnah, Sapru, and Vithalbhai Patel. The usually moderate Motilal was in militant mood: he claimed 'there was no difficulty about having full Dominion Status at once'. Irwin replied that this was unreasonable, and suggested that 'the true function of the [projected] Conference would be to discuss the difficulties in the way of conferment of full Dominion Status'. Motilal was unimpressed: 'He gave it as his opinion that no Indian would be satisfied with less than Dominion Status. He saw no difficulties in the way himself.'[29] The Irwin initiative was over. Inadequately prepared, unimaginatively received, both in Britain and India, it remains a historical irrelevance.

Gandhi moved on to the offensive. His Salt Satyagraha was launched in March 1930 and soon India was in ferment. Although Irwin was reluctant to arrest Gandhi, this became inevitable, and before long 60,000 political agitators were in jail. The police and security services were stretched almost to breaking point.

Nothing seemed to go right for the Simon Commission and it was against this unpromising background that their *Report* appeared: Volume I, the *Survey*, in mid-June and Volume II, *Recommendations*, at the end of the month. The *Survey* assessed the working of Dyarchy, at the Centre and in the Provinces, and probed into almost every aspect of 'the Indian problem'. C. F. Andrews complained that the Report 'deals much more with that old India which I knew when I first went out nearly thirty years ago . . . it shows no understanding of the Young India which we see rising today'.[30] But most criticism was concentrated on Volume II which even Irwin felt was lacking.[31]

Because the Report was so heavily criticised, especially in India, it is scarcely ever evaluated at its real worth; it was an outstanding achievement on the instalment plan model. The reforms Simon advocated actually went as far as the real constitutional advance up to 1939. Simon called for the separation of Burma from India: this was implemented. He advocated full provincial autonomy 'in which the provincial Cabinet will be answerable to the legislature over the whole provincial field', the legislature to be wholly elected by a much wider franchise. The official element was removed. All this was later accepted, but not until the 1935 Act became operative in 1937. In one passage the Report considers: 'Suppose that the first elections for the new provincial councils take place at the end of 1931 so that they meet in January 1932.'[32] Suppose, suppose . . . The first new-style elections actually took place early in 1937 and the first Congress governments took office in July 1937. If those wasted five-and-a-half years had been used, the Congress would have found how much real power they had acquired and the British would have been compelled to respond to Indian pressures. This did not happen: given only two years (1937 – 9) before they were compelled to resign by the Congress High Command, these provincial governments were not consolidated. Pakistan (undreamed of by Jinnah in 1930) became the challenge. India was partitioned.

A vital opportunity was lost, but then Gandhi and Nehru always rejected the instalment plan formula. They were almost equally hostile to the Round Table Conference formula which now took over. And, of course, the Simon Commission really sabotaged their own proposals by accepting the Conference formula.

The Labour government persisted with plans for the Conference even though there could be no Congress participation. They were more concerned about the basis for British participation. Benn assured Irwin that it was vital to maintain 'a Three Party truce in Indian matters . . . questions of Indian policy are to be free from subjection to the exigencies of party politics at home and debates . . . should be conducted in a non-partisan manner. Since 1919 the government has consulted the opposition on Indian policy.'[33] A Cabinet Paper — 'Round Table Conference: Composition of the British Delegation', dated 15 July 1930 — proposed including Opposition representatives 'with a genuine purpose of cooperating and not, as some Indian leaders are likely to apprehend, for the purpose of wrecking the Conference in advance'. This was indeed suspected: Jinnah cabled MacDonald on 19 July, 'Inclusion representatives opposition disaster please don't agree.' Benn also informed Irwin that Lloyd George and Austen Chamberlain were pressing for Simon to be in the British team: 'Not as representing any party but as an independent figure.' Irwin was all against this: India would deduce that the Conference was restricted to going through the Commission's proposals.[34]

When the Cabinet considered these matters at two consecutive meetings they agreed that Simon should be excluded. The British group should contain six to eight members of the Cabinet, four Conservatives and four Liberals.[35] It was privately agreed between Labour and Tories that Baldwin should be discouraged from participating because if he were included Lloyd George would insist on coming in. The manoeuvre worked, and Benn was able to tell Irwin that the Liberal delegates were likely to include Reading and Samuel (who would be 'very welcome') and perhaps Crewe: 'with Simon out of it and LG a possible non-starter we may get a decent [Liberal] team'.[36]

There were sixteen British delegates to the conference: eight representing the Government (led by MacDonald, Sankey and Benn) and four Tories (with Peel as nominal leader and Hoare as the real driving force). The Liberals were led by Reading, with his unrivalled prestige. Their M.P.s were Sir Robert Hamilton and Isaac Foot, a Plymouth solicitor whose persistent efforts to enter Parliament twice succeeded (1922 – 4 and 1929 – 35). The fourth was Philip Kerr, who had recently inherited the Lothian peerage. Prominent in the *Round Table* group, he was Lloyd George's private secretary during the critical years of his premiership (1916 – 21). He had been a frequent visitor to India.

It had been announced that the Round Table Conference would be a 'free' conference, not limited at all to Simon's recommendations. But in which direction would it go? The *Manchester Guardian* was keen on an all-India federation. Colonel Haksar, plenipotentiary for some of the Princes, indicated that his clients favoured this solution in conversation with J. T. Gwynn, the scholarly former Civilian who was the *Guardian*'s resident correspondent. The Liberal newspaper came out with this proposal on 5 November, just a week before the King opened the proceedings. Federation became the main talking-point among Indian delegates.

In the course of the set speeches that followed the formal opening of the conference (12 November) a surprising degree of agreement was emerging among the Indians present — Liberals, Muslim League, Independents and

Princes. In order to go beyond the provincial autonomy Simon recommended they envisaged an all-India federation. On 19 November a Cabinet memorandum took this further. The Labour government and the British Liberals were ready for an advance in this direction. Reading was the most cautious of his quartet. At meetings of the Liberal delegation, Lothian, Hamilton and Foot spoke of the Indian demand as 'the legitimate child of English liberalism'. Reading agreed, 'English Liberals were the lawful inheritors of the democratic tradition and must certainly act up to their character as such'.[37] On 5 January 1931 he announced he 'was prepared to agree to a responsible Federal Government in India, provided it was subject to certain safeguards'. [38] His speech carried the day. The Tories did not dare dissent for fear of being isolated. As Benn ruefully informed Irwin, Reading was 'the hero of the Conference and creamed the milk the Prime Minister was due to deliver'. Lloyd George scrapped any tendency to pursue a conservative line and fulsomely congratulated Reading; it was a triumph 'of historic Liberal doctrine guided throughout by your great knowledge of Indian affairs, by your statesmanship, and by your great personal influence and prestige . . . It will always be reckoned one of British Liberalism's foremost achievements in the realm of constructive statesmanship.'[39]

Two weeks later MacDonald announced that 'responsibility for the government of India should be placed upon Legislatures, Central and Provincial, with such provisions as may be necessary . . . during a period of transition' (the formula had Reading's prior approval). The conference dispersed amid mutual compliments: but of course it had been a performance of *Hamlet* without the Prince. Unless Gandhi could be persuaded to discuss the concept of federation between British India and Princely India it was but a 'Paper Federation'.

Most of the Conservative party accepted what their delegates had concurred in, but not the Churchill faction, the Diehards. Parliament debated the question on 26 January. MacDonald declared that they would now move forward. Gandhi and his fellow prisoners had been unconditionally released the previous day (civil disobedience was spluttering out). To those who were doubtful, the Prime Minister declared the alternative was 'repression and nothing but repression'. Hoare supported him; all-India federation had become 'a practicable programme'. They must maintain all-party unity. India must not become 'the pawn of party politics'; 'I should be very sorry to see the Indian question go the way of the Irish question.' Isaac Foot echoed these sentiments; the choice was 'between a friendly India and an alienated India'. He recounted the comment made by M. R. Jayakar about Reading's crucial speech: if the rest of India could have heard him, 'suspicions and difficulties . . . would have disappeared like mist before the sun'.

So far all was harmony. Simon introduced a critical note: 'There is a tremendous amount of work still to be done.' Regarding some difficulties — he cited the position of the Depressed Classes — 'nothing has as yet been accomplished at all'. However, it was Churchill in a bludgeoning speech who launched a head-on attack. The trouble had started with Irwin's 'uncalled for' statement. This had caused a breach between Parliament and the Commission: the Simon Report had been 'completely shelved' and its author 'invidiously excluded' from the Conference. Churchill endeavoured to arouse Lloyd George. He cited an article LG had written for the *Daily Mail* a year previously headed 'Jerry Building for a Smash in India'. He appealed to the old warrior 'on this Indian matter to come to the rescue of the country as he did in wartime days'. LG looked startled, and for once was at a loss for words. He was backing Reading and reform and kept silent.

It was left to Wedgwood Benn to sum up. He believed Churchill was left in isolation so he concentrated on the task ahead. They had so far only sketched an outline of the solution: which 'has to be filled in and not rubbed out'. 'On this occasion . . . one thinks of many acts of foresight and of significant courage. I think naturally of the name of Mr. Edwin Montagu who thirteen years ago laid the foundation.' Two elements were needful: 'One thing is sincerity and the second is speed.' If India was not ready now for self-government would it be ready in ten or twenty years' time? The change in Lloyd George's thinking about India was, in fact, part of a general change of strategy. His previous plan of trying to exploit an opening to the centre gave way to a strategy of going for an opening to the Left. In this he was at odds with Simon and others. This was not yet the final parting of the ways, but it served as an ominous warning.

In India, there were talks between Viceroy and Mahatma, and on 4 March a settlement was concluded. Civil disobedience was called off, and Congress agreed to participate in the next round of discussions on constitutional reform. The great question remained unanswered: would Gandhi come to London? He professed to receive no answer from his Inner Voice. The *Manchester Guardian* tried to dissolve the impasse. Why should not they invite Gandhi to visit Britain as their guest so that he could assess the situation at first hand? James Bone, their London editor, put the idea to Benn's Private Secretary, William Croft, but the Government of India advised that the *Guardian* 'had better not barge in', and Benn added, 'I agree.'[40] The *Guardian* kept its eyes steadily on the future. In an editorial 'Nature Abhors a Vacuum' (4 June 1931) the paper declared, 'We have our duty now in India — to further by every means in our power the establishment of self-government there . . . We have governed India and now we must help India to govern herself.'

At last, on 27 August, Gandhi announced that he would come to the next session of the Round Table Conference. His timing was disastrous. Riven by indecision about how to tackle the gathering international financial storm, the Labour government fell apart. MacDonald became the head of a new 'National Government'; he was joined by the Liberals and Tories. Most Socialists repudiated this 'betrayal'. When the new government was announced on 24 August the Cabinet of sixteen included five Liberals, with Reading as Foreign Secretary and Samuel as Home Secretary. MacDonald retained three Labour colleagues: there were also seven Conservatives, including Sir Samuel Hoare as Secretary for India. Conservative predominance became even more evident when a General Election was called on 27 October, after intense Tory pressure and Liberal protest. The verdict was even more lopsided than in 1918: 473 Conservatives were elected and only 52 Socialists. Most of the former Front Bench were defeated, including Wedgwood Benn. Those who claimed the Liberal label included 33 followers of Herbert Samuel, and 35 Liberal Nationals (later called National Liberals), followers of Simon who accepted the Protectionist policy which Simon had adopted. Finally, there was the Lloyd George family; four in number, they still commanded the loyalties of north Wales. They sat with the diminutive Labour opposition. In this new National government there were four Labour Ministers as before, nine Conservatives, and six Liberals (but only if two National Liberals were counted in). Simon replaced Reading as Foreign Secretary. Among those demoted was the Marquess of Lothian; in the first brief National Government he was in the Cabinet; now he accepted the lesser post of Under Secretary for India. It was a magnanimous act (he had been a contemporary of Hoare at Oxford) but it was in line with his strong commitment on India.

This was the background to the second Round Table Conference which opened on 7 September. Many of the British participants were preoccupied, for Britain went off the gold standard on 21 September. It soon became evident that most of the Indian delegates were determined to raise the question of the minorities in the new legislatures. Instead of leading the discussion towards the issue of independence, Gandhi was compelled to carry on bargaining sessions with leaders of the Muslims and others. His difficulty was evident when he paid a visit to the 85-year-old C. P. Scott who posed the question: 'Don't you think it is due to British rule that there is unity in India?' Gandhi meekly replied that 'pressure from above' had induced that unity but that it was now threatened by 'disruptive forces'. In an attempt to reach a satisfactory formula, Gandhi spent a weekend at Oxford as guest of the Master of Balliol along with C. F. Andrews, Lothian, and Malcolm MacDonald. They reached agreement on a fresh approach to the problem but their proposals were unacceptable to the other delegates.[41]

In addition to the communal disagreements, the Princes were also going cold on federation. When the Conference closed on 1 December Gandhi repeated that 'Congress alone claims to represent the whole of India, all

194

interests'. They were only divided by 'the wedge in the shape of foreign rule'. Ramsay MacDonald drew what consolation he could: 'The discussions . . . have been of value in showing us more precisely the problems we have to solve.' If Indians could not resolve their communal differences themselves the British government would have to work out what 'checks and balances' were required. Gandhi returned to India, announced the resumption of civil disobedience, and was promptly arrested and jailed. India was back where it had been before.

The day after the conference was adjourned, Ramsay MacDonald told Parliament they would prepare a new constitution based upon the Simon Report. Three important questions had arisen at the Conference. The 'most important' concerned the extension of the franchise: how should this be effected? Perhaps by making *panchayats*, village committees, the means of election; perhaps by a system of proportional representation (British governments have always been keen on PR for everywhere except Britain). The second big question was about the future of separate communal representation: the Conference had been divided. The third question concerned the relation between Princely and British India.

The debate provided the first occasion for Attlee to speak on India since he had signed the Simon Report. He reflected that their report had revealed the 'enormous complexity' which was India: 'problem seems to overlap problem.' There were changes since they began their inquiry; however, the Simon Report should not be 'brushed aside . . . it has been utilised as a jumping off place for further advance, as one always expected that it would be.' The report had emphasised the need for safeguards: 'I want to see safeguards for the people who are economically and educationally backward.' Attlee sat down, having reconciled to his own satisfaction his essentially moderate stance with the more radical views of some of his Socialist colleagues. From among them, Josiah Wedgwood condemned the Round Table Conference; it would create 'an oligarchy of princes'. He harked back to Montagu's Declaration of 1917: 'The finest act of statesmanship that Great Britain has produced.'

One of the newly-elected Liberals, the writer and traveller Robert Bernays, gave it as his own experience that the old India was passing away. The peasant masses now had 'a great national advocate' in Gandhi. It was vital 'to proceed to the goal [of self-government] with steps as swift and as firm' as difficulties allowed. The debate was concluded by Baldwin, claiming, 'We have got to the point that we have reached with still a practical unity of parties.' That this was a pious hope was shown when Churchill forced a division, and 43 of his supporters voted against the government: however, 369 voted in favour, including Attlee and many of the Labour men.

Lord Lothian was appointed to head an Indian Franchise Committee to determine how the new legislatures would be elected. They left almost at once for India, but before departure Lothian met a delegation of British women who pressed for a special effort to ensure that the women of India would have their rightful place in the new legislatures. The leader of the delegation was Margery Corbett Ashby, President of the Women's National Liberal Federation, and with her were other Liberals, Lady Layton and Lady Hartog. Lothian was able to assure them that his committee would include a woman.

The eight members of the Franchise Committee included the pugnacious Socialist Major Milner and the suave Conservative R. A. Butler; on arrival in India they were joined by twelve Indian members. The Simon commission error was not repeated. The Indian Liberals were particularly anxious to move forward quickly. Lothian hastened to reassure them:

> As regards the work of the Franchise Committee I entirely agree with your point of view that the sooner it can be completed the better . . . I hope that by the middle of April we shall have arrived at agreement as to how the electorate under the new system is to be constituted . . . Both the Prime Minister and Sir Samuel Hoare are as anxious as you that the whole work of the constitution should be carried through as rapidly as possible.[42]

The Committee went ahead, enduring the Congress boycott, and before the end of April Lothian was able to inform the *Times* correspondent in India:

> I have been overwhelmed with work in the preparation of our Report. We have got it done . . . It anyhow provides a foundation upon which responsible government can be erected if communalism does not tear it to pieces and if India can throw up the political leaders necessary to work a democratic system . . . Things are hanging fire pending the production of the new Constitution and meanwhile the wretched consequences of civil disobedience work out their weary way in ordinances and police action. Everything now depends on whether the British Government now gets on quickly with its job.[43]

For the provincial electorate, the effect of the recommendations (which were later adopted) was to increase the number of voters from less than 6½ million to about 35 million (or 27 per cent of the adult population). Moreover, female voters, less than 320,000 under the 1919 Act, now numbered more than 6 million. For the central legislature the voting qualification was higher, though still representing a substantial increase. On 27 June 1932 the government announced there would be one Bill to provide full autonomy and a federation of British and Princely India. The question of separate representation for Muslims and other minorities was settled by a unilateral Communal Award by the Prime Minister. Then the whole momentum slackened. British Liberals were in trouble; but so were the Conservatives because Churchill threatened to weaken Baldwin's hold over the party, making India the issue.

Participation by the Samuelite Liberals had been shaky since the Tories and Simonites declared for Protection at the 1931 election. In August 1932 the government announced a series of protective duties under the Ottawa agreement. Samuel summoned a meeting on 7 September to 'discuss the serious situation that arises'. It was decided that the Liberal Ministers resign, though the party would still support the National Government. When the decision became effective on 28 September, Lothian resigned with all the rest (except for Walter Runciman).

The Conservatives — the party with the power — went into bottom gear on the India Bill to frustrate Churchill. Hoare referred the draft legislation to a Joint Select Committee of both Houses of Parliament *before* introducing his Bill. The real Diehards (Churchill, Page Croft, Lord Lloyd) declined to join, but Conservatives like Lord Salisbury and Austen Chamberlain were included and adopted a hard line. Of the 32 Committee members (16 from each House) only four were Liberals (Reading, Lothian, Foot, Hamilton) and four were Labour (Attlee, Morgan Jones, F. S. Cocks, Lord Snell).[44] The Tory hardliners were Hoare's main worry now.

The 1930s seemed to the older generation of Liberals quite bewildering. Viscount Gladstone lamented to Reading, 'The great Liberal ideas with which my father's name is associated are not very prominent today in the newspapers.' They really ought to promote better publicity 'in case the present National Government should fall into disfavour' so that 'a safe Liberal alternative' was still available to 'crude Socialism'. Reading assured Gladstone: 'I believe that the country in the main still supports the great principles of liberty and Liberalism always associated with the name of your father. With your views on the Labour Party I am in complete agreement, yet I hear that a number of Liberals are inclined to dally with Labour.' While expressing agreement he felt unable to be of much help in promoting Liberal periodicals.[45]

However, the Liberal point of view was still cogently expounded in the *Manchester Guardian*. In an editorial 'The North West Frontier Province' the paper condemned the use of air power to suppress tribal unrest (6 April 1933). There were grumbles within the India Office. Sir Findlater Stewart described the editorial as 'rough stuff', adding that Gwynn was no longer writing the leaders: 'One Moggridge has taken his place who knows a good deal less about his job.'[46] The grumbles continued and H. Macgregor of the India Office Information Department wrote to the *Guardian*'s London editor: 'Strictly between your editor and myself we hear that certain woolly-minded people in this country have been instigating the Congress leaders to use the *Manchester Guardian* to stir up public opinion against the [Joint Select] Committee's recommendations.' The result was likely to be a 'strengthening and hardening of Conservative tendencies among British parliamentarians'. The Diehards were the threat, not the Radicals. Whoever these 'woolly-minded people' were, they might have included an idealistic gentleman in the Liberal Party Organization, Mr. Hawkins, who suggested that Gandhi might be invited to stand as a Liberal candidate for Parliament![47]

The Joint Select Committee lumbered on from April 1933 to November 1934. They held 154 meetings and examined 120 witnesses. Hoare strove to preserve the framework which had been erected by all the conferences and committees but in several respects the original White Paper proposals were weakened. One important change was that both houses of the central legislature, directly elected under the Lothian Committee's plan, were deprived of direct representation and instead were to be filled by indirect election from the various provincial legislatures. When the Liberals on the Committee proposed direct election (on 6 July 1934) they were defeated, 18 – 5. Those in the minority were Reading, Lothian and Foot, with two Labour members — Morgan Jones and Cocks. When a vote was taken subsequently to substitute indirect election, six voted against the majority: they included the Archbishop of Canterbury. In these votes Attlee was for indirect election, perhaps because he had endorsed this as a recommendation in the Simon Report to which he remained so loyal.[48]

When the Joint Committee finally ended its deliberations, Hoare could take considerable credit for bringing the vessel to port, even if a little battered. Throughout these proceedings, Sir Malcolm Hailey, the greatest Indian Civilian of his day, was at his elbow. He told the new Viceroy, Lord Willingdon:

> He has changed greatly from the very cautious and conservative attitude which I saw him taking in 1930 and . . . he has attracted to his own head the brickbats which a short time ago used to be directed at Lord Irwin. It is indeed curious that we should find a small band of Conservative politicians who are pleading the Indian cause with all the fervour . . . which was once displayed by Mr. Montagu and who seem willing to run the dangers which fell to his lot.[49]

Hoare was in no danger. Baldwin and the solid centre of the Conservative party stood firm. That the revolt was led by Winston Churchill, the Liberal renegade (almost as dangerous as Lloyd George), strengthened the Baldwinites. The gradual shift by the Labour party into opposition to the new measure was unexpected: but in contemporary parliamentary arithmetic Labour's threat was less dangerous than the Diehard revolt. The Samuelite Liberals were even smaller in number, so their decision to provide support was not essential. Lloyd George's decision that his little group would opt out of the debate took away from the drama but had no effect on the result. It seemed that LG had decided that the time had come to negotiate with the real Indian leaders. Recalling his own experiences in Ireland, when Redmond was extinguished by Sinn Fein, he had decided that the only man who counted was Gandhi. Moreover, he had reached the conclusion that in England Liberalism 'was more or less dead'. He turned his back upon his party and upon India to launch the Council of Action which was going to bring peace and prosperity.[50]

When the House of Commons considered the recommendations of the Joint Select Committee on 10 and 12 December 1934 the future pattern of the debate on the Bill became discernible. Attlee dissociated his party from it on the grounds that Dominion Status was not defined as a goal and there was no share for the workers and peasants in the constitution. Isaac Foot bemoaned the loss of direct elections at the centre, rebuking Attlee for his lack of interest. He condemned the excessive attention given to safeguards: 'Our first concern must be not for ourselves but for India.' Graham White, another Liberal, expressed the need for action: 'In the policy of doing nothing, of standing still, there is no risk but certainty of disaster.' Simon made an intervention (he did not take part in later debates). He complained that this was the first time that the House of Commons 'has even devoted five minutes to discussing the report of the Statutory Commission'. He argued that everything in the bill was implicit in their report, compiled 'without a dissentient Minute'. He questioned whether direct election was really a 'fundamental principle' or 'just a question of electoral mechanics'. This must have irritated those members of his old party to whom 'electoral mechanics' in the form of proportional representation had come to mean so much.

Finally, Churchill declared that the new Bill was just 'the plan of the Socialist Government'. That innuendo did not prevent Labour going into the same lobby as the Diehards — as they were to do so frequently during the coming months. The motion to accept the Joint Select Committee's Report was carried by 410 votes (Liberals included) to 127 votes (Diehard and Labour).

The Bill was to occupy a major part of Parliament's time from 6 February 1935 until it was enacted on 2 August. Thirty days were devoted to the Committee stage (taken on the floor of the House), three days to the Report stage, and two days to the Third Reading. Before they began this marathon, the leading contenders were invited to address the public on the radio. Hoare opened the series and Baldwin had the last word. Isaac Foot spoke for the Liberals while Dorothea Layton also took part 'from the woman's point of view'.

The talk Foot gave with the title 'Cooperation Implies Consent' contained most of the arguments he was to employ during the weary weeks ahead. He insisted: 'We . . . welcome the demand for self-government and the expressed desire for representative institutions and see in this movement not the failure but the success of our efforts. In India, as elsewhere, we reap as we have sown' (his text contained many such biblical allusions). Freedom should not be 'grudgingly conceded' but offered 'to the fullest extent'. As Liberals they felt that the Joint Select Committee had not given

199

enough; but 'our duty . . . was to help in finding a central body of agreed opinion, an area of solid ground upon which could be built a bridge between politically-minded India and politically-minded Britain. . . . The whole basis of our position in India is the consent of the Indian people. If that consent is withheld, our moral and legal right to govern India . . . disappears.' Foot deprecated the emphasis upon 'safeguards' in the Bill: 'we may yet have to get rid of that word lest it should become a tyrant.' He ended on an optimistic note: 'I cannot believe that Indian politicians are going to throw away the immeasurable opportunity that the new constitution will give them.' Britain would still have a role in India: 'But I would like to emphasize not only India's need of us but also our need of India . . . We need all the friends we can get . . . especially in Asia . . . We in this country may have to fight a big battle . . . for the defence of Freedom, for the maintenance of representative institutions, and for the preservation of the most precious elements in our civilisation. In that struggle we shall need all the allies we can get . . . India is qualified to contribute to this mighty undertaking.' [51]

And so began the debate in which the contestants repeated and repeated their viewpoint. Hoare commenced by promising that the Bill would 'ultimately' make India one of the 'fully self-governing members of the British Commonwealth'. Then why, Attlee inquired drily, was not Dominion Status mentioned in the Bill which began baldly: 'To make further provisions for the Government of India'? Once again he praised the Simon Report where it was foreseen that 'what was required was flexibility and growth. That does not exist in this Bill.'

Samuel opened for his party, declaring that the Bill was 'of the purest milk of the word Liberalism'. He regretted that there was no reference to Dominion Status and he condemned the substitution of indirect for direct elections at the centre. He rejected the notion of trying to impose safeguards for British exports. Though Samuel sat for a constituency with a textile industry he insisted it was 'useless to attempt to rely upon holding or acquiring trade by Act of Parliament'. He rejected holding India by repression. 'If the Empire is to be maintained merely by military force, a democracy cannot do it.'

On the next day Robert Bernays warned the government against capitulating to Tory dissidents, observing sorrowfully, 'I can speak for a Party who know something about Party splits and we know what disastrous effects they have.' He joined in the attack on indirect elections: 'Turning New Delhi into Old Sarum.' The alternative to passing this Bill was recourse to 'The methods of Hitler . . . establishing concentration camps from one end of India to the other'. He foretold that Congress would work for the new legislatures: 'Responsibility has a tremendously sobering effect . . . I do not think the politicians will refuse to work the constitution.' It was a speech which foreshadowed much that would come to pass.

Churchill made the first of innumerable interventions. He regretted the absence of Lloyd George: 'He seems to have lost interest in this all-important matter in which he has played so important a part.' He also deplored the absence of MacDonald (as did others) and alleged that Simon had been 'taken care of'. Churchill's amendment obtained the support of 133 Members against 404. Those marching into the minority lobby were an incongruous band: Brendan Bracken and Nye Bevan, Lord Henry Cecil and Stafford Cripps, the Marquess of Hartington and George Lansbury.

Then the House went on to consider the Bill clause by clause (there were 478 altogether). Throughout this time the attendance thinned out unless Churchill or another star performer was on his feet. During the tedious, often long-winded speeches by all those with something to say, Isaac Foot sat waiting on the Liberal bench, ready to leap up with a question or inter-jection. Early on he reminded Parliament that 'the whole of Indian history in the last twenty-five years has been a comment on being too late'. There had been delay from 1917 to 1919, but much worse between 1930 and 1935, giving ample opportunity for 'mischief makers'.

The Liberals' big day came on 6 March when they endeavoured to reverse the choice of indirect election at the centre. Samuel objected that this was 'definitely and deliberately contrary to Indian desires'. He countered the argument that the electorate would be vast and unmanage-able by suggesting that Indian society was held together by caste and other associations: 'public opinion is the result of group movements.' It was inevitable that in the long run direct election would prevail. Hoare's reply was dismissive and cynical: 'Whatever system of election you have, you get much the same kind of people returned.' Inevitably, Samuel's amend-ment was lost, 57 against 262, but the cross-voting on this occasion was more bewildering than in almost any other vote. Churchill, in a nostalgic gesture towards his lost Liberalism, voted for the amendment.

Churchill exploited every tactical opportunity. When he received word that the Princes had come out against the federal scheme (on 20 March) he proposed that the remaining sections of the Bill, which dealt with the Centre, be omitted from consideration. Foot insisted they must go on. The concessions to the Princes were, if anything, over-generous: they were promised 33 per cent of seats in the lower house and 40 per cent in the upper house. Parliament, said Foot, was telling India: 'This is the House that we have constructed. It is for you to say whether that House should be occupied by you.' He issued a prophetic warning: 'It will be a disastrous day for the Princes if they fail to seize this opportunity.' There was a division, and Churchill's ploy was rebuffed by 270 to 94 votes.

Under the strain of it all, Hoare fell ill and the main burden was assumed by R. A. Butler, who had succeeded Lothian as Under Secretary. During the Report stage the Liberals made another vain attempt to restore direct elections at the Centre. They pointed out that as a member of the Franchise

Committee Butler had voted for the direct method though he had reversed his stand in the Joint Select Committee. Butler offered the prospect that the mode of election was 'to be regarded as open to future review'. It was not much, and a Labour Member, E. A. G. Bailey, urged the government to accept the 'very reasonable Liberal amendment': 'After all, they have been very faithful to the government in these discussions. I do not know what the government would have done but for the support they have had from the Socialist and Liberal votes'. Perhaps Mr. Bailey was being sarcastic. The Liberal amendment was defeated: 200 against, 61 in favour. Once more, the allies of the Liberals were a motley band.

On the Third Reading, Samuel, with uncharacteristic astringency, characterised the 'unholy alliance' between Ultra-Tories and Socialists as 'between those who would die hard and those who would live dangerously'. He added, ominously, 'If this measure does not succeed in the working it cannot endure. It will be swept away . . . on the demand of the Indian people.' Wedgwood was totally against the Bill: better to leave things as they were; 'The leading strings that were devised by John Morley and Edwin Montagu have suddenly been converted into fetters.' However, Churchill would have none of it. 'You offer this bouquet of faded flowers of Victorian Liberalism which, however admirable in themselves, have nothing to do with Asia and are being universally discarded throughout the continent of Europe.' The last vote was taken: Ayes, 386; Noes, 122.

The passage of the Bill through the House of Lords aroused no drama. Lothian called their debate 'a mare's nest', and accused the government of retracting pledges made to the Round Table Conference. He moved a number of amendments designed to extend the franchise, but without success. Unexpectedly, and illogically, a new Section was introduced by Lord Zetland to elect the new upper house, the Council of State, by direct vote. The electorate would number about 10,000. Lothian pressed unavailingly for this concession to be granted to the lower house. While Lothian sensed that there was 'no great enthusiasm' for the measure either in Britain or India he felt, paradoxically, that this was a good omen. There was 'an immense fund of ability and an immense quantity of public spirit in India'. They must hope to achieve cooperation: if Indian politicians worked the new constitution then there would be 'steady and inevitable progress' to Dominion Status.

The response of political India ranged between the sceptical and the hostile: 'Satanic' was to be the standard epithet. This reception was aroused not by the Act itself (which Gandhi admitted he never read) but by India's suspicion of the motives of British political parties. The Tories had come out clearly for 'safeguards': they had encouraged reactionary Princes. But were the others any better? 'Why should we expect much from the British Labour Party?' wrote Nehru at this time.[52] It was in this embittered atmosphere that Lord Lothian tried to persuade Nehru to view the new constitution more positively.

First, there was another general election to be fought in Britain and when the hour came in November 1935 the Liberal result was the worst yet: 21 M.P.s remained, including the little Lloyd George clan. The National Liberals, indistinguishable from Tories, won 33 seats and the Conservatives 387. Labour, despite shedding Lansbury and Cripps from their team, increased their numbers to 154. Absent from the returning Liberals were Samuel (who might have lost votes at Darwen because he opposed 'safeguards' against Indian tariffs) and Foot who lost Bodmin. Margery Corbett Ashby failed to win Hemel Hempstead. Isaac Foot wrote to Lord Reading: 'The majority against me was so heavy that if the Archangel Gabriel had spoken on my behalf I don't think it would have made any difference.'[53] In the new House of Commons there was no Liberal with a special interest in India; for Sir Archibald Sinclair, the next leader, it simply was not on his map.

This account has concentrated on the response of individual politicians because this was how India chiefly impinged on British politics. Both the Liberal and Labour parties were committed to self-government on the instalment plan; but this was not central to their political philosophy. Among the Liberals, only Montagu acquired a deeper vision. And in the Labour ranks there were only a few to whom India was preeminent — Josiah Wedgwood, Fenner Brockway, Reginald Sorensen. And in their party they were seen as harmless eccentrics.

Perhaps more surprisingly, the Tories, the Party of Empire, were also quite pragmatic. Only for one or two — Sir Reginald Craddock, the ex-governor, the Duchess of Atholl perhaps — was the mission of the Raj sacrosanct. They swallowed the 1935 Act and in 1947 they were to swallow independence. India was of major importance to Britain — as an export market (especially for cotton) and as the biggest source of military manpower within the Empire. Yet India never became an inter-party issue in British politics as Ireland was, in the most divisive terms, for over thirty years. In the 1930s peace and unemployment were the over-riding issues. Already, as Churchill wound down his India campaign, he was beginning his campaign for rearmament. Under these circumstances, indirect influence and personal contacts were all that remained to the Liberals.

Lord Lothian, for example, set himself to soften Jawaharlal Nehru's revulsion against the 1935 Act by arguing that Congress could not have devised a plan except by making 'in fundamentals . . . the same kind of concessions to communalism, to the princes, and to property as are contained in the present constitution'. It was important, Lothian insisted, that India, as had been the infant United States, 'is being launched on its self-governing life on the basis of a written constitution which can be moulded, easily, but not too easily, to meet her developing needs'. He had suggested that there were dangers in India from the separatist tendencies of religion, race and language. Nehru minimised these arguments, saying that communalism in India was less than in Ireland: 'It is overemphasized.' [54]

In 1937 the provincial elections had been contested by Congress, who won 716 of the 1585 general constituencies but only 26 of 482 Muslim seats. They formed Ministries in eight provinces. The predictions of Lothian, Foot, Bernays, and other British Liberals had been fulfilled. Thanks to the folly of the Princes the federal layer of the constitution was not activated.

With the outbreak of war the Congress High Command ordered the Ministries to resign and the whole experiment came to an abrupt end. Everything was now in the melting pot. Lord Zetland, Secretary for India, tried to prod the War Cabinet: 'When Parliament accepted Dominion Status as the goal, the feeling was that the journey was a long one; but the effect of the outbreak of war has been to bring us hard up against the implications of Dominion Status for India.' [55] But nothing was done, and when Churchill became Prime Minister if anything the deadlock hardened. Sir Archibald Sinclair was Secretary of State for Air in Churchill's administration and was a confidant of the great man, but he had nothing to say on India. Sinclair was present at all the crucial meetings in 1942 when the idea of the Cripps mission was discussed, and after its failure, when it was decided to arrest and intern Gandhi and the other Congress leaders. The record does not suggest that he made any positive contribution.

The last occasion in which a Liberal leader impinged on Indian events was equally oblique. On 6 April 1943, Lord Samuel (as he now was) delivered a long speech on India. Regretting the Congress decision to withdraw from the provincial legislatures he alleged that Congress 'has to a great extent thrown over democratic philosophy . . . It shows signs of turning to totalitarianism'. Samuel averred that Congress did not speak for the whole of India: they 'can claim at best barely more than half the population'.

So the long years of war dragged by, and as victory at last came into view people began to discuss the postwar world. As part of this forward vision, Sir Walter Layton addressed an international gathering at Oxford. In his sweeping survey, he said, 'India has been promised the right to decide her own constitution after the war . . . She will be free. Even if a self-governing India decides to remain in a special association with the British Commonwealth, these relations can never be quite the same as those of existing Dominions. Unless our world order provides for the sharing of responsibility, there will one day be a clash between white and the other races.' [56]

Liberals were saying the right things: but it no longer fell to them to implement Liberal ideas. When India did achieve freedom — through division — their role was simply to watch from the sidelines. At the 1945 general election their parliamentary representation was cut to twelve.

Woefully, the *Manchester Guardian* wrote of 'the submergence of the Liberal Party . . . Under the present system its hopes must be slender' (27 July 1945). Liberal M.P.s joined in facilitating the passage of the Indian Independence Bill through Parliament: but so also did the Conservatives, rediscovering the inter-party unity which had greeted Montagu's reforms. As Independence Day approached, scarcely anyone remembered that it was he who had first foreseen this day.

Notes

1 For reasons of space citations have not been provided for Lords and Commons debates. My thanks are due to Dr. S. R. Ashton who supplied me with materials from the India Office Records.

2 In his first book, Stephen Koss identified the twentieth-century Liberal weakness as an 'ideological inheritance which by its self-contradictions and uncertainties, proved as irrelevant to the Indian situation as it did to other urgent problems': a harsh judgment, which he never recanted, though there was always a tone of regret in his censure. (*John Morley at the India Office, 1905–1910*, p. 212).

3 *Rufus Isaacs, First Marquess of Reading*, by his son, ii, (London, 1945), 353. For Hailey's comment see note 49.

4 S. D. Waley, *Edwin Montagu; a memoir and an account of his visits to India* (London, 1964), p. 235, Montagu to Willingdon, 9 September 1920.

5 Sir Algernon Rumbold, *Watershed in India, 1914–1922* (London, 1979), p. 99.

6 P. G. Robb, *The Government of India and Reform; policies towards politics and the constitution, 1916–1921* (London, 1976), attempts to award a larger share in the reforms to Chelmsford.

7 Waley, p. 180, and Rumbold, p. 124.

8 For Lloyd George's anti-imperial background, see Koss, ed., *The Pro-Boers; the anatomy of an antiwar movement*, esp. pp. 251–6.

9 For an account of the Punjab in 1919 from the Indian viewpoint, see Hugh Tinker, *The Ordeal of Love: C. F. Andrews and India* (Delhi, 1979), pp. 151–7, 159–61.

10 Waley, Ch. XVII. For Aurangzeb, see p. 246.

11 *Rufus Isaacs, First Marquess of Reading*, Vol. 2, p. 220.

12 Waley, Ch. XIX, and Rumbold, Ch. XVI.

13 Rumbold, p. 303, and *History of the Times*, p. 656.

14 No exact count on party lines in the 1920s is possible. Koss (*Asquith*, p. 256) emphasises 'the confused state of party politics' and shifts in allegiance.

15 C. V. Wedgwood, *The Last of the Radicals* (London, 1951), p. 147. On Reading and Olivier see *Rufus Isaacs, First Marquess of Reading*, ii, 293–7.

16 Tinker, *The Ordeal of Love*, pp. 205, 222.

17 Tinker, *Separate and Unequal; India and the Indians in the British Commonwealth* (London, 1976), p. 81.

18 Earl of Birkenhead, *Halifax: the Life of Lord Halifax* (London, 1965), pp. 237–9.

19 *History of the Times*, iv, Part II, p. 865.

20 The Government of Burma produced a statement 590 pages long: about average.

21 Simon to Dawson, 12 January 1929, *History of the Times*, p. 869. The Conservative members were Lord Strathcona, Lord Burnham, E. C. G. Cadogan and Colonel G. R. Lane Fox. The Labour members were Vernon Hartshorn and C. R. Attlee.

22 The negotiations previous to the Dominion Status announcement are on file: IOR:MSS EUR F77/41, and include the quotations which follow.

23 *Rufus Isaacs, First Marquess of Reading*, ii, 522. An account of the events in the summer of 1929 is given by R. J. Moore, *The Crisis of Indian Unity, 1917–1940* (Oxford, 1974), Ch. 2.

24 The two letters are printed in the Preface to Vol. I of the Commission's *Report* (Cmd. 3568 of 1930). They are dated 16 and 25 October, though the document describing these manoeuvres (Resumé of Negotiations Regarding Interchange of Letters) records that the actual exchange of the signed letters took place on 30 October.

25 *The Transfer of Power, 1942 – 7*, eds. Nicholas Mansergh and Penderel Moon (HMSO), iv, (1974), 329.

26 For Simon's own version of these events, see Viscount Simon, *Retrospect* (London, 1952), pp. 150 – 5. For a version emphasizing the ulterior motives of LG see Moore, *Crisis of Indian Unity*, pp. 82 – 7.

27 Harold Nicolson, *King George the Fifth; his life and reign* (London, 1952), p. 505.

28 Perhaps he had little option: according to his autobiography, *As It Happened* (London, 1954), p. 81, MacDonald at no time ever consulted him about India.

29 Jinnah's copy of the Minutes of the meeting as cited by Stanley Wolpert, *Jinnah of Pakistan*, (New York, 1984), p. 112.

30 Tinker, *The Ordeal of Love*, p. 244.

31 Birkenhead, *Halifax*, p. 287.

32 *Indian Statutory Commission, Report*, vol. II, p. 114.

33 Telegram, Benn to Irwin, No. 2247 (11 July 1930). Round Table Conference File: IOR: L/PO/16, from which items following are also taken.

34 Benn to Irwin, telegrams 2358 and 2359 (22 July), and Irwin to Benn No. 659 (23 July). The Viceroy emphasized that all the Governors were opposed to Simon's inclusion.

35 Cabinet Conclusions: Cab(46)30 and Cab(47)30, both on 30 July 1930.

36 Personal letter, Benn to Irwin, 20 August 1930.

37 Minutes of Liberal delegation meeting (19 November 1930), quoted Moore, *Crisis of Indian Unity*, pp. 152 – 3.

38 *Rufus Isaacs, First Marquess of Reading*, vol. 2, p. 356.

39 Benn to Irwin (15 January 1931); Lloyd George to Reading, (4 February 1931): see Moore, *Crisis of Indian Unity*, p. 153.

40 Bone to Croft (28 May 1931); Note by Benn (12 June): IOR:L/I/1/284.

41 Tinker, *The Ordeal of Love*, pp. 251 – 2.

42 Lothian to Sapru and Jayakar (Delhi, 31 January 1932): IOR:Q/IFC/1.

43 Lothian to Alexander Inglis (Simla, 28 April 1932): IOR:Q/IFC/1. For the *Report*, and 4 volumes of evidence, see Cmd. 406, 1932; Recommendations on electorate, Cmd. 4998, 1932.

44 In addition to the 32 British parliamentary Committee members there were 27 Indian assessors — 20 from British India and seven from the States.

45 Viscount Gladstone to Marquess of Reading (27 August 1934); Reading to Gladstone, (17 September 1934): IOR MSS EUR F/118/22 – 26. Among those suspected of 'dallying' with Labour were Sir Walter Layton and his *News Chronicle* (Koss, *The Rise and Fall of the Political Press in Britain*, ii, 2).

46 IOR: L/I/1/284. Stewart was out of date: Muggeridge had already left to be *Guardian* correspondent in Moscow. For the role of Muggeridge at the *Guardian*, see Koss, ibid., p. 497.

47 Tinker, *The Ordeal of Love*, p. 288, n. 2.

48 Simon assured Parliament in December 1934 that Attlee was personally 'responsible for a good deal of what is in these volumes'. This might have appeared as an attempt to bid for his support but the same claim also appears in Attlee, *As it Happened*, p. 81.

49 Hailey to Willingdon (26 April 1933). Quoted in J. A. Cross, *Sir Samuel Hoare; a political biography* (London, 1977), pp. 166 – 6.

50 For LG's insistence that the man who counted was Gandhi, see *ibid.*, p. 176, and A. J. P. Taylor, *W. P. Crozier: Off the Record; political interviews, 1933 – 43* (London, 1973), p. 26. For Liberalism 'dead', *ibid.*, p. 28. For the Council of Action, see Koss, *Nonconformity in Modern British Politics*, Ch. 9.

51 Reprinted in *The Listener*, 30 January 1935.

52 Jawaharlal Nehru, *An Autobiography* (London, 1936), p. 582.

53 Foot to Reading (20 November 1935) IOR MSS EUR F118/22?26.

54 Jawaharlal Nehru, *A Bunch of Old Letters* (Bombay, 1958), pp. 136, 145.

55 Tinker, *Separate and Unequal*, p. 175.

56 'The British Commonwealth and World Order' (speech to inaugural meeting of the Liberal International): IOR:L/I/1/1441.

11

Seeing the Future:
British Left-Wing Travellers
to the Soviet Union, 1919-32

F. M. Leventhal

No event in the twentieth century was more enthusiastically welcomed by the British left than the overthrow of the Tsarist tyranny in 1917. Not only had a democratic republic replaced the hated Romanovs, but its call for peace without annexations or indemnities rekindled hopes for a prompt cessation of hostilities. A jubilant Ramsay MacDonald told an Independent Labour Party conference that 'a sort of spring-tide of joy had broken out all over Europe',[1] while H. N. Brailsford, no less resolute a critic of British war involvement, proclaimed that 'the whole earth has become a more habitable planet since the Russian autocracy has been destroyed.'[2] Despite the allegiance of a militant minority in Great Britain, much of the initial euphoria was dissipated when the Bolsheviks seized power and concluded a separate peace with Germany in violation of previous pledges. However critical of revolutionary tactics, the British left was united in denouncing allied intervention as an unwarranted intrusion into the affairs of another country.

Belligerent relations between Great Britain and the Soviet Union impeded communication during the first years after the Bolshevik revolution. As a corollary to economic blockade, the British sought to restrict the flow of information to and from the Soviet Union by refusing passports to British citizens. Soviet authorities were equally keen to exclude suspicious foreigners, especially journalists, many of whom were believed to be engaged in espionage. A few sympathetic correspondents who happened to be in Russia at the outbreak of the revolution, including M. Philips Price of the *Manchester Guardian* and Arthur Ransome of the *Daily News*, continued to send dispatches, but most newspapers relied on sources outside Russia who flagrantly misrepresented the new regime.

By 1920 allied intervention had subsided, and Lenin was becoming more receptive to foreign observers. In increasing numbers journalists, politicians, and trade unionists travelled to the Soviet Union, bringing back information on the regime to an eager audience. From then until the purge trials in the 1930s disenchanted much of the British left with Stalinism, a steady stream of travellers, individually and in groups, came to discover and frequently to extol the revolutionary achievements. Accounts of journeys to the Soviet Union became almost a literary genre with common traits. In so far as they can be categorized, these published reports fall into two groups. Of least value were those written by Communists or 'fellow travellers', so fulsome in their apologetics as to belie credibility. From Sylvia Pankhurst to Hewlett Johnson, their aim was to vindicate the Soviet regime in British eyes. On the other hand, there are those accounts, to be considered here, which at least aspired to critical detachment and whose purpose was primarily to articulate rather than to acclaim. Such distinctions are, however, not always clear. Although neither Communists nor fellow travellers, George Lansbury and the Webbs betrayed astonishing credulity in their writings on Russia, believing most of what their hosts told them and shutting their eyes to contradictory evidence.

Recent critics, strongly influenced by post-war Kremlinological scepticism, disparage most of the early travellers as gullible enthusiasts, so biased in favour of the Soviet system that they allowed themselves to become victims of calculated deception.[3] Soviet officials became adept at manipulating visitors, forestalling negative impressions by ensuring exposure only to those features which would portray the regime favourably. Many travellers connived at their own seduction, rationalizing defects as temporary aberrations or explaining them in terms of historical backwardness which the Soviets were struggling valiantly to overcome.

Reading these largely forgotten accounts today, one is struck as much by what they failed to observe as by what they reported. Even since the revelations of the Twentieth Party Congress, it has been impossible to view the Soviet regime with the naive expectations prevalent among the left in its early years. Yet to condemn these early observers for failing to disclose forced labor camps or to anticipate the purge trials is to convict them with hindsight. If they were over-credulous, they were often aware of the distorted information provided, the filtering out of jarring images, and tried to form their own impressions, deliberately evading the surveillance of guides and interpreters. Despite socialist affinities, few of the writers idealized the Soviet regime, although many exaggerated the noble purpose that motivated its leaders. As socialists, they regarded

210

Communism as an alternative version of their own goals, inapplicable to England, but a hopeful experiment for a nation emerging from an autocratic, economically underdeveloped system.

I

The earliest travellers arrived shortly after the upheaval, when the Bolsheviks, battling internal and foreign enemies, exhibited signs of a siege mentality. With its future still in question, British visitors searched for indications of the regime's viability and, for the most part, accepted constraints on political liberty as an inevitable condition of survival. Writing for a largely uninformed audience, they tried to disentangle myth from reality, describing details of everyday life and refuting the monstrous images of revolutionary leaders perpetrated in the right-wing press.

Among the first visitors was one already familiar with the Russian scene. Arthur Ransome, now chiefly remembered as the author of children's stories, had gone to Russia in 1913 and remained there through most of the war as correspondent for the *Daily News*. When allied intervention made it unfeasible for him to remain in Russia, he escaped to Stockholm, where he maintained ties with Maxim Litvinov while gathering information for the British Foreign Office. In February 1919 he returned to Russia despite the objections of Trotsky, who regarded him as an imperialist spy.

His *Six Weeks in Russia in 1919*, a hastily compiled journal rather than a systematic treatment, was the first eye-witness account published in England. Like other early reports, it testified to the privations endured by the inhabitants of Petrograd and Moscow, where food, fuel, and clothes were in short supply. On the other hand, compared with the previous year, these cities were now peaceful, and armed men no longer roamed the streets. Public transport, disrupted during the revolution, was functioning again, and the streets seemed cleaner that at any time since its outbreak. Much of the book recapitulates interviews with prominent officials invariably depicted as conscientious administrators grappling with economic contingencies, not as fanatical revolutionaries. Attending the Moscow Soviet, Ransome discovered that 'the political excitement of the revolution [had] passed' and later decided that the masses were 'settling down under the new regime'.[4] Although hunger was ubiquitous, schemes for dispensing food had been improvised, taking the edge off popular discontent. Theatres were crowded with workers, shabbily dressed, but able to enjoy the plays and concerts from seats formerly monopolized by the wealthy. Nor was there yet any indication of religious persecution: churches were open and worship went on unimpeded.

In recounting conversations with political opponents of the regime, he

211

provided evidence that the instrument of terror had not wholly stilled the voices of malcontents. While sharing their doubts about the efficacy of Bolshevik methods, Ransome was clearly sympathetic to what the leaders sought to accomplish against overwhelming odds. Nowhere does this emerge more strongly than in his portrait of Lenin, 'the first great leader who utterly discounts the value of his own personality'.[5] The set piece Lenin interview became a staple of travel reports during 1919 – 20. The Bolshevik leader tried to ingratiate himself with foreign visitors, and the informality of such encounters did much to humanize the image of the revolutionary hero as well as to distance him personally from the excesses of the Red terror.

It was almost a year later that George Lansbury, the editor of the *Daily Herald*, having secured a visa to Finland, smuggled himself into Russia. Once there, he was treated as an honoured guest, welcomed by Chicherin, Lunacharsky, Zinoviev, and, most importantly, by Lenin. Like other visitors, he was struck by the lack of ostentation in Lenin's surroundings and by his 'straightforward, honest manner'. It was the selflessness of this 'great impersonal soldier' that impressed his visitor. Seeing Lenin as the embodiment of a new, creative spirit, Lansbury scoffed when his anarchist friend Kropotkin castigated the regime as 'a class government and as tyranny'.[6] Conversations with several priests was sufficient testimony that there was 'perfect freedom to worship God'. Shortages of food and medical supplies, responsible for so much suffering, were attributable to the blockade, not to deficiencies in Soviet administration. It took only a few visits to workshops to convince him that industry was being reorganized more efficiently amid civil war. The only obstacle was the scarcity of raw materials, a problem that would be alleviated once the blockade was lifted and transport could be shifted to non-military uses.

Nothing impressed the ardent English suffragist more than the Soviet treatment of women. Equal pay in industry and generous maternity benefits confirmed that nowhere else in the world were women 'so free and so respected and cared for'.[7] Despite limited resources an ambitious educational program had been initiated, providing nurseries and boarding schools as well as adult-classes. In contrast to England or Germany, children were being taught to regard education not as a means for personal aggrandizement but for social service.

Lansbury's biographer contends charitably that 'he may have been dazzled, he was not blinded'.[8] While he grudgingly conceded that the regime might be coercive, he found it all too easy to condone and to take the protestations of officials at face value. Dzerzhinskii, the head of the Extraordinary Commission, assured Lansbury that by containing bribery, corruption, and brigandage, as well as dissent, the secret police were reducing violence and protecting lives. Nor was the sacrifice of a few malcontents an exorbitant price to pay for genuine popular democracy.

As a socialist he felt impelled to applaud and to rectify his readers' mis-apprehension about the nature of the regime: 'In my judgment, no set of men and women responsible for a revolution of the magnitude of the Russian Revolution ever made fewer mistakes or carried their revolution through with less interference with the rights of individuals, or with less terrorism and destruction.' Such hyperbole detracts from the credibility of his impressions. While he recognized imperfections, he generally blamed them on factors, such as the war or the blockade, beyond the control of Soviet leaders. Too willing to accept intention for result, he seemed oblivious to the capacity for ruthlessness or guile among men who, 'actu-ated by purely moral and religious motives', were 'striving to build the New Jerusalem'.[9]

It was in a spirit of inquiry rather than solidarity that the Trades Union Congress suggested that an impartial delegation be appointed. The Allied council consented to issue passports, and the Soviet Foreign Ministry agreed to the proposed visit. The nine delegates, representing the Labour Party and the T.U.C., arrived in Petrograd in May 1920 and during the next six weeks visited Moscow, Nizhni Novgorod, and Saratov. In the course of their trip they met government officials and trade unionists, educators and opposition politicians; they attended innumerable receptions and reviewed parades; and they toured factories, schools, and hospitals. Their visit became the prototype of subsequent officially-sponsored group tours, crowded with events calculated to show the regime to advantage, but also to underscore good will towards British workers. The authors of the report claimed that they enjoyed freedom of movement and were unimpeded in their individual investigations, but Ethel Snowden, one of the delegates, later complained that they were watched and accompanied everywhere by official guides who deflected awkward questions.

The report granted that much of the town population was enjoying a greater share of national wealth than before, but social equalization had not yet been attained. Although glaring inequalities common in the West had been eradicated and new cultural opportunities created, certain groups — soldiers, manual workers, and bureaucrats — enjoyed distinct advantages. The delegates were impressed by the enlightened attitudes towards children — an invariable reaction among English visitors — and by the cooperative spirit that inspired voluntary, unpaid labour to help rebuild devastated towns. At the same time they felt impelled to assert that this social progress had been achieved at an inordinate cost, not merely in con-comitant violence, but in the methods employed by the Communist Party to perpetuate its dominance. Even though the rigours of the terror had receded, personal liberty and free speech were severely curtailed; arrests persisted for alleged political offences; and the activities of the Extra-ordinary Commission evoked a 'pervading fear' that dissent would lead to imprisonment for counter-revolutionary activity.[10] Yet they were equally

213

certain that there was no viable alternative to Communist rule except a return to autocracy. Much as the delegates deplored the repressive features in the system, they demanded unconditional recognition of the present government. Appealing for a renewal of peace and friendship, they warned that 'to puruse a policy of blockade and intervention is madness and criminal folly which can only end in European disaster'.[11] Unhesitant in condemnation of British policy, they were able to balance Soviet accomplishments against more glaring defects. Unlike Lansbury, they could evaluate dispassionately, giving credit where due, without losing their perspective. The report set a standard for objectivity that later observers found difficult to emulate.

Such sobriety was not a feature of the subjective accounts that individual participants hastened to publish upon their return. Mrs. Snowden, one of two women in the delegation, produced a highly impressionistic version that mingled insight and inanity in equal measure. Often derided as a social climber,[12] the avowedly anti-Bolshevik wife of I.L.P. pioneer Philip Snowden ascribed much of Russian misery to Lenin's seizure of power. Conversations with remarkably candid dissidents confirmed her estimate that there was 'not an ounce of democratic control in the politics of Russia'.[13] The much-vaunted social equality was a misnomer: peasants welcomed the dissolution of the big estates, but servants continued to be mistreated, and party members, who constituted a new aristocracy, enjoyed special privileges.

However valid this assessment, it was based largely on hearsay. When Mrs. Snowden commented on what she had observed personally, her remarks were more favourable. Despite the undeniable hunger, dirt, and disease, strides had been made towards the equitable distribution of food; drunkenness had vanished; art was now within the reach of the poorest classes. She too had found no sign of social disorder: it was possible to walk the streets in absolute safety. In view of bureaucratic incompetence, mass illiteracy, the habit of violence, 'the wonder [was] not that they have failed to establish Socialism, but that they have successfully accomplished so much that is good'.[14]

Resentful about attempts to exploit the propaganda value of the British visit, Mrs. Snowden did not hesitate to reprove her hosts for seeking to erect a system upon class hatred. Although Lenin's 'engaging frankness' and twinkling eyes attracted her, she felt it incumbent upon herself to disabuse him of the notion that British workers were on the verge of adopting Communism. Like other delegation members, whose visit was trumpeted as a sign of solidarity, she avowed repeatedly that they had come as objective inquirers, not in order to endorse Communist methods.[15]

Bertrand Russell, who accompanied the group as an independent observer, was even more hostile than Mrs. Snowden, but far more penetrating in his critique. As he described his reactions many years later,

For my part, the time I spent in Russia was one of continually increasing nightmare. . . . Cruelty, poverty, suspicion, persecution, formed the very air we breathed. . . . I felt that everything that I valued in human life was being destroyed in the interests of a glib and narrow philosophy, and that in the process untold misery was being inflicted upon millions of people. With every day that I spent in Russia, my horror increased, until I lost all power of balanced judgment.[16]

Russell's objections were fundamental and unmitigated. His sceptical rationalism could not brook the doctrinal nature of Bolshevik ideology; its dogmatism offended his commitment to scientific inquiry and to the liberation of mankind from superstition. Nor could he accept its supposed benevolence: Bolshevism had erected a cruel dictatorship which concentrated authority in the hands of a self-constituted elite. As sole possessors of power, party members enjoyed material advantages that made a mockery of egalitarian pretensions. By imposing industrial conscription, the government, ostensibly the friend of the protelariat, had established 'an iron discipline, beyond the wildest dreams of the most autocratic American magnate'.[17] Unlike those travellers who yielded to Lenin's charm, Russell found him narrowly orthodox and opinionated, but agreed that he was honest, courageous, and 'destitute of self-importance'.[18]

Despite his antipathy, even Russell recognized that daily life in the Soviet Union bore little resemblance to the unmitigated horror depicted by the reactionary press. There was little disorder; women were safe from molestation; theatres were crowded. All this helped to foster an impression of 'virtuous, well-ordered activity', although in comparison with England, ordinary existence was 'drab, monotonous and depressed'.[19] Yet contrasts were significant: historically unprepared for democracy, Russia was also crippled industrially by war and woeful inefficiency. However repugnant to liberal sensibilities, the harsh dictatorship was performing 'a necessary though unamiable task'. Although Russians were inured to misery, the restoration of peace and commerce was essential not merely to ameliorate hardship, but to prevent the Soviet government from resorting to imperialist expansion in Asia for the sake of self-preservation.[20]

Charles Roden Buxton, secretary to the British delegation and a well-known recruit from Liberalism to the Labour Party, published his own study of a typical Russian village in 1922. Exhausted by the official round of receptions and exhibits, he had resolved to 'get right off the beaten track alone'. His choice of an obscure village east of the Volga seems to have been purely arbitrary and was certainly not dictated by Soviet officialdom. Containing nothing very startling, his modest book demonstrated the possibility, even in 1920, of independent exploration. It was a useful corrective to the urban focus of most early travel reports and confirmed the impression that hunger in the cities was less the result of food shortages than of peasant recalcitrance. In homes Buxton visited there was ample provision of such scarce items as eggs, butter, and even meat. On the other hand the dearth of manufactured goods, so notable in the major cities, was clearly evident in Ozero as well.

Buxton tried to convey to his British readers the ambivalence towards the government he perceived among the Ozero peasants. When the landlords' estates were divided among the villagers in 1917, no one receiving more than he and his family could work, the peasants applauded the revolution. But satisfaction of land hunger did not transform them into Communists. They complained that the Communists 'go too fast' and that the local Soviet 'is always taking things from us'. As far as Buxton could determine, the peasants felt obliged to the government for redistributing land but complained bitterly about the shortages and compulsory requisitions. Yet however much they protested, there was no evidence that they wished to replace the regime. 'They were for the Revolution; and for the moment Soviet power was the embodiment of the Revolution. They grumbled and cursed at it; but when the opportunity was offered to overthrow it, they said "No". ' [21]

Initially hostile to the Bolshevik takeover, H. N. Brailsford found his attitude mellowing considerably during the course of an eight-week visit in the autumn of 1920. A noted journalist, whose articles appeared regularly in the *Herald*, the *Nation*, and the *New Republic*, he was not intending to transmit dispatches during his trip for fear of offending his hosts. Perhaps as a consequence he was able to travel alone wherever he wished, unhindered by protocol or surveillance. Brailsford divided his time between Petrograd, Moscow, Minsk, and the central province of Vladimir, where he was the first foreign visitor in six years. Having intended to spend only a few days in Vladimir, he became so fascinated that he remained for a fortnight, learning more about Russia there than in the other six weeks. Here was able to observe a provincial Soviet in session. Without deceiving himself as to its influence, he was impressed by the practical experience in self-government. But it was clear that here, as in Moscow, Communist dictatorship prevented the development of any genuine representative system.

Throughout his journey he noted the emphasis on making culture accessible to the masses and especially to children. The educational progress indicated that the regime was 'ripening the whole Russian people for responsibility and power'.[22] Although distrust of intellectuals led the government to recruit teachers from the proletariat, the determination to break barriers of class and poverty pervaded all that he saw. With the proliferation of libraries, theatres, and concerts, the regime might well claim 'a better record in its relations to art and culture' than any other civilized government.[23] While applauding the cultural strides, the dedication of teachers, soldiers, and provincial administrators, and the visionary experiments to uplift this backward nation, he was apprehensive about the exercise of power in the Soviet Union. The hostile environment in which the

216

Bolsheviks had seized power, the resistance to their grandiose plans explained the source of the terror, but 'nothing can excuse [their] cruelty. To save the revolution, [they] are ruining Russia.'[24]

H. G. Wells was the most celebrated figure yet to visit the Soviet Union when he arrived in September as the guest of Maxim Gorki. During his stay he was invited to address to Petrograd Soviet, where he was introduced with fulsome praise and exhorted not to emulate Mrs. Snowden or Bertrand Russell by repaying their hospitality with sharp criticism. Speaking not as a Marxist, but as a 'Collectivist', Wells told his audience to look to liberal opinion rather than to social revolution in the West as the instrument of peace.

Having visited Russia six years before, he was appalled by the 'vast irreparable breakdown' of the social and economic system. The shops in Petrograd had 'an utterly wretched and abandoned look'; wooden houses were being demolished for firewood; ill-clad, hurrying people, all carrying loads, gave the impression that 'the entire population was setting out in flight'.[25] The government was unable to supply sufficient food to sustain healthy life, and in spite of covert trading of material goods, most people were shockingly underfed. Wells was especially dismayed by the plight of artists and intellectuals. Thanks to his friend Gorki, their suffering had been partially alleviated: a House of Science and a House of Literature and Art had been established to provide for their physical needs and to salvage cultural life. Although the writing of new books had ceased, writers were now being employed on a Russian encyclopedia; an Expertise Commission had begun the cataloguing of the abandoned art treasures of the previous regime.

Yet Wells never blamed the misery or even the disorganization of civilized life on the failures of Communism. The Russian catastrophe resulted from the collapse of a bankrupt system, the moral insufficiency of the ruling classes before the revolution, and exhaustion after six years of war. He was not certain that the Bolsheviks could achieve the superhuman task of restoring the nation, but he was convinced that the Soviet government, secure in its power, was the only force capable of staving off total collapse. While bemoaning its monumental inefficiency and its obsession with proletarian science and art, he found at least a glimmer of hope. Much as other visitors that year had done, Wells noted that Russian streets were safe and that, despite gigantic difficulties, the number and quality of schools had risen dramatically. Above all, it was his interview with Lenin which convinced him that Bolshevik leaders might actually succeed in establishing a new social order of a civilized type. If he did not quite measure up to Wells's image of the 'samurai' who would rule his idealized Utopia, Lenin offered Wells a vision of reconstructed industry, electrification, town planning, and improved transportation, assuring him that Communism could be 'enormously creative'. He failed to persuade

217

Lenin that social revolution in England was not imminent, but he ended his trip more convinced than when he arrived that radical steps were needed to prevent the collapse of Russian civilization. Unless the Western powers recognized the Bolshevik government and furnished material aid, it seemed likely that Russia would disintegrate into a peasant society, convulsed by petty civil wars, recurrent famine, and epidemics that might engulf the rest of Europe.[26]

II

After a spate of publications the pace of travel reports slackened. The viability of the regime, a point of contention during 1919 – 20, was no longer seriously questioned. In Russia the desire for a breathing space led to the formulation of the New Economic Policy; revolutionary ardour was sacrificed to the hope of economic revival and strenuous efforts to stimulate trade with the West. The containment of revolutionary goals, later embodied in the concept of socialism in one country, made the Soviet Union seem less menacing to Western socialists, but at the same time party dictatorship, bureaucratic rigidity, and repression of dissent could no longer be dismissed as transitory responses to the exigencies of war. As its more objectionable features came to be recognized as permanent, travellers preferred to focus their attention on the ways in which the regime was consolidating its hold on the country, stressing economic gains rather than political deficiencies. The death of Lenin in January 1924 and the almost simultaneous diplomatic recognition by the Labour government rekindled interest in travel to the Soviet Union, which was encouraged by its leaders who recognized the propaganda value of such visits. Russian authorities became more adept at revealing only those features of the regime they wished to publicize, and inquisitive British visitors had greater difficulty in circumventing restrictions on movement and personal contacts. It is clear that in some cases they allowed themselves to be deceived by the elaborate stratagems devised by those officials who stage-managed the reception of foreign visitors. Not only were the hazards of economic development concealed, but far less attention was focussed on the role of Stalin than on Lenin. In contrast to 1920, when Bolsheviks strove to defend their tactics, later visitors encountered leaders confident of their power and willing to trust to a selective presentation of their achievements to make the desired impression.

In November 1924, shortly after the fall of the Labour government, the T.U.C. sent a delegation to Russia whose members included Herbert Smith, of the Miners' Federation, and Ben Tillett. A. A. Purcell, then Vice Chairman of the T.U.C. General Council, led the group, and George Young, a left-wing writer on foreign affairs who accompanied the 1920 deputation, accompanied them as an adviser and later wrote most of the report. Throughout their trip they were met by 'enthusiastic groups of workers, who rushed forward to meet us, and expressed spontaneously their gratitude to us for visiting them'. Those who had visited Russia four years earlier noted that there were no longer signs of extreme poverty; children seemed well cared for, although many older people had 'evidently passed through a period of great trial, oppression, and persecution'. While in Moscow the delegation visited Lenin's mausoleum, attended performances at the Opera House, toured the Kremlin, and were guided through prisons in which criminals were humanely treated and given occupational training. During the next month they investigated industries, mines, workshops, and housing as they toured Kharkov, the Don Basin, Rostov, Baku, and Tiflis. They marvelled at aristocratic estates transformed into convalescent homes for workers and model villages constructed near the Grozny oilfields.[27]

The authors of the report took great pains to affirm their objectivity. Although given every facility needed to pursue their inquiry, they relied on the findings of their own experts and claimed to check official pronouncements with members of the opposition. While it is not clear that they encountered many dissidents or that those they met were free to express their views, they insisted that the delegation 'came well provided with means of getting into touch with opposition opinion and was kept continuously in contact with it'. However sympathetic, it was impossible to deny the total control over political machinery, the press, schools, and the army. At the same time they contended that this did not constitute dictatorship as ordinarily understood. If elections differed from the West, there was no evidence that the regime had undermined the representative power of the Soviet system. It was responsive to criticism, willing to recognize failure and to permit changes in personnel and policy without the periodic oscillations of democratic politics. If the rulers of the Soviet Union survived in power, it was because they governed with the 'tacit consent of a great majority of the electorate'.[28] There was even less hesitation in their pronouncements about Soviet justice: unlike the Cheka, repressing counter-revolutionaries, the GPU in its efforts to preserve public order resembled the British C.I.D. In contrast to Tsarist cruelty, the ordinary criminal was now confined not for punitive reasons, but with a view to educating him to become a useful citizen. In several areas the delegates were willing to take intention for achievement. The new educational system eliminated sex distinctions, emphasized science and foreign languages, but was hampered by the lack of competent teachers. The majority of workers had obtained better housing, but there was still overcrowding, and improvements in the cities mainly affected the higher grades. Not only was the Soviet worker free to follow any trade, but he was better able than anywhere else to advance himself occupationally and to take advantage of educational opportunities. The report predicted that wastage of talent, so lamentable a feature of the capitalist society, would disappear in the Soviet Union.

Although the document was not a total whitewash, it is clear that the delegates allowed themselves to be hoodwinked. Dazzled by carefully choreographed demonstrations, they interpreted lack of protest as a sign of mass approval. While noting that no attack on the Communist Party was tolerated, they argued that considerable latitude was allowed in the form of open discussion of social and economic questions and even maintained that Russian citizens enjoyed freedom of self-expression. It is clear that the Soviet authorities succeeded in their purpose: seeking to project an image of a stable society in which workers enjoyed wider social benefits than under capitalism, they guided the perceptions of the British delegation to ensure that they would return a favorable verdict.[29]

Brailsford had a second glimpse of the Soviet Union when he returned there in the spring of 1927 for the *New Leader*. His first trip had fired his enthusiasm, but he had questioned whether the revolutionary impetus — or indeed the regime itself — would survive. These doubts had been dispelled by the time he returned six and a half years later, determined to be impressed by what he saw. Above all, it was the improved living conditions, the easing of the stern puritanical tension of the civil war, that he noted. In Moscow, where vodka once again flowed freely, the people were no longer subsisting on herring broth and potato parings. The change was even more remarkable in Vladimir, the high point of his earlier trip. In 1920 shops had been open only a few hours a day until their meagre stocks were exhausted; now the windows, crammed with goods, beckoned customers. The Sobinka factory, with barely enough cotton to keep workers busy in 1920, had been replaced by a vast new mill, well-equipped, powered by electricity, and humming with activity.

Brailsford was no less struck by evidence that the regime had won acceptance from the people. In the factories he visited, the workers' council seemed to have gained full control over the social institutions, and the distinctions of the past had been eliminated. In contrast to the atmosphere of suspicion prevailing in 1920, he now discovered factory newspapers publishing complaints against the bureaucracy. Villages managed their own affairs through elected soviets, an indication that the people were 'realizing the earliest and simplest conception of democracy'.[30]

As in 1920, he refused to restrict himself to tourist sights or to rely on official propaganda to form his impression. Unlike many British visitors, he was familiar enough with life in Eastern Europe to appreciate the contrasts with pre-revolutionary conditions. Yet he allowed his enthusiasm to shape his judgment. Never deluded about authoritarian elements, he still maintained that 'the mass of the population, even in the villages, accepts the leadership of the Communist Party with feelings that vary from

220

acquiescence to enthusiasm'.[31] Genuine social progress obscured the rigours of dictatorship; his credulity allowed him to believe that the promise would be fulfilled. That the regime provided a framework for democratic criticism, that it perceived itself as a federation of socialist republics did not prevent a centralized, totalitarian state from emerging. Whatever his misgivings, he was ready to conclude that even the absence of political liberty was 'a small loss compared with this inestimable gain of social freedom'.[32]

III

The third phase of travel accounts, dating from 1930 – 32, coincided with the onset of depression and galloping unemployment in Great Britain. Through the device of the Five Year Plan the Soviet Union launched a massive struggle to transform its economy by rapid industrialization and forced collectivization in agriculture. What left-wing observers in England saw, at least at first, was not the coercion of resistant peasants or the subordination of consumer demand to industrialization, but the efficacy of planning to achieve the kind of growth needed to ensure full employment. With socialist goals at home sacrificed to the imperatives of international finance and the dole queues growing every year, the Soviet experiment became increasingly appealing, especially as long as the most unsavoury aspects of Stalinist tyranny could be concealed.

By the 1930s English travellers had learned that their Soviet hosts were less than candid about the defects of the regime and ordinarily displayed only the triumphs of Communism. When Aneurin Bevan, John Strachey, and George Strauss toured the Soviet Union in the summer of 1930, they reported that 'we saw everything we wanted: not necessarily what the Russians wanted to show us'. This determination to circumvent the constraints of the authorized tour led them to inspect Leningrad slums as well as new housing estates. They found that despite huge enterprises launched under the Five Year Plan, 'the side of economic life which caters for the people's needs has been comparatively neglected'. Alongside staggering industrial progress, there was persistent 'suffering, difficulty and dislocation in daily life'.[33] During their three-week trip they visited the dam and power station at Dniepostroi, an engineering plant in Leningrad, the Schacti mines, an agricultural machinery factory near Rostov, and several collective farms. Without underestimating the discomforts and privation, they were impressed by the 'keenness and intensity of labour'. Sceptical of optimistic output predictions, they seemed oddly oblivious to the extent of the agricultural crisis which the Soviet authorities took such pains to deny. Rather than question forced collectivization, they insisted that, inefficiency and disorganization notwithstanding, it was 'raising the whole

221

standard of Russian agriculture' and constituted 'the greatest change which has taken place' since the revolution.[34] Although cautious in their enthusiasm, the three British politicians tended to exaggerate the social benefits of the Five Year Plan, naively acccepting assurances that coercion had already been abandoned. The tangible achievements, not merely collectivization and industrial growth, but the new cultural life for the workers as well, were 'so far-reaching and so valuable to the Russian people' that it was inconceivable to imagine their disappearance.[35]

The celebrated visit of George Bernard Shaw and Nancy Astor attracted most of the publicity in July 1931, but Shaw wrote little about the actual visit aside from a ludicrous letter to *The Times* in which he equated Communism and Fabian Socialism.[36] Far more instructive was Julian Huxley's account of a visit during the same summer with a party of doctors and scientists under the auspices of the Society for Cultural Relations. Huxley exhibited the cultural relativism notable in many English visitors when he warned readers to 'discard some of [their] bourgeois ideas about democracy, religion and traditional morality' and refrain from judging Russians by British standards.[37] In spite of continuing economic and social inequality, Communist society represented a distinctive experiment in collective living, working, playing, and thinking. He welcomed the stress on sport and exercise, which contributed to health and efficiency, and praised the Park of Culture and Rest in Moscow where workers could relax or attend the cinema or enjoy community singing and dancing. A visit to a Moscow bathing place caused him to marvel at the splendid physiques and at the naturalness of the setting where, separated only by a fence, men and women bathed naked. Looking at the workers of Moscow and Leningrad, he formed the distinct impression that their health and physiques were better than those of British working people.

As a scientist he was particularly interested in the primacy of planning with scientific research as an essential component. Unlike England, where budgetary constraints impeded scientific progress, Russia devoted a larger proportion of national income to research than England had done even during prosperity. He found the vast scale of the Institute of Plant Industry astonishing and denied that pure science was stifled by the utilitarian focus of research activity. The accomplishments in agricultural research were more notable than those in public health, still hampered by lack of trained personnel and ignorance of hygiene among the masses, but he commended the Russians for having raised standards, eliminated epidemics, and provided excellent medical care for workers.

Huxley's conclusions were mixed. He realized that the Soviet Union had not yet fulfilled its promise, but he had little doubt that it was headed in the right direction, especially in the areas of scientific research and health policy where it was already in advance of other countries. He found aesthetic judgment stifled by rigid orthodoxy; architectural design was dull and mediocre, raising doubts in his mind whether Communism was compatible with cultural creativity. Despite the forcible repression from above, which he freely admitted, there was a good deal of genuine popular enthusiasm in what had become a land of workers. The educational opportunities for the young, the increased provision of leisure facilities, the seeming efficiency of the People's Courts, the improvements in medical care helped to explain why 'in spite of all its difficulties, Communist Russia is a going concern, thoroughly alive . . . and prepared to endure more for the realization of its Plan'.[38]

In 1932 the New Fabian Research Bureau decided to send an investigating team of a dozen men and women to Russia. Unlike the triumphal progress of the Webbs in the spring, their four-week tour of Leningrad, Moscow, and the Ukraine was a much more low-key affair, a serious effort by experts from within the Labour movement to probe particular problems in Soviet life. The group, coordinated by Margaret Cole, was broadly representative of English socialism, ranging from the moderate politician and economist Hugh Dalton to the fellow-travelling lawyer D. N. Pritt. The report published the following year was not a collective summary but distinct essays, each written by a participant on his or her speciality: finance, agriculture, the legal system, architecture, women and children, film, the media, and industry, among others. Its authors believed their work to be impartial, but Mrs. Cole later conceded that it was nothing of the kind. While few of the chapters were as laudatory as Pritt's encomium to Soviet justice, the investigators celebrated the sense of collective purpose and minimized what they did not wish to admit. 'We went to the U.S.S.R. believing it to be the hope of the world,' she wrote, and there was little opportunity amid the arranged, chaperoned tours to revise their extravagant estimations.[39]

Since the First Five Year Plan was drawing to a close, the investigators were concerned to evaluate the effect of state planning. Dalton, a keen advocate of planning if no great admirer of the Soviet Union, clearly approved of the fact that planning had become the dominant principle in Russian economic life and traced its impact in the rapid advance of heavy industry and electrification. On the other hand inefficiency abounded, and the standard of living of most workers had been sacrificed to the imperatives of construction. In their essays Graeme Haldane and John Morgan underscored Dalton's scepticism about whether the gap between goal and achievement could be bridged. Haldane observed that despite the emphasis on rapid electrification, transportation and communication, equally essential for industrial growth, had been neglected. Although the state was providing facilities for training and education, the shortage of skilled workers was a serious impediment. In order to compensate for the lower efficiency of Russian workers, factories operated on three shifts around the clock, and a six-day work week had been universally instituted in violation of standards implemented after the revolution. In his analysis of Soviet agriculture Morgan argued that the land was failing to meet the food requirements of the nation because official policies deterred peasant initiative. Only by assuring some economic benefits to the peasant would resistance to collectivization be overcome. He frankly admitted that shortages were at least as much a result of faulty government policies as they were the consequence of bad harvests or the decline in commodity prices.

In other areas their approval was more unqualified. G. R. Mitchison depicted Soviet factories as social units, whose managers were accessible and where wall newspapers testified to the freedom to criticize. Margaret Cole stressed the changing status of women, the improved facilities for children, and the fall in infant mortality. The architect Geoffrey Ridley condemned the monotony of Soviet buildings and lamented the continued failure to relieve overcrowding, but blamed failures on the legacy of the past and shortages of skilled labour. Whatever their defects, the new housing developments provided not merely salubrious homes for workers, but communal dining rooms, laundries, and kindergartens, improvements which ought to be incorporated into British standards of town planning.

In many ways the Fabian group typified the viewpoint of British travellers in the 1930s. It was not that they were blind to the defects of the regime or that they failed to recognize that repression was intrinsic to Soviet rule under Stalin. But the humanitarianism reflected in the social services, especially in relation to women and children, the priority ostensibly placed on social equality suggested that socialist principles were being implemented. That censorship persisted and that living standards were being at least temporarily sacrificed qualified, but did not undermine their enthusiasm. If they were prejudiced in favour of the Soviet Union, it was in part because the British government was remiss in providing for many of the needs the commissars were prepared to address. Conditions were harsh, particularly for dissidents, but no efforts were spared to promote scientific research, public health, education, and social welfare, all dear to the hearts of British socialists, especially in the aftermath of the second Labour government. Leaving a depressed England with its insoluble unemployment problem, they found 'a country which was tremendously excited, with an excitement which could not possibly be feigned, over the huge social experiment which it was making and which it believed was the people's own experiment'.[40]

Kingsley Martin, recently appointed editor of the *New Statesman*, was in the Soviet Union at the same time as the Fabian group, but his account, complementing David Low's satirical cartoons, was somewhat more frivolous in tone. He found little to romanticize in the discomfort and shortages of food and consumer goods, the overcrowding and lack of privacy. Leningrad reminded him of 'a French town behind the lines, drab, pinched, but concentrated for victory, which must surely come if you can

224

hold out long enough'.[41] On the other hand, certain aspects of the regime were superior to conditions in the West: there was no advertising of sex or violence; birth control information was easily accessible; abortion was legal; homosexuality was not criminally penalized; no stigma was attached to illegitimacy. In contrast to the exploitation of prurience in Western capitals, the Soviet government had 'got rid of the constant titillation which seeks for commercial purposes to stimulate sexual desire without offering the means of satisfying it'.[42]

If Martin's idiosyncratic analysis emphasized enlightened sexual mores, he also celebrated the apparent receptivity to criticism, which suggested not so much tyranny, as a readiness to sanction 'public washing of foul linen', at least in regard to inefficiency or slackness. While conceding some appalling failures, he was optimistic that the Soviets had discovered solutions to the employment problems that had eluded Western nations. While capitalism relied on the scourge of hunger to stimulate production, communism was able to appeal to the collective spirit, to the hope that by constantly striving they might inhabit a New Jerusalem. Martin questioned whether ordinary people might tire of the struggle, but not whether the inescapable repression betrayed its sense of purpose.[43]

After 1932 travel reports appeared less frequently, at least within the non-Communist left. Many impartial observers, like Walter Citrine, who went to Russia in 1935, objected openly to the constant propagandizing, the extravagant assertions of improving conditions that were belied by queues, squalour, and poor workmanship.[44] Malcolm Muggeridge claimed that sympathetic critics of the regime had done more to enhance its prestige than subsidized publications, but his vehement denunciation of the Soviet Union hardly redressed the balance.[45] Without turning its back on the Soviet experiment, the British left found it more difficult to disregard the unremitting tyranny, the exaggerated boasts about a workers' paradise, and the relentless proselytizing of Communist sympathizers in England. Much that was written between 1919 and 1932 was wrong or misguided, but dispassionate judgment was never entirely sacrificed. Travel literature fulfilled a necessary function by helping to inform opinion in the face of strong anti-Communist prejudice. If the views expressed erred on the side of indulgence, they were never as blind to the realities of Soviet life as Muggeridge averred. By shedding light, they helped to dispel illusions and may actually have done more to instill caution than the anti-Soviet tirades of the right-wing press. The avoidance of deification helped to ensure that for most readers of Russian travel accounts Communism never became the God that failed.

Notes

1 Quoted in David Marquand, *Ramsay MacDonald* (London, 1977), p. 208.

2 *Herald*, 24 March 1917.

3 Paul Hollander, *Passionate Pilgrims: Travels of Western Intellectuals to the Soviet Union, China and Cuba 1928 – 1978* (New York, 1981), p. 153. For a less tendentious interpretation, see the earlier work by Stephen Richards Graubard, *British Labour and the Russian Revolution, 1917 – 1924* (Cambridge, Mass., 1956). *Russian Bolshevism and British Labor 1917 – 1921* (New York, 1984) by Morton H. Cowden adds very little.

4 Arthur Ransome, *Six Weeks in Russia in 1919* (London, 1919), pp. 46, 72.

5 Ransom, p. 82.

6 George Lansbury, *What I Saw in Russia* (London, 1920), pp. 24, 28 – 9.

7 Lansbury, pp. 51, 73.

8 Raymond Postgate, *The Life of George Lansbury* (London, 1951), p. 204.

9 Lansbury, pp. xii – xv.

10 *Report of the British Delegation to Russia 1920* (London, 1920), pp. 6 – 10, 26 – 29.

11 *Ibid.*, p. 31.

12 Bertrand Russell reported that in Petrograd, where the former imperial limousine was put at the disposal of the delegates, Mrs. Snowden drove about 'enjoying its luxury and expressing pity for the "Poor Czar"'. See *The Autobiography of Bertrand Russell 1914 – 1944* (Boston, 1968), p. 141. Also see Norman and Jeanne MacKenzie, eds., *The Diary of Beatrice Webb*, Vol. III (1905 – 1924) (London, 1984), p. 385.

13 Mrs. Philip Snowden, *Through Bolshevik Russia* (London, 1920), p. 141.

14 *Ibid.*, p. 181.

15 *Ibid.*, pp. 43 – 4, 50, 116.

16 Russell, *Autobiography*, pp. 141 – 3.

17 Bertrand Russell, *The Practice and Theory of Bolshevism* (London, 1920), p. 96.

18 *Ibid.*, p. 36.

19 *Ibid.*, pp. 92, 97.

20 *Ibid.*, pp. 107 – 9.

21 Charles Roden Buxton, *In a Russian Village* (London, 1922), pp. 9, 41 – 2, 47 – 8.

22 H. N. Brailsford, *The Russian Workers' Republic* (London, 1921), p. 73.

23 *Ibid.*, p. 88.

24 *Ibid.*, p. 115. For a fuller assessment, see F. M. Leventhal, *The Last Dissenter: H. N. Brailsford and His World* (Oxford, 1985), pp. 164 – 7.

25 H. G. Wells, *Russia in the Shadows* (New York, 1921), pp. 17 – 18, 21 – 3.

26 Wells, pp. 158 – 61, 172 – 3.

27 *Russia. The Official Report of the British Trades Union Delegation to Russia and Caucasia Nov. and Dec. 1924* (London, 1925), pp. xiii – xx.

28 *Ibid.*, pp. 2 – 4, 17.

29 See Sylvia R. Margulies, *The Pilgrimage to Russia: The Soviet Union and the Treatment of Foreigners, 1924 – 1937* (Madison, Wisc., 1968), pp. 149, 181. A stridently anti-Soviet former Belgian consul later claimed that the authorities deliberately staged events for the delegation. At the Rostov railway works politically unreliable workers were given temporary leave in anticipation of the British visit and replaced by members of the Rostov GPU posing as workers. On another occasion, as a train carrying the British delegates passed a factory, peasants were mobilized to burn wet straw to give the illusion of black smoke from a thriving industry (Joseph Douillet, *Moscow Unmasked* (London, 1930), pp. 23 – 4).

30 H. N. Brailsford, *How the Soviets Work* (New York, 1927), p. 51.

31 *New Leader*, 23 March 1927.

32 Brailsford, *How the Soviets Work*, p. 157. Also see Leventhal, *The Last Dissenter*, pp. 205 – 8.

33 Aneurin Bevan, John Strachey, George Strauss, *What We Saw in Russia* (London, 1931), pp. 8 – 10.

34 *Ibid.*, pp. 16 – 19. Also see Hugh Thomas, *John Strachey* (London, 1973), pp. 84 – 7.

35 *What We Saw in Russia*, p. 28.

36 Letter to the Editor, *The Times*, 13 Aug. 1931.

37 Julian Huxley, *A Scientist Among the Soviets* (New York, 1932), pp. 4 – 5.

38 *Ibid.*, p. 55.

39 Margaret Cole, *Growing Up into Revolution* (London, 1949), p. 159. See Margaret Cole, *The Story of Fabian Socialism* (London, 1961). pp. 227 – 9. The N.F.R.B. report was published as *Twelve Studies in Soviet Russia*, Margaret I. Cole, ed. (London, 1933).

40 Cole, *Growing Up into Revolution*, p. 160.

41 Kingsley Martin, *Low's Russian Sketchbook* (London, 1932), p. 28.

42 *Ibid.*, p. 68.

43 *Ibid.*, pp. 82 – 3, 90, 108 – 11.

44 Sir Walter Citrine, *I Search for Truth in Russia* (London, 1936), pp. 177 – 80, 214. 143.

45 Malcolm Muggeridge, *Winter in Moscow* (London, 1934), pp. vi – vii. Also see John Bright-Holmes, ed., *Like It Was: The Diaries of Malcolm Muggeridge* (New York, 1982), pp. 19 – 42.

12

Henry Moore and the Blitz

Peter Stansky

The outpouring of cultural activities and achievements in England during the years of the Second World War, notable at the time, seems in retrospect a truly remarkable, even unparalled phenomenon. The achievements at their most impressive, and, as it has turned out, at their most enduring, have transcended national boundaries and historical circumstances. They have become a permanent part of Western culture in the twentieth century. Even the most selective list would include Virginia Woolf's *Between the Acts*, George Orwell's *Animal Farm*, T. S. Eliot's *Four Quartets*, the poems of Dylan Thomas gathered in *Deaths and Entrances*, the wartime films by Humphrey Jennings, especially *Fires Were Started*, the 'Shelter Drawings' by Henry Moore, and Benjamin Britten's first true opera, *Peter Grimes*. These, I emphasize, are the examples that immediately come to mind but they were not isolated achievements. Rather, one sees them as the most outstanding in their respective genres, surrounded by an impressive array of work approaching them in quality.

Indeed, to have so distinguished a creative outpouring in a period of six or seven years would be remarkable at any time. That it should have occurred in wartime, in a country engaged in a war that threatened its very existence, seems almost incredible. Nothing on a comparable scale had happened during the First World War. Wartime culture then would largely have meant propaganda, recruiting posters, patriotic popular songs, idealistic verse, escapist fiction to distract the attention of civilians in England from the horrifying realities of life in the trenches of France. (And of course it was in those trenches that the war poetry we think of still as the most important artistic work of the first war had its origins.) In the

228

postwar aftermath, in the disillusioned 1920s and the embittered 1930s, the notion of a linkage between war and an enrichment of culture would have seemed a far-fetched paradox. Yet what happened in 1939 was precisely that, and it provides a rich field of evidence for the social and cultural historian. It was a new phenomenon, certainly unprecedented, and it deserves to be studied, celebrated and perhaps explained.

There seems to have been, from the first, a determination — on the part of such responsible and farseeing public figures as John Maynard Keynes and Kenneth Clark, of such editors as John Lehmann of *Penguin New Writing* and Cyril Connolly of *Horizon*, and of such senior authors as E. M. Forster and Osbert Sitwell — a determination that 'culture' was not to be put aside for the duration; in the act of fighting to save England, English culture must not be sacrificed. The commitment of the government to art in all its manifestations was established as a principle early on. The creation of the War Artists' Advisory Committee, under Clark, and of the Committee for the Encouragement of Music and the Arts, under Keynes, would play a significant role in bringing art to the people of England even as the Blitz brought the war itself into their lives. The 'Home front,' a cozy-sounding phrase, was anything but cozy as the bombs fell night after night on London, and Manchester, and Coventry. Life in the wartime years went on at something like battle pitch. The emotional level was high, and it was a level at which it was possible for artists, composers and writers to create works of art — not as a way of escape, but of expressing the tension under which they lived.

My aim here is not to cover a broad canvas, but to focus instead on one of the most extraordinary artists of the war and the work he was inspired to produce then: the 'Shelter Drawings' of Henry Moore, how they came about and their significance, then and now.

On September 1, 1939, the German army invaded Poland: in effect, if not quite yet officially, the Second World War had begun. That date — September 1, 1939 — was affixed as a title to a poem by W. H. Auden, who had emigrated to America in January 1939 with the intention of becoming a citizen of the United States. The poem, too well known to need extensive quotation, begins:

> I sit in one of the dives
> On Fifty-second Street
> Uncertain and afraid
> As the clever hopes expire
> Of a low dishonest decade . . .

One of those hopes, of course, was that a *second* World War would never occur. Another hope, equally strongly felt, and very often by the same people who were anti-war, was that Nazi-Fascism might be contained, defanged, somehow be made to disappear. September 1, 1939, the date not the poem, made it clear that the two hopes were irreconcilable: that to be against war and fascism was a contradiction too deep to be papered-over by rhetoric or wishful thinking.

At ten o'clock on the morning of September 3, at Monk's House, their house in Rodmell, Sussex, a half-hour's drive from the English Channel, Leonard and Virginia Woolf were waiting for the Prime Minister, Neville Chamberlain, to speak to the nation. In the previous October he had spoken to the nation upon his return from meeting with Herr Hitler in Munich. He was, he had said, bringing 'peace with honour ' — he had the assurances of Herr Hitler that this was so.

Now, at ten o'clock in the morning, Virginia Woolf, who let hardly a day pass without writing in her diary, took it up and wrote.

This is I suppose certainly the last hour of peace. The time limit is out at 11. P[rime] M[inister] to broadcast at 11.15. L[eonard] & I "stood by" 10 minutes ago. . . . We argued. L. said Greenwood was right. . . . [This was a reference to Arthur Greenwood, the Deputy Leader of the Labour Party in the House of Commons. Urged to 'speak for England', he had insisted that the time for compromise was past and that England's duty was to honour her guarantee of aid to Poland.] I argued its 'they' as usual who did this. We as usual remain outside. If we win, then what? L. said its better to win, because the Germans . . . are what they are. . . . All the formulae are now a mere surface for gangsters. So we chopped words. I suppose bombs are falling on rooms like this in Warsaw. A fine sunny morning here; apples shining. . . .[1]

The mood at Monk's House was a compound of resignation, acceptance and weariness. In the diary Mrs. Woolf notes that 'sewing [blackout] curtains was an anodyne. pleasant to do something; but so tepid & insipid.'[2] That mood was not peculiar to the Woolfs, something comparable was pretty general throughout England. 1939 was not 1914, there were none of the confident high spirits that had marked the onset of the earlier conflict.

It is hard to believe that the prevailing mood on the 3rd of September at the small house in Kent where Henry Moore and his wife, Irina, lived, when not in London, was any more cheerful. If there is no documentation, such as an entry in a diary, there is the evidence of a drawing, done in pencil, pen and ink, chalk, crayon, and watercolour, signed and dated with unusual emphasis on the day, 'Moore Sept 3rd/1939.' (Usually, he signed his drawings simply with 'Moore' and the year.) Odd, enigmatic, and surrealistic, this drawing of September 3 offers a degree of literary content and particularly of detail that make it very different from most of Moore's 'Ideas for sculpture' and his other drawings of the period. It challenges us to decipher its meaning. What we see, beginning at the lower part of the drawing, are eight women bathing in the sea, submerged to their breasts, their heads confined in what appear to be gas-masks or, possibly, divers' helmets. Behind them is a strip of empty beach. Filling the upper half of the drawing, a great wash of dark cliffs encloses the scene, with only a marginal glimpse of empty sky above. The effect is alarmingly claustrophobic: as though these women with their strange headgear might have been dropped down in the sea — who are they? where have they come from? and why? — with no way out (not a footprint on the beach, not a path or stairway up the cliffs) of the predicament imposed upon them.

When this drawing was included in the comprehensive exhibition, 'The Drawings of Henry Moore', that began in Ontario in 1977, went on to three cities in Japan, and ended at the Tate Gallery in London in June 1978, Alan Wilkinson, who wrote the catalogue, provided this explanatory note.

> On 3 September, the day war was declared, the Moores were bathing off the Shakespeare Cliffs at Dover. He remembers hearing an air raid siren, an ominous prelude to the day and night warnings in London a year later during the Blitz. In this recreated scene of bathers with the cliffs in the background, the strange heads of the figures, evoking the world of science fiction, were probably suggested by the familiar form of gas masks. Standing chest high in the water, these forbidding women, alert and watchful, look across the Channel towards the French coast.[3]

This is clearly helpful; but since an enigma never admits of a final answer, it seems permissible to suggest that the scene is more likely to have been created than recreated, and that the images who populate it were almost certainly drawn from the artist's unconscious. France, across the Channel on this first day of the Second World War, would have deep, latent evocations for Moore; so too the gas masks that he imposed upon the women in the drawing — and that, in reality, in the year preceding the outbreak of war, were being distributed in London by authorities who feared a gas attack from the air. Moore himself had been a volunteer soldier in France in the First World War; he had worn a gas mask and had been under gas attack on the Western Front. So one may legitimately wonder if the drawing of these 'Henry Moore women', half submerged in the sea, is not a kind of symbolic recognition — or pre-recognition — of the changes that war might lead to for him as an artist. That of course the First War had not done, for he was not then an artist at all, though he wanted to be. But to understand what happened then, and would happen now, we must go back for a glance at the beginning of the story.

Henry Moore, the seventh of eight children of Raymond and Mary Moore, was born in 1898 in Castleford near Leeds in Yorkshire, where his father was a coal miner, and later a mining engineer. (Moore himself would not go down a mine until he did his drawings of miners during the Second World War.) The father encouraged his youngest son in his studies, and hoped that he would grow up to become a teacher, as an older brother and sister were to do. Henry went first to the local elementary school, and perhaps more importantly, in terms of his ultimate vocation, to the local Sunday school. For it was there, when he was ten, that he decided that he would become a great sculptor: 'Our Sunday School teacher told us how, when Michelangelo was carving his Head of a Faun, someone said, "But that's an old faun; surely an old faun would have lost some of his teeth?" Michelangelo took up his chisel and knocked two of the teeth out. "There you are," our teacher said. "There's the greatest sculptor in the world ready to take advice." What went click in my mind was not the moral but the fact that this was the greatest sculptor who ever lived. I'd always liked our drawing classes, and I'd carved bits of wood and stone. Now, instead of saying I wanted to be an engine driver, I said I wanted to be a sculptor.' The poet Donald Hall, who reported this story in 1966, went on to comment, 'He is still competing with Michelangelo.'[4]

Two years later at the age of twelve Henry won a scholarship to the Castleford Grammar School, where he received particular encouragement from the art teacher, Alice Gostick, one of the decisive figures in his early years. If his father's plan had been fulfilled, he would have gone on from grammar school to a Teacher Training College but the war intervened. In February 1917 he went into the army, served in France, and was gassed at the battle of Cambrai in December 1917. One can accept as a characteristic understatement his remark forty-four years later that, for him, 'the first world war passed in a kind of romantic haze of hoping to be a hero'.[5]

When he was finally demobilized in February 1919 he returned to teach at Castleford for a short time; then, using a grant available to him as an ex-service man, he studied at the Leeds School of Art for two years, from 1919 to 1921. There he had the valuable experience of getting to know well the avant-garde art collection of Sir Michael Sadler, at that time Vice-Chancellor of the University. In 1922, he went on from Leeds to study at the Royal College of Art in London for a further three years, during which he became familiar with the antiquities in the British Museum that were to have so significant an influence upon his development as a sculptor. Of his coventional art education, he was later to say: 'I'm terribly grateful that I didn't get to Leeds till I was old enough not to believe what I was told by teachers.'[6]

In 1922 he went to Paris, the first of more or less annual trips abroad. In 1924 he was appointed an instructor at the Royal College, where he taught until 1931, and then at the Chelsea School of Art where he was when the war broke out. In 1925 he had gone to the Continent on a travelling scholarship: his visit to Italy that year was surely the most important part of the trip, for it was then that he had his first encounters with the works of the early Renaissance painters and sculptors, Masaccio in particular, and, as one would expect, with the overwhelming achievements of Michelangelo. When he came back to London, he continued to haunt the galleries of the British Museum, studying the primitive, the pre-Columbian, the Egyptian, Etruscan, African and other antiquities there.

Moore had, and always would have, an abiding interest in nature, in stones and natural shapes, a belief in 'truth to materials'. Yet at the same time, he was then, and continued to be, by temperament and inclination, an artist with no wish or need to adopt the traditional realist approach of English art. From very early on, his genius as a sculptor expressed itself first in the act of carving, in discovering the form that he wanted in the block of stone or wood; and second in his extraordinary gift for abstraction. What emerged from the stone was not the portrait or effigy or likeness of a particular woman, but, as it were 'woman herself' or one might even say 'womanness.' And the two motifs that continued throughout his life are the reclining figure (virtually without exception of a woman), and the seated figure of a woman, holding her child. In his early experimental days before he had found his true style, he had to come to terms with the great variety of influences to which he had been subject. And there was a continuing tension between his admiration for the works of the Renaissance he had seen in Florence and his instinctive responsiveness to primitive sculpture he was seeing the British Museum. But the greatest demand that he made upon himself was to reconcile abstraction with the expression of emotion.

In *Heads Figures and Ideas*, there is a postcard photograph of an Egyptian head. Under it, Moore wrote 'XVIII Dynasty Egyptian — Head of a Woman (princess?) in the Archaeological Museum, Florence. I would give everything, if I could get into my sculpture the same amount of humanity & seriousness; nobility & experience, acceptance of life, distinction, & aristocracy with absolutely no tricks no affectation no self consciousness looking straight ahead, no movement, but more alive than a real person.'[7] (This, I contend, is what he was to achieve in his work in the Second World War.) He himself has recognized his wartime drawings as achieving 'perhaps a temporary resolution of that conflict which caused those miserable first six months after I had left Masaccio behind in Florence and had once again come within the attraction of the archaic and primitive sculptures of the British Museum'.[8]

In many ways, his most powerful sculptural works, once he had assimilated and surmounted his influences, were those that he carved himself in the early part of his career, especially in the 1930s, with their abstract but intuitive suggestion of fundamental forms of the human figure. But the 'humanity and seriousness' for which, as he said, he would 'give everything,' were still in the future.

Moore had his first one-man show in 1928, of 30 drawings and half a dozen sculptures. The young Kenneth Clark — he was then 25 — whose career would be intimately involved with Moore's, bought a drawing from the show for one pound. (Speaking conservatively, it would by now

233

have appreciated by some 10,000 per cent.) Others who came to that first exhibition to see, to admire, and even to buy included the painters Augustus John and Henry Lamb, and the sculptor Jacob Epstein. In fact, Moore was launched as an artist. From that time forward, his was a steady ascent to fame and recognition. Certainly the earliest and most remarkable act of recognition came from the distinguished critic, historian, and apostle of modernism, Herbert Read. In 1931, in his book *The Meaning of Art*, he proclaimed the stature of Henry Moore: 'We may say without exaggeration that the art of sculpture has been dead in England for four centuries; equally without exaggeration I think we may say that it is reborn in the work of Henry Moore, [who] in virtue of his sureness and consistency, is at the head of the modern movement in England.'[9]

In 1931 this must have seemed as much a manifesto and a prophecy as it was an evaluation of Moore's achievement thus far. But by the end of the decade, the prophecy had been fulfilled. Among admirers of modern art, he was the foremost sculptor in England. But in England then, modern art was still being viewed with a good deal of hostility and incomprehension — a sculpture in the Moore style, a reclining woman with holes punched through her, was a suitable subject for laughter in *Punch*. Although Moore had many purchasers for his work, he still needed to teach to survive financially, and in 1939 he was still on the staff at the Chelsea Art School.

This sketchy and compressed, but I hope intelligible, summary of Moore's early career brings us to the coming of the war, which was to change so much. But for Moore, as for so many others in England, the changes came more slowly than they had anticipated. The next several months turned out to be the period of the phoney war, or the great bore war, that Evelyn Waugh satirized in his novel *Put Out More Flags*, and that came to an end only in April 1940 with Hitler's invasion of Denmark and Norway. Moore more or less continued as before, remaining in his Kent cottage, where he was able to sculpt outdoors, as he preferred to do, while going up to London two days a week to teach at the Chelsea School of Art. Kenneth Clark invited him to stay at his house in Gloucestershire, but the Moores saw no reason not to stay on at their cottage. Moore was at work on an exhibition to be held in Leicester Galleries, in London, in February 1940, consisting of 20 sculptures and 31 drawings, which would prove very successful in terms of sales.

Increasingly, however, the war began to interfere. It became harder to acquire the stone necessary for his work, and even harder to arrange for its transport. He worked on small lead figures. In the spring of 1940, he turned exclusively to drawings. With the threat of invasion, the area around Dover was likely to become a restricted zone and the Moores gave up their cottage, first moving into their studio in London and then to a nearby one, at 7 Mall Studios in Hampstead. As he wrote to James Johnson Sweeney in 1943: 'Up to the Fall of France . . . there were no difficulties

234

over going on doing sculpture just as before, and except that one was intensely concerned over the war and greatly worried about its course and eventual outcome, it had no new or direct visual experiences for me which had any connection with work. But when France fell and a German invasion of England seemed more than probable, I like many others thought the only thing to do was to try to help directly.' [10]

Moore, casting about for a way to help in the war effort, had, along with Graham Sutherland, applied to take a course in precision toolmaking at the Chelsea Polytechnic, but, as there were many more applications than positions, they heard nothing. When the Chelsea Art School presently moved itself to Northampton, Moore did not follow it. Expecting to be called up any day for some sort of service, he worked only on drawings, which could be done in the short run. Of course he had always made drawings as part of the preparation for sculptures, and some independent portraits, such as a famous one of Stephen Spender, made around 1937. His tendency, when working on a drawing as a preliminary for a sculpture, was to start with a more realistic version and then progressively simplify it. But, as he would point out: 'The great value and purpose of drawing from life, from nature, is to intensify one's observation, to concentrate on looking, and so increase one's knowledge, understanding and appreciation of the object.' [11] But now, he was, because of a combination of circumstances, to devote himself exclusively to drawings. Later, he would explain: 'There seemed no point in starting work on a new sculpture and so I concentrated on drawings. Then came the Battle of Britain . . . and the blitz began.' [12]

Up until this point, he had not had any interest — nothing that he wanted to do artistically — in joining the War Artists Scheme, despite the urgings of his friend Kenneth Clark, the chairman of the War Artists' Advisory Committee. The official role of War Art had been, after much difficulty, well established during the First World War. Artists were to provide a record of the war; and in some instances, though it was very much a lesser consideration, they might even create something of greater artistic merit. This had certainly been true of such painters as Paul Nash, Stanley Spencer, and Wyndham Lewis. So there was little resistance to the thought that something of a similar nature should happen during this war as well. In August 1939, Clark proposed a committee to the Ministry of Information and it came into being the following January.

A few artists' organizations outside the Government had been already formed by that time, such as Paul Nash's Oxford Art Bureau. Nash was concerned that artists might too rapidly be called up as servicemen, and he established a Panel of Authorities — John Betjeman, Lord David Cecil, Lord Berners and John Piper — to compile lists of artists who might be appropriate, and the lists were sent to ministries. But Nash's efforts were superseded by the War Artists' Advisory Committee, which would appoint certain artists as official artists and have the right of first refusal for all their work.

Clark wished to have almost all approaches and sorts of artists in the scheme, but his particular concern was with those who might be regarded as too advanced, too experimental, and hence not be appropriate for the scheme. In his autobiography, he explained, 'I was not so naive as to suppose that we should secure many masterpieces, or even a record of the war that could not be better achieved by photography. My aim, which of course I did not disclose, was simply to keep artists at work on any pretext, and, as far as possible to prevent them from being killed.' [13] Indeed, the artists to whom he was closest — Graham Sutherland and Henry Moore — emerged as the most important artists of the Second World War. If it were not for his particular interest, they might not have been urged, being more abstract than academic, to turn their artistic interest to the war, or, even worse, been put upon some inapproriate task.

Thanks to the War Artists scheme important work was done outside England by such painters as Anthony Gross, Eric Ravilious, Edward Bawden, Leonard Rosoman, and Edward Ardizzone. Yet it is striking that the greatest art work of the war should have been done on the home front. Not only Moore and Sutherland in London, but Stanley Spencer in the shipyards on the Clyde, Paul Nash in his extraordinary paintings of fighter planes in the air war over Britain, culminating in the greatest single oil masterpiece of the war, *Totes Meer (Dead Sea)* of wrecked German planes. It was perhaps the most extensive patronage scheme for British artists that has ever existed, and it resulted in nearly 6,000 works of art, eventually most of them distributed to museums, with the Tate Gallery and the Imperial War Museum having the first pick.[14] It also resulted in a higher evaluation placed by the public and those who were seriously concerned with art, upon British art not only of the present but of the past.

Clark, looking back, admitted he 'did not suppose that the war artists scheme would produce many outstanding works of art'. In fact, he added with justifiable pride, 'it did. . . . John Piper was the ideal recorder of bomb damage, and Graham Sutherland transferred his feelings for the menacing forms of roots and trees to twisted girders and burned out bales of paper. Above all the tube shelters gave Henry Moore a subject that humanised his classical feeling for the recumbent figure, and led to a series of drawings which will, I am certain, always be considered the greatest works of art inspired by the war.' [15]

Despite Clark's urgings, Moore had not been particularly interested in becoming a war artist for there was nothing that ignited even a spark of inspiration. But then came the Blitz in September 1940, and Moore changed his mind. 'Then,' as he remarked: 'there were things happening in London.' [16] And the artist responded.

The use of the underground or tube stations as shelters was a development for which the people of London themselves were responsible. The government was explicitly opposed to the idea, however logical it might seem, fearing what was called a 'deep shelter complex'. Moreover, 'Crowded shelters, besides being a perfect breeding place for various physical infections, would encourage every form of mass hysteria from defeatism to panic.'[17] But such objections were overridden by events. On September 12, five days after the Blitz had started, the poor, increasingly demoralized, took action into their own hands and descended into the tubes.[18]

Tube shelters might not be particularly desirable — hygienically, or psychologically — but people had gone down into them for safety during the air raids of the First World War, and were determined to do so again. There was no legal way by which the government could prevent people from buying penny-halfpenny platform tickets and seeking shelter from the nightly raids. And of course they would do this early in the day. When the raids began, it would have taken longer to reach a tube shelter than the seven minutes allowed between the first warning sirens and the beginning of the raid. Eventually the government was forced to follow the lead of the populace and attempt to improve the standard of comfort and sanitation in the underground cities of the tubes, providing lavatories and building tier bunks for children. Food and medical services rapidly improved. But when Moore saw the shelters first they were still in their most primitive state.

In a way, the situation was emblematic of the war: tube-platforms full of shelterers at the same time that ordinary life went on, and the trains continued to run, although on schedules affected by the raids. People would start to queue up early in the morning to get on the platform and establish their territory. Up until 7.30 in the evening they had to keep eight feet from the edge, from 8.00 until 10.30, four feet, and then when the trains stopped running they could take over, even slinging hammocks over the rails. Even so, of course, sleep was difficult, men averaging 4½ hours and women 3½ hours. 'Sleep replaced food as the simplest, most everyday, object of desire.'[19] Not so surprisingly then, many of the most dramatic and moving of Moore's drawings would depict people sleeping.

Londoners sheltering in the tubes was what Moore discovered fortuitously on that now legendary evening in the history of British art, early in September 1940. In his account of the moment, Moore writes:

We owned a little Standard coupé and as a rule we used it when going into town. But one evening we arranged to meet some friends at a restaurant and for some reason or other went into town on the 24 bus instead of going by car. We returned home by Underground [because the buses had stopped running] taking the Northern Line train to Belsize Park station. It was a long time since I'd been down the tube. I'd noticed that long queues were forming outside Underground stations at about seven o'clock every evening but hadn't thought much about it, and now for the first time I saw people lying on the platforms at the stations we passed: Leicester Square, Tottenham Court Road, Goodge Street, Euston, Camden Town, Chalk Farm. It happened to be the first night on which a big anti-aircraft barrage was put up all round London. I think it was done to help the morale of Londoners more than anything else: it made a terrific noise and gave the impression that we were hitting back at the raiders in a big way. When we got out at Belsize Park we were not allowed to leave the station because of the fierceness of the barrage. We stayed there for an hour and I was fascinated by the sight of people camping out deep under the ground. I had never seen so many rows of reclining figures and even the holes out of which the trains were coming seemed to me to be like the holes in my sculpture. And there were intimate little touches. Children fast asleep, with trains roaring past only a couple of yards away. People who were obviously strangers to one another forming tight little groups. They were cut off from what was happening up above, but they were aware of it. There was tension in the air. They were a bit like the chorus in a Greek drama telling us about the violence we don't actually witness. [20]

He now had a purpose — to record what he had seen that night and would see again night after night. His interest was in drawings as finished works in themselves and not as preliminary studies for sculpture. 'The first year of the shelter drawings was for me a very exciting and unique period,' he remembered forty years later. 'The tremendous excitement of seeing, the morning after the raid, the blitzed buildings that had been whole the day before. If the drawings of this period reflect my feelings it is because I was completely occupied in *only drawing* at this period. To me at that time it seemed that nothing had ever happened in the world like that before. Unlike anything that had ever happened in other wars. . . . All those hundreds of people huddled together in the Underground were rather like what one imagined were the people huddled in the bottom of a slave ship. I felt here was a group of people — having things done to them, and being absolutely helpless.' [21]

Robert Melville has compared Moore's going down into the tubes to Turner's rush to the burning Houses of Parliament in 1834. 'It led directly to a series of drawings which record the strangest aspect of the most critical months in our history and which constitute one of the greatest pictorial achievements of British art.' [22]

The next morning he started his drawings, and in succeeding nights continued to go down into the tubes. He would not disturb the privacy of the shelterers but made notations of what he saw on the back of envelopes intending to work on the drawings later, in his studio in Hampstead. 'After all,' he explained, 'the shelterers were leading private or family lives. . . . To have sketched them would have been an intrusion . . .' [23] 'You couldn't sit in the shelters and draw people undressing their children — it was too private.' [24] Soon he was doing as many as three drawings a day. It was a time of extraordinary artistic activity: the conjunction of the pressures of war and inspiration. At last, as he told Kenneth Clark, he was ready to join the War Artists scheme. Altogether

238

he would fill two sketch books, part of a third, and finish about sixty-five large drawings.[25]

When Clark saw the first sketch book, he felt that it was a natural coming together of Moore's qualities. 'In 1939 he was known purely as an 'abstract' artist, but I had fortunately seen one or two groups of draped figures that he had done in 1938 which suggested that the problem of representing huddled, sleeping forms would appeal to him technically; while the human qualities of courage and stoicism would appeal to his warmth of heart.'[26]

Meanwhile, Moore was to experience directly in his own life something of the consequences of the bombings. He and his wife had been staying for the weekend with friends, Leonard Matters, a Labour M.P., and his wife, in the village of Much Hadham in Hertfordshire. The Matters urged them to stay longer in the comparative safety of the countryside, though it was only thirty miles from London, and they could see the fiery glow of the air raids lighting up the sky. But Moore wished to return to London to work on the drawings. 'We left them on the Monday morning in the little Standard Coupé that we had in those days, and for which I had a small petrol ration, being a war artist. When we got to Hampstead, the road leading to our studio was cordoned off by the police because of an unexploded bomb. A policeman said "You can't go this way. Where do you live?" I said "7 Mall Studios," and he said "Oh, they're flat to the ground" with almost a kind of enjoyment in the devastation.'[27] 'We found that the warden had mistaken Parkhill Studios for Mall Studios, but although our place was not down it had suffered badly from the blast. The doors were blown out all the windows and top lights smashed. Fortunately, only one of the sculptures was damaged — a reclining figure in brown Hornton. . . . We managed to cover up the sculpture, but it was impossible to sleep there and we asked Leonard Matters if we could stay at his Much Hadham place until we found somewhere else to live.'[28]

In Much Hadham they discovered that they could rent half of a house called Hoglands. 'It was in a pretty tumble-down state, but anywhere was good enough in those days. On the first night we slept there, the nose of an anti-aircraft shell came through the roof.'[29] A month or so later, they were offered the whole house and the Moores used £300 to put down a deposit: precisely the sum that the surrealist artist, Gordon Onslow Ford, had recently paid him for an elm wood reclining figure.

Much Hadham served as a base for the shelter drawings. He would drive the thirty miles into London for two days each week, spend the night in the shelters making observations, then sketch for two days. 'The rest of the time I spent working on drawings to show the War Artists Committee. I would show them eight or ten at a time and they would choose four or five leaving me to do what I liked with the rest.'[30] He had his favourite among the underground stations, those that excited a particular visual response, Cricklewood, and especially Liverpool Street underground extension. It was a newly constructed tunnel in which the rails had not been put down and 'at night its entire length was occupied by a double row of sleeping figures'.[31]

It was a time of extraordinary artistic concentration for Moore. The first three or four months were the most intense, but he was at work on the 'Shelter Drawings' for about a year; that is, more or less the entire period of the Blitz. It was his way of fully participating in the war, and he had created eternal images of what the war was like for the Londoner while the city was burning. Here he took the themes of his earlier sculpture — particularly reclining women — and raised their humanity to a new level. He had discovered a huge city in the depths of the earth, a sort of counter-city to the one above, and he revelled in its chaos and confusion, the sense of the people both being oppressed, and coping, with a certain nobility, with their situation. All of his previous years concentrating on life-drawing for the uses of his abstract sculpture prepared him to render these figures from life he found in the London underground in the year of the Blitz.

Today we are more than forty years beyond the war, the Blitz, the underground shelters — everything that inspired and occasioned the drawings. Having survived the historic past, they have won a secure place among the great works of the century. Scholars, critics, estheticians, and analysts of the collective unconscious feel free to range among them. They are variously associated with Egyptian tombs, Etruscan funeral sculpture, the Nazi death camps, and Jungian archetypes. But the one relationship that was essential to their existence — their relationship to Britain at war in 1940 — tends nowadays to be under-emphasized or even ignored. Admittedly we are living in an age when historical memory is short — if this is true of politics, as it is, when so many of our leaders seem to be suffering from amnesia, then why should it not be true for the work of art, which too often is treated as though it had been created in a vacuum? As a historian, I regret the tendency: hence I have given this circumstantial and factual account of how the shelter drawings came into being. For the same reason, I will conclude with a brief account of the significance of the drawings in Moore's own life and career, and their immediate sequel.

In fact, it was with the 'Shelter Drawings' that his fame became general, at home and abroad. In 1941, a show of British art at the Museum of Modern Art in New York included four of the drawings — his launching in America. The next year, Kenneth Clark, as director of the National Gallery in London, arranged to display there a large number of the drawings. The English, starved for art — the Gallery, for safety reasons, had had its collections of paintings removed and stored in a mine in Wales — flocked to the Moore exhibition and its impact was considerable. Londoners, ordinary people, had no difficulty in recognizing something that many of them had known imtimately. Moore's art was no longer an experience for the few; and, as critics were quick to point out, he had achieved his effects at no sacrifice or compromise of his individual genius.

Perhaps the most significant visitor to the show at the National Gallery was an Anglican clergyman, the Reverend Walter Hussey of Saint Matthew's Church in Northampton. Hussey, a collector of modern art, had long felt that the Church should once again resume its historic but long neglected role as a patron of artists. He himself had already made a start in that direction by commissioning a Cantata, 'Rejoice in the Lamb', from Benjamin Britten. Hussey was strongly moved by the drawings; it occurred to him, seeing those figures of women, cowled in draperies, often holding a child, that Moore might be persuaded to carve a Madonna and Child for Saint Matthew's. He wrote to him proposing the commission and, in due course, Moore accepted. This was to be his first new major sculpture since the war began, and, as it turned out, the last that he would actually carve himself for many years. (Most of his postwar sculpture would be small moulded clay or plaster maquettes, which were then cast in bronze and brought up to immense size.) The 'Madonna and Child' that Moore produced in 1944 for Saint Matthew's, Northampton, directly and fully attains the 'humanity and seriousness, the nobility and experience' that he so valued, and had achieved before, most memorably, in the 'Shelter Drawings'.

It is one of the paradoxes of life and art that these two great achievements should have been produced under the urgent, dangerous conditions of war — not war as something far off that one might read about in a headline, but as a part of ordinary life in a city that had become a target for destruction. In retrospect, one sees that the 'Shelter Drawings' and the 'Madonna and Child' occupy a unique place in Moore's career which would continue in a different direction when the war was over. They form a category of their own, and as such are unrivalled: the war works of Henry Moore.

Notes

1 Anne Oliver Bell, ed., *The Diary of Virginia Woolf, V: 1936 – 1941* (London, 1984), p. 223.
2 *Ibid.*
3 Alan G. Wilkinson, *The Drawings of Henry Moore* (London, 1977), p. 103.
4 Donald Hall, *Henry Moore* (London, 1966), p. 32.
5 Vera and John Russell, 'Conversation with Henry Moore', *Sunday Times* December 17, 1961, pp. 17 – 18.
6 *Ibid.*
7 Henry Moore, *Heads Figures and Ideas* (London, 1958), n.p.
8 Quoted in Joseph Darracott, *Henry Moore War Drawings* (?London, ?1975), n.p.
9 Herbert Read, *The Meaning of Art*, pp. 250 – 57, quoted in *Henry Moore: The Reclining Figure* (Columbus, Ohio, 1984), p. 130.
10 James Johnson Sweeney, *Henry Moore* (New York, 1946), pp. 64 – 7.
11 *Henry Moore Drawings 1969 – 79* (New York, 1979), pp. 6 – 7.
12 J. Hedgecoe and H. Moore, *Henry Spencer Moore* (New York, 1968), pp. 132 – 3.
13 Clark, *The Other Half* (New York, 1977), p. 21.
14 See Sarah Griffiths 'War Painting: a no-man's land between history and reportage', *Leeds Art Calendar*, lxxviii (1976), 24 – 32.
15 Clark, pp. 23 – 4.
16 Henry Moore 'Interview', April 13, 1983.
17 Constantine FitzGibbon, *The Blitz* (London, 1957), p. 15.
18 See Joanna Mack and Steve Humphries, *London At War* (London, 1985), p. 53.
19 Angus Calder, *The People's War* (London, 1971), p. 173.
20 Henry Moore, *Shelter Sketch-Book with 80 facsimile collotypes* (Berlin, 1967), n.p.
21 Henry Moore, *80th Annversary Exhibition* (Bradford, 1978), n.p.
22 Robert Melville, *Henry Moore Shelter Sketch-Book 1940 – 42* (London, 1972), p. 95.
23 Wilkinson, *The Drawings*, p. 31.
24 Gemma Levine, *Henry Moore: The Artist at Work* (London, 1978), p. 25.
25 Wilkinson, *The Drawings*, p. 32.
26 Kenneth Clark, 'Hindsight' in Tom Hopkinson, ed., *Picture Post* (London, 1984), p. 140.
27 Levine, p. 25.
28 Moore, *Shelter Sketch-Book*, n.p.
29 *Ibid.*
30 Hedgecoe and Moore, *Moore*, p. 140.
31 *Ibid.*

13

Churchill in British Politics 1940-55

Paul Addison

With good reason, the career of Winston Churchill is usually associated with the history of warfare and international relations. There is no need to dispute the emphasis, but it does mask the significance of Churchill in other respects. All his life Churchill was concerned as a professional politician with questions of authority, order, hierarchy and stability. Even when he was not pursuing them, they were pursuing him.

Churchill's active political life spanned the period from 1900 to 1955. Throughout that time the authority of the traditional governing class — the Liberal and Conservative élite which ran the country at the end of the nineteenth century — was repeatedly challenged on two fronts. At home the challenge came from the labour movement, a term that embraces the trade unions, socialists, and their joint creation, the Labour Party. Overseas the challenge took the form of nationalist and separatist movements within the British Empire. These were as diverse as the Empire itself and gave rise to major conflicts in South Africa, Ireland, Egypt and India.

The internal politics of Britain and the politics of the British Empire were separate spheres, but linked by the responsibility of Cabinet and Parliament for both. In each of the two spheres the traditional governing class was confronted by popular movements and pressures from below, and most leading politicians devoted as much time to the multitude of imperial problems as to home affairs. Some actually served as imperial governors or proconsuls at some point in their careers. And though the issues and structure of domestic politics were so different from the realm of imperial affairs, politicians tended to be psychologically consistent in moving from one world to the other. One has only to picture the response of Lord

243

Halifax to the Labour Party, to be reminded of his demeanour as Viceroy of India towards the Congress movement.

One of the most striking features of Churchill's character was the co-existence of tough and tender elements in his outlook. Irrespective of the party to which he belonged at the time, he could be more liberal than the Liberals in his compassion for the downtrodden, yet more stern than the Tories in the repression of challenges to authority. In a governing élite which operated by the judicious manipulation of the carrot and the stick, these were conspicuous and valuable qualities if brought into play at the right moment. One of the interesting aspects of Churchill's career was the fact that he so often applied them, in the opinion of his colleagues, at the wrong moment.

But these were psychological constants. Churchill's attitudes also varied over time. In a politician's career, issues tend to interlock, and this was true of social and imperial issues as they affected Churchill. From this point of view his career fell into three main phases, with the two world wars as the watersheds dividing them. Up to 1914, and leaving aside his wild oats as a young Tory, Churchill addressed social and imperial problems as a Liberal. There were indications after 1910 that the various symptoms of the 'strange death of Liberal England' were propelling him towards the Conservatives, but he was still contained within a Liberal Cabinet.

The second phase of his career began, as Maurice Cowling has described, in the aftermath of the First World War. The Liberal Party was broken and Churchill was on the loose. The Bolshevik revolution was threatening to sweep into central Europe and a crisis of order at home was matched by a triple crisis in the British Empire, with revolts in Ireland, Egypt and India. Reacting violently against the collapse of the world he had known before 1914, Churchill took up a line of militant resistance on a range of issues from anti-Bolshevism abroad to anti-socialism at home. And though he eventually compromised over Ireland, he was all the more determined to shoulder the white man's burden in Egypt and India. By 1922 Churchill was an imperial diehard. As Chancellor of the Exchequer in the Baldwin government of 1924–9, Churchill tried to re-establish himself as a progressive in social and economic affairs, but failed and relapsed during the world slump into his passionate but ill-judged India campaign. The Churchill of the mid-1930s, half in love with continental fascism and calling for a retreat from universal suffrage, was an embittered and isolated reactionary.

But then, about 1936, Churchill stumbled into the third and final phase of his career. He began to subordinate all other issues to the single campaign of resistance to Nazi Germany. He thrust the Indian question to the back of his mind, called off his propaganda campaign against the Soviet Union, ceased to be rude to the Labour Party, and instead of

244

lamenting the deficiencies of parliamentary democracy, glorified it as the common cause of Britain and France against Germany.

Churchill's stand against Hitler had great repercussions on his position in social and imperial affairs. In rescuing him from failure, and converting him into the hero of 1940, the Second World War also restored him to a moderate and even progressive role in British politics. The price Churchill paid was that he had to accept the responsibility, as Prime Minister and leader of the Conservative Party for changes that were not always welcome. On the one hand he was obliged to abandon his resistance to the Labour Party in home affairs. On the other he was almost powerless to resist the destruction of the moral authority of the British in the Far East. These two factors converged early in 1942 when the combined pressure of Roosevelt and the Labour ministers forced Churchill into a declaration that India would be given the right of self-determination after the war. Of course he planned to wriggle out of it if possible: but no power on earth could have prevailed upon him to make such a declaration before.

Churchill, then, had to adjust to major changes in social and imperial affairs. On the imperial side the adjustment proved extremely painful. Churchill fought a prolonged rearguard action over India and as late as March 1946 there was talk of his intention, never carried through, of leading an 'anti-capitulation' campaign against Attlee.[1] A second rearguard action, this time over the evacuation of the Suez Canal Zone, led to a series of clashes with Anthony Eden, the Foreign Secretary, during the peacetime premiership of 1951 to 1955. Characteristically, Churchill was generous in defeat and praised India for remaining in the Commonwealth. But in this respect he seems to have ended his life with a sense of failure, since all his efforts to prevent the decline of the Empire had proved unavailing.

So much by way of general introduction. As its title indicates, this particular essay deals with Churchill's role in the politics of social and economic change from 1940 to 1955. In home affairs Churchill was much more successful in adapting to circumstances. Indeed he must qualify as one of the creators of that almost mythical entity, the post-war consensus. Churchill made two major contributions to this. Firstly as Prime Minister, and leader of the first post-war Conservative government, he led the party towards the welfare state and the appeasement of Labour. But in the general election of 1945 he set out a second aim: the rolling back of state socialism. With hindsight we can see that he was less successful in this latter aim than in the former. Yet Churchill did seek to follow through his anti-socialist policies after 1951 and did preside over a partial restoration of private enterprise.

It is often remarked that Churchill's knowledge of social and economic affairs was superficial, and that he was not interested in these areas of policy. In one respect this is correct. Churchill never intended to master

245

the detail of social and economic policy, which would have bored him. He relied on others to brief him on the salient points. But Churchill was deeply interested in the party political implications of policy, and kept a watching brief on sensitive issues. When in office it was his custom to begin the day by combing through the press for items of domestic news which might embarrass the government, with the result that many a minute calling for action landed on ministerial desks. Allied to his political concern was an erratic but genuine interest in the problems of ordinary people, on whose behalf he was ready to act as a self-appointed Ombudsman.

The second observation often made about Churchill is that by the 1940s his underlying political beliefs were antiquated and irrelevant. Harold Macmillan, for example, writes of Churchill's period in opposition: 'His general views on economic affairs were not substantially changed from his Victorian upbringing. While he was always ready to study new ideas, and generously accepted the suggestions of his followers, he was not capable or desirous of initiating new concepts of financial, monetary or economic policy.'[2] The same might be said of Churchill's concepts of Empire. But whereas Churchill's imperial ideas were often at odds with reality, and had to be suppressed by heroic efforts of self-restraint, his ideas about British society still had an archaic relevance to the character of Britain. In responding to the impact of Labour after 1940 Churchill referred back to the Tory Democracy of his father, Lord Randolph, and the Edwardian Liberalism of labour exchanges and social insurance. These inspirations were of positive assistance to Churchill in mapping out his course. If Tory Democracy was valuable as a myth — and one in which Churchill believed — the new Liberalism of the Edwardian period offered a more positive view of the role of the state in social policy and industrial relations. A conscious revival of Edwardian values gave Churchill a new sense of direction as Britain evolved from the collective experience of wartime to the 'new Elizabethan age' of the early 1950s.

To explore the argument in more detail we must begin with Churchill as the head of the wartime coalition government formed in May 1940. In October Churchill was 'elected' leader of the Conservative Party. In reality he appointed himself in order to gain control of the majority party in the House of Commons. He took little interest in sustaining the Conservative cause of preparing the party for post-war politics. On the contrary, Churchill neglected the party organisation and allowed a policy vacuum to develop on the Right. When he first addressed a party gathering in March 1941 it was to proclaim the desirability of maintaining national unity after the war 'in certain practical measures of reconstruction and social advance to enable this country to recover from the war and, as one great family, to get into its stride again'.[3] This passage strongly suggests that Churchill was already contemplating a post-war coalition and conscious that social reform would be the condition Labour attached. But Churchill was quite vague about his post-war ambitions at this stage, and often talked of retirement when Hitler was beaten.

Until 1943 Churchill took the line that war and peace were separate operations, and ruled out any plans for social reconstruction until the end of the war. But the embargo was overcome by William Beveridge, whose report was published in Decembeer 1942, and R. A. Butler, whose plans for education were almost ready at about the same time. Realising that the unity of the coalition depended upon a forward move in reconstruction, Churchill broadcast in March 1943 a speech proclaiming what he called his Four-Year Plan, and ranging over health, education, social insurance, and employment policy. This programme he now linked to post-war politics by proposing that it should be put to the electorate 'either by a National Government, formally representative as this one is, of the three parties in the State, or by a National Government comprising the best men in all parties who are willing to serve'.[4]

Churchill knew that the Labour Party might not agree to serve with him after the war. But the prospect of a post-war coalition continued to attract him and he was particularly keen to retain the support of organised labour by renewing his alliance with Ernest Bevin, the Minister of Labour. Since 1940 Churchill had wielded undisputed power as a national leader. He could address Stalin or Roosevelt in the knowledge that a united House of Commons, and for all practical purposes a united people, stood behind him. As an international statesman he had nothing to gain from the revival of party politics and class anatagonisms. Though confident that he could if necessary fight and win a general election on party lines, he sought a post-war platform that would command the widest possible consent, and kept the door to a coalition open. In October 1943 he delighted his Labour colleagues by the fillip he gave to plans for the transition from war to peace. Food and employment were to be the priorities, all was to be set down in a series of plans compiled on the model of the War Book, and nothing was to be ruled out because it was controversial.[5]

If Churchill warmed to the politics of social reform, this was also because he found them congenial. They blended with his natural paternalism and fitted the autobiographical self-portrait he was forever composing in his mind. Churchill had always taken pride in the fact that as Lloyd George's lieutenant, he had pioneered labour exchanges and social insurance and 'brought the magic of averages to the rescue of the millions'. And the record after 1918 demonstrated that however reactionary he was in other respects, he continued to believe, as Kenneth Morgan writes in his study of the Lloyd George coalition, in 'free enterprise with a human face'.[6] As he declared in a speech in the depths of the world slump, in August 1933: 'I have more hope in Mr. Roosevelt than in Mr. Norman.'[7] There need be no doubt that Churchill was converted to social reconstruction in 1943 and intended, as his election manifesto promised, to carry through the main principles of his 'Four-Year Plan'.

Churchill's attempt to appropriate the welfare state needs to be taken in conjunction with a second strand in his wartime outlook. Churchill fully recognised the necessity in wartime of a centralised state economy based on emergency powers and the curtailment of personal liberty. Yet there was an undertone in his war premiership of suspicion of creeping bureaucracy. He was on his guard lest civil servants or Labour politicians introduce controls for controls' sake. Running through his wartime minutes is a picturesque concern for the burdens of a civilian population groaning beneath the weight of restrictions. Fearful that an excess of austerity would undermine morale, he resisted on several occasions proposals by the Ministry of Food and the Board of Trade to extend rationing. Thus in July 1942 he remonstrated with Lord Woolton, the Minister of Food, over plans for poultry rationing: 'the hen has been part and parcel of the country cottager's life since history began . . . What is the need for this tremendous reduction to one hen per person?'[8] Having at first accepted, in the spring of 1942, the case for coal rationing, Churchill turned sharply against it, persuaded, no doubt, that it was a socialist plot by Hugh Dalton, the President of the Board of Trade. The Prime Minister's attitude to fuel economies was pungently expressed in a minute to Cherwell in October 1942:

> The climax of folly seems to be reached by the gentleman who writes to the papers proposing that the use of lifts should be restricted, pointing out that if you walk up eight flights of stairs you save the use of electricity for the lift which would keep an electric light burning for so many hours. But this takes no account of the condition of exhaustion of people made to climb several times a day up many flights of stairs, and the bad effect on their office work. If it comes to that, why not stop the trains and let people walk and carry their baggage with them, as they did in the good old days? We are a modern community at war, and not Hottentots or Esquimaux.[9]

When Churchill's thoughts turned towards post-war policy, he drew a sharp distinction between the expedience of controls in wartime and their undesirability in peace. In this he was egged on by Bracken and Beaverbrook, whose goal was to throw off wartime restrictions as quickly as possible. In addition he read, or somehow obtained the gist of, Friedrich Hayek's *The Road to Serfdom*, published in 1944, which vigorously restated the case for laissez-faire liberalism. Hayek argued that the march of centralised planning was threatening to turn Britain into a totalitarian state. This prompted Churchill to warn, in the general election campaign of 1945, that a socialist government, incapable of tolerating dissent, 'would have to fall back on some form of Gestapo, no doubt very humanely directed in the first instance'.[10] By 1945, then, Churchill was committed on the one hand to a programme of 'work, food and homes', while on the other he was fired by the idea of liberating trade and industry from controls.

After 1945 the Conservatives had to decide how to define and present the long-term policy of the party. According to the orthodox version Harold Macmillan and R. A. Butler took the lead in reformulating a more progressive Toryism and, although they encountered much resistance, they won lasting victory with the acceptance by the party of the Industrial Charter of 1947. This led on to the enlightened Conservatism of the managed economy and the welfare state which broadened the appeal of the party and led to its electoral recovery.

The impression we have of Churchill in this transition is that he was largely irrelevant to it. His instincts were backward, his role in policy-making negligible, and his career as leader of the Opposition notable chiefly for achievements in other fields: the composition of the first four volumes of his war memoirs, and the speeches he delivered in the course of his campaign for a united Europe.

It would be quite misleading to present Churchill as a great leader of the Opposition. His attendance at the House of Commons was patchy and he was not an effective leader of the parliamentary party. The Opposition front bench was ill co-ordinated and Churchill's colleagues were never quite sure when he would intervene or what line he would take. Often he took no line at all. He spoke, for example, in none of the debates on nationalisation until the introduction of the Iron and Steel Bill in the autumn of 1948. More than ever, Churchill seemed to look down on the party from an Olympian position of quizzical detachment. When the parliamentary party came under attack at the end of 1945 for the feebleness of its tactics, Churchill responded by putting down a motion of censure on the Attlee government, and proceeded' to deliver an attack on the follies of the administration. Duty done, he then packed his bags for three months' holiday in the United States, during which he delivered his speech on the Cold War at Fulton, Missouri.

It would also be true to say that Churchill's approach to Opposition was negative in other senses. Churchill believed that an Opposition with a detailed programme would be at a disadvantage. The task of an Opposition was to make as much political capital as possible out of the Government's mistakes by tripping up ministers in the House of Commons. Churchill disliked the idea of making pledges in Opposition which might become an embarrassment in government. And as far as possible he wanted to keep his own hands free to direct a future government as he wished, according to whatever circumstances might prevail when he took office.

In the aftermath of the party's defeat a clamour arose from the back-benches and the rank-and-file for a positive definition of party policy. A typical view, expressed at a conference of young Tories in April 1947, was that of a Miss Margaret Roberts from Oxford (better known in later years as Margaret Thatcher), who said that 'to people at the moment Conservatism meant nothing more than anti-socialism. We must have a clear and unified statement of policy.' [11]

At the first post-war conference of the party at Blackpool, in October 1946, the demand for a reformulation of policy was so great that Churchill responded by appointing a committee of the shadow cabinet, under the chairmanship of R. A. Butler, to draw up a statement on economic and industrial affairs. (The other members of the committee were Oliver Stanley, Oliver Lyttelton, Harold Macmillan and David Maxwell-Fyfe.) But, as Butler recorded in 1949, Churchill 'gave the strictest injunctions that no detailed policy was to be published'.[12] As a consequence of this directive, the Industrial Charter was long on generalisation and short on specifics. The Conservative Party issued no full-length programme until the publication of 'The Right Road for Britain' in July 1949.

Apart from swashbuckling opportunism in the House of Commons, Churchill saw his role in the Opposition as rhetorical, the definition of broad propaganda themes for the party. In social policy his theme was the attachment of the Conservative Party, and himself in particular, to the welfare state. Labour stood to gain electorally from higher social insurance benefits and the new National Health Service. Churchill, who had promised to introduce similar changes himself, felt that he had been robbed: Labour had caught him bathing and run away with his clothes. Time and again he stressed that the social legislation of the Labour governments had been prepared by the wartime coalition. As far as possible he tried to appropriate the credit for the Conservatives and, having decided on this tack, went the whole hog. It was fair enough to maintain that the Education Act of 1944 had been the work of R. A. Butler. But it was poetic licence to claim that Lord Woolton had written the 1944 White Paper on employment policy, and the tale of his own record on social policy was much improved in the telling. Here is Churchill addressing a conference of Conservative women in April 1948:

> I have worked at national insurance schemes almost all my life and am responsible for several of the largest measures ever passed. The main principles of the new Health Schemes were hammered out in the days of the Coalition government, before the party and personal malignancy of Mr. Bevan plunged health policy into its present confusion. The Family Allowance Act was passed by the Conservative Caretaker Government. School milk was started in 1934 by a Conservative Parliament. The Education Act was the work of Mr. Butler. The idea of welfare foods was largely developed by Lord Woolton . . . These facts should be repeated on every occasion by those who wish the truth to be known.[13]

This social theme in Churchill's rhetoric owed little or nothing to the Industrial Charter, which was primarily concerned with economic and industrial policy. It was simply a continuation of the line he had taken since

1943. Nor did Churchill intend to outbid the Labour government by promising more ambitious welfare schemes. He probably regarded the 'welfare revolution' as complete and merely wished to stress that it harmonised with Tory tradition and would therefore be safe under a future Conservative government. In 1950 he remarked to R. A. Butler that in future there would be 'much less politics in social reform' because the workers would have to pay.[14] Nonetheless Churchill was compelled shortly after this to accept, with some reservations, a major new commitment.

The one weak spot in the Labour government's record in social policy was the housing policy. Though nearly a million houses were built between 1945 and 1950, there were still more than four million families sharing accommodation.[15] Housing was also doctrinally contentious. Aneurin Bevan, the minister responsible, was a dedicated socialist who severely restricted the building of private houses. Of all new houses and flats constructed between 1945 and 1951, four out of five were built by local authorities for rent. Calling instead for a 'property-owning democracy', the Conservatives demanded more scope for private building, and the acceleration of the local authority programme by the relaxation of standards and regulations. At the party conference in October 1950 a resolution was carried in favour of a specific pledge to build a minimum of 300,000 houses a year.

Churchill had been intermittently interested in housing since 1918. The 'cottage homes' of the people occupied a prominent place in his vision of domestic politics. In the final stages of the war he attached a high priority to the building of prefabricated homes and he greatly resented the incoming Labour government's allegation that no effective preparations had been made. Aneurin Bevan, the minister in charge of the housing programme, was a bête noire whose record Churchill attacked with particular venom. But, though Churchill made much play with the housing statistics, he was careful, in accord with his general tactics in opposition, not to commit himself to an alternative figure. When the party conference forced him to declare a position he announced that he accepted the target of 300,000 as 'our first priority in time of peace'. But he was speaking during the Korean war — and he qualified his pledge by reference to the possible effects of the rearmament programme upon industry and finance.[16]

Churchill's rhetoric in social policy derived from the Edwardian era and the concept of the national minimum. Indeed Churchill consciously repeated the language he had learnt before the First World War. Here, for example, is Churchill speaking in March 1947 to a meeting of the Central Council of the National Union:

We accept and affirm the principles of minimum standards of life and labour and the building up of those standards continuously as our resources allow. But above these

251

minimum standards the British people must not be fettered or trammeled. There must be competition upwards — not downwards.[17]

Churchill had learnt his economics during the free trade campaign of 1904 – 5. Thereafter his faith in the capacity of competitive enterprise to generate wealth for the masses was robust and frequently expressed. From the New Liberalism of social reform he took the concept of a safety net, or minimum standard of living guaranteed by the state, to protect the casualties of the system. But social reform was treated in his Edwardian speeches as the antithesis to socialism, a formula Churchill never forgot. After 1945, as before, Churchill tended to be a paternalist in social policy but a libertarian in economics.

What was the relevance of Churchill's anti-socialism to the revival of the post-war Conservative Party? Churchill was often criticised at the time for taking a purely negative line — a description likely to be applied to anyone in the 1940s who advocated laissez-faire economics. According to Samuel Beer and others, we are supposed to read the history of the Conservative revival after 1945 in terms of the acceptance of a mixed and managed economy. On this analysis, the Industrial Charter was the critical turning point. The Charter did indeed accept a strategic role for the state in the economy, admitted that much of Labour's nationalisation programme was irreversible, and pledged the party to the maintenance of full employment. Churchill, though not exactly brimming over with enthusiasm for the Charter, had no difficulty in digesting this message into his rhetoric. As he pointed out, it squared with the statement he had made in 1943 predicting an expanding role for the state in the economy.

But the dominant note in Churchill's speeches was full-blooded support for the restoration of private enterprise. In December 1945 Churchill hit on the phrase, 'set the people free.' This was to be his constant refrain and this, in his view, was the long-term alternative to socialist planning and controls. In 1945 the language of free enterprise was out of tune with the times. Enlightened and educated opinion, ranging far beyond the Labour government, was convinced that the economic crisis inherited from the war could only be resolved through coherent and centralised planning. Ministers claimed to be introducing a planned economy and could point to the steady procession through Parliament of the bills nationalising the Bank of England, coal, gas, electricity, railways, long-distance road haulage, and iron and steel. Meanwhile, through the network of wartime regulations, they continued to exercise a battery of powers over the import programme, the allocation of raw materials, prices, and the rationing of consumer goods.

Throughout his period in opposition Churchill let no opportunity slip for condemning this machinery of control. By conflating controls and nationalisation, equating them both with socialism, and blaming the socialist system for cuts in the standard of living and crises in the economy, Churchill assembled a polemic that served him well. Though the state of the economy was mainly due to the 'total war' Churchill had waged, he shifted the blame and did so with conviction.

Churchill's anti-socialist campaign succeeded in refreshing the parts of Conservatism that others did not reach. While Butler and Macmillan supplied the rationale for the revival of Conservatism among the Oxbridge élite, a rougher revival was in progress lower down the social scale. A middle class and businessmen's revolt broke out against economic controls. The first sign of the rebellion was that curious organisation, the British Housewives' League, which began as a genuine protest by middle class women against the power of officialdom and was rapidly converted by the Conservative Party into a major propaganda campaign against rationing. It is too easy, when reading the subtle and civilised memoirs of Butler or Macmillan, to forget the smouldering animus against the Attlee governments felt by sections of the Tory nation, and fanned into flames by the Kemsley, Rothermere and Beaverbrook press. Churchill's 'Gestapo' speech is laughed at by historians but it expressed what many of the middle classes came to feel after 1945.

Churchill, therefore, as so often in his career, was prescient in his attack on controls and anticipated a major shift of opinion. In 1945 the initiative in politics lay with socialists and planners. By the end of the 1940s the initiative lay with Keynesians and businessmen. In 1948 John Jewkes, an economist working on Keynesian assumptions, supplied theoretical chapter and verse to Churchill's critique of Whitehall socialism in his book *Ordeal By Planning*. The shadow of the Cold War cast a chill of socialist thought in Britain, and Churchill's emphasis on the freedom of the individual from the state was suddenly fashionable. In the autumn of 1948 the introduction of the government's bill to nationalise iron and steel touched off a fierce anti-nationalisation campaign. Though the government pressed on and nationalised the industry in 1950, the Labour Party's enthusiasm for nationalisation in general was wilting. By 1951 the Attlee government was moving rapidly away from the command economy of wartime to the managed economy of Keynes. As Professor Cairncross writes: 'Whereas in 1947 and 1948 30 per cent of consumer expenditure was on rationed goods, by 1950 the percentage had fallen to 11. For raw materials the corresponding proportions of industrial input covered by allocating schemes were 83 per cent in 1947 and 47 per cent in 1950.'[18] The Churchill government, when it took office in 1951, had only to accelerate this process of change.

Churchill's language in opposition was often so extreme as to suggest that he himself was an extremist. In November 1947, for example, he predicted that under socialism 'at least a quarter of those who are alive today will have to disappear in one way or another after enduring a lowering of standards of food and comfort inconceivable in the last fifty years'.[19]

253

But Churchill loved a touch of bogus melodrama, and there is no need to be distracted by it. By 1950 Churchill occupied a position in the middle ground of politics.

The result of the general election of February 1950, which left the two main parties almost level in terms of popular support, and the Labour government balancing on a knife-edge majority, reinforced Churchill's commitment to the politics of the Centre. He was keen to capture the Liberal vote and tried to organise an electoral pact with the Liberals. He spoke for Lady Violet Bonham-Carter, who was unopposed by a Conservative, in the general election of 1951.

It was also clear that Churchill was anxious for good relations with the trade unions. He was sensitive to his reputation in the labour movement as a class warrior and anxious to live it down. The Industrial Charter had proposed legislation to outlaw the closed shop in the public sector, and re-introduce contracting in. In the general election campaign of 1951, a speech by David Maxwell-Fyfe, one of the authors of the Charter, suggested that the Conservatives were intending to introduce trade union reforms. Churchill swept all this away, announcing that no legislation affecting trade unions would be introduced in the next Parliament. In an election address on October 2, 1951, he declared, 'What we need is a period of steady, stable administration by a broadly-based Government, wielding the national power and content to serve the nation's best interest rather than give party satisfaction . . . There will be no vindictive triumph for Tories over Socialists, no dull exclusion of Liberal and independent forces, but rather a period of healing and revival.' [20]

Once restored to office, Churchill was in a position to define precisely the position his government should adopt. As his very first moves demonstrated, he intended his government to rest on the broadest possible basis, with a high priority accorded to the appeasement of labour. The decision to send R. A. Butler to the Treasury instead of Oliver Lyttelton; the appointment of Walter Monckton to the Ministry of Labour instead of Maxwell-Fyfe; the appointment of Harold Macmillan as Minister of Housing, were all signals of the course Churchill intended to follow. No less indicative, though it was not to occur until the following May, was the unexpected promotion of Iain Macleod to be Minister of Health. [21]

On the Labour benches the signals were understood. Richard Crossman wrote in his diary:

. . . the real free enterprise and deflationists seem to have been kept out and there is a good deal in view that the general make-up of the Churchill Cabinet means that it will be only very slightly to the right of the most recent Attlee Cabinet. Just as Attlee was running what was virtually a coalition policy on a Party basis so Churchill may well do the same. [22]

Similarly Hugh Gaitskell reflected: 'What the intelligent Tories will, of course, want to do is to be able to say to the electorate when the election comes, "No war: no unemployment: no cuts in social services. Just good government." ' [23]

There are two circumstantial explanations for the course Churchill set. Firstly the Conservatives had an overall majority of only 17 seats, and the total Conservative vote was nearly a quarter of a million below that of the Labour Party. While a majority of 17 may look quite secure in retrospect, it appeared fragile at the time. This anxiety was rooted in a second factor, a legacy of the Korean war and the overblown rearmament programme of the Attlee Cabinet. The Churchill government inherited a balance of payments deficit of nearly £700 million, and rapidly diminishing dollar reserves. To restore the balance, economies in public expenditure and cuts in the import programme were essential. These in turn made it imperative to win the co-operation of the trade unions in preventing industrial disputes. And once in charge himself, Churchill began to count the cost of the party warfare he had organised so vigorously while in Opposition. His doctor, Lord Moran, heard him say that Britain was divided into two equal halves: 'If they worked together they might survive. But they won't. They are set on tearing the heart out of one another.' [24]

In its first months, therefore, the Churchill government led an apprehensive existence. The mood can be gauged from a memorandum written in November 1951 by Churchill's economic and scientific adviser, Lord Cherwell, the Paymaster-General, on the imperative of higher coal production:

> Deliberately to make the miners a privileged class, perhaps with a guaranteed wage differential, would of course be a very big decision requiring most careful consideration. But I am inclined to believe it is a decision we should take, and take quickly. A 'New Deal for the Miners' would have to be put across to the country as a major part of Government policy . . .
>
> We must always remember that a coal strike lasting even one week would be disastrous; a fortnight would compel us to surrender. [25]

So at the very beginning of the government, Churchill sought for and obtained an informal social contract with the trade unions and with the Labour Opposition. But the strategy was very nearly wrecked in the early stages. In February 1952 an attempt was made by officials in the Bank of England and the Treasury to bounce the Cabinet into 'Operation Robot', a plan to make sterling convertible and float the pound. The pound, it was argued, would then depreciate to the point at which the balance of payments would be rectified. R. A. Butler was converted, and so, momentarily, was Churchill, captivated by the phrase 'setting the pound free'.

Much has been written about the debate over Robot, which revolved around a variety of technical and political arguments. [26] For present purposes the salient point is that both supporters and opponents of the plan accepted that it would mark a clean break in the pattern of domestic politics. As Butler explained to Churchill:

> It will be seen that this new course in our external policy requires a complete rethinking of the whole of the economic policies which have been in operation, fundamentally with the support of all parties, during the last few years . . . the basic idea of internal stability of prices and employment, which has dominated economic policy for so long, will not be maintainable.[27]

The plan divided the Cabinet and it was decided at meetings on February 28 and 29 to postpone a decision and review the position later. But a few days later Cherwell, a strong opponent of 'Robot', overheard Churchill musing on the attraction of 'setting the pound free'. He wrote to the Prime Minister:

> I hope you will be under no misapprehension as to what this all means. It means that whenever our exports fail to pay for our imports, the value of the pound will fall until imports diminish . . . If this fails to close the gap the Bank Rate will have to be raised until more firms close down and dismiss their workers, leading to a further fall in demand for imported materials and food. If a 6% Bank Rate, 1 million unemployed and a 2s loaf are not enough, then there will have to be an 8% Bank Rate and a 3s loaf . . .
> To rely frankly on high prices and unemployment to reduce imports would certainly put the Conservative Party out for a generation.[28]

If Churchill had thrown his weight behind 'Robot', the plan would have been put into action. But Churchill hesitated. His thoughts on the topic are obscure, but this, perhaps, was a juncture at which his inclination to free market forces was at odds with his desire for social appeasement. (Paradoxically the 'Robot' plan would have involved fresh controls over imports and the sterling balances of non-residents, but that is another story.) Whatever the explanation, Churchill drew back from the brink and the politics of consensus were preserved.

It might be supposed that Churchill, who was 77 on his return to office, aimed simply for a quiet life in home affairs so that he could devote his remaining energies to defence and foreign policy. This may be so, but a quiet life had to be organised. The mood and the tone had to be set and, to judge from the record, Churchill was surprisingly active in setting them.

On the industrial front Churchill took particular care to establish cordial relations with the General Council of the TUC. Hence the occasion when Arthur Deakin was in hospital, and Churchill suggested to Tom O'Brien and Will Lawther that his own doctor, Lord Moran, be called in.[29] In July 1952 a delegation from the General Council went to Downing Street to put the case for a million workers covered by wages councils in the distributive and allied trades. The report in *The Times* captures the flavour of the event:

256

Mr Churchill listened attentively to all that the TUC representatives had to say. In promising to give full consideration to their arguments he recalled that when he was President of the Board of Trade, over forty years ago, he was responsible for the legislation which established trade boards to protect conditions of employment of the lowest paid workers, and added that he had always taken a close personal interest in the subject.[30]

In June 1952 Churchill was alarmed by the rise in the unemployment figures, which threatened to exceed 500,000. He therefore appointed a Cabinet committee to propose measures, such as public works, for the creation of more jobs. In the event the committee proved to be unnecessary, as unemployment totals fell again, but the very fact that it was set up in the first place shows how seriously Churchill took the Conservatives' pledge to maintain full employment.[31]

It is well known that, as Minister of Labour, Walter Monckton held a brief from Churchill to buy off industrial unrest at the price of moderately inflationary wage settlements. Yet it is still something of a surprise to discover the lengths to which Churchill took this. Here he is addressing the Cabinet on the subject of the threatened rail strike of December 1953:

> The Prime Minister said that he had been wondering whether the Government might not help in this by relieving the Commission of some part of the interest charges with which they had been saddled on nationalisation. If a part of the capital sum were transferred to the National Debt, the Railway Staff National Tribunal could then be invited to review railwaymen's wages in the light of this improvement in the financial position of the railways.[32]

The Cabinet were horrified by this proposal and turned it down, but all the same the dispute was resolved on terms favourable to the rail unions.

In social policy, too, Churchill set the scene for appeasement. There was a prolonged dispute in the summer of 1952 between the Treasury and Harold Macmillan over the scale of capital investment in the housing programme. Churchill summed up in favour of Macmillan, determined that the party must redeem its pledge to build 300,000 houses a year.[33]

While Churchill insisted on continuity in the welfare state and employment policy, he was no less keen to follow up his anti-socialist rhetoric and 'set the people free'. To a great extent the process of decontrol was the work of ministers like Peter Thorneycroft at the Board of Trade or Harold Macmillan at the Ministry of Housing. Churchill's contribution was to ginger up ministers he thought were lagging behind. He was keen to get on as fast as possible with the abolition of food rationing and the officials responsible for enforcing it. On the subject of meat rationing he urged Lord Woolton, who was overlord of Food and Agriculture, to 'make a plan to deration pork and let it rip'.[34] He was keen on bananas and wrote a picturesque minute to the Minister of Food and the Colonial Secretary bemoaning their absence:

257

When Joseph Chamberlain was Foreign Secretary, he introduced a striking feature into our life, 'the banana on the street barrow'. I suggest to you that you try to make a plan for this. There was a Liverpool merchant called Jones, long since dead, who ran a line of ships especially for the banana trade during the particular season of the year. The banana is a valuable food for the people, as well as being a variation. I am sorry that it seems to have vanished from the scene.[35]

As the terms of trade shifted in favour of Britain, and the balance of payments moved into surplus, food rationing was gradually removed. In this respect Churchill was lucky: he came into power at the right time. But on the industrial front the process of liberating free enterprise was a more qualified success. Churchill was eager to carry through the party's pledge to denationalise long-distance road haulage and insisted on early legislation. Similarly he pressed for early legislation to denationalise iron and steel. It was a measure of the initial lack of self-confidence of the government that this proposal aroused opposition in the Cabinet. In July 1952 a number of ministers were so worried about the foreign exchange position that they proposed to abandon the denationalisation of steel. They argued that in the circumstances the government should do everything in its power to create a spirit of national unity, and this meant avoiding a bitter controversy over steel. Churchill summed up in favour of going ahead, stating that he thought an agreement with the Labour party on this issue out of the question.[36] And, in due course, steel was denationalised.

In spite of this, and the greater freedom allowed to private enterprise in other areas, the restoration of industrial capitalism was only a very qualified success. Though the Conservatives had criticised the structure of the nationalised industries, they did little to reorganise them. The inflationary policies resulting from the appeasement of the unions helped to make British industry less competitive. The trade unions themselves exercised the power of veto over trade union reform.

Such right-wing dissent as existed was fragmentary. Brendan Bracken, who had refused office in 1951, was convinced that the boards in charge of nationalised industries were incompetent, and tried to rally Churchill on the subject: in vain, of course.[37] In December 1952 the journalist Collin Brooks recorded a conversation with Ralph Assheton, a backbench M.P. and former chairman of the party:

> He is as impatient of the 'wets' in the Party as I am — the wets including Anthony and Rab. He could, he knows, muster a score of supporters against Rab, and might even wring out and dry another 50 backbench 'wets'. But, he says, the only issue would be tax reduction, and there Rab would have socialist support.[38]

Nothing came of this. Butler succeeded in disarming potential critics by cuts in income tax and an overall reduction in public expenditure. Now and then a minister would express dissent over some aspect of the government's social and industrial policies, but there was never a likelihood that a right-wing critique would crystallise. A reassuring blanket of Churchillian tranquillity was descending on government and people.

There are many ways of interpreting Churchill's final administration and they are not mutually exclusive. To some extent it was a revival of the wartime coalition but without the formal apparatus of an all-party government. In Churchill's mind it was also a revival of the more benign and optimistic aspects of Edwardian Liberalism. It was testimony, even in Churchill's old age, to his continuous capacity to adapt to change, develop fresh political strategies, and interpret the present in the light of the past.

In spite of his immense aristocratic distance from the social realities of the classes below, Churchill displayed considerable intuition in divining the direction of social and economic change. One of the greatest insights of his last years in office was the potential significance of coloured immigration. Responding to stories in the press, he instituted in November 1952 a series of inquiries into the number of such immigrants in Britain, and the social tensions resulting. In this area of policy, Churchill's social and imperial views converged in a pessimistic diagnosis. So let us conclude with Churchill as reported in the Cabinet minutes for February 3, 1954:

> The Prime Minister said that the rapid improvement of communications was likely to lead to a continuing increase in the number of coloured people coming into this country, and their presence here would sooner or later come to be resented by large sections of the British people. It might well be true, however, that the problem had not yet assumed sufficient proportions to enable the Government to take adequate counter-measures.[39]

Notes

Early drafts of this article were delivered as papers to the Colloquium in Modern British History at Durham and to the Seminar on Twentieth Century British Policy and Administration at the Institute of Historical Research in London. I am grateful to all who put questions or comments to me on these occasions. I am also grateful to Mr. Iain Campbell for additional research on my behalf at the Public Record Office.

1 David Carlton, *Anthony Eden: A Biography* (London, 1981), p. 266.

2 Harold Macmillan, *Tides of Fortune, 1945 – 1955* (London, 1969), p. 45.

3 Robert Rhodes James (ed.), *Winston S. Churchill: His Complete Speeches*, vi, 6364 (New York, 1974).

4 *Ibid.*, vii, 6759 (broadcast of 21 March 1943).

5 Ben Pimlott (ed.), *The Second World War Diary of Hugh Dalton 1940 – 1945* (London, 1986), p. 656 (entry for 21 October 1943).

6 Kenneth Morgan, *Consensus and Disunity: The Lloyd George Coalition, 1918 – 1922* (Oxford, 1979), p. 182.

7 Rhodes James (ed.), *Complete Speeches*, v, 5293 (speech of 12 August 1933).

8 Winston S. Churchill, *The Second World War: The Hinge of Fate* (London, 1951), p. 781 (minute of 18 July 1942).

9 Cherwell Papers (Nuffield College, Oxford) F245, Prime Minister's Personal Minute to the Lord President of the Council and the Minister of War Transport, 21 October 1942.

10 Rhodes James (ed.), *Complete Speeches*, vii, 7172 (broadcast of 4 June 1945).

11 *Daily Herald*, 2 April 1947.

12 R. A. Butler, *The Art of the Possible. The Memoirs of Lord Butler* (London, 1979), p. 150.

13 Rhodes James (ed.), *Complete Speeches*, vii, 7629 (speech of 21 April 1948).

14 John Ramsden, *The Making of Conservative Party Policy* (London, 1980), p. 147.

15 Macmillan, *Tides of Fortune*, p. 403.

16 Rhodes James (ed.), *Complete Speeches*, viii, 8106 (speech of 14 October 1950).

17 *Ibid.*, vii, 7463 (speech of 14 March 1947).

18 Alec Cairncross, *Years of Recovery: British Economic Policy, 1945 – 1951* (London, 1985), p. 23.

19 Rhodes James (ed.), *Complete Speeches*, vii, 7573 (speech of 6 December 1947).

20 *Ibid.*, viii, 8248 (speech of 2 October 1951).

21 I am greatly indebted, in my remarks on Churchill's peacetime administration, to the excellent book on the subject by Anthony Eden, *Churchill's Indian Summer: The Conservative Government 1951 – 1955* (London, 1981).

22 Janet Morgan (ed.), *The Backbench Diaries of Richard Crossman* (London, 1981), p. 30 (entry for 31 October 1951).

23 Philip M. Williams (ed.), *The Diary of Hugh Gaitskell 1945 – 1956* (London, 1983), p. 307 (entry for 23 November 1951).

24 Lord Moran, *Winston Churchill: The Struggle for Survival* (London, 1966), p. 379 (entry for 25 February 1952).

25 Cherwell Papers J 110, Cherwell to Churchill, 15 November 1951.

26 See in particular, the Earl of Birkenhead, *The Prof in Two Worlds: The Official Life of Professor F. A. Lindemann, Viscount Cherwell* (London, 1961), pp. 283–94, and Cairncross, *op. cit.*, Ch. 9.

27 Public Record Office (PRO), PREM 11/40, Memorandum on 'External Action' by the Chancellor of the Exchequer attached to letter of R. A. Butler to Churchill of 21 February 1952.

28 PRO, PREM 11/137, Cherwell to Churchill, 18 March 1952.

29 Moran, *Churchill*, p. 384.

30 *The Times*, 25 July 1952.

31 PRO, CAB 11/13. The Committee reported on 19 November 1952. It was then dissolved and future responsibility for checking unemployment passed to the Economic Policy Committee.

32 PRO, CAB 128/26, Part 2, Cabinet of 15 December 1953.

33 Macmillan, *Tides of Fortune*, p. 411.

34 MS Woolton, Bodleian Library, 25, Prime Minister's Personal Minute to the Lord President of the Council and the Minister of Food, 25 March 1952.

35 PRO, PREM 11/44, Prime Minister's Personal Minute to Secretary of State for Colonies and Minister of Food, n.d., but arising out of a report in the *Manchester Guardian* of 20 June 1952.

36 PRO, PREM 128/25, Cabinet meetings of 14 and 15 July 1952.

37 Beaverbrook MSS (House of Lords Records Office) C57, Bracken to Beaverbrook, 7 January 1953. 'Churchill doesn't want to change anything in his Government,' Bracken wrote, 'and one cannot blame him for taking this line which is one that has been taken by most of his predecessors.'

38 The diary of Collin Brooks, entry for 17 December 1952.

39 PRO, PREM 11/824 (various correspondence beginning 12 November 1952, and Cabinet conclusions for 3 February 1954).

14

The Labour Left and the General Election of 1945

Jonathan Schneer

In the summer of 1945 the British Labour Party scored a landslide election victory. With 393 Members in the House of Commons it had converted a minority of 195 against the Conservatives into an absolute majority of 146 over all other parties combined. This overwhelming triumph was the sweeter for being nearly totally unexpected. Few, even among Labour's supporters, had supposed that it would be possible to drive the great war-time leader Winston Churchill, or his party, from office.[1]

Surprising as it was at the time, Labour's triumph has sparked little controversy among historians. As Paul Addison has argued in *The Road to 1945*, the party's victory affirmed a new 'Butskellite' consensus based upon Keynesian economic policies at home and collective security (mainly with the Americans) abroad. The new consensus had been forged during the war, experience of which converted a majority of the intelligentsia to belief in the virtues of 'planning', and a majority of the working class to in-sistence upon government guarantees of vastly improved economic and social conditions, while convincing both sectors of the population of the need for collective security against dictatorships and the threat of war. To a greater or lesser extent all the main parties advocated these ideals and aspirations in 1945, but because Labour espoused them most forthrightly it reaped its reward in the General Election of that summer. In so doing it set the seal upon British politics for more than a generation.[2]

This essay is intended to suggest a different interpretation of Labour in 1945. It was not necessarily apparent to contemporaries that the party's victory had established a moderate (Butskellite) consensus. Conservatives like Oliver Lyttelton 'feared for my country' after the General Election,

262

because he expected revolutionary action from the new Government. Labour's left wing believed the Attlee Administration would peacefully transform both foreign and domestic relations and thereby achieve 'socialism in our time'. As Emrys Hughes, son-in-law of the socialist pioneer Keir Hardie, put it on the morrow of victory: 'Britain has risen and the day is here.'[3]

Historians have paid scant attention to the Labour Left during the 1945 General Election. At the time, however, Labour Party leaders could not exclude it from consideration. Labour's left wing, which has always maintained a distinct, occasionally powerful, presence within the party, in fact helped to set the tone of the contest. Examination of its role during the campaign suggests a revised interpretation of perhaps Britain's most important twentieth-century election.

II

The background to the General Election is uncontroversial, but there is one point of significance which often has been forgotten. The flat-out contest for supremacy between Labour and Conservatives which took place during the campaign might not have occurred, had it not been for the Labour Left.

On May 23, 1945, Churchill announced the termination of the Coalition, which had governed Britain since the resignation of Neville Chamberlain five years before. He proclaimed the formation of a Conservative 'Caretaker Government', which would carry on during a General Election campaign of three weeks duration, beginning on June 15 and ending on polling day, July 5. Election results would not be known or broadcast, however, until July 26, in order to leave time for Service votes to be assembled from overseas and distributed by constituency.

Neither Churchill nor a majority of the Cabinet wanted an end to the electoral truce that had been more or less in effect in Britain since the beginning of the war. Most of the Labour Ministers hoped the Coalition Government would remain in power at least until victory over Japan had been won, and not knowing of the atomic bomb thought this victory might take several years to achieve. That Labour fought the General Election of 1945, not to improve its position against the Conservatives in the Coalition but in hopes of achieving outright victory, was largely a result of pressure emanating from the party rank and file, most forcefully articulated by Harold Laski, Aneurin Bevan and Emanuel Shinwell, representatives of the left on Labour's National Executive Committee. They convinced Herbert Morrison and William Whitely, Labour's chief whip in the House of Commons, that the party would not accept the continuation of Coalition Government. Attlee, Bevin and Dalton, who argued to the

263

contrary, were outvoted at a meeting of Labour's National Executive Committee. Thus the most successful General Election in Labour Party history was due in part to a victory of the rank and file, and of the Labour Left, over the party leaders.[4]

There is general agreement about the course of the campaign. Labour was quickest off the mark, having been meeting in annual conference while the decision was being made to terminate the Coalition. Labour candidates fanned out into the constituencies with the exhortation of retiring party chairman, Ellen Wilkinson, ringing in their ears: 'Fight clean, fight hard, and come back with a solid majority for a Labour Government.'[5] Once the campaign was on, the leadership, though it doubted victory, showed no signs of its previous indecision. The Conservative leadership, experiencing no such doubts, appeared at least equally determined. Churchill made a notable intervention in a radio broadcast of June 5, predicting that a Labour victory would lead to Britain being governed by a Gestapo. This and other charges he levelled during the campaign, for example that Post Office savings of the poor would be jeopardized if Labour won, are generally held to have been counter-productive. On the other hand, many observers believed that his cross-country motor tour was a triumphal success. If Churchill the party leader was not universally admired, it seemed that Churchill the national symbol and great wartime statesman was.

A critical moment in the campaign came on June 15 when Churchill invited Attlee to accompany him to Potsdam for the pending Three Power talks. Harold Laski, the London School of Economics professor who had replaced Ellen Wilkinson as chairman of Labour's N.E.C., intervened. 'If Mr. Attlee attended' the conference, Laski warned, he should do so only as an observer: 'Labour's foreign policy does not in many respects tie up with a Coalition dominated by the Tories. . . . The Labour Party and Mr. Attlee can hardly . . . accept responsibility for agreements which . . . will have been concluded by Mr. Churchill as Prime Minister.'[6] Laski's statement provided the Conservatives with two openings. First, they pointed out that the professor, although a member of Labour's Executive, was not responsible to the general electorate. Thus his presumed directive to Attlee, the party leader, was evidence that an undemocratic caucus controlled the Labour Party and, if Labour should win the Election, would control Britain too. Secondly, they held that Churchill's position at Potsdam would be weakened if it became known that Britain was divided over foreign policy. Therefore Laski's comments had been unpatriotic.

In a series of public letters to Churchill, Attlee smoothed the matter over, to Labour's advantage it is generally held, by repudiating the doctrinaire and impractical left-wing academic, while chiding Conservatives for their ignorance of Labour's constitution, and reaffirming his party's belief in 'continuity in foreign policy'. The N.E.C., he maintained, had no power over the party leader in such a matter. He accepted the Prime

Minister's invitation: 'There seems to me to be great public advantage in preserving and presenting to the world at this time that unity on foreign policy which we maintained throughout the last five years.'[7]

When they have written about this episode and its immediate aftermath, historians have agreed unanimously that Attlee used it to demonstrate an approach to foreign policy which Conservatives need not fear, as well as the dismissive manner with which he would confront pressure from his party's left wing. At the time, however, his conduct may have been viewed differently.

The basis for the common historical interpretation seems to be first, the Labour Government's traditional approach to foreign policy after the General Election and second, the famous last line of a private letter which the new Prime Minister sent to Laski on August 20: 'a period of silence on your part would be welcome'. It is tempting to read back into June 1945 tensions within the Labour Party which became explicit only later. No doubt they were implicit at the time. But people interpret politics mainly on the basis of some kind of public record. On that basis a reasonable person (especially of the Labour Left) could have concluded in 1945 that neither Attlee nor the party leadership had repudiated Laski's doubts about Conservative foreign policy. In fact, it would have been reasonable to conclude that they had been endorsed.

Laski opposed 'continuity in foreign policy' on the grounds that the approach of a socialist party to international affairs must be different from that of a Conservative party. Later the Labour Left fiercely criticized Attlee's Foreign Secretary, Ernest Bevin, for following the main lines of Churchill's traditional foreign policy, rather than embarking upon a new 'socialist' one. Like many other phrases, however, 'continuity in foreign policy' was subject to more than one interpretation, perhaps especially during that politically charged summer. A close reading of Labour campaign speeches suggests that in June and July 1945 the phrase could have held connotations quite the opposite of what eventually became its generally accepted meaning.

The three most publicized elements of the Coalition's foreign policy had been total defeat of the Axis powers, alliance with America and the Soviet Union, and the support of a new and powerful United Nations Organization to keep the peace after the war. During the summer of 1945, Labourites often maintained that a purely Conservative Government would be unlikely to continue striving for a strong U.N.O. or close relations with Russia. They even suggested that total victory could not be assured if the 'men of Munich' were returned to power. In this context the meaning of 'continuity in foreign policy' is far from clear.

Its ambiguity seems most obvious with regard to Anglo-Soviet relations. As Tom Braddock, Labour candidate for Mitcham, and a future critic of the Government's anti-Soviet alliance with America, put it in his

265

Election Address: 'It is impossible not to see that Russia is unpopular with big business cartels and monopolies, and with the Tory Government. It is only natural that it should be so. Russia is not run for the profit makers.'[8] Under Labour, Braddock predicted, Great Britain would not be run for profit either. Labour, then, was better qualified than the Conservative Party to maintain the Coalition's policy of friendship with the Soviets. The party leadership agreed, explicitly and on numerous occasions. Here is one instance taken from many, Stafford Cripps, speaking at Oxford on June 26: 'We must have a progressive, forward looking Government if we are to enter into the reconstruction of Europe hand in hand with the Soviet Union. Mr. Churchill's and Mr. Eden's policy has been good, but it has been the outcome of a Government of all parties. It would be a completely different proposition were we to have a Tory Government in power.'[9]

Which party, then, was opposed to 'continuity in foreign policy'? Already on June 23 the *New Statesman* had concluded that 'if there is a breach in the continuity of the policy of good relations with Russia, it is far more likely to come from a Tory administration' than from Labour.

But it was not only with regard to Russia that such conclusions about continuity could be drawn. For example Attlee argued vigorously for maintaining Coalition support for U.N.O. which, according to him, the Conservatives might abandon. This was also the burden of Philip Noel-Baker's June 18 B.B.C. election broadcast. Before the war, he argued, Conservatives had weakened the League of Nations. Only with the advent of Labour in the government had support for U.N.O. and the principle of collective security become a major theme of British foreign policy. Ernest Bevin, too, seemed to argue on the B.B.C. that 'continuity in foreign policy' meant continuation of Labour's ideals, including support of U.N.O., which Churchill and the Conservatives might jettison. 'I repeat,' Bevin declared: 'the foreign policy being pursued at the moment was devised by the Coalition Government, not by the Tory Members alone but by a combined effort, and is based upon collective security, a policy for which Labour has always stood.' Such statements, though emphasizing the tripartite nature of coalition foreign policy, were by no means necessarily repudiations of Laski's warnings about continuity. It all depended on what was being continued. Laski himself, while reiterating that 'the Socialist Party has principles different from Tory policy', professed himself content with these and similar Labour pronouncements.[10]

What, then, of Attlee's reaction to Churchill's attempts to pin him down on the 'continuity' issue? On June 16, as we have seen, he informed the Prime Minister that he hoped to maintain 'that unity on foreign policy' which had characterized party relations during the war. He then added: 'I do not anticipate that we shall differ on the main lines of policy which we have discussed together so often. I understand, of course, that responsibility must rest with the government, but I take it that we should consult

266

together upon the issues that arise in order to present a policy consonant with the views of the great majority of the people of this country.' Laski's response to this statement should be noted: 'Now that the sphere of responsibility has been defined the position is entirely satisfactory.'[11]

In retrospect it is clear that the professor was indulging in wishful thinking. But the question is what Labour supporters, and particularly the Labour Left, might have thought *at the time*, and thus what Labour's electoral victory meant to them. We must not read cold war tensions and suspicions of the Soviets among rank and file Labour voters into the Britain of 1945. Perhaps the Russian threat and the overriding need to maintain friendly. relations with America were the issues which, in fact, Attlee and Churchill had 'discussed together so often'. In June or July 1945, however, it would have been reasonable to infer from Attlee's statements that, during the war, the Coalition Government had carried out a foreign policy to which Labour had made the distinctive contribution, and that he was attending Potsdam to ensure that it continued to do so.

At the close of the campaign, Attlee responded again to Churchill over the 'continuity' issue:

> With regard to continuity in foreign policy, it is obvious that a Labour Government will follow a policy in accordance with the principles in which it believes, and on which its members in the House of Commons have been elected. This is sound constitutional doctrine. Presumably a Conservative Government would do the same. The fact that in the late Government members of all parties were in accord on the main lines of our foreign policy does not alter the fact that the complexion of the new House of Commons will decide the course of future policy as it did before the war when you and I both disagreed with the policy of the Conservative Government.[12]

This seems almost an explicit endorsement of Laski's argument that Labour would strive for international different objectives from the Conservatives'. Attlee's meaning hinges upon the phrase 'main lines of our foreign policy'. In retrospect, we can see that he may have meant suspicion of Soviet intentions, the need to maintain a 'special relationship' with the United States, and continuation of Britain's world role which, in fact, became the Labour Government's foreign policy. At the time, however, an intelligent voter could reasonably have thought he meant complete victory over fascism, development of the U.N.O., and the maintenance of friendly relations with America and the Soviet Union. This was the conclusion reached by the *New Statesman* on July 14. According to its editor, Kingsley Martin, the Three Power meeting would provide Attlee with an opportunity to 'indicate what continuity of foreign policy will really mean if interpreted in terms of 1945', namely the 'evolution from inter-Allied war planning to inter-Allied planning for reconstruction'. Far from opposing Attlee's presence at Postdam, then, the Labour Left had come to endorse it.

Of what else did the Labour Left believe a 'socialist foreign policy' would consist? Again, Laski was prominent in formulating objectives. He believed that World War II was not primarily a defensive struggle of the democracies against rapacious fascism, as commonly was maintained. Rather, in his opinion, it was a positive revolutionary war in which the European working classes could succeed, finally, in defeating capitalism. The primary aim of a British Labour Government, therefore, must be to establish friendly relations with new, revolutionary regimes, where they had already taken power, and to aid revolutionary movements in those countries where victory had not yet been achieved. During the General Election, this became a common Labour Left theme. Konni Zilliacus, a former staff member of the League of Nations in Geneva who now was standing for Labour at Gateshead, said:

> Throughout Europe the resistance movements derive their main strength from the workers and their allies, and are largely under Socialist and Communist leadership. Their reconstruction programmes are based on sweeping advances toward Socialism. Europe can be reconstructed . . . and democracy revived, only on the basis of a new social order. . . . Only a British government friendly to Socialism can join effectively in making peace in Europe.

The young Denis Healey, soon to be appointed Labour's International Secretary, concurred. As he told Labour's 1945 Annual Conference at Blackpool: 'The Socialist revolution has already begun in Europe and is already firmly established in many countries in Eastern and Southern Europe. The crucial principle of our own foreign policy should be to protect, assist, encourage, and aid in every way that Socialist revolution, wherever it appears.'[13]

In these sentiments too, the Labour Left thought it heard agreement in speeches of the party leadership. Cripps, who had been a prominent left critic of the leadership before the war, was, perhaps, most explicit. As he explained at Oxford: 'If we are to have any hope of a peaceful reconstruction of Europe it must be on the basis of Left Governments that are rising in Europe today.' He professed to be 'terrified of the result if the old Conservative clique got back into power'. He had not forgotten, nor, Labour candidates made certain, had the electorate, Churchill's counter-revolutionary zeal after 1917. 'Was there not a danger,' Cripps asked an audience in Cardiff, 'that a Tory Government would try to reimpose the reactionary governments which would endanger the whole reconstruction of Europe?'[14] There is no evidence that the Labour leadership sought to restrain this sort of rhetoric. Perhaps the most famous line to come from Labour's 1945 Annual Conference was Bevin's: 'Left understands Left but Right does not.' This was commonly understood to mean that a Labour Government could work more easily with the Soviets and other left-wing governments in Europe than the Conservatives. Bevin encouraged this assumption again, on July 26 at the Central Hall in London, where his audience was composed of Labour M.P.s from the metropolis and outlying arreas. Expecting Attlee to appoint him Chancellor of the Exchequer, he described how, as master of England's finances, he would assist every anti-fascist organization in Europe (including the communists) which had contributed to the defeat of Hitler, thus completing the socialist revolution launched on the continent in the anti-Nazi resistance. He was cheered to the echo.[15]

One does not want to go too far with this line of reasoning. It is not meant to suggest that the Labour Party leadership were professing revolutionary sentiments in 1945. On the other hand, one can see that the Labour Left had grounds for thinking that the party leadership shared its main foreign policy goals. In that case, however, the Butskellite consensus of 1945 appears problematic. At the least, different wings of the Labour Party might read different meanings into their great electoral victory. The Labour Left in 1945 was mistaken, but had reason to suppose that their Government would cooperate with the Soviets and continental revolutionary movements in reconstructing Europe on a socialist basis.

III

The Labour Left attitude towards the party's domestic program likewise was based upon perhaps mistaken, but hardly groundless, expectations. Before the opening of the election campaign it had greeted the party platform with restraint. *Let Us Face The Future* was a 'well written, simply worded document', according to the *New Statesman*, 'embodying a clear [if] limited policy of immediate objectives'.[16] Such judiciousness, however, did not survive Churchill's rapid and unexpected conversion from national to Conservative Party leader. Among the Labour Left the response to his Gestapo charge, and to the attack upon Laski, was an almost instinctive rallying behind the party leadership, and a perhaps natural inclination to identify its own attitudes with those of the party as a whole.

Polarization between the two main political parties led the Labour Left to accept, perhaps uncritically, a belief in the epochal nature of the contest. As one Labour Left candidate, Dr. Santos Jeger of South East St. Pancras, put it: 'It is not a simple question of Box replacing Cox. We have to settle by our votes who is to control the wealth and resources of Britain and in whose interests.' In Wales, Aneurin Bevan was sharper. The election was, in his view, 'a real struggle for power . . . between Big Business and the People'. But this was the line taken by the leadership to which Bevan soon would be promoted. As Herbert Morrison, the number two man in the party, after Attlee, put it on June 29 on the B.B.C.:

269

The election is about who is going to organise the producing power of our country, and how, and for what ends. It's about whether a great national plan can win the peace as it won the war, or whether the speculators, the buccaneer barons of Fleet Street, the sluggish leaders of big business, monopolies and cartels, are to sit comfortably — on our backs — for another shameful period of national decline.

Attlee too presented the Election nearly in apocalyptic terms. 'It was the duty of all Labour men and women,' he admonished an audience at Coventry 'to keep to the fore the question of vital importance: "was Britain in the future to be a country in which the prime object of industry, agriculture and trade was to provide the best possible life for all the people, or was it to be a country which was primarily a field of opportunity for private profit, the general good of the nation being a secondary consideration?"' Given the circumstances of the campaign, even for Attlee to pose the question so starkly may have suggested to the Labour Left that he favoured answers more radical than the party leadership usually advocated.[17]

Perhaps this reading of the leadership's intentions prompted Labour Left candidates to voice assessments and aspirations which, probably, the party's highest officials neither shared nor intended to fulfil. 'I believe,' said Stanley Awberry, Labour candidate for Bristol Central, that 'the time has arrived for the [present economic and social] system to be entirely changed.' Richard Acland, speaking on behalf of the Common Wealth Party, but already on the verge of joining Labour, spelled out on the B.B.C. what such a transformation would mean: 'All the resources of our country, the banks, the land, the mines, railways, insurance companies, shipping lines and all substantial industries and factories of any kind, must cease to be owned by big business and must be owned by all of us in common; run to meet the human needs of the many, not to make the profits of the few.' This, of course, went beyond Labour's official program. But the Labour Left was confident that eventually their party would enact such measures. As Walter Monslow put it in Barrow-in-Furness: 'Only a complete Socialist transformation of society can solve the economic problems of our age. . . . We can no longer patch and tinker . . . A Socialist government with the firm backing of the common people will introduce Socialist measures that would pave the way for a new classless society from which poverty and insecurity would be forever banished.' Perhaps such predictions appear utopian or naive to a later generation. But they seemed to many in 1945 to follow from the terms in which the Labour leadership presented the General Election in the first place.[18]

Throughout the campaign, Labour Party leaders expressed themselves in language which the left could reasonably consider its own. It was not simply 'planning' which the leadership endorsed (and which Liberals and some Conservatives advocated as well), but the socialist promise of democratic control of the economy. Attlee himself was capable of warning: 'if the community did not control the powerful economic forces . . . it would be controlled by them. The fight for economic freedom had yet to be won. The control over men's lives by great trusts and combines could be as oppressive as the rule of the barons in the past.' Such words were reminiscent of British socialism's late nineteenth-century heroes, verging on a Marxist interpretation of historical stages. Other party leaders referred to more specific forms of democratic control of industry which Labour would introduce. Hugh Dalton, Attlee's future Chancellor of the Exchequer, predicted that under a Labour Government the mines would be 'owned by the people and conducted in the interests of the country as a whole, with the miners themselves taking a full share of the responsibility for the control of the industry'. Emanuel Shinwell, Attlee's future Minister of Fuel and Power, agreed: 'We are working on details of coal legislation so that a Labour Coal Minister should not depend on Civil Servants, but should have the benefit of the ripe experience of those men who know the industry.' Such rhetoric, although vague, must have encouraged less well-known Labour candidates likewise to speculate upon the forms which 'economic freedom', as Attlee had called it, might take. 'Under common ownership,' predicted R. W. G. Mackay, the Labour nominee in North West Hull, 'and working within a broad national plan, the direction and administration of industry will be decentralised into the hands of local communities, and of the workers and technicians within the factories. Only thus can democratic cooperation replace bureaucratic red tape and control.' This seems about as far removed from the supposed moderate consensus of 1945 as may be.[16]

With so much apparently at stake, the pitch of electioneering became extreme. 'If the nation has to give marching orders to big business,' Morrison warned in his June 29 address, 'The nation must give them. . . . Big business has got to toe the line of public need — and the phrase is — got to. . . . the building rings are tough and powerful. . . . Who is likely to be toughest with them? And . . . what about the land? Who do you think is likely to make a radical attack on the problem of the control of the use of land and community planning?' One senses in such rhetoric appeals not merely to class consciousness, which were common on the Labour side during the campaign, but perhaps even to the possibility of class war. Why else did Morrison choose a semi-military term, 'marching orders', and implicitly threaten to use force if 'big industry' refused 'to toe the line'? Listeners on the Labour Left who were hungry, perhaps, for such language can be excused for thinking that the party leadership intended more swingeing measures than it ever enacted, and that there could never be consensus between Labour and Conservative. Labour Left candidates, at least, drew such conclusions. In Liverpool the redoubtable Bessie Braddock refused to shake hands with the Lord Mayor 'or with any of them — none

271

of the Conservatives', and promised, if elected, only to represent the working people of her district and 'no business interests'. In Chippenham, the Labour candidate, Andrew Tomlinson, advised British soldiers in Greece to turn on their Tory officers and mutiny, this being 'the only logical action left to them'.[20]

By the close of the campaign even the shrewdest and most cautious champions of the Labour Left believed that the party's election program constituted 'a direct challenge to . . . capitalist society'.[21] When, later, Butskellite compromises were worked out between the two main parties, these former optimists had grounds for complaint. Whatever the leadership had in mind, the Labour Left, at least, had recognized no such consensus during the summer of 1945. If anything its members had believed that the most powerful figures within Labour's ranks favoured their own more militant and radical outlook.

IV

After the votes had been counted and the full extent of Labour's victory became known, the party's left wing was jubilant. Believing, as Kingsley Martin wrote in the July 28 *New Statesman*, that 'the country has voted for Socialism', they assumed the party leadership shared this interpretation of its mandate, and would fulfil it. They appear to have accepted at face value the most radical pronouncements to which the leaders had given voice during the campaign. Geoffrey Bing, the Labour Left candidate in Hornchurch who had campaigned on a platform of 'straight out Socialism', assured local supporters that 'the policy of the Labour Party would be put into force without delay. There was not going to be any soft pedalling of the programme.' Moreover, he declared confidently, 'his conscience and Labour Party policies would never come into conflict'. Harold Laski, in an interview with American correspondent Edward R. Murrow, predicted that Labour was 'going, in a straightforward and orderly fashion to socialise the ownership, stage by stage, on a carefully considered plan of priority, of the vital instruments of production upon which the life of this nation depends.' Emrys Hughes concurred: 'The things that Keir Hardie stood for have now become practical politics.' Hughes, who had to wait six months until a by-election in Ayrshire gave him an opportunity to join others on the Labour Left in Parliament, could not but 'rub my eyes and wonder whether I am asleep or awake' once he got there. What particularly pleased him was 'recognizing ever new faces of personalities who were prominent in the old I.L.P.', which had disaffiliated from Labour in 1932, claiming that the larger party was no longer sufficiently Socialist. In 1945, hoping to stem the flood of members like Hughes who had quit to rejoin Labour, the I.L.P. petitioned, unsuccessfully, to re-affiliate.

Likewise members of Common Wealth were following Hughes's example. Almost immediately after the votes had been counted in July, its founder, Richard Acland, applied to Transport House. As he explained in *Reynolds's News* on September 23, he still believed that 'all the great resources of our country . . . and every substantial industry and factory . . . must be owned . . . by the community as a whole'. But he added: 'I believe that since the election, the effective growing point for one hundred percent Socialism is inside the Labour Party and not elsewhere.' [22]

The Labour Left believed that it had been empowered by the election victory. Historians such as Henry Pelling have argued that Attlee's Cabinet appointments were cautious and conservative. Perhaps so, yet the Labour Left rejoiced when men and women with whom they had identified in the past, Aneurin Bevan, Emanuel Shinwell, Stafford Cripps and Ellen Wilkinson, were invited to join. In *Left News* Victor Gollancz noted that the new Government was composed mainly of former Left Book Club authors: Attlee, Cripps, Wilkinson, Bevan, Strachey, Noel-Baker, and Lord Addison; and that those who had written for him during the 1930s were also well represented on the back benches (Foot, Edelman, Elwyn Jones, J. P. W. Mallalieu, Swingler, Zilliacus). To many this must have represented a revolution of sorts, at least in the sense that the old establishment had been blasted from power and their former critics elevated instead. In such unprecedented circumstances what was not possible? Laski entertained hopes of being appointed British ambassador in Washington. The veteran I.L.P.ite, Sydney Silverman, imagined that he might be made a junior minister in the Home Office. He was supported by Shinwell who mentioned his name to Attlee. Barbara Castle, George Wigg, J. P. W. Mallalieu, Donald Bruce, all of whom had been active on the left during the pre-war popular front agitation, were chosen as Parliamentary Private Secretaries. [23]

Amid the rejoicing on the Labour Left, a few notes of caution, or even of misgiving, might be heard. In Huddersfield the victorious candidate, J. P. W. Mallalieu held an impromptu rally when the results of the poll were announced, 'an open air meeting of 10,000 people. As I spoke the voice of an elderly man kept coming from the crowd, repeating the age old fear of the British working class: "Don't let us down, Lad! Don't let us down!"' Fred Longden, Labour Member for Deritend in Birmingham, voiced the opposite fear: that the party was in advance of the rank and file. 'People have not voted for us because they are socialists conscious of what they are doing. I know very well that most people voted Labour from fear of the interwar years being repeated.' And in *Reynolds's News*, on August 12, Tom Driberg, the columnist and Member for Maldon, commented unenthusiastically on Attlee's Cabinet choices: 'On the whole it is a Government of the Right rather than the Left of the Labour Movement.' Amid the celebrations, however, such voices were barely audible. And

273

even their owners attempted to still these small doubts. Driberg believed the Labour Right dominated Attlee's government, 'but it is well balanced politically as well as in other ways, and deserves the staunch support of all socialists'.[24]

V

Thus the Labour Left during the summer of 1945, 'English Socialism's blissful dawn', as Michael Foot called it many years later. They believed that finally their hour had struck, that the British people had voted for a peaceful socialist revolution to which the leadership of the party was committed. The famous Laski incident did not signify, in their eyes, Attlee's repudiation of his party's left wing. Rather the Labour Left believed that the new Government was determined to maintain the best aspects of Coalition foreign policy, and to reconstruct Europe along socialist lines. On the home front it believed the Government would take control of the 'commanding heights of the economy' as Bevan was to call them some years later, and that it would not merely extend state responsibility for the provision of welfare, but also make possible true 'economic freedom' as Attlee had called it, by which was understood democratic control at all levels.

Later the policies of Attlee's governments gave rise to doubts, tensions, heartsearchings and outright dissent on the Labour Left. These constitute a formative chapter in its post-war history, and in that of the larger party to which it belonged. They help explain the Bevanite rebellions of the 1950s, New Left disenchantment with official Labour during the 1960s and 1970s, and even, possibly, current tensions between Bennites and the followers of the party leader Neil Kinnock. They were prompted, however, by the Government's policies as they evolved, especially after 1947, not by the program laid down in 1945. The Labour Left insisted, in fact, that it had remained true to those policies and principles, while the Government was failing to carry them out.[25]

The General Election of 1945 did not mark the triumph of moderate reformism over 1930s Conservatism, which is how usually it is remembered. At the time many thought, with reason, that it presaged more fundamental changes. Perhaps hidden differences existed during the campaign within the Labour Party itself. But the gulf which separated Bevanites and Gaitskellites only a few years later did not yet exist. In 1945, for once, the party leadership said more than enough to satisfy the Labour Left.

Notes

Earlier drafts of this paper were presented at the Modern History Seminar, Institute of Historical Research, University of London, and at the Social History Seminar, King's College, Cambridge University. In addition to thanking their convenors and members for many helpful comments and suggestions, I wish to thank Chris Clark, Jim Cronin, Paul Kennedy, Fred Leventhal, Standish Meachum, R. K. Webb, and Peter Weiler for reading and commenting on this piece. Sadly, Stephen Koss, upon whose critical judgement and friendly advice I always had relied previously, was no longer able to help me.

1 It is true that the polls predicted a Labour victory, but few people paid attention to them. Churchill predicted a majority of over sixty. See Henry Pelling, *The 1945–51 Labour Governments* (London, 1984), p. 27. He adds that 'most political observers expected . . . the Conservatives and their allies would have a lead in the end.' On the Labour side, Dalton foresaw 'either a small Tory majority or deadlock.' Chuter Ede, Bevin and Bevan thought Churchill would be unbeatable. See Kenneth O. Morgan, *Labour in Power, 1945–51* (London, 1984), p. 39. Strangely enough, it appears that among Labour Party notables only Harold Laski believed Labour would win the election. See Kingsley Martin, *Harold Laski, 1893 – 1950, A Biographical Memoir* (London, 1953). p. 172.

2 Paul Addison, *The Road to 1945* (London, 1975), p. 280. 'Butskellism' was a term coined during the 1950s to suggest the similarity of economic policies followed by Labour Chancellor Hugh Gaitskell and Conservative Chancellor R. A. Butler. Other works which have treated the 1945 General Election from the same perspective include Morgan, *op. cit.*, Pelling, *op. cit.*, and Pelling, 'The 1945 General Election Reconsidered,' *Historical Journal*, xxiii (1980). 399 – 414. The other standard works on the subject are R. B. McCallum and A. Readman, *The British General Election of 1945* (London, 1947) and Angus Calder, *The People's War* (London, 1969). Calder criticizes the Labour Party precisely for establishing the new consensus.

3 *Glasgow Forward*, August 4, 1945.

4 For the split within the Labour Party over the timing of the General Election see Pelling's article cited above. He does not mention Laski. However, *The Times* of June 25, 1945, quotes Randolph Churchill: 'It is notorious that at the Blackpool Conference last month Professor Laski was among the most assiduous in forcing Mr. Attlee and his colleagues to leave the Government.'

5 Quoted in McCallum and Readman, *op. cit.*, p. 132.

6 *The Times*, June 15, 1945.

7 *Ibid.*, June 16, 1945.

8 File on Tom Braddock compiled by the editors of the *Dictionary of Labour Biography*. I am grateful to Dr. Joyce Bellamy and Professor John Saville for opening these to me.

9 *The Times*, June 26, 1945.

10 *Ibid.*, July 5, 1945; for other statements by Laski see *ibid.*, June 15, June 16, and June 20, 1945.

11 *Ibid.*, June 16, 1945.

12 *Ibid.*, July 3, 1945.

13 For Zilliacus see Labour Party papers at Walworth Road, 1945 General Election file; *Labour Party Annual Conference*, 1945 p. 114.

14 *The Times*, June 26, June 18 and July 2, 1945.

15 For this Central Hall speech I am indebted to John Platts Mills, who sent me a private letter describing it; also to Ernest R. Millington, then the sole Common Wealth M.P., who granted me an interview, and also described the effect of Bevin's speech.

16 *New Statesman*, May 19, 1945.

17 For Jeger see Labour Party 1945 General Election file; Bevan is quoted in McCallum and Readman, *op. cit.*, p. 113; Attlee in *The Times*, June 22, 1945.

18 For Awberry and Monslow see Labour Party 1945 General Election file.

19 Attlee quoted in *The Times*, June 22, 1945; Dalton, *The Times*, June 28; Shinwell, *The Times*, June 27, 1945. For Mackay see British Library of Political and Economic Science, Mackay Collection, 25/6.

20 Millie Toole, *Mrs. Bessie Braddock* (London, 1957), p. 126; for Tomlinson see Labour Party, N.E.C., vol. 91, p. 71, February 28, 1945. The N.E.C. forced Tomlinson to retract this statement.

21 *New Statesman*, June 2, 1945.

22 For Bing see *Romford, Hornchurch and Upminster Recorder*, August 3, 1945; for Laski, *Daily Herald*, August 2, 1945; for Hughes, *Glasgow Forward*, January 12, 1946.

23 *Left News*, September 1945; Silverman's aspirations are recorded by Emrys Hughes in *Sydney Silverman. Rebel in Parliament* (London, 1969), p. 89.

24 Mallalieu recorded this incident in *Sunday Pictorial*, March 23, 1947; Longden is quoted in the *Labour Pacifist Fellowship Bulletin*, November 1945.

25 For a thorough treatment of the evolution of Labour Left attitudes towards the Attlee Governments see my *Labour's Conscience: The British Labour Left, 1945 – 51* (forthcoming, Allen and Unwin).

15

The Rise and Fall of Public Ownership in Britain

Kenneth O. Morgan

'Socialised industry in one country' — the key to the rejuvenation of a dying capitalist order in Britain and to the economic advance of the working classes throughout the world. This battle cry in 1933 by the young left-wing publicist and ideologue, A. L. Rowse, encapsulates much of the grandeur and tragedy of modern British socialism.[1] At least as an aspiration, the public ownership of major industries, utilities and natural resources was inseparable from the socialist idea in Britain from the foundation of Keir Hardie's Independent Labour Party in 1893 down to the Second World War. It reached its heady climax with the Attlee government of 1945 – 51 when seven major measures of nationalization went through and twenty per cent of the economy was taken into public hands. Equally, the relative electoral decline and flagging morale of the British left, from the high noon of the late 1940s to the anxious twilight of the early 1980s, were intimately bound up with a diminishing primacy for nationalization as the coping stone of labour's programme, and an eroding confidence in either the methods or achievements of public ownership at least as traditionally conceived. No one reacted more violently against these earlier left-wing shibboleths than did A. L. Rowse himself in his later incarnation as academic historian, insatiable author on Shakespeare and the Elizabethan world, and pessimistic patriot who abjured the social enthusiasms of his youth. A brief analysis of the rise and decline of public ownership as a radical panacea, therefore, with a particular emphasis on the subtle subterranean changes that took place in the status and ethic of public ownership in the Attlee years of 1945 – 51, is central to an understanding of the political and social culture of modern post-imperial Britain that

Stephen Koss did so much to illuminate. It takes us close to the heart of the strengths and weaknesses of the British version of socialism in our time.

The dream of nationalization had been current in left-wing circles since the 1880s.[2] Radicals advocated the public ownership of land, partly in response to the agrarian protests widespread in Ireland (and, to a lesser extent, Wales and Scotland) at the time. The miners became strongly committed to the principle of nationalization of the coal-mines ('the mines for the miners') after the turn of the century, and it was formally adopted by the Labour Party and the T.U.C. from 1906 onwards. The nationalization of the railways was also endorsed at Labour annual conferences before the First World War.

But public ownership at this early stage was an aspiration rather than a programme. It was largely the outcome of deteriorating labour relations in major British industries, at a time of serious class conflict and growing economic difficulties, rather than of a carefully worked-out blueprint for social change or technical modernization. Little interest was taken in the mechanics of nationalization by trade unionists themselves. The miners of south Wales, for example, were uncertain as to the rival merits of bureaucratic state ownership on the German model or syndicalism or other forms of industrial devolution.[3] A young miner like Aneurin Bevan grew up apparently espousing both these contradictory creeds at the same time. Most of the serious advocates of public ownership before 1914, in fact, were not workers at all. They were mostly middle-class socialists of a theoretical or intellectual bent, ranging from Marxists in the S.D.F. to the more centrist Fabians, such as the Webbs, who pressed the cause of 'municipal socialism' side by side with central state ownership as part of the gospel of gradualism. The First World War, however, gave public ownership a considerable boost. In particular, the unions now came to see it as synonymous with those central controls which had regenerated industrial production in wartime. As a result, the Labour Party constitution of 1918 included the famous clause (later renumbered as clause 4) which committed the party to the public ownership of the means of production and distribution, with some vague reference to notions of workers' control or joint consultation thrown in as an incidental embellishment.

Despite this apparent priority given to nationalization, however, its role in Labour's policies in the twenties remained vague in the extreme. Even what it meant was uncertain. R. H. Tawney, one of Labour's sages and moral inspirations, adopted a deliberately eclectic view in *The Acquisitive Society* (1921). While public ownership could mean a central board being set up to manage an industry on national lines (as proposed by Tawney himself for the coal industry in a famous scheme of 1920), he also proclaimed the merits of the co-operative system, the purchase of shares by the state or various forms of 'industrial self-government'.[4] Nationalization was but one route towards socialism, alongside educational reform, the

278

redistribution of capital, the ethic of equality and much else besides. The objectives of nationalization were also not clear. Efficiency considerations relating to major industries and services where a high degree of monopoly prevailed; the urge for more harmonious labour relations and greater industrial democracy; demands for higher wages and shorter hours; straight class hatred of private tycoons like coalowners and railway bosses all played their part. When the Fabians urged nationalization, they had in mind a functional collectivist model. But when the miners or railwaymen called for the 'the mines for the nation' they implied an industry in some sense owned by themselves and run for their own benefit. 'Nationalisation,' avowed Tawney, was 'not an end but a means to an end.'[5] But both the method and the objective were singularly lacking in substance.

If the purpose and method of public ownership were unclear, so, too, were the precise areas of the economy to be taken over. When Labour came to power for the second time in 1929, only coal nationalization was proposed with any seriousness. Even that was not pursued with much resolution. Earlier plans for the public ownership of the land, power, rail transport or the Bank of England fell by the wayside. Labour's manifesto in 1929 was strong on social reform, the defence of trade unionists, the revival of employment, and a generalized compassion that could appeal to idealistic ex-Liberals, or enthusiasts for the League of Nations. But on public ownership, the jewel in the crown for dedicated socialists, Marxist and non-Marxist alike, the party's lack of grasp was painfully clear long before the financial and political débâcle of 1931 exposed it for all the world to see. When Labour lost office in 1931, it was still a party committed to social welfare and a generalized defence of the workers' interests rather than to socialism.

The real history — as opposed to the prehistory — of public ownership began in 1931. Between then and 1937, Labour and the T.U.C. for the first time in their history evolved a clear democratic socialist programme, with nationalization central to it. *Labour's Immediate Programme* (1937) outlined a precise list of industries and services to be taken over by a future Labour government, very much on the lines of that pursued after 1945. There were also viable models for nationalization now in existence. Herbert Morrison's highly influential book, *Socialisation and Transport* (1933), used the precedent of the London Passenger Transport Board to uphold the idea of the autonomous public corporation, free equally from parliamentary interference and internal dictation by the workers.[6] Earlier he had denounced such bodies as 'capitalist soviets'. The T.U.C. in 1932 eventually came to favour much the same kind of approach, although Ernest Bevin for one wanted more emphasis on the principle of having trade union members on the board of directors of the new publicly-owned industries.

The main reason, however, why public ownership suddenly became the

279

new conventional wisdom of the British left was that a new school of university-trained democratic socialist economists appropriated public ownership as part of their rationale. Hugh Dalton's *Practical Socialism for Britain* (1935) contained a lengthy treatment of nationalization, including the Bank of England whose sinister role during the alleged 'bankers' ramp' in 1931 had been widely condemned.[7] On the other hand, a much younger writer like Douglas Jay in the *Socialist Case* (1937) placed significantly less emphasis on nationalization and concentrated largely on Keynesian-style economic management, the planning of investment and the reform of taxation to redistribute wealth. Jay's book contained only four pages referring directly to public ownership, and even they focussed on the relatively narrow issue of the compensation of private stock-holders.[8] The same was broadly true of the various writings of Evan Durbin, another prominent Oxford-trained economist at the time, whose views in part reflected the trade-cycle theories of Hayek at the London School of Economics.[9] He did argue, however, that replacing a private employer with a manager appointed by a democratically-elected government would remove the social gulf in industrial relations.

On balance, though, the basis for the new appeal of public ownership in the thirties lay in the fact that it was harnessed to the idea of planning. It became part of the attempt by some gifted young intellectuals to fuse Keynesianism and the mixed economy with the moral imperatives of democratic socialism. Public ownership for them was part — perhaps not the most important part — of an organically-conceived machinery of planning to co-ordinate and control production, distribution, investment, pricing policy and (within limits) consumption, and to rectify the inefficiencies, perhaps even more the inhumanities of the market economy. The vogue for planning in the 1930s gave public ownership a new credibility. Even Chamberlain's 'national' government shared in this enthusiasm to some degree, with the state ownership of coal-mining royalties in 1938 and the creation of the British Overseas Airways Corporation in 1939 following on such earlier instances of state enterprise as the Central Electricity Board.

The Second World War, of course gave the notion of public ownership an enormous boost. The support of the unions became even more committed, especially among miners and railwaymen. The newly-launched National Union of Mineworkers in January 1945 included the nationalization of the mines, on corporatist lines, as their first objective. There was, however, significantly less enthusiasm from steel workers, although they, too, were now formally committed to nationalization rather than to the central planning board for steel they had advocated in the thirties. In addition, a variety of middle-class groups were also strongly pledged to growing state intervention in the economy. The wartime thrust towards centralized planning; the redistribution of industry to restore employment in depressed communities such as Tyneside and South Wales; the wartime control of industries like coal and shipping; the introduction of nationalization into munitions production with the takeover of Short Aircraft by Stafford Cripps in 1943[10] — all helped advance the cause of public ownership. Professional, technical, managerial and administrative groups, through such organizational voices as the Town and Country Planning Association and P.E.P., became strongly dedicated to public rather than private enterprise. They were anxious not to repeat the errors of decontrol and the wanton return to private ownership such as had occurred after the First World War in 1919 – 21. The wartime surge towards planning and social direction chimed in with Labour's creed of public ownership, while young socialists like Gaitskell, Jay and Durbin all served in important posts in the civil service (Jay at the Board of Trade to work on regional development) to push their ideas further. But throughout, as in the writings of ideologues like G. D. H. Cole at this period, the call for nationalization was advocated primarily in terms of practical objectives of efficiency and modernization rather than the beguiling vision of socialism.

The Labour Party itself reflected this new commitment. There were fears, indeed, that Labour's leading ministers in the Churchill wartime coalition government — Attlee, Morrison, Greenwood and Bevin — were veering towards the watered-down idea of central control rather than state ownership of basic industries. There were angry protests by Labour M.P.s in the Commons in 1942 when the government's white paper for the mining industry, to which Attlee and Morrison had given their blessing, suggested a form of dual control of the mines during the war years rather than outright public ownership.[11] The wartime emphasis, indeed, appeared to be on compromise schemes for state control rather than uninhibited nationalization. On the left flank, Harold Laski urged on the 1942 Party conference the need to take the banks, land, shipping, transport and civil aviation into public hands, along with sources of energy such as coal, gas and electricity.[12] The main tendency of wartime economic policy, however, was rather to favour a pragmatic extension of the financial controls and physical planning of the wartime emergency, but to leave the capitalist substructure intact. The socialist utopia was still far off, while Emanuel Shinwell blandly admitted to the 1943 party conference that the major details of Labour's public ownership proposals still had to be worked out. 'We are not yet in a position to submit a final report.'[13]

An instructive episode took place at the Labour Party's annual conference in December 1944.[14] It was typical of the way in which political activism at the grass roots continued to mount between 1940 and 1945. When the Labour Party national executive, with Noel-Baker and Shinwell as their spokesmen, tried to push through a generalized motion on behalf of a more controlled and integrated economic policy, an amendment from the Reading Labour Party, moved by Ian Mikardo, and strongly endorsed

281

by James Callaghan, prospective candidate for Cardiff South,[15] was carried without a vote. This committed Labour unambiguously to public owner- ship. Indeed, the amendment included iron and steel as well, which the N.E.C. had tried desperately to omit. The Executive had to give way. In April 1945, despite strong opposition from Herbert Morrison, the N.E.C. drafted a strong, precise policy of nationalization, including iron and steel, for its forthcoming election manifesto.[16]

Labour, therefore, for the first — and only — time in its history went before the electors in July 1945 with the nationalization of major industries and utilities as a major objective. On the other hand, it is highly significant what the list did not include. Some of the proposals outlined in *For Socialism and Peace* in 1934 were omitted, notably the land, the joint-stock banks and cotton-spinning. Labour showed throughout much reluctance in moving into manufacturing industry or in dealing with the private banks or other financial institutions.[17] From the start, it had a precise, but limited and finite programme. It was committed to working out the old agenda of the thirties, rather than looking forward to new fields for state ownership.

Judged from an international perspective, Labour's schemes down to 1945 remained highly distinctive. The programme and the models for nationalization followed, in the main, domestic ideas such as those of the Fabians or native prototypes such as the public corporation enshrined in the L.P.T.B. in 1933 or B.O.A.C. in 1939. It was a pragmatic, national approach, heavily influenced by theories of planning derived from the 1930s and reinforced by the experience of a victorious war in which Britain, almost alone amongst the countries of western Europe, was not occupied by German troops. Nationalization in a curious way was thus associated with a kind of patriotism, with the social unity newly created by a people's war.

Within this context, European ideas of workers' control had little in- fluence on the British labour movement which, from Ernest Bevin downwards, was committed to traditional policies of collective bargaining in which the unions maintained their historic role of representing the workers. French-style 'syndicalism' of pre-1914 days, which had found some echoes in the Welsh mining valleys and in Clydeside in Scotland amongst engineering and shipyard workers, faded from the scene in the 1920s. Nor did Italian-style corporatism have an influence in Britain (apart from a few fascist fringes). The only continental country that had much impact at all on Labour's planners, indeed, was one more geographically isolated — Sweden, a potentially socialist state with a Social Democratic government from 1934. A book edited by Margaret Cole and Charles Smith for the New Fabian Research Bureau in 1938 sang the praises of Swedish social democracy. The authors noted that in Sweden, alone in Europe apart from the Soviet Union, the socialized sector was already extensive. It included the Post Office, most railways, most electric power, forests, the Riskbank, air transport, radio, tobacco, liquor and even some iron-ore mining. Even so, the main appeal for young socialists, such as Hugh Gaitskell, lay rather in its inter-weaving of exchange rate policy, deficit budgeting and a public works programme as part of its 'middle way'.[18] In any case, apart from the marginal case of Sweden, the idea of nationalization in Britain was largely conceived in insular terms. Much of its later history can be explained by reference to this fundamental, historic fact.

The political situation in July 1945 determining the history of nationalization in Britain was a most remarkable one. Labour won the general election with a huge landslide majority, winning 394 seats as against the Conservatives' 210. Nationalization, therefore, was the product of a massive political revolution in which the Labour government could carry all before it.[19] Apart from the great enthusiasm within the Labour Party and amongst trade unionists such as the miners and transport workers, the programme of public ownership carried out in 1945 – 7 seemed to win broad agreement across the political spectrum. The Conservatives did not resist nationalization measures to any particular extent until they began to oppose the 1947 Transport Act, mainly over road haulage. After all, in industries like gas, electricity and civil aviation there was already a high degree of public intervention, national or municipal. In addition, coal and the railways were industries with bad records of modernization and industrial relations during the decades of private ownership. Many government inquiries, such as the McGowan report on electricity or the Heyworth report for gas, called for public control on technical grounds. The civil service, notably the planners like James Meade in the Economic Section of the Cabinet, a stronghold of Keynesianism, also showed much initial enthusiasm for nationalization while the press and public seemed more than prepared to acquiesce. An historic measure like the nationalization of the coal mines on January 1 1947, aroused passionate rejoicing in mining communities from Scotland to Kent.

The programme of public ownership in the 1945 – 7 sessions, as has been seen, went through with relatively little controversy. One feature that is apparent throughout is the comparatively moderate nature of many of the changes adopted. In the case of the Bank of England, only a modest reform was effected. No public control of capital movements or the flow of investment was attempted, and the governor of the Bank continued to behave in much the same fashion as he had done prior to nationalization. In some industries there was already a high degree of municipal ownership (in electricity, and in the later case of gas). The same applied, it might be added, to the more centralizing aspects of Aneurin Bevan's National Health Service, which nationalized all hospitals.[20] There was widespread bipartisan agreement on the principle of public ownership as in the cases of civil aviation, cable and wireless, and the electricity supply and distribution industry. In addition, there were remarkably generous scales of compensation paid to private stock-holders, especially in the case of the railways, in accordance with pre-war decisions that there would be no overt confiscation of assets.[21]

In every case, too, the Morrisonian pattern of the public board was broadly adopted, with in each instance a modicum of workers' or trade union representation amongst the directors. The public board was the sacrosanct model at this time, with old socialist ideologues like Harold Laski and G. D. H. Cole giving it their blessing. Cole's former enthusiasm for 'Guild Socialism' was now a thing of the distant past. This commitment to the public board method was strongly endorsed in each case by the Labour Cabinet's Socialisation of Industry Committee, chaired by Morrison, throughout the 1945 – 8 period.[22] The public board approach seemed to follow naturally from the wartime experiments in public planning and full employment policy. There was no trade union enthusiasm at all for workers' partnership, let alone workers' control. The giants of the T.U.C., men like Arthur Deakin of the Transport Workers or Will Lawther of the Miners, felt, like all trade union leaders before them, that their role would be fundamentally compromised if union leaders turned into bosses. If trade unionists became members of boards of nationalized industry, as when Walter Citrine became chairman of the Electricity supply industry, or when Ebby Edwards of the N.U.M. became a director of the National Coal Board, they had to resign their trade union posts, to avoid any possible conflict of interests or confusion of identity. In Britain, unlike Western Germany or Austria for instance, a broadly adversarial view of the relation between workers and capitalist employers continued to predominate, a legacy of the pattern of industrial relations as it had evolved since the Victorian era.

However, the other point to be made about nationalization in Britain in 1945 – 7 is that the idea of consensus and inter-party agreement can be exaggerated. The post-war schemes for coal and transport went distinctly beyond the wartime proposals for planning and control. In some cases, notably coal, the most radical option available was taken up. But the results were not always happy. In the case of coal, the highly centralized system of management and of industrial relations led to many problems, and to the resignation of Sir Charles Reid as director in May 1948.[23] Emanuel Shinwell, Minister of Fuel and Power in 1945 – 7, was a frequent, caustic critic of the lack of care and attention paid to the details of nationalization and of the over-centralization, lack of industrial democracy and adequate machinery of consultation within the coal industry.[24] He later complained that, when he set about nationalizing coal in 1945, all he could find for guidance in the Labour Party's files was a pre-war document by James Griffiths written in Welsh! It might be added, though, that since

Shinwell himself had served at the Mines ministry in 1924 and 1929, and had been chairman of Labour's Reconstruction Committee in the latter stages of the Second World War, he was foremost among the guilty men responsible for this neglect. In the event, the achievement of the great prize of nationalization in a major industry like coal mining was the product of much last-minute hustling and muddle, rather than of purposive long-term planning. Many of the future problems of the British coal industry, including many of the background factors in the terrible miners' national strike of March 1984 – March 1985, can be related to the unsatisfactory nature of the nationalization structure adopted back in 1947.[25] In many ways, the French approach to nationalization in 1944 – 7, more varied in technique and perhaps more flexibly adapted to the needs of particular industries and utilities, survived the test of time and economic hammer-blows rather better.

As has been noted, coal was the greatest emotional triumph for British nationalization. Vesting day on January 1, 1947, was hailed by mining villages throughout the land, and evoked much enthusiasm amongst workers in France and other continental countries. Yet it was also coal that became associated with the first serious doubts about nationalization as a policy. The advent of nationalization coincided with a terribly cold winter of prolonged freezing weather, from January to March 1947. This led to immense coal shortages, a huge cutback in energy supplies and industrial production, and much temporary unemployment. It was perhaps unfair to blame all these problems on the newly-nationalized industry: part of the trouble lay in transport difficulties rather than in coal production. But it did draw attention to manpower shortages and the low level of productivity in the coal industry.[26] From the fuel crisis of early 1947, British nationalization was partially tainted with the stigma of failure. The planners had simply failed to plan. Shinwell, the Minister of Fuel and Power, who had blithely discounted fears about coal shortages in 1946, as late as November of that year, was one of the victims. He was finally removed from the Cabinet altogether in October 1947, to be replaced by his enemy, the bourgeois figure of Hugh Gaitskell.

Apart from the disaster of coal, in Britain, as in France, 1947 saw a growing mood of *anti-étatisme*, as the emotion of wartime unity gradually evaporated. After a glorious period in which nationalization, the ethic of equality, planning and the common weal had swept all before them, there was mounting public discontent with controls, bureaucracy and the continuing austerity and restriction on personal liberty in the post-war period. To the general public, coal and railways, two declining industries with long-term structural problems, were symptomatic of a wider decay in the socialist ideal.

Added to this psychological mood, Britain, like other western countries, was gravely afflicted by the economic crises of 1947. In the case of Britain, there was a mounting balance of payments crisis and a huge outflow of funds on the capital as well as the current account, culminating in the disaster of convertibility of sterling in July – August 1947. The American loan of 1945, supposed to help Britain until 1951, would, at the present rate of loss, be completely used up by the end of 1947. Hence Marshall Aid, O.E.E.C. and the European recovery programme, as a salvage operation mounted in dire necessity. In itself, Marshall Aid did not directly influence the Labour government's will to nationalize, which was shaped by internal party priorities and assumptions. Paul Hoffman of the U.S. European Recovery Program did voice concern with British steel nationalization in 1948,[27] but this played no part in determining British policy. Marshall Aid to Britain, which came through in vast quantities down to the end of 1950, went partly to maintaining food supplies, partly to building up the infrastructure of British industry and services, public and private. However, the nature and volume of U.S. assistance helped confirm a reluctance to tamper with the character of British industry at a time of acute financial crisis, as grave as 1931. It encouraged widely-expressed doubts about the lack of confidence in socialism in terms of economic achievement and productive effect, as opposed to moral ideals of social equality or human justice.

All these doubts surfaced in full in the great Cabinet debates about the nationalization of iron and steel in the spring and summer of 1947. No issue showed more clearly the implicit limits to Labour's commitment to nationalization as a concept and an ideal. The case of iron and steel was significantly different from that of industries and services previously nationalized. In the first place, steel would take British nationalization into manufacturing industry, including engineering. This was a radical new departure, and one viewed with lack of enthusiasm by most members of the government. Secondly, the steel industry was not easy to criticise on grounds of poor productive performance. It had done very well during the war, while the Iron and Steel Control Board, a kind of half-way house for nationalization set up in 1946, performed very efficiently with rapidly rising steel production in 1946 – 7 and major new steel works like the Steel Company of Wales plant near Port Talbot in South Wales coming into operation. The chairman of the Control Board, Sir Andrew Duncan of Steel House, was praised by Labour's Chancellor of the Exchequer, Hugh Dalton, as a 'great executive' who was half a socialist himself.[28] Thirdly, it was well known that steel workers were less zealous for nationalization than were the miners or railway workers. The history of labour relations in the steel industry in the 1930s had been good, despite bitter memories of the closure of Jarrow and the hunger march of 1936. There was not the legacy of conflict that had plagued coal mining for forty years past. Lincoln Evans, president of the Iron and Steel Confederation, the main trade union, made it very plain that he personally did not want nationalization at all.[29]

Finally, and crucially important, key figures in the government, including Attlee and Morrison, did not favour steel nationalization. Morrison had opposed its being inserted in the party manifesto at all in 1945. It was also highly significant that steel was postponed until almost all the other proposed nationalization measures had been passed before it was considered ripe for legislative action. Even a figure like Emanuel Shinwell was reluctant about steel nationalization since the steel industry was the major customer for the coal and coke supplies which concerned him as Minister of Fuel and Power. Ernest Bevin himself, the Foreign Secretary and the most powerful living trade unionist, was also less than wholly committed by now.

Bitter arguments over iron and steel preoccupied the Labour Cabinet in many private sessions between April and August 1947.[30] The records of these meetings are fully available in the Public Record Office at Kew, with the opinions of individual ministers clearly attributed. In the end, the steel industry was overshadowed by the terrible financial crisis of the convertibility of sterling in the summer of 1947, which increased still further the doubts about the merits of introducing so controversial a measure at a time of great economic emergency. Morrison was hostile to nationalization throughout, and he proposed a kind of compromise semi-control scheme (Cabinet Paper [47]212) which fell far short of nationalization. He was supported by other ministers, both in the Cabinet and outside. Among them was John Wilmot, the Minister of Supply who had responsibility for steel nationalization, and who proved strangely reluctant to challenge the steel barons. When Wilmot was removed from office in October 1947, he was to be succeeded by George Strauss, a man with a strong record as a man of the left (he had been expelled, with Cripps and Bevan, from the parliamentary Labour Party in 1939 for advocating a Popular Front). Yet he, too, was to prove a somewhat timid nationalizer in practice.[31] After much anguished ministerial debate, gas nationalization was given priority for the 1948 sessions, with iron and steel postponed to the 1948 – 49 session, to allow for a measure to be introduced to cut down the delaying powers of the House of Lords over legislation passed through the House of Commons from two years to one.[32] All this meant that iron and steel nationalization might not now pass through parliament before another general election.

The entire ministerial debate showed clear and unmistakable doubts within the Cabinet, to the dismay of the Labour Left in parliament and in the country. Morrison obviously did not want steel nationalization at all — even though, ironically enough, he was urging this very thing, along with Bevin, for the steel industry of the British-occupied zone in western Germany at the same period. Evidently he felt more confidence in the British steel owners than he did in the heirs of Krupp, Stinnes and Thyssen.[33] Attlee also showed much uncertainty, and his general attitude led to an overt challenge to his leadership, led by Cripps, in September 1947, which the Prime Minister survived with difficulty. One civil servant advised Attlee in August 1947 that seven ministers were against nationalization, and another eight wanted a postponement, while only three (Bevan, Tomlinson, Strachey) wanted the immediate nationalization of steel.[34] But there were still some powerful voices on behalf of steel nationalization, too. Cripps, the President of the Board of Trade, retained his old commitment as a man of the left. So, more forcibly, did Hugh Dalton, the Chancellor of the Exchequer. Aneurin Bevan, Minister of Health, who sat for a steel constituency in Ebbw Vale, was vehement on behalf of steel nationalization throughout. Yet it was noticeable that much of the argument on behalf of it was ideological rather than empirical. With Bevan, as with the left-wing journals *New Statesman* and *Tribune* (the latter edited jointly by Bevan's wife, Jennie Lee), it was less a case of the technical, economic merits of nationalizing the steel industry. Rather, steel had become a touchstone of the government's socialist intentions, a beacon of hope in a hostile capitalist world.[35] It was also tacitly assumed, even by Bevan, that steel would in any case be the last measure of nationalization, at least for some considerable time. There would be no 'second wave' as there was in France over air and maritime transport in 1947 or in Austria with the electricity proposal of 1947. British nationalization was in retreat, and it would never have the same glamour again.

From the autumn of 1947 the retreat of nationalization, from the gates of Moscow as it were, was clearly under way. Gas nationalization went through in 1948, with Gaitskell in charge, while steel nationalization eventually was passed through the House of Lords in December 1949. It was noticeable, though, that the form of public ownership adopted meant no remodelling of the structure of the 107 firms to be taken over by the state.[36] This meant that it could very easily be denationalized by a future Conservative government — as was to happen in 1954.

The retreat from nationalization is in many ways easy to understand, if not, perhaps, to justify. Labour's main theoreticians had long implied that nationalization would be limited in scope. Now that the original 1945 list had been achieved, there was no cause to advance much further. In his book, *The Politics of Democratic Socialism* (1940), Evan Durbin had emphasized, as did many other Labour authors, the need to limit growth of nationalization on grounds of personal freedom. He always stressed the priority of a pluralist society and a mixed economy in libertarian terms.[37] Further to the left, G. D. H. Cole, writing on 'The Socialisation Programme' in 1948, assumed that the bulk of industry and finance would remain in private hands, though it would be a private enterprise more humane and acting more responsibly — and perhaps purified by anti-monopoly policies by the Board of Trade. Cole also suggested trying a variety of techniques in pushing through nationalization, instead of the uniform public board model — the co-operative method and the purchase of equity shares by the state were other measures that he proposed as alternatives. A similar view was to be taken by Aneurin Bevan in 1952 when he upheld the mixed economy and condemned excessive nationalization.[38] A much younger Oxford economist like Anthony Crosland was to stress, following the American, James Burnham, in his *Managerial Revolution*, the growing divorce between ownership and management in industry, which in effect diminished the unique case for nationalization and made it seem increasingly irrelevant.[39]

On the National Executive of the Labour Party, discussions on industrial policy from November 1947 onwards showed a clear halt to the drive towards further public ownership. Herbert Morrison, the chairman of the party Policy Committee and the key link between the Cabinet and the party machine, criticised the policy document 'Socialism and Private Enterprise' as too doctrinaire. 'We definitely do not want to nationalise the small man — the shop around the corner,' Morrison declared, with the approval of most of his fellow executive members.[40] The public arguments about Labour's plans, in its Transport Bill in 1947, to nationalize smaller private road haulage operators, holding C licences (which covered distances of less than forty miles), had brought the government into bad odour and made it seem illiberal.[41] As has been seen, Emanuel Shinwell, one of the more left-wing members of the government, had made public his doubts about the nature and pace of nationalization to date. Even Aneurin Bevan, the most committed socialist in the Cabinet, admitted the need to improve on the productive performance of industries and services already nationalized, and to improve on their public relations side.[42] Bevan also well knew that the record of labour relations in the newly nationalized industries was already a somewhat mixed one. In the coal industry, recent damaging strikes in the pits around Grimethorpe in south Yorkshire and some evidence of 'go-slow' working in his own South Wales collieries showed no dramatic improvement in the industrial climate compared with the days of private ownership.

The retreat from nationalization was further reinforced by the ascendancy in the government of Sir Stafford Cripps, who became Chancellor of the Exchequer in November 1947 and remained in that key post until October 1950. This may seem strange, since Cripps enjoyed a long-established status as an ideologue of the left, and had been expelled from the parliamentary party for his left-wing views in 1939. But he had moved to a far more centrist position during the war years, while his period at the Board of Trade in 1945 – 7 (when, for instance, he resisted any attempt to nationalize the cotton-spinning industry in Lancashire) had accentuated this tendency. Cripps was, above all, anxious to boost exports, to make Britain financially self-sufficient, and to avoid any further financial crisis of the kind that had almost brought the government down during the convertibility crisis of August 1947. This meant partnership with private industry, and the use of indicative planning within a mixed economy through Sir Edwin Plowden and the newly-formed Economic Planning Board, guided by the Economic Committee and Productive Committee of the Cabinet, both recent creations also. Cripps had the crucial support now of American Marshall Aid, reinforced by the Intra-European Payments Agreement through which Britain's position as a creditor nation with other western European nations was financed. The objective of making Britain self-sufficient commercially and industrially — an objective which showed encouraging signs of being realised when Britain's balance of payments moved back into surplus by the end of 1948 — was not compatible with domestic political controversy over nationalization.

As the general election of 1950 approached, Labour's attitude towards nationalization was hesitant and piecemeal. While the remaining stages of steel nationalization were forced through by the end of 1949, Labour otherwise went to the electors with a bizarre mixture — or 'shopping list' — of separate proposals. Cement, water supply, meat wholesaling, sugar refining were all added to the list at random, whereas brickmaking and the chemical industry were turned down as candidates for public ownership.[43] It all had a harmful effect on Labour's prospects, especially the curious proposal to nationalize the sugar refining enterprise of Tate and Lyle, an admitted monopoly. This threat brought the cartoon figure of 'Mr Cube' on to every packet of sugar on the breakfast table, a formidable domestic weapon against nationalization in every household.

More significant was the debate on the party national executive in 1949 about the nationalization of industrial assurance, as a complement to the 1946 National Insurance Act, which implemented the schemes of the Beveridge Report for social security. Nationalization of private insurance companies, with their huge funds, seemed, even to a moderate like James Griffiths, a necessary part of creating the welfare state.[44] He was strongly backed by Aneurin Bevan, the Minister of Health. But this plan was opposed by Morrison, many trade unionists, and also by Cripps, aware of the crucial role of private insurance in boosting Britain's 'invisible exports' through its operations in the United States and many other countries.[45] The Co-operative Society, which had its own insurance activities on an extensive scale, also was strongly hostile.[46] In the end, a modified form of 'mutualization', or control by the policy-holders, was placed on the party manifesto for 1950. It did Labour no electoral good at all. It meant that every private insurance agent in the land was a potential anti-Labour propagandist from now on. On balance, the 'shopping list' of nationalization measures was probably a straight vote-loser. Nationalization played no significant part in the 1951 session of parliament, after Labour's narrow return to power with its majority reduced to six only. Only the final, weary stages of putting the iron and steel nationalization into effect survived from former controversies. In the 1951 campaign, Labour made no positive commitment to nationalization at all, other than pledging itself vaguely to taking over unnamed industries that might in future be 'failing the nation'. Calls from the left, such as from Ian Mikardo, later a leading 'Bevanite', for the nationalization of aircraft production, machine tools or parts of the car industry, somewhat on the French model, were ignored.[47] For the aircraft industry, ministers like Morrison argued that technical advance required freedom from state control; instead, Morrison proclaimed the need for something called 'Competitive Public Enterprise' which might revitalize private enterprise through the spirit of competition.[48] On the other side in 1951, the Conservatives and their business allies in the organization 'Aims of Industry' attacked nationalization for bureaucracy and controls, for inefficiency and waste. In six years, therefore, Labour's priorities had totally changed. Nationalization, once a great asset and inspiration for the party, had become something of an electoral liability — or even worse, a plain irrelevance.

The long-term success or failure of the nationalization measures in Britain in 1945 – 51 raise far wider issues. Certainly, many of the criticisms of the nationalized industries were unfair. For instance, the financial losses incurred by the coal industry or the railways arose from the policy of keeping down prices and fares as part of an anti-inflation programme. These industries could easily have made a large profit if they had been allowed the same freedom to operate enjoyed by private enterprise, and if nationalized enterprises had not been viewed as social services. For all the difficulties in some aspects of labour relations, it could hardly be denied that, at least down to the early 1970s, the relationship between management and the workforce, in the coal industry for instance, showed a dramatic improvement by comparison with the class confrontations of the past.

In fact, there was very little denationalization by the subsequent Conservative governments of 1951 – 64. Only road haulage and steel were denationalized in the early 1950s; the rest of Labour's achievement was broadly left alone. The publicly-owned industries did well in the economic expansion and consumer affluence enjoyed in Britain in the 1950s and 1960s. Not until the mid-1960s did they come under attack as the British economy showed signs of slowing down, and government was forced to act increasingly in determining the pricing and investment policies of state enterprises.[49] The public sector was also accused of fuelling the wage inflation that characterized Britain during the 1960s and early 1970s. When state ownership again emerged as an issue after 1974, after the election of another Labour government, first led by Wilson, then by Callaghan, the cause was advocated in terms of trying to bail out dying enterprises, such as

Rolls Royce, British Leyland or the various clients of the National Enterprise Board, rather than the bold expansion and forward-looking planning dreamed of in the heady days of 1945. In practice, the policies of the 1970s made the public image of nationalization rather worse. On balance, from 1945 to the mid-1970s, there seemed to exist a broad consensus amongst the political parties and the social groups mobilized during the wartime years to sustain the mix of the economy achieved after 1945, and to remove nationalization from public controversy. So things remained until the 'privatization' policy of the Thatcher government after 1979, when its overt rejection of the post-1945 consensus and its zeal to roll back the frontiers of the state took nationalization back into the domain of public controversy.[50]

One major consideration is how the British nationalization programme relates to the experience in western Europe generally after the Second World War. This is not altogether easy to determine; but, on balance, the impact of direct influence from public ownership experiments in France, Austria or elsewhere after 1945 (or after 1936 in France) seems relatively small. British nationalization, like so much else of British history in the twentieth century, appears now like an exercise in splendid isolationism. There was some direct involvement with nationalization on the European continent after 1945. For instance, as has been seen, proposals for British coal or steel nationalization to some degree became caught up in plans to nationalize the coal and steel industries of the Ruhr in the British-occupied zone in western Germany at the same period. But little direct interest was shown by British governments in continental experiences from 1945 onwards; even the modified *dirigisme* of the Monnet Plan in France from 1947 excited relatively little interest either in the Cabinet or the economic planning sections of the civil service, at least at this period.[51] The British government showed precious little enthusiasm for the economic policies of post-war French governments, even left-wing ones, and refused to accept the Monnet plan as the basis for the European Recovery Program.

When pressure built up in 1948–9 for a more integrated approach towards European economic co-operation, a clear lack of any community of outlook showed itself between British socialists, and their French, Belgian and Dutch comrades. The British idea of 'western union' and the French concept of 'European unity' were fundamentally different.[52] While Britain and Bevin led the way in the functional arrangements of O.E.E.C. and later the European Payments Union, the 1950 Schuman plan for an integrated coal and steel industrial system in western Europe was strongly rebuffed by the Labour Cabinet and the unions, even though Cripps and some right-wing figures like Gaitskell and Kenneth Younger showed some sympathy. As Schuman and the French government no doubt expected in May 1950, Britain's socialist movement continued to emphasize its geographical and ideological detachment from the continent and to proclaim its wider links with the Commonwealth and the USA instead.[53] In a curious way, public ownership, and the idea of socialist planning that it was still felt to embody, was a part of that proud detachment.

British nationalization under Labour, then, was very British, very insular — perhaps, indeed, very English since ideas once current in South Wales for forms of syndicalism or theories of workers' control emanating from the shop stewards' movement in Clydeside in Scotland were firmly set aside. The whole debate about nationalization in 1945 – 51 (as in 1931 – 45) was largely conducted in domestic terms. After 1945, British industrial authority and leadership in a war-ravaged western Europe was taken for granted. The impact of worldwide commercial or monetary pressures upon British industry, whether nationalized or in private hands, was seldom adequately considered by Attlee and his colleagues. Such industries and utilities as were nationalized were largely allowed to function on a basis of managerial autonomy rather than as part of an integrated, planned socialist economy. By 1951, even the essentially shorter-term forms of planning adopted after the war were visibly in retreat, as the public mood rebelled against continuing wartime controls.[54] Despite the massive programme of nationalization, therefore, the British economy and society changed less profoundly than did those of France, West Germany or other continental countries in the post-war years. Nationalization was debated and implemented in an atmosphere of domestic conservatism and complacency. For this, Britain in the 1980s continues to pay a heavy cost.

Even in 1985, there were prominent centrist trade union leaders such as Alan Tuffin of the Union of Communication Workers who still called, not only for the renationalization of British Telecom, Britoil and Enterprise Oil by a future Labour government but for nationalization to be restored as 'the main vehicle for investment and jobs. Labour's economic programme should be promoted so as to highlight this prominence.'[55] Such voices, however, were relatively rare even on the far left fringe. Labour's new leadership in the Kinnock-Hattersley era from 1983 onwards, visibly gave public ownership an infinitely more humble role in future Labour programmes. Enterprise boards run by metropolitan local authorities were one alternative mooted. Meanwhile, the columns of Marxism Today contained suggestions that the far left, or some of it, went along with a view that rejected bureaucratic, paternalistic state ownership — especially as personified in the rigid and unappealing figure of Ian MacGregor of the N.C.B. — as any kind of route to socialism.[56] The general drive of Labour's policy pronouncements — if only through its silences — was only to confirm the diminished confidence in public ownership as a panacea, that had been detectable in Labour's ranks from the time of the pivotal debates over steel in 1947 onwards. Both Kinnock and Hattersley in early 1986 affirmed that there would be no further nationalization by a future Labour government, and that even renationalizing concerns 'privatized' by the Tories would not be a major priority. Party leaders were anxious to reassure small investors in British Telecom shares that they would be amply compensated.

Precisely why public ownership should so have lost esteem — in contrast, say, with others of Labour priorities such as the idea of a welfare state — is open to debate. Opponents of the very concept of governmental interference in the management of industry could argue that the history of nationalization since 1945 merely confirmed the inherent evils of monopoly, whether public or private, as inevitably tending to inefficiency and the raising of costs for the consumer.[57] But there were, naturally, very few in the Labour movement who would accept this case. After all, even Crosland's *Future of Socialism* (1956), while focussing on other themes such as the promotion of equality, still gave nationalization a significant role. Indeed, the total failure of Hugh Gaitskell to secure the elimination of Clause Four from Labour's constitution in 1959 was testimony to the enduring mystique of public ownership as a principle and source of inspiration to party activists.[58] No subsequent Labour leader had dared to risk his position in the way that Gaitskell managed to do. In many ways, too, the failure of public ownership to command more support is paradoxical and puzzling, in view of the inability of private enterprise (covering over eighty per cent of the economy) to apply itself at all effectively in coping with Britain's industrial and commercial decline between 1951 and 1985. It is not obviously faith in capitalism and the market economy — especially in its abrasive Thatcherite form — that has eroded the faith of the British centre and left in the traditional nostrum of public ownership.

The explanation may lie in something more deeply rooted in the British psyche in the later twentieth century. Public ownership, we have seen, was conceived in a spirit of insularity, even of national self-confidence. Its model, going back from Gaitskell and Durbin in the 1930s, through the Webbs to Chadwick and Bentham, was that of the detached, unemotional public servant, altruistically pursuing the path of duty, running economic and social institutions in a way that would transcend sectionalism and invest them with a kind of Platonic purity. It was a domestic, progressive version of the model of colonial rule offered to the young Attlee at Haileybury and to the Wykehamists who joined his administration after 1945,[59] a form of social imperialism with the common touch, not so much Kiplingesque as Rudyard Hardie. Amongst the thirties generation of socialists, Gaitskell was the son of an Indian civil servant whose brother developed irrigation schemes in the cotton fields of the Sudan; Jay's brother served with distinction on the Yangtse; Durbin was the son of a Baptist minister who had been a missionary in Ceylon. If the Victorian empire (much admired by Bevin, Morrison and other ministers in 1945 – 51) had been Joseph Chamberlain's Birmingham writ large, the

National Coal Board, British Rail, B.O.A.C., and even the B.B.C. were Chamberlain's empire writ small, with their chairmen (often retired industrialists or even generals) cast as the Cromer or Lugard *de nos jours*. After 1945, however, the cocoon of confident insularity within which the debate over nationalization took place soon dissolved. The underlying structural weakness of the British economy, whatever its pattern of ownership, became embarrassingly plain to see. At home and abroad, the state lost much of its moral authority; equally the mystique of the detached public servant, the patrician symbol of the governing élite, deferentially obeyed by native and workers alike, became outdated, even discredited. The decline of public ownership in Britain thus mirrored — and partly grew out of — the downfall of empire overseas. The attendant economic, financial and commercial disintegration of that empire reinforced the decay at home. In the end, internal colonialism took the same path to perdition as did its external counterpart. It had become one with Nineveh and Tyre, paradise mislaid rather than lost, and was likely to remain so.[60]

Notes

The author wishes to thank Sir Henry Phelps Brown for some valuable comments on this article.

1 A. L. Rowse, 'Industry in the Transition to Socialism' in Stafford Cripps *et al.*, *Where Stands Socialism Today?* (London, 1933), p. 126.

2 See E. Eldon Barry, *Nationalism in British Politics* (London, 1965).

3 Kenneth O. Morgan, 'Socialism and Syndicalism: the Welsh Miners' Debate, 1912', *Bulletin of the Society for the Study of Labour History*, xxx (1975), 22 – 36.

4 R. H. Tawney, *The Acquisitive Society*, pp. 152 – 7. Also see Rita Hinden (ed.), *R. H. Tawney: the Radical Tradition* (London, 1966), pp. 123 – 43; Ross Terrill, *R. H. Tawney and His Times* (London, 1973), esp. pp. 151 – 2.

5 Tawney, *Acquisitive Society*, p. 149.

6 Herbert Morrison, *Socialisation and Transport* (London, 1933), pp. 149ff.

7 Hugh Dalton, *Practical Socialism for Britain* (London, 1935), pp. 93 – 180.

8 Douglas Jay, *The Socialist Case* (London, 2nd ed., 1946), pp. 198 – 202.

9 Elizabeth Durbin, *New Jerusalems* (London, 1985), esp. pp. 136 – 46.

10 See D. E. H. Edgerton, 'Technical Innovation, Industrial Capacity and Efficiency: Public Ownership and the British Military Aircraft Industry, 1915 – 48', *Business History*, xxvi (1984), 266 – 8.

11 *Parl. Deb.*, 5th ser., ccclxxx. 1093 ff. and 132ff. (10 and 11 June 1942).

12 *Report of the Forty-First Annual Conference of the Labour Party*, 1942, pp. 110 – 112.

13 *Report of the Forty-Second Annual Conference of the Labour Party*, 1943, pp. 180.

14 *Report of the Forty-Third Annual Conference of the Labour Party*, 1944, pp. 160ff.; 'Short Term Programme' presented to N.E.C. (Labour Party archives).

15 Peter Kellner and Christopher Hitchens,*Callaghan: the Road to Number Ten* (London, 1976), pp. 16 – 17.

16 Hugh Dalton's diary, April 11, 1945 (British Library of Political and Economic Science, Dalton Papers).

17 Cf. Sidney Pollard, 'The Nationalisation of the Banks', in David E. Martin and David Rubinstein (eds.), *Ideology and the Labour Movement* (London, 1979), pp. 167 – 90.

18 Hugh Gaitskell, 'The Banking System and Monetary Policy', in Margaret Cole and Charles Smith (eds.), *Democratic Sweden* (London, 1938), pp. 96 – 107. Other contributors included Cole, Postgate and G. R. Mitchison.

19 For general developments, see Kenneth O. Morgan, *Labour in Power, 1945 – 1951* (Oxford, 1984), pp. 94 – 141.

20 Cabinet conclusions, October 18, December 20, 1945 (Public Record Office [PRO], CAB 128/1).

21 See Nicholas Davenport, *Memoirs of a City Radical* (London, 1974), pp. 180 – 1.

22 Minutes of Committee on Socialisation of Industry, 1946 – 8 (PRO, CAB 134/687 – 8).

23 *New Statesman*, May 22, 1948.

24 e.g., Shinwell's speech to the Co-operative Congress, reported in *The Times*, May 3, 6, 13, 1948. See also Norman Chester, *The Nationalization of British Industry, 1945 – 51* (London, 1975).

25 Cf. R. Kelf-Cohen, *British Nationalisation, 1945 – 73* (London, 1973).

26 Cabinet conclusions, January 7, 1947 (PRO, CAB 128/8); Shinwell's paper on 'The Coal Position', February 21, 1947 (PRO, PREM 8/ 8449).

27 Morgan, *Labour in Power*, p. 272 and n.

28 Dalton, Memorandum on Iron and Steel, May 1946 (PRO, T 228/74).

29 Lincoln Evans to Morgan Phillips, October 2, 1950 (Labour Party archives, GS 23/1).

30 Cabinet conclusions, April 28, July 24, July 7, August, 1947 (PRO, CAB 128/9, 10).

31 Hugh Dalton's diary, January 4, 1951 (Dalton papers, I/39); Cabinet conclusions, December 2, 1948 (CAB 128/13).

32 Cabinet conclusions, August 7, 1947 (PRO, CAB 129/10).

33 Cabinet conclusions, May 7, 1946 (CAB 128/5).

34 W. S. Murrie to Attlee, August 4, 1947 (CAB 21/2243).

35 Cabinet conclusions, July 31, 1947 (CAB 128/10).

36 Cabinet conclusions, June 7, 14, 1949 (CAB 129/12).

37 See Evan Durbin, 'The Economic Problems Facing the Labour Government', in Donald Munro (ed.), *Socialism: the British Way* (London, 1948), pp. 3 – 29.

38 G. D. H. Cole, 'The Socialisation Programme for Industry', ibid., pp. 30 – 56; Aneurin Bevan, *In Place of Fear* (London, 1952), p. 118.

39 Anthony Crosland, *The Future of Socialism* (London, 1956), especially pp. 462ff.

40 Labour Party Policy Committee minutes, November 25, 1947.

41 Socialisation of Industry Committee, minutes, March 8, 1946 (CAB 134/687); Cabinet conclusions, July 7, 1946 (CAB 128/5).

42 Labour Party Policy Committee minutes, November 25, 1947 (Labour Party archives).

43 *Ibid.*, February – November 1949.

44 *Ibid.*, May 30, July 7, October 24, 1949.

45 Cripps to Dalton, March 16, 1949 (Dalton papers, 9/7/9).

46 Meetings of Policy Committee with Co-operative Society representatives, July 27, October 24, 1949 (Labour Party archives).

47 Ian Mikardo, *The Second Five Years: a Labour Programme for 1950* (London, 1948).

48 *Annual Conference of the Labour Party*, 1949, p. 155.

49 Kelf-Cohen, *British Nationalisation*, pp. 139ff.

50 See Jacques Leruez, *Le Thatchérisme: Doctrine et Action* (Paris, 1984), pp. 41 – 56. British Gas was proposed for denationalisation in 1985, but this would await the next election.

51 Personal information from Sir Robert Hall, director of Economic section of the Cabinet from 1947.

52 Record of International Socialist conference at Selsdon Park, March 21 – 22, 1948 (Labour Party archives, International department); material in R. W. G. Mackay papers, section 8, file 3 (British Library of Political and Economic Science).

53 Cabinet conclusions, June 2 1950 (CAB 128/17); record of meeting of Cripps and Monnet, 15 May 1950 (PRO, FO 371/85842, CE 2338/2141/181).

54 Jacques Leruez, *Economic Planning and Politics in Britain* (London, 1975).

55 Alan Tuffin, 'How State Control could be a Winner', *The Guardian*, April 19, 1985.

56 Gareth Stedman Jones, 'Paternalism Revisited', *Marxism Today* (July 1985), p. 26.

297

57 George Watson, *Nationalization: the end of an illusion* (Unservile State Papers, ?1983 [n.d.]).

58 Philip Williams, *Hugh Gaitskell* (London, 1979), pp. 537ff. Even Gaitskell was prepared to endorse public ownership on a pragmatic basis, for instance in the case of urban building land (*ibid.*, p. 545).

59 See A. F. Thompson, 'Winchester and the Labour Party: Three Gentlemanly Rebels', in Roger Custance (ed.), *Winchester College: Sixth Centenary Essays* (Oxford, 1982), pp. 489 – 503, for comments on Gaitskell and Crossman.

60 In July 1986, Labour's Policy Committee endorsed a modest 'social ownership', in place of the Morrisonian corporation which was deemed 'unresponsive' and 'monolithic'.

Stephen E. Koss:
A Bibliography*

I   Books

1   *John Morley at the India Office, 1905 – 1910*
(New Haven and London: Yale University Press, 1969).

2   *Lord Haldane: Scapegoat for Liberalism*
(New York and London: Columbia University Press, 1969).

3   *Sir John Brunner: Radical Plutocrat 1842 – 1919*
(Cambridge: Cambridge University Press, 1970).

4   *Fleet Street Radical: A. G. Gardiner and the Daily News*
(Hamden, Connecticut: Archon Books, 1973)
(London: Allen Lane, 1973).

5   *Nonconformity in Modern British Politics*
(Hamden, Connecticut: Archon Books, 1975)
(London: Batsford, 1975).

6   *Asquith* (New York: St. Martins Press, 1976)
(London: Allen Lane, 1976; reissued, Hamish Hamilton, 1985).

7   *The Rise and Fall of the Political Press in Britain: The Nineteenth Century*, Vol. I
(Chapel Hill, North Carolina: University of North Carolina Press, 1981)
(London: Hamish Hamilton, 1981).

8   *The Rise and Fall of the Political Press in Britain: The Twentieth Century*
(Chapel Hill, North Carolina: University of North Carolina Press, 1984)
(London: Hamish Hamilton, 1984).

II   Anthology

9   *The Pro-Boers: The Anatomy of an Antiwar Movement*
(Chicago and London: University of Chicago Press, 1973).

III   Scholarly Articles

10   'John Morley and the Communal Question,' *Journal of Asian Studies*, xxvi (May 1967).
381 – 87.

11   'Morley in the Middle,' *English Historical Review*, lxxxii (July 1967). 553 – 61.

12   'The Destruction of Britain's Last Liberal Government,' *Journal of Modern History*, xl (June 1968). 257 – 77.

13   'Morley and Kitchener: A Private War,' *The Quarterly Review of Historical Studies*, viii (1968 – 69). 32 – 38.

14   'British Political Biography as History,' *Political Science Quarterly*, lxxxviii (December 1973). 713 – 24.

---

* I am indebted to Elaine Koss for generous access to materials, hospitable working conditions and, most of all, sage advice. Thanks are also due to Mr. Charles Seaton of the *Spectator*, Mr. Anthony Howard of the *Observer* and Mr. Jeremy Treglown of the *TLS*.

15 'Lloyd George and Nonconformity: The Last Rally,' *English Historical Review*, lxxxix (January 1974). 77 – 108.

16 '1906: Revival and Revivalism,' in A. J. A. Morris, ed., *Edwardian Radicalism 1900 – 1914* (London and Boston: Routledge & Kegan Paul, 1974). 75 – 96.

17 'Wesleyanism and Empire,' *Historical Journal*, xviii (March 1975). 105 – 18.

18 'Asquith versus Lloyd George: The Last Phase and Beyond,' in Alan Sked and Chris Cook eds., *Crisis and Controversy: Essays in Honour of A. J. P. Taylor* (London: The Macmillan Press Ltd., 1976). 66 – 89.

IV Reviews in Scholarly Journals

19 Denis Judd, *Balfour and the British Empire*, *Jewish Social Studies*, xxxi (July 1969). 224 – 25.

20 Afaf Lutfi al-Sayyid, *Egypt and Cromer: A Study in Anglo-Egyptian Relations* and Walter Nimocks, *Milner's Young Men: The 'Kindergarten' in Edwardian Imperial Affairs*, *American Historical Review*, lxxv (October 1969). 124 – 26.

21 Paul Barton Johnson, *Land Fit for Heroes: The Planning of British Reconstruction, 1916 – 1919*, *ibid.*, (October 1969). 126 – 7.

22 Angus Calder, *The People's War: Britain — 1939–1945*, *ibid.*, lxxv (June 1970). 1457 – 58.

23 Jeffrey Butler, *The Liberal Party and the Jameson Raid* and Peter Rowland, *The Last Liberal Government: The Promised Land, 1905 – 1910*, *Journal of Modern History*, xlii (September 1970). 428 – 31.

24 D. M. Schreuder, *Gladstone and Kruger. Liberal Government and Colonial 'Home Rule,' 1880 – 85* and John W. Cell, *British Colonial Administration in the Mid-Nineteenth Century: The Policy-making Process*, *ibid.*, xlii (December 1970). 683 – 85.

25 Zara S. Steiner, *The Foreign Office and Foreign Policy, 1898 – 1914* and Peter Lowe, *Great Britain and Japan, 1911 – 1915: A Study of British Far Eastern Policy*, *Political Science Quarterly*, lxxxvi (June 1971). 325 – 27.

26 Max Beloff, *Imperial Sunset*, Vol. I *Britain's Liberal Empire, 1897 – 1921*, *ibid*, lxxxvi (September 1971). 522 – 23

27 P. F. Clarke, *Lancashire and the New Liberalism*, *Journal of Modern History*, xliv (June 1972). 293 – 94.

28 Roy Douglas, *The History of the Liberal Party 1895–1970*, *American Historical Review*, lxxvii (October 1972). 1126 – 27.

29 A. J. P. Taylor, ed., *Lloyd George: Twelve Essays* and Cameron Hazlehurst, *Politicans at War, July 1914 to May 1915, A Prologue to the Triumph of Lloyd George*, *Political Science Quarterly*, lxxxvii (December 1972). 678 – 80.

30 Neal Blewett, *The Peers, the Parties and the People: The British General Elections of 1910*, *American Historical Review*, lxxviii (June 1973). 696 – 97.

31 D. A. Hamer, *Liberal Politics in the Age of Gladstone and Rosebery: A Study in Leadership and Policy*, *Political Science Quarterly*, lxxxviii (June 1973). 309 – 310.

32 George Watson, *The English Ideology: Studies in the Language of Victorial Politics*, *History*, lix (June 1974). 287.

33 Chris Cook and John Ramsden, eds., *By-Elections in British Politics*, *Political Science Quarterly*, lxxxix (Fall 1974). 697 – 99.

34 Michael Foot, *Aneurin Bevan: A Biography, 1945 – 1960*, *Journal of Modern History*, xlvi (December 1974). 716 – 18.

35 Maxwell Philip Schoenfeld, *The War Ministry of Winston Churchill*, *American Historical Review*, lxxix (December 1974). 1558.

36 E. L. Tapin, *Liverpool Dockers and Seamen, 1870 – 1890*, *Labour History*, xvi (Spring 1975). 299 – 300.

37 Philip N. Backstrom, *Christian Socialism and Co-Operation in Victorian England: Edward Vansittart Neale and the Co-Operative Movement*, *ibid.* (Fall 1975), 556 – 58.

38 Norman St. John Stevas, ed., *The Collected Works of Walter Bagehot*, Vols. V – VIII, *The Political Essays*, *Victorian Studies*, xix (June 1976), 534 – 36.

39 David Cresap Moore, *The Politics of Deference: A Study of the Mid-Nineteenth Century English Political System*, *Political Science Quarterly*, xcii (Summer 1977). 352 – 53.

40 Harold Wilson, *The Governance of Britain*, *ibid.* (Autumn 1977). 555 – 57.

41 David Marquand, *Ramsay MacDonald*, *American Historical Review*, lxxxii (December 1977). 1256 – 57.

42 Asa Briggs and John Saville, eds., *Essays in Labor History 1918 – 1939*, Sheila Lewenhak, *Women and Trade Unions: An Outline History of Women in the British Trade Union Movement*, Standish Meachem, *A Life Apart: The English Working Class, 1890 – 1914*, and William D. Muller, *The Kept Men? The First Century of Trade Union Representation in the British House of Commons*, *Labour History*, xix (Summer 1978). 434 – 42.

43 Christopher Thorne, *Allies of a Kind: The United States, Britain and the War Against Japan, 1941 – 45*, *Political Science Quarterly*, xciii (Summer 1978). 352 – 54.

44 Francis H. Hinsley, ed., *British Foreign Policy Under Sir Edward Grey*, *The Historian*, xli (November 1978). 119 – 20.

45 Richard O. Cosgrove, *The Rule of Law: Albert Venn Dicey, Victorian Jurist*, *Journal of Modern History*, liv (March 1982). 111 – 13.

46 D. W. Bebbington, *The Nonconformist Conscience: Chapel and Politics, 1870 – 1940*, *Albion*, xiv (Spring 1982). 92.

47 Kenneth O. Morgan, *Keir Hardie: Radical and Socialist*, *Labour History*, xxiii (Summer 1982). 455 – 58.

48 P. J. Waller, *Democracy and Sectarianism: A Political and Social History of Liverpool 1868 – 1939*, *Journal of Modern History*, liv (December 1982). 781 – 83.

49 Alan Hankinson, *Man of Wars: William Howard Russell of The Times*, *American Historical Review*, lxxxix (June 1984). 767 – 68.

50 J. A. W. Gunn, *et al.*, *Benjamin Disraeli Letters: 1815 – 1835* and *Benjamin Disraeli Letters: 1835 – 1837*, *Journal of Modern History*, lvi (September 1984). 534 – 35.

51 W. R. P. George, *Lloyd George: Backbencher*, *Welsh History Review*, xii (December 1984). 282 – 83.

V Reviews in Literary Journals

52 'Alien Hordes.' Bernard Gainer, *The Alien Invasion: The Origins of the Aliens Act of 1905. New Statesman*, 6 October 1972, 474 – 75.

53 'Pick a Bag of Oakum.' José Harrris, *Unemployment and Politics: A Study in English Social Policy 1886 – 1914*, *ibid.*, 8 December 1972, 868 – 69.

54 'Sorcerer's Apprenticeship.' Kenneth O. Morgan, ed., *Lloyd George Family Letters 1885 – 1936*, *ibid.*, 2 March 1973, 307.

55 'Rad Libs.' H. V. Emy, *Liberals, Radicals and Social Politics 1892 – 1914*, *ibid.*, 30 March 1973, 466 – 67.

56 'Shaw's War.' Stanley Weintraub, *Bernard Shaw 1914 – 1918: Journey to Heartbreak* and Bernard Bergonzi, *The Turn of a Century*, *ibid.*, 11 May 1973, 698 – 99.

57 'Point of No Return.' Michael Kinnear, *The Fall of Lloyd George: The Political Crisis of 1922*, *ibid.*, 6 July 1973, 24.

58 'Face to Face.' A. J. P. Taylor, ed., *Off the Record: Political Interviews 1933 – 1943* (by W. Crozier), *ibid.*, 3 August 1973, 155 – 58.

59 An Amateur Sport.' A. B. Cooke and John Vincent, *The Governing Passion: Cabinet Government and Party Politics in Britain 1885 – 1886*, *ibid.*, 8 March 1974, 330 – 31.

60 'Cavalier.' Peter Fraser, *Lord Esher: A Political Biography* and Nicholas D'Ombrain, *War Machinery and High Policy: Defense Administration in Peacetime Britain 1902 – 1914*, *ibid.*, 19 April 1974, 551 – 52.

61 'Honours Czar.' Tom Cullen, *Maundy Gregory*, *ibid.*, 17 May 1974, 701.

62 'Triple-Decker.' Stephen Roskill, *Hankey: Man of Secrets*, Vol. III, *ibid.*, 12 July 1974, 50 – 51.

63 'Encompassing Churchill.' Henry Pelling, *Churchill. Times Literary Supplement*, 26 July 1974, 781 – 82.

64 'Socialists and anti-Socialists.' Kenneth D. Brown, ed., *Essays in Anti-Labour History: Responses to the Rise of Labour in Britain* and Joyce M. Bellamy and John Saville, eds., *Dictionary of Labour Biography*. Vols. I and II, *ibid.*, 23 August 1974, 894 – 95.

65 'Webb's Wonders.' J. M. Winter, *Socialism and the Challenge of War: Ideas and Politics in Britain 1912 – 1918. New Statesman*, 23 August 1974, 257 – 58.

66 'Socialism and Saintliness.' Ross Terrill, *R. H. Tawney and His Times. The Listener*, 29 August 1974, 281 – 82.

67 'The Story of O.' Robert Gathorne-Hardy, ed., *Ottoline at Garsington. New Statesman*, 20 September 1974, 386 and 388.

68 'Genuine Yankees and True John Bulls.' Henry Steel Commager, ed., *Britain Through American Eyes. TLS*, 27 September 1974, 1041 – 42.

69 'Gloomy Editor.' Alfred F. Havighurst, *Radical Journalist: H. W. Massingham. The Listener*, 12 December 1974, 784 – 85.

70 'The Meshes of Impurity.' M. R. D. Foot and H. C. G. Matthew, eds., *The Gladstone Diaries*, Vol. 3: *1840 – 1847* and Vol. 4: *1848 – 1854. TLS*, 14 March 1975, 266 – 67.

71 'One of the Lost Boys?' Robert Skidelsky, *Oswald Mosley. New Statesman*, 21 March 1975, 376 and 378.

72 'Dear Diary.' Colin Cross, ed., *Life with Lloyd George: The Diary of A. J. Sylvester*, *ibid.*, 2 May 1975, 597 – 98.

73 'The Evangelism of Progress.' Robert E. Dowse, ed., *The Socialist Ideal. TLS*, 9 May 1975, 515.

74 'From Walpole to Wilson.' Herbert van Thal, ed., *The Prime Ministers*, Vol. I *Sir Robert Walpole to Sir Robert Peel* and Vol. II *Lord John Russell to Edward Heath*, *ibid.*, 16 May 1975, 526.

75 'For the Record.' Chris Cook, ed., *Sources in British Political History 1900 – 1951*, Vol. I: *A Guide to the Archives of Selected Organisations and Societies*, *ibid.*, 30 May 1975, 609.

76 'A Bear in the Hornet's Nest.' Martin Gilbert, *Winston S. Churchill*, Vol. 4. *1916–1922*, *ibid.*, 6 June 1975, 625.

77 'Tremendous Tories.' Robert J. Taylor, *Lord Salisbury* and E. J. Feuchtwanger, *Gladstone. The Observer*, 3 August 1975, 21.

78 'The anti-Turkish Crusade.' R. T. Shannon, *Gladstone and the Bulgarian Agitation 1876. TLS*, 22 August 1975, 941.

79 'Unchanging Plot.' Maurice Cowling, *The Impact of Hitler: British Politics and British Policy, 1933 – 40* and Francis L. Loewenheim, Harold D. Langley and Manfred Jonas, eds., *Roosevelt and Churchill: Their Secret Wartime Correspondence. The Listener*, 25 September 1975, 407 – 8.

80 'The Very Private Secretary.' A. J. P. Taylor, ed., *My Darling Pussy: The Letters of Lloyd George and Frances Stevenson 1913 – 1941. TLS*, 10 October 1975, 1169.

81 'Dizzy Fancies.' Helen M. and Marvin Swartz, eds., *Disraeli's Reminiscences*. *New Statesman*, 24 October 1975, 510.

82 'The Matrix of Fabian Doctrine.' Willard Wolfe, *From Radicalism to Socialism: Men and Ideas in the Formation of Fabian Socialist Doctrine 1881 – 1889*. *TLS*, 21 November 1975, 1390.

83 'Speaking of the Past.' Paul Thompson, *The Edwardians: The Remaking of British Society, ibid.*, 5 December 1975, 1435 – 36.

84 'Revisionism is a Serious Business.' Gillian Peele and Chris Cook, eds., *The Politics of Reappraisal 1918 – 1939* and Robert J. Scally, *The Origins of the Lloyd George Coalition: The Politics of Social-Imperialism 1900–1918, ibid.*, 5 March 1976, 256.

85 'Everybody Out.' G. A. Phillips, *The General Strike: The Politics of Industrial Conflict, ibid.*, 14 May 1976, 568.

86 'A Charmed Life.' Robert Rhodes James, *Victor Cazolet: A Portrait, ibid.*, 28 May 1976, 638.

87 'Boilermaker.' John Mahon, *Harry Pollitt. New Statesman*, 28 May 1976, 719 – 20.

88 'The Obsessions of Imperialism.' B. L. Reid, *The Lives of Roger Casement* and John Marlowe, *Milner, Apostle of Empire*. *TLS*, 9 July 1976, 838.

89 'When the Bombs Fell.' Tom Harrison, *Living Through the Blitz. The Observer*, 1 August 1976, 21.

90 'Rantipoling Wives.' Kirsty McLeod, *The Wives of Downing St, ibid.*, 8 August 1976, 21.

91 'The Vagabond Prince.' Christopher Hibbert, *Edward VII. TLS*, 17 September 1976, 1151.

92 'Winston in the Wilderness.' Martin Gilbert, *Winston Churchill*, Vol. 5 *1922 – 1939, ibid.*, 29 October 1976, 1361 – 62.

93 'The First '68,' Christopher Harvie, *The Lights of Liberalism: University Liberals and the Challenge of Democracy 1860– 86. The Listener*, 10 February 1977, 189 – 90.

94 'Daughter of Marx.' Yvonne Kapp, *Eleanor Marx*, Vol. II, *ibid.*, 24 March 1977, 370.

95 'The Pioneers in Person.' Joyce M. Bellamy and John Saville, eds., *Dictionary of Labour Biography*, Vol. 3. *TLS*, 25 March 1977, 380.

96 'Swastikas in Retaliation.' David Pryce-Jones. *Unity Mitford: An Inquiry Into Her Life and the Frivolity of Evil. New York Times Book Review*, 8 May 1977, 10 and 45 – 47.

97 'Hon and Red.' Jessica Mitford, *A Fine Old Conflict. The Observer*, 15 May 1977, 28.

98 'The Middle-Class Talking Shop.' Norman and Jeanne MacKenzie, *The First Fabians, TLS*, 1 July 1977, 793.

99 'The Uninspired Member for Chelsea.' John A. Cross, *Sir Samuel Hoare: A Political Biography, ibid.*, 8 July 1977, 829.

100 'Mr. Asquith's Crossman.' Edward David, ed., *Inside Asquith's Cabinet: The Diaries of Charles Hobhouse. The Listener*, 18 August 1977, 219 – 220.

101 'The Westminster File.' Chris Cook, ed., *Sources in British Political History 1900 – 1951*, Vols. ii – iv, *TLS*, 19 August 1977, 996.

102 'Out-Harolding Harold.' Harold Wilson, *A Prime Minister on Prime Ministers, ibid.*, 11 November 1977, 1320.

103 'The Duchess of Omnium.' Edna Healey, *Lady Unknown: The Life of Angela Burdett-Coutts, New Statesman*, 6 January 1978, 18 – 9.

104 'Locust Years.' Chris Cook and John Stevenson, *The Slump, ibid.*, 3 February 1978, 156 – 57.

105 'Crossing the Party Lines.' David Butler, ed., *Coalitions in British Politics. TLS*, 14 July 1978, 792.

106 'Gladstone at the Threshold.' H. C. G. Matthew, ed., *The Gladstone Diaries*, Vol. v, *1855 – 1860* and Vol. vi, *1861 – 1868. The Listener*, 2 August 1978, 155 – 56.

107 'Annals of the Gutter.' G. A. Cronfield, *The Press and Society: From Caxton to Northcliffe. TLS*, 11 August 1978, 915.

108 'Vixens in Velvet,' Brian Harrison, *Separate Spheres: The Opposition to Women's Suffrage in Britain. The Listener*, 17 August 1978, 222.

109 'Girth & Mirth.' Margaret Canovan, *G. K. Chesterton: Radical Populist. New Statesman*, 1 September 1978, 273 – 74.

110 'In the Imperial Context.' John Barnes and David Nicholson, eds., *The Leo Amery Diaries*, Vol. i, *1896 – 1929. TLS*, 13 October 1978, 1168.

111 'From Zenith to Zenith.' John Grigg, *Lloyd George: The People's Champion, ibid.*, 27 October 1978, 1252.

112 'The Next Age.' Peter Clarke, *Liberals and Social Democrats. New Statesman*, 15 December 1978, 824.

113 'The Last Ditch.' Gregory D. Phillips, *The Diehards: Aristocratic Society and Politics in Edwardian England, ibid.*, 2 March 1979, 292.

114 'Ren & Ref.' Quentin Skinner, *The Foundations of Modern Political Thought*, 2 Vols. *New Statesman*, 23 March 1979, 409 – 11.

115 'Thirtyish.' A. L. Rowse, *A Man of the Thirties* and Telford Taylor, *Munich: The Price of Peace. Spectator*, 8 September 1979, 22.

116 'Tall Tales.' Michael Balfour, *Propaganda in War 1939 – 1945: Organisations, Policies and Publics in Britain and Germany. New Statesman*, 28 September 1979, 462 – 63.

117 'Ll. G's Coalition.' Kenneth O. Morgan, *Consensus and Disunity: The Lloyd George Coalition Government 1918 – 1922. Spectator*, 3 November 1979, 22 – 23.

118 'Labour in Travail.' Philip Williams, *Hugh Gaitskell. TLS*, 23 November 1979, 12.

119 'In Black and White.' George Boyce, James Curran and Pauline Wingate, eds., *Newspaper History: From the Seventeenth Century to the Present Day* and James Curran, ed., *The British Press: A Manifesto, ibid.*, 14 December 1979, 118.

120 'Fair or Free?' Alan Sykes, *Tariff Reform in British Politics 1903 – 1913. Spectator*, 2 February 1980, 18.

121 'When the Swinging Had to Stop.' Christopher Booker, *The Seventies: Portrait of a Decade. TLS*, 29 February 1980, 225.

122 'National Nutshell,' David Butler and Anne Sloman, *British Political Facts 1900 – 1979, ibid.*, 18 April 1980, 448.

123 'A Double Life.' Arnold Bennett, *Sketches for Autobiography*, edited by James Hepburn, *ibid.*, 2 May 1980, 488.

124 'Kings of the Jungle.' Hugh Cudlipp, *The Prerogative of the Harlot: Press Barons and Power, ibid.*, 16 May 1980, 549.

125 'The Cataclysm as Catalyst.' James Trevise, James Glen Stovall and Hamid Moulane, *Watergate: A Crisis for the World, ibid.*, 30 May 1980, 602.

126 'Practitioner in Politics.' Kenneth O. Morgan and Jane Morgan, *Portrait of a Progressive: The Political Career of Christopher, Viscount Addison* and John Turner, *Lloyd George's Secretariat. Spectator*, 31 May 1980, 17 – 18.

127 'Mannerism.' Max Egremont, *Balfour, ibid.*, 21 June 1980, 22 – 23.

128 'Holidays in the Head.' Peter Conrad, *Imagining America. Quarto*, July 1980, 7.

129 'Conciliations.' John D. Fair, *British Interparty Conferences: A Study of Conciliation in British Politics 1867 – 1921. Spectator*, 12 July 1980, 21.

130 'There Was Always a Touch of Scorn in Him for Obvious Creeds.' John Joliffe, *Raymond Asquith: Life and Letters. The Listener*, 17 July 1980, 83 – 84.

131 'Anglo-American Attitudes.' James D. Startt, *Journalism's Unofficial Ambassador: A Biography of Edward Price Bell 1869 – 1943. TLS*, 25 July 1980, 832.

132 'Enemy Aliens.' Ronald Stent, *A Bespattered Page? The Internment of 'His Majesty's Most Loyal Enemy Aliens'* and Peter and Leni Gillman, *'Collar the Lot!' How England Interned and Expelled Its Wartime Refugees. Spectator*, 16 August 1980, 19 – 20.

133 'Friends of Fascism.' Richard Griffiths, *Fellow Travellers of the Right: British Enthusiasts for Nazi Germany, 1933 – 39* and James J. Barnes and Patience P. Barnes, *Hitler's MEIN KAMPF in Britain and America: A Publishing History 1930 – 39. TLS*, 24 October 1980, 1193.

134 'GOM ex-FBA.' A. J. P. Taylor, *Politicians, Socialism and Historians. Spectator*, 1 November 1980, 19 – 20.

135 'Tangled Wires.' Paul Kennedy, *The Rise of the Anglo-German Antagonism 1860 – 1914. Spectator*, 29 November 1980, 17 – 18.

136 'A Historian For Our Times.' Chris Wigley, *A. J. P. Taylor: A Complete Annotated Bibliography and Guide to His Historical and Other Writings. TLS*, 12 December 1980, 1405.

137 'Good Old C.B.' Bruce K. Murray, *The People's Budget 1909 – 10* and Patricia Jalland, *The Liberals and Ireland: The Ulster Question in British Politics to 1914. Spectator*, 14 February 1981, 22 – 23.

138 'Contrari-wise.' Richard Jay, *Joseph Chamberlain, ibid.*, 14 March 1981, 21 – 22.

139 'From the Social Point of View.' Harold Perkin, *The Structured Crowd: Essays in English Social History. TLS*, 17 April 1981, 439.

140 'Progress of the Principality.' Kenneth O. Morgan, *Rebirth of a Nation: Wales 1880 – 1980, ibid.*, 8 May 1981, 503 – 4.

141 'Heavy Going at the House.' Nancy E. Johnson, ed., *The Diary of Gathorne Hardy, Later Lord Cranbrook, 1866 – 1892. Political Selections, ibid.*, 4 September 1981, 1010.

142 'Putting Our Best Face Forward.' Philip M. Taylor, *The Projection of Britain: British Overseas Publicity and Propaganda 1919 – 39, ibid.*, 16 October 1981, 1187 – 88.

143 'The Whirling Tory Dervish.' R. F. Foster, *Lord Randolph Churchill: A Political Life, ibid.*, 20 November, 1981, 1343 – 44.

144 'Forced Destinies.' Jean Goodman, *The Mond Legacy: A Family Saga, ibid.*, 16 April 1982, 430.

145 'Art in the Socialist Utopia.' Ian Britain, *Fabianism and Culture. The Observer*, 4 July 1982, 28.

146 'Emulating Aubrey.' Alan Watkins, *Brief Lives, ibid.*, 26 September 1982, 34.

147 'Manful Perseverance.' Norman and Jeanne MacKenzie, eds., *The Diaries of Beatrice Webb*: Vol. 1 *1873 – 1892, ibid.*, 17 October 1982, 32.

148 'Keeping the Loins Girded.' Richard Shannon, *Gladstone*: Vol. 1 *1809 – 1865* and H. C. G. Matthew, ed., *The Gladstone Diaries: With Cabinet Material and Prime Ministerial Correspondence*, Vol. 7 *January 1869 – June 1871* and Vol. 8 *July 1871 – December 1874. TLS*, 22 October 1982, 1151 – 52.

149 'Print of Cloven Hoof.' Piers Brendon, *The Life and Death of the Press Barons. The Observer*, 7 November 1982, 28.

150 'The Prime Minister's Pole-Star.' Michael and Eleanor Brock, eds., *H. H. Asquith: Letters to Venetia Stanley. TLS*, 26 November 1982, 1289.

151 'The Gadfly of History.' A. J. P. Taylor, *A Personal History. The Observer*, 29 May 1983, 30.

152 'Standing to Reason.' Vernon Bogdanor, ed., *Liberal Party Politics. TLS*, 3 June 1983, 564.

153 'Like Alfred the Great and Peter Pan.' William Manchester, *The Last Lion. Winston Spencer Churchill. Visions of Glory: 1874 – 1932. New York Times Book Review*, 5 June 1983, 11 and 30 – 31.

154 'In a Claude-glass.' Christopher Mulvey, *Anglo-American Landscapes. The Listener*, 16 June 1983, 26.

155 'The Big Apple.' Michael Leapman, *The Companion Guide to New York*. *The Observer*, 19 June 1983, 31.

156 'The Battle Begins.' Martin Gilbert, *Finest Hour: The Biography of Winston S. Churchill 1939–1941*. *TLS*, 1 July 1983, 689.

157 'The Honeytime of Fabianism.' Norman and Jeanne MacKenzie, eds., *The Diary of Beatrice Webb*: Vol. 2 *1892–1905*. *The Observer*, 16 October 1983, 33.

158 'The Rise of a Bounder.' John Campbell, *F. E. Smith. First Earl of Birkenhead*. *TLS*, 23 December 1983, 1419–20.

159 'Making It.' David Sinclair, *Dynasty: The Astors and Their Times*, *ibid.*, 3 February 1984, 107.

160 'Losing an Empire and Finding a Role.' Alan Bullock, *Ernest Bevin: Foreign Secretary 1945–51*. *New York Times Book Review*, 6 May 1984, 13–4.

161 'The Master's Last Years.' Leon Edel, ed., *Letters of Henry James*, Vol. 4 *1895–1916*. *The Observer*, 13 May 1984, 23.

162 'No Man's Mistress.' Daphne Bennett, *Margot: A Life of the Countess of Oxford and Asquith*. *London Review of Books*, 5–19 July 1984, 12–3.

163 'The Firm of Webb.' Lisanne Radice, *Beatrice and Sidney Webb, Fabian Socialists*. *The Observer*, 22 July 1984, 21.

164 'Wigan Peer.' John Vincent, ed., *The Crawford Papers: The Journals of David Lindsay, 17th Earl of Crawford and 10th Earl of Balcares, During the Years 1892 to 1940*. *London Review of Books*, 15 November – 6 December 1984, 3.

VI Miscellaneous Journalism: Current Affairs, Theatre Reviews, Etc.

165 'A Netherlands Notebook.' *TLS*, 28 November 1975, 1424.

166 'The Bernhard Affair.' *The Listener*, 2 September 1976, 258–60.

167 'Indira Gandhi: 'I Will Be Good,' *ibid.*, 24 January 1980, 90–100.

168 'The Relics of Dizzi-Ben-Dizzi.' Review of 'Dizzy and Beaconsfield' Exhibit, Low Memorial Library. *TLS*, 13 February 1981, 166.

169 'Only Forty Watts.' Review of Woody Allen's 'The Floating Light Bulb.' Vivian Beaumont Theatre, New York, *ibid.*, 29 May 1981, 602.

170 '"Nickleby" in New York,' *ibid.*, 6 November 1981, 1299.

171 'Family Happiness.' Review of Jules Feiffer's 'Grown Ups,' Lyceum Theatre, New York, *ibid.*, 1 January 1982, 11.

172 'Dryasdust.' Review of Enid Bagnold's 'The Chalk Garden,' Roundabout Theatre Company, New York, *ibid.*, 21 May 1982, 557.

173 'Forum' in *History Today* 34 (September 1984). 5–6. ("Stephen Koss questions whether the press has ever truly mirrored public opinion.")